HEAVY HANDS

An Introduction to the Crimes of Domestic Violence

Denise Kindschi Gosselin

PEARSON
Custom
Publishing

PEARSON
Prentice
Hall

Taken from:

Heavy Hands: An Introduction to the Crimes of Domestic Violence
by Denise Kindschi Gosselin
Copyright © 2000 by Prentice-Hall, Inc.
A Pearson Education Company
Upper Saddle River, New Jersey 07458

This special edition published in cooperation with Pearson Custom Publishing.

Printed in the United States of America

10   9   8

ISBN 0–536–66683-0

2004540044

DG

Please visit our web site at *www.pearsoncustom.com*

PEARSON CUSTOM PUBLISHING
75 Arlington Street, Suite 300, Boston, MA 02116
A Pearson Education Company

Contents

Part Two _____

Part Three

Part Four

Crime Identification   253

CHAPTER 9   **Recognizing Child Abuse   255**

Part Five

The Future   347

Preface

Thousands of police officers across the country routinely come face to face with domestic violence. With little direction they face the challenges that researchers and academics ponder. Rarely are they part of the intellectual discourse on abuse and neglect. This book is a small step toward bringing us all together.

My first domestic call came shortly after graduation from the Massachusetts State Police Academy in 1980. Impressed with my accomplishments, the call was a rude awakening. To this day I remember the gut-wrenching feeling when going through the front door of that home. I did not have a clue about what should be done. More surprisingly, the victim was a man, over 6 feet tall. He had just announced that he was moving out and his girlfriend didn't want him to leave. When he was on the phone with the police, she had grabbed the phone and struck him over the head with it. Blood was everywhere and he required numerous stitches. Afterwards I returned him to the house and counseled them both. The resolution never seemed quite right!

Fortunately, the movement to intervene in family violence had begun and I became a part of that change. W. Michael Ryan, the Northwestern District Attorney, was instrumental toward developing my interest in domestic abuse. I owe him a debt of gratitude for the training and support that this office supplied while I was a detective assigned to his organization. We developed the first multidisciplinary team in Massachusetts to screen and investigate child abuse allegations. Struggling through the new legislation on mandated reporting, the office was inundated with complaints of sexual and physical abuse. Working together with the Department of Social Sciences, prosecutors, physicians, victim witnesses, and mental health agencies, an increase in successful prosecution was accomplished.

Our success was due in part to the aggressive investigation of family violence. It was treated like any other *major* crime. Child victim statements were routinely video-taped to assure the defense of their accuracy. Adult victims were treated equally and with respect regardless of their sexual orientation, gender, race, or the makeup of the offender. Evidence to corroborate the statement was collected through search warrants whenever possible. Perpetrators were arrested and prosecuted only after a thorough investigation. Interviews and interrogations were the norm in every case.

After twelve years on the state police force I became an educator at Western New England College in Springfield, Massachusetts. My passion to understand the dynamics of family violence and the role of criminal justice led me to develop a course on the topic in 1992. It has been offered numerous times since then, with minor revisions each time. My approach is sociolegal, with a leaning toward the criminal justice perspective. It is now a permanent course offering at our institution and has been cross-referenced and may be taken at the undergraduate level as a criminal justice or sociology course. There is so much to learn that this book can provide only a comprehensive beginning. It includes information on all forms of family violence.

The book is designed to follow in content the course that I have offered over the years. It is meant to assist both educators with no field experience and those with professional backgrounds to meld the theory and practice of domestic violence for students of the social sciences. It is meant to tear down myths about both victims and offenders. Women and men have been victimized. Elderly and children are present as both perpetrators and victims as well. Heterosexuals and homosexuals can both be violent; dating relationships can be dangerous. To leave anyone out is to ignore the pain and suffering that domestic violence brings.

Students of criminal justice tire quickly when hearing about the mistakes of the profession. Therefore, I wrote this book with an eye toward the future, without dwelling on the past. It is my desire that crimes of domestic violence be identified and the consequences understood. As much as possible, the perpetrators are characterized and victimization is illustrated. My purpose is to provide a positive and instructive book from the criminal justice perspective, bringing together the causes and consequences of domestic violence and law enforcement response. The text addresses the following questions: What is domestic violence? Why does it happen, and what are the consequences? Who are the offenders, and who are the victims? What legislation exists relative to family violence? How does the criminal justice community respond? How do you get help? What resources are available?

More human misery has been caused by domestic relationships than all of the wars in history combined. The very nature of these relationships dictates that they will be imperfect, fluctuate, and perhaps end. Yet it is not the unhappiness caused by a failed or flawed relationship that we find egregious. What is unacceptable is when one human being purposely inflicts pain upon another and does so by design. This is when the inevitable human discord crosses the line into abuse and one party chooses to apply a heavy hand to the other. It does not matter one bit whether the abuse takes the form of physical, emotional, or sexual violence. This type of act is such that it can and is being regulated by recently enacted laws in countries that are advanced in areas of public policy and criminal law enforcement. It is the wave of the future. More laws will follow; more countries will follow; more of us will agree. Heavy hands are wrong!

Writing this textbook has been a labor of love.

Acknowledgments

Thank you to the many victims who have confided in me about atrocities too horrible to recount. I remember you. You taught me the value of dignity and the importance of equal enforcement of the law. To the women, men, boys, and girls who have suffered from domestic crimes, I marvel at your resilience and applaud your survival.

I owe a debt of gratitude to Kathy Arenstam, whose contribution since the beginning of this project provided consistency. Thank you, Danielle D. McIntosh, for the research on elder law. Cynthia Kindschi, always there when I needed your support! A very deep appreciation to my parents, Elizabeth and Gerald Feldmann, whose love and guidance have provided a positive basis for comparison. To Robert Gosselin, without whom this book would not have been possible, my love.

To my friends and colleagues at Western New England College, who encouraged my efforts, thank you. In particular, Professor Janet Bowdan, whose reading and editing was invaluable.

About the Author

A pioneer in law enforcement, the author became the first uniformed female officer for her hometown, Lunenburg, MA, the first female campus police officer at the Community College she had attended. The Massachusetts Senate honored her in 1978 as the first woman appointed constable for the city of Fitchburg. In 1979 she was named an Outstanding Young Woman of America.

Trooper Gosselin graduated in the 61st Recruit Training Troop of the Massachusetts State Police in January, 1980. During the twelve years that followed she served as a uniformed officer performing route patrol activities; as an instructor at the Massachusetts State Police Academy; and as a major crime detective. Recognized as a local expert in Child Abuse Investigation she spoke on cable television and on radio. She and Trooper Gibbons appeared on *America's Most Wanted* when John Walsh presented their fugitive case on the show. Additionally, she has made many presentations at professional meetings with the Department of Social Services, Department of Mental Health, and for the Office of the District Attorney. Trooper Gosselin has testified on numerous major crime cases, both in Criminal Court and in Civil hearings.

Like many police officers, her education was fragmented, interrupted over the years by demanding work and family responsibilities. Denise holds an Associate in

Science in Law Enforcement from Mt. Wachusett Community College; her Bachelor and Masters Degrees in Criminal Justice were awarded from Westfield State College. At the University of Massachusetts she studied at the doctoral level in the Political Science department. She was awarded a scholarship to attend the first Child Abuse and Exploitation Investigative Techniques Training Program at the Federal Law Enforcement Training Center. Denise has additional training in homicide investigation, rape, search and seizure, and stalking. In 1995 she studied at the International Institute for the Sociology of Law in Onati, Spain.

From 1991 to the present the author has lectured at Greenfield Community College, Holyoke Community College, and Westfield State College as an adjunct. For five years, she has been on the faculty of the Criminal Justice Department at Western New England College in Springfield, Massachusetts. Her research efforts have concentrated on Domestic Violence, Juvenile Law, and Interviewing/ Interrogation. She developed the curriculum for courses in Domestic Violence and Interviewing/Interrogation that have been made permanent course offerings at WNEC. Recently Mrs. Gosselin taught Domestic Abuse for the 74th Massachusetts State Police Recruit Training Troop.

In August, 1999 the author returned to law enforcement as a Trooper with the Department of State Police in Massachusetts.

Part One

Domestic Violence Crime:
Definition, Prevalence, and History

Domestic violence is a familiar phrase to most people today, but what does it really mean? How often does it occur? Is domestic violence a new phenomenon? Do any countries other than the United States view domestic abuse as problematic? These and many other questions are answered in Part One.

In Chapter 1, "Violence in the Family," we provide a base for future chapters to build upon. This is where you learn the meaning of common terms and look at the prevalence rates for the various forms of domestic violence. What are the recognized illegal acts? How are the relationships defined? Are all forms of domestic violence criminal behavior? Are there separate laws that forbid violence between people that are related by blood or marriage? Every discipline has a unique vocabulary so those professionals can communicate within the field; familiarization of the terminology allows students to join in the dialogue.

In Chapter 2, "A Global View of Family and Social and Legal Relations," we broaden the foundation for future chapters. Domestic violence is recognized as a current social problem of epidemic proportions affecting millions of women, men, and children. Here domestic violence is put into perspective both historically and globally. How widespread is family violence? Beyond the people who are victimized and those who perpetuate the violence, a larger picture emerges. Has society only recently begun to legislate against violence committed within the family? Have laws that were poorly designed and sporadically enforced actually encouraged and contributed to the problems that we face today? Have we discovered something new, or are we looking at unresolved issues of the past? Additionally, we examine the concerns of foreign nations on the issues of family violence. Is domestic violence particular to our society? We look from the past to the present without being confined to our own society.

Violence in the Family

INTRODUCTION

This book is about terror, fear, confusion, and despair: a hopelessness that characterizes the victims caught in a web of domestic violence. Consider this: The person you love is your tormentor. You walk through the door of your home wondering what is going to happen to you today. Will it be a good day, or a bad day? The unpredictability heightens your fear. Domestic violence is a reality. Domestic violence is a crime. The victims are from every walk of life, rich and poor, of every race. The majority of victims are women, but men are terrorized in their homes as well. Intimate dating partners are battered and raped, setting the stage for a life of anguish. Lesbian and homosexual domestic partners may be threatened and beaten as well. Children and spouses victimize the elderly, who thought they knew their abusers. As if that were not bleak enough, adults are not the only victims. Children are physically abused and sexually molested by the adults who "care" for them. Victims are being stalked, and some are being killed. Who is doing these horrible things? Loved ones, parents, and children are the perpetrators. For example:

- A biological father on numerous occasions during visitations raped his 14-year-old daughter. Her 22-year-old sister was also his victim; she had been impregnated by her father when she was 15. The family never talked about it, but the resulting baby was a constant reminder of the physical and emotional pain caused by the rapes.

- A 6-year-old girl complained that her stepbrother who lived with her was hurting her. Physical examination of the child confirmed that she had been raped. The 13-year-old boy was found guilty of rape and sodomy, which had occurred over a two-year period.

- An 11-year-old boy told his social worker that his mother's boyfriend had hit him over the head with the handle of a machete, and that he was having headaches. His mother insisted that her son was not telling the truth. An investigation by the police determined that the boyfriend had repeatedly beaten the boy with a belt on at least one occasion. Another time the man forced the child to stand in front of a door that had a poster picture of Mickey Mouse on it. He fired numerous shots from a handgun at the child, both above his head and at his feet, yelling "you're dead, you're dead!" Afterward, the man took a razor blade and cut him on the little finger, telling him, "When you die, I am going to be the one to kill you." When a search warrant was executed on the home, the poster of Mickey Mouse was found under a mattress, and eleven bullet holes were located on the floor and in the wall.

- An old woman was reluctant to report that her grown son was stealing her money. She was afraid because of his drug habit and believed that he might take what little she had left in her life. At 70 years old, she knew there was no other way to keep from having to go into a nursing home; she had to remain self-sufficient. That meant turning her son in for larceny.

The investigation into multiple sexual assaults on the young woman was difficult. She came forward as an adult because it had taken time for her to get away from her cruel stepfather who physically assaulted her as well. Unfortunately, it took her too long to break free. The assaults against her were beyond the statute of limitations; the stepfather could not be prosecuted! The case prompted the local prosecutor to submit a proposal to change the law, extending the statute of limitations in Massachusetts. Future sexual assault victims will now have 10 years after reaching majority to come forward with complaints.

- What about her mother? When asked to take her picture, I found the face so swollen that it was barely recognizable. Her eyes were blackened, her nose was swollen twice its size, her lips were grotesque. It would be years after this particular incident before the woman could bring herself to testify against him in court for the years of battering. During her marriage she had suffered broken bones, broken teeth, and a detached retina, among other injuries too numerous to mention. She walks with a cane due to the many times that he kicked her on the ground and twisted her legs around the kitchen table till they snapped. Even worse, she had suffered psychological abuse that ranged from cruel to bizarre. Coming home to find the bloody head of her horse on the walkway was just another way he intimidated and kept control of her.

- The 15-year-old girl pushed her father down the stairs yet another time. She had injured her mother in the past, also. It was not that the parents were elderly, just older than most parents. They were tired from fighting with their growing child and embarrassed that anyone would find out. She was the child of their dreams turned into a nightmare.

These are just a sample of the cases that come to mind when domestic violence is discussed. For victims of domestic violence, life is lived in hell, with the perception that there is no way out. Their home is a prison.

Yes, we have noticed the problem. We talk about it. Most people know, or think they know, what domestic violence is. Daily newspapers, magazines, and television report on domestic violence. Stories about famous people in sports, politics, and Hollywood are linked with whispers and screams of family violence. Articles appear on the Internet and in academic journals. Researchers are examining the signs and symptoms of domestic violence. Sitting in coffee shops or in boardrooms, people are talking about it. Still, people laugh and tell jokes about domestic violence! People say that if it is so bad, the victim ought to leave. Plain and simple: Just leave. If they don't leave, it can't really be that bad. Or can it?

On the other hand, *domestic violence* is a term frequently used to describe acts that are not violent, such as mental and verbal abuse. By themselves, these forms of abuse are not illegal. It is difficult to separate mental and verbal abuse from the portrayal of a domestic violence victim. The power and control exercised in a relationship are part of the battering syndrome. They warn of the potential for a violent relationship or the existence of one. Mental and verbal indignities are the signs and symptoms of an abusive relationship. They are the tools used to break the spirit and overcome the will. Noncriminal acts of violence must be documented because they increase the creditability of the victim, particularly in cases where the greater injuries may not be visible. Professionals with the duty to respond must understand the crime and make the distinction between criminal and noncriminal domestic violence.

Domestic violence is a crime. Still, some people think that domestic violence legislation is just one more way for the government to interfere in a citizen's private life. A person once asked if he needed to get written permission from his wife to have sexual relations. The man was afraid of being accused of rape! He felt that laws designed to prevent domestic violence were akin to having a police officer in every bedroom.

Whether the perpetrator is a stranger, husband, lover, or parent, rape is a criminal act. It is the act that determines the crime, not the relationship. An act is defined as illegal through legislative statutes or through case law. It is the relationship between the offender and the victim that determines if the crime is domestic. Legislation to prevent domestic violence is a social as well as a legal statement. It is a commitment to enforcement of existing statutes for all persons, regardless of their relationship to the offender. Some states have created special court orders designed to protect victims of domestic abuse. Looking closely, one would find similar orders of protection from strangers when the need occurs. Recognizing a domestic relationship does not excuse an otherwise illegal act. It empowers the victim and in turn empowers society. Misinformation and misunderstanding of the issue have become problems, which must be corrected.

Recognition of all victims of domestic violence is not meant to undermine the immensity of the problem faced by millions of female victims. All forms of domestic violence will be addressed fully in this book to examine the dynamics of family battering. Assaults against men by their female partners are not infrequent. However, women who are victimized in domestic violence usually suffer more severe injuries than do male victims. Females batter other females in lesbian relationships. Men victimize other men in homosexual and bisexual relationships. Violence is present in many intimate relationships in the United States. Sexual abuse against men and boys is more common than we want to admit. Fear and embarrassment often inhibit a victim from coming forward.

An arrest is not routinely made when the perpetrator of abuse is a woman. Why? Police officers occasionally suggest a range of excuses for not taking action when probable cause exists to do so. These run the gamut from "he would be embarrassed" to "she didn't hurt him that badly." If domestic violence is to be taken seriously, gender cannot be the determining factor for law enforcement action. Research documenting male battering has been unpopular in the past and should be reexamined. There is no readily available law enforcement documentation of the numerous abuse calls where the male is the victim and no action is taken. Domestic violence intervention offers legal protection for all victims, regardless of their relationship to the perpetrator or their gender.

Feminist organizations are responsible for having brought the issue to the forefront, where it can no longer be ignored. Credit must be given to the dedicated women and men who pioneered efforts to understand the dynamics of spousal battering and to protect those victims of abuse. Domestic violence is now recognized as a major social problem. Having identified the problem, people seek ways to do away with it. Federal and state funding has been established for research, protection, and education on domestic violence. Legislation was passed to provide necessary protection for the victims. Criminology, victimology, and family violence courses are offered in colleges and universities to address the issues and discuss solutions. We have taken enormous strides toward understanding the various ways in which we hurt the ones that we "love."

Where has all the media hype, research, and dialogue brought us? Quite frankly, back to the beginning. What we know about domestic violence is anything but complete. There is no easy way to abolish it, no pill to take to make it better. Experts debate implications of this festering illness that breeds among us and weakens family structure. Theorists discuss possible explanations: cultural, social, psychological, biological, and learned. In the recent past, people routinely did not want to acknowledge that incest and physical abuse to children existed. It was difficult to accept that the elderly were being battered and neglected by their own children. Spousal abuse was also readily denied. Now that these forms of domestic abuse have been identified, the dialogue will continue.

The criminal justice community has been identified as the most logical source of protection and empowerment for the domestic violence victim. New legislation and public policy, which now mandate a law enforcement response, are in effect. Police officers are delineated as the primary first responder in the war to eradicate and control this disease, at least until another option is discovered. Simultaneously, researchers and policy makers must remain concerned by the pitfalls of an inadequate response by the criminal justice system to domestic violence. The law enforcement community is charged with dealing with this serious problem. Educational avenues must be explored tht may assist us to meet the formidable task.

This book is about meeting that challenge. It will be rewarding for every person who is interested in the factors involving domestic violence in the United States. What do we know about it? What has been done to control domestic violence? How do we recognize battering, and what action should be taken? The purpose of this book is to bring a detailed explanation of domestic violence and prevention efforts to those who have been tasked by society to intervene and to those who want to become involved.

WHAT IS DOMESTIC VIOLENCE?

The Roxbury Dictionary of Criminal Justice (Champion, 1997) offers the best available definition for the criminal justice professional:

> **Domestic violence:** any spousal altercation or interfamilial conflicts of sufficient nature to justify law enforcement intervention; spousal abuse is most frequently cited. May involve parent–child conflict, either physical or psychological.

Take out the term *spousal* and replace it with *domestic partner* for a general definition of abuse. Federal and state laws recognize that domestic relationships include partnerships where people live together but are not legally married. Same-sex relationships and roommates may also constitute domestic partners.

The California Family Code defines domestic violence as abuse or violence that is perpetrated against any person in a legally recognized domestic relationship. It is important to note that many forms of abuse are socially unacceptable and are part of the violent relationship but do not rise to the level of criminal violations. Other domestic abuse situations clearly constitute crimes and require law enforcement intervention. Domestic violence situations are often not easy to interpret legally and are always unpleasant. Sometimes it is difficult to determine exactly who has done what! The response role is not limited to law enforcement, however. Noncriminal abuse and neglect will also often come to the attention of law enforcement officers. In these situations, police officers can play an important role by referring the apparent victim to appropriate health or social service agencies. There may be children involved who desperately need someone to intervene on their behalf.

In many cases, the law requires that the first responder take action when he or she is a service provider or law enforcement officer. When police, medical, and educational professionals become aware of child abuse, all states require them to report the matter to a designated agency, whether it be an appropriate child welfare agency or law enforcement agency.

Crimes against the Person

Domestic abuse is a classification containing many crimes that are committed against the person, where that person has an intimate or a familial type of relationship with the offender. Examples of crimes committed against the person include the following:

- Assault
- Assault and battery
- Assault with a dangerous weapon
- Aggravated assault
- Murder
- Rape
- Stalking

As stated earlier, these acts are illegal if committed against a stranger; therefore, it is the relationship of the perpetrator to the victim that often characterizes these crimes as domestic violence. Individual states have outlined which relationships will be considered as "domestic" through legislation. When domestic abuse situations that do not constitute criminal activity come to the attention of criminal justice practitioners, they should take proper alternative action. It is essential that criminal justice personnel recognize signs and symptoms of abuse so that the response might be appropriate. (See Figure 1–1.)

Forms of Domestic Violence

Domestic violence comes in many different forms (Figure 1–2). The severity of an act or the extent of harm is routinely the measuring tool used by the police to determine whether or not the act is criminal. The author suggests that this approach is outdated and should be changed to reflect contemporary knowledge of domestic violence: It is meant to hurt, intimidate, control, or place the victim in fear of the abuser. With this understanding, the physical extent of harm becomes moot. Probable cause that a crime has been committed is the standard of every other law enforcement action and therefore must continue to be applied equally when domestic crimes are being investigated.

Arrest of the perpetrator should not be viewed as the punishment for domestic crimes; it is simply the legal intervention when a crime has been committed. This form of intervention should be taken whenever the law of the state determines it to be appropriate. The courts will ultimately resolve the matter. The examples below suggest some types of violence that might be considered criminal conduct that is prohibited by law. Fredrica Lehrman suggested the following list of domestic violence forms (Lehrman, 1997):

Figure 1–1   Alcohol and drug use are frequently associated with crimes of domestic violence. They are not a cause, however. Substance abuse does not cause a nonbattering person to become violent. (*Photo courtesy of Mark C. Ide.*)

- Beating
- Pulling hair
- Shoving
- Striking
- Pulling
- Punching
- Slapping
- Kicking
- Hitting

- Choking
- Biting
- Pointing weapons
- Throwing things
- Threatening
- Harassing
- Sexual abuse
- Stalking
- Homicide

ABUSE PREVENTION ACTS

Recent legislation to prevent domestic violence attempts to address problems specific to intimate and familial relationships and provide additional protections to the victims of abuse. They represent a strong statement of public policy: that domestic violence is a serious crime and cannot be dismissed as merely family business. Legislation varies slightly from state to state, but its content is similar, defining domestic violence or abuse relationships recognized by the particular state and including general

Figure 1-2   Pointing a weapon at a domestic partner is one of numerous forms of domestic violence. *(Photo courtesy of Mark C. Ide.)*

descriptions of criminal conduct that is domestic in nature. Of particular importance are the remedies provided to protect the victim, in addition to criminal sanctions. Court-issued protection orders are now commonly issued in accordance with *abuse prevention acts.* Violation of protection orders is a criminal act. *Domestic abuse acts* (as they are sometimes called) also provide clear instructions to law enforcement on the intent of the law, outlining the responsibility of police officers. Mandated arrest and preferred arrest policies are routine for domestic violence–related crime and are covered in depth later in the book.

RELATIONSHIPS

There is no uniform understanding of what constitutes a domestic relationship. Legal definitions vary slightly from state to state. Some common ground exists, and generally the domestic relationships are defined via marriage. These include:

- Persons who are or were legally married: a spouse or former spouse
- Persons who reside together without marriage: a cohabitant or former cohabitant
- Persons related through marriage: any person related by consanguinity or affinity within the second degree, related by blood or through marriage

- Persons who share a child in common: where the presumption applies that the male is the biological father of the child and the female is the biological mother (whether they were ever legally married or not)
- A woman who is pregnant and the man who is presumed to be the father
- Persons who are having or have had a substantial dating or engagement relationship
- Biological children or stepchildren
- Biological parents or stepparents

The category of persons who simply reside together is controversial. This may be interpreted to include apartment dwellers and students who share dorm accommodations, depending on the jurisdiction. It definitely includes persons who share a house or apartment, regardless of whether they are married. Some, but not all states include substantial dating relationships as a category where violence would be viewed as domestic violence. Same-sex relationships where the persons reside as if they were married are considered to be domestic. Remember that it is not the gender of the victim or the relationship of the people that determines the crime; it is the act committed.

DEFINITIONS OF COMMON TERMS

These definitions are provided as guidelines for identifying the problems associated with abuse. They provide insight into the various types of abuse that criminal justice professionals encounter. Each specific type of abuse is defined by federal and state law and varies from jurisdiction to jurisdiction. Researchers and practitioners may use different definitions for the types of abuse detailed below.

Physical abuse: use of force or threat of force that may result in bodily injury, physical pain, or impairment. The signs of physical abuse may be external, internal or both. Physical injuries that are untreated in various stages of healing might indicate an approximate time of injury. External signs of physical abuse include, but are not limited to, bruises, welts, marks, burns, bleeding, missing or pulled hair, ripped clothing, crying, wincing, and the appearance of a drug-induced state. Broken blood vessels or unequal pupil dilation in the eyes may indicate physical child abuse. Additional signs of physical abuse may be human bites, strangulation, immersion in scalding water, and poisoning. Internal signs of physical abuse include, but are not limited to, internal tissue or organ injuries, bone fractures, broken bones, bleeding, sprains, and dislocations.

Sexual abuse: nonconsensual sexual contact of any kind. Sexual contact with a person incapable of giving consent is also considered sexual abuse. A minor is presumed unable to give informed consent; therefore, any sexual contact with a minor is sexual abuse. Sexual conduct includes, but is not limited to, unwanted touching, rape, sodomy, coerced nudity, and sexually explicit photographing. Force, threat of force, or implied force may accomplish sexual abuse. Physical signs of abuse and the use of force are not always present in relationships where one person is dominant and the power is inherent in the position rather than the person. Physical signs of sexual abuse are the exception rather than the rule. They include bruises around the breasts or genital area, venereal disease or genital infections, vaginal or anal bleeding, and clothing that is torn, stained, or bloody.

Emotional or psychological abuse: intentional infliction of anguish, pain, or distress designed to control the victim. The verbal or nonverbal forms of emotional/psychological abuse include, but are not limited to, verbal assaults, insults, threats, frightening, intimidation, humiliation, and harassment. With the exception of threats, this category of abuse is rarely illegal. It is often evidenced along with other forms of abuse. Over extended periods of time, emotional/psychological abuse may be the "force" by which other forms of abuse occur. Emotional or psychological abuse can be more damaging than physical violence. It may deprive the victim of self-worth or self-confidence, making the victim vulnerable to further domestic violence victimization (Figure 1–3).

Figure 1–3   Emotional or psychological abuse can rob a person of self-worth or self-confidence, increasing his or her vulnerability to future domestic violence victimization. *(Photo courtesy of Mark C. Ide.)*

Neglect: failure or refusal to provide care or services for a person when there is an obligation to do so. This form of abuse carries with it a resulting harm due to the action or inaction of the caregiver. Examples of neglect are failure to provide to a minor or elder life necessities such as food, water, clothing, or shelter. Leaving a young child unattended or unsupervised may also be considered neglect. Signs of neglect include, but are not limited to, dehydration, malnutrition, untreated bed-sores, untreated health problems or conditions, unsanitary living conditions, a failure to thrive, or abandonment.

Financial exploitation: illegal or improper use of an elder's funds, property, or assets. Theft, fraud, and unfulfilled promises of care in exchange for assets are examples of financial exploitation. Substantial monetary or property gain to another person is considered exploitation when the elderly victim consented to enrich that person as a result of misrepresentation, undue influence, coercion, or threat of force.

Wife abuse: physical, sexual, mental, and emotional abuse to a married woman at the hands of her husband. Its use should be restricted to research as a way to limit and narrowly define the population of study.

Spouse abuse: common substitute for wife abuse. The term is gender neutral and refers to wife or husband battering. Use of the term without definition is problematic because it excludes partners who live together and are not legally married.

Domestic partner abuse: most comprehensive designation that refers to any violence between intimates. It includes all adult intimate relationships between people regardless of sexual preference, marital status, or age of the intimates.

Battering: initially used to describe a form of domestic abuse, hitting; now commonly used to refer to the pattern of violent and coercive behavior used to gain control in an intimate relationship. The control may be accomplished through economic forms, such as withholding or denying access to money or other basic resources, or sabotaging employment, housing, or educational opportunities. Social isolation is quite common, including the denial of communication with friends and relatives or making communication so difficult that the victim chooses to avoid it, prohibiting access to the telephone or transportation; and denying access to needed health care. Verbal and emotional forms of assault and control include intimidation, coercion, threats, or degradation. Physical and sexual assaults may occur. Victims of battering include women, men, and lesbian or homosexual partners. Individual acts do not constitute battering; it is the violence in general, regardless of the form, relationship, living arrangement, marital status, or age of the intimates.

Child abuse: includes nonaccidental physical injury, sexual abuse or exploitation, emotional or psychological injury, and neglect or maltreatment to a person under the age of 18 (or the age specified by the law of the state). It is a general term that includes all abuses involving minors. Child abuse is frequently the term used to describe abuse by caregivers (e.g., legal guardians, teachers) and abuse by family members. Incest is the sexual abuse of children by a family member.

Elder abuse: may be physical, sexual, or emotional/psychological and involve neglect, abandonment, or financial exploitation. Most researchers agree on two general categories of elder abuse: domestic and institutional. Domestic elder abuse refers to any of several forms of maltreatment of an older person by someone who has a special relationship with the elder, such as a spouse, a sibling, a child, a friend, or a caregiver in the older person's home. A caregiver is one who is responsible for the elder due to a legal or contractual arrangement. Institutional abuse is any form of abuse that occurs in residential facilities for older persons, such as nursing, foster, or group homes. Perpetrators of institutional abuse are usually persons who have a legal or contractual obligation to provide elder care and protection. A significant amount of elder abuse is believed to be in the category of self-neglect. Further, elder abuse may involve both the purposeful or active abuse and passive abuse that results in negligence due to ignorance or an inability to provide care. It is important that professionals who respond to elder abuse understand the legal definitions in their state. Classifications of elder abuse as criminal, civil, or requiring social service intervention vary greatly from state to state.

PREVALENCE OF DOMESTIC VIOLENCE

Battering

Domestic violence is the single most frequent violence that police officers encounter, according to Lawrence Sherman (Figure 1–4). Police respond up to 8 million times per year to violence that involves a spouse or lover (Sherman & Rogan, 1992). At one time it was considered the most dangerous police call; now it is generally accepted as the most frequent form of violence in the United States.

The battered woman is by far the most frequent victim of domestic violence. She is typical of any woman that you encounter in public, but the danger for her is in her own home. She comes from every walk of life, every age, race, ethnicity, and social class. Women's battering has reached epidemic proportions in the United States and is considered a major social problem. Domestic violence is the leading cause of injury and death to American women, causing more harm than vehicular accidents, rapes, and muggings combined. Although many expect domestic violence victims to be poor, uneducated women, the picture is inaccurate. Their partners victimize many professional women. This is true even though a number of the female victims earn more money than their abusers earn (Goode, 1996). According to the Commonwealth Fund 1998 Survey of Women's Health: "One of six women experienced physical and/or sexual abuse during childhood. The equivalent of three million women nationwide

Figure 1–4   Domestic violence is believed to be the single most frequent violence that police officers encounter. *(Photo courtesy of Mark C. Ide.)*

reported experiencing domestic abuse in the past year. Nearly two in five women had at some point been physically or sexually assaulted or abused, or had been a victim of domestic violence in their lifetime. One in five said she had been raped or assaulted in her lifetime" (Collins et al., 1999).

Each year, an estimated 30 percent of women who become homicide victims die at the hands of men with whom they have a family (Brody, 1992). Husbands or boyfriends killed 28 percent of female murder victims in 1994 (Perkins & Klaus, 1996). Many people fault the battered woman who does not leave her abuser. Yet women do leave abusive relationships. It is at the time of separation that the women are most vulnerable to being beaten and killed. Women who leave their abusive partners are at greater risk of being killed, up to 75 percent greater than for those who stay. A woman is most likely to be murdered when trying to break off an abusive relationship (Sonkin & Durphy, 1997).

Abuse of pregnant women is the leading cause of birth defects and infant mortality, according to the March of Dimes. Lenore Walker has reported a high degree of battering during first, second, and third pregnancies (Walker, 1984). Determining the extent of marital rape is complicated by the fact that some states still do not legally recognize marital rape, while others have extended their definitions to include cohabitors (American Society of Criminology, 1977). Walker has also found a strong correlation between marital rape and battered women; 59 percent of her sample stated that they were forced to have sex with their spouses (Walker, 1984). Studies have indicated that as many as 1 in 10 wives may have been sexually assaulted by their spouses at least once. The majority of domestic violence perpetrators have prior criminal records, according to numerous National Institute of Justice studies (Figure 1–5). A Minneapolis study in 1984 found that 60 percent of domestic violence abusers had prior criminal records (Sherman & Berk, 1994). In 1992, Hirschel reported finding 79 percent of domestic abusers were criminals (Hirschel et al., 1992). Consistent with these findings, a large study conducted in Massachusetts (Klein, 1993) found that 78 percent of men brought before the court for restraining orders in 1990 had at least one prior criminal complaint, the average being 13. The majority of offenders in the Massachusetts study had already been prosecuted for failing to obey a court or Registry of Motor Vehicle injunction. The implication is that many domestic violence perpetrators have indicated through prior legal proceedings that they are inclined toward noncompliance (Klein, 1993). This finding is problematic since the primary response of the court is to protect the domestic violence victim through court order. The average abuser brought to police attention is 32 years old, with two-thirds between their mid-20s and early 40s.

Some researchers suggest that the incidence of male battering may be as high as female battering. Most experts, however, typically accept the incidence rate of male battering by females to be approximately 5 percent of domestic violence. Steinmetz

Figure 1–5   Numerous studies have found that most domestic violence offenders have prior criminal histories. (*Photo courtesy of Mark C. Ide.*)

first reported the problem as the *battered husband syndrome* in 1978 (Steinmetz, 1978). Two national surveys conducted in 1975 and 1985 by Straus and Gelles suggest that domestic violence by women is increasing and violence by men is decreasing (Straus & Gelles, 1986). An earlier study indicated that spousal abuse is almost gender-neutral in most categories of violence (Straus et al., 1980). Recently, Straus reiterated that every study of married and cohabiting couples that was not self-selective found a rate of assault by women on male partners to be the same as the rate of assault by men on female partners (Straus, 1996).

The prevalence of husband battering is an issue of considerable controversy. Some researchers altogether deny the existence of a battered husband syndrome (Hattendorf & Tollerund, 1997). Because the acknowledgment of a male syndrome would be in contrast to the theoretical explanations for wife battering, the position may be a legitimate one. Feminist theorists suggest that it detracts from the importance of the immense problem of female battering. Law enforcement officers, however, would disagree. There is reluctance by law enforcement to arrest female perpetrators, indicating a smaller percentage of perpetrators than in reality. The Kenosha Domestic Abuse Intervention Project (Hamberger, 1990) indicated that after institution of a domestic violence mandatory arrest law, women exhibited a 12-fold increase in arrests relative to pre-mandatory arrest compared to a twofold increase for men during the same period (Hamberger & Potente, 1996). The author of the project cautions that women and men do differ in their rate of violence and that self-defense is most often the underlying cause for domestic violence by females.

Often cited as a precursor to spouse abuse, dating violence and acquaintance rape have received considerable national attention lately. The sexual climate on college campuses has been identified as nothing less than treacherous for women. As reported by Copeland and Wolfe (Copeland & Wolfe, 1995):

- In a survey of 3,187 college women, 478 reported having been raped; of these, 10.6 percent were raped by strangers; 24.9 percent were raped by nonromantic acquaintances; 21 percent were raped by casual dates; and 30 percent were raped by steady dates.
- More than half of college rape victims had been attacked by dates.
- Studies of high school and college students conducted during the 1980s reported rates of dating violence ranging from 12 to 65 percent.

For incidents other than rape, a number of studies have confirmed that females self-report a higher incidence of violence toward men than do men toward women in their dating relationships (Straus, 1996). A study in 1991 indicated that female college students were more likely than males to resort to using violence to control, show anger, or retaliate for emotional hurt (Follingstad et al., 1991).

Vallerie Coleman has recently demonstrated that lesbian violence is a significant problem, noting the reluctance by both lesbians and mainstream society to recognize violence between women (Coleman, 1996). In *Domestic Partner Abuse* she reviews the available literature and concludes that "the prevalence and severity of lesbian batter-ing are comparable to that of heterosexual relationships...rates of violence in lesbian relationships ranging from 25% to 48%." Coleman cites a study (Gardner, 1989) that compared rates of violence among couples that were heterosexual, lesbian, and gay. No significant differences in prevalence were found in partner abuse; heterosexual couples evidenced the lowest rate of abuse, at 28 percent; gay men had a rate of 38 percent; and lesbian couples had the highest rate, 48 percent.

Another form of intimate violence, gay domestic violence, is slowly coming to the surface. This form of violence is difficult to determine due to societal preconcep-tions about a battered victim. We expect that one will be larger and stronger than the other. Frequently, we view battering between men as normal aggressive behavior. Issues in gay relationships are forcing us to reconceptualize domestic violence. Battered gay and bisexual victims often respond to battering by striking back, which also occurs in male–female relationships. Typically, this attempt at self-protection is mutual physical aggression. When the perpetrator and victim are roughly of the same physical size and strength, the violence is misperceived as "mutual" (Letellier, 1996).

Of all forms of domestic violence, this one is the least known of all: children bat-tering their parents. How much battering goes on can be left to one's imagination. Parents who are physically or sexually assaulted will rarely report their child. It is a source of shame and confusion. Statistics on the numbers of parents that are killed by their adolescent children have been documented. Between 1977 and 1986, the killing of a parent was an almost daily event in the United States, with over 300 parents killed each year (Heide, 1992).

Heide conducted an in-depth analysis of the FBI Supplementary Homicide Report data for this period, which revealed that parents and stepparents murdered were typically white and non-Hispanic. Further, in the majority of cases, the child who killed was also a white, non-Hispanic male. More than 70 percent of those killing fathers, stepfathers, or stepmothers were under 30 years of age, while almost 70 per-cent of those killing mothers were between 20 and 50. Sons and daughters under age 18 killed 15 percent of murdered mothers, 25 percent of fathers, 30 percent of step-mothers, and 34 percent of stepfathers.

CHILD ABUSE

Child abuse is neither uncommon nor newly discovered (Golden, 1997). Children have always been abused and neglected by one or both parents. Rarely is child abuse a single physical attack or a single act of deprivation or molestation. For a child, emotional abuse includes excessive, aggressive, or unreasonable parental behavior that places demands on a child to perform beyond his or her capabilities. Sometimes emotional abuse is not what a parent does, but what a parent fails to do. Children who receive no love, no care, no support, and no guidance will carry the scars into adulthood.

Until recently, few considered that the treatment of children in the United States was a concern or problem. It came to public attention, however, with the coining of the phrase *battered child syndrome* in 1962 by C. Henry Kempe. Since that time, parents have killed 50,000 children, and at least 25 million more have been abused, neglected, or sexually exploited (Helfer & Kempe, 1988). Although we don't know the exact numbers of children abused or neglected, private- and government-sponsored research has given us some insight into the extent of the problem. In 1988, the National Committee for Prevention of Child Abuse estimated that there were 1,225 reported child abuse fatalities in the United States (Whitcomb, 1992). Approximately 1,046 children, or three children per day, died in 1995 and again in 1996 as a result of child abuse and neglect (National Committee to Prevent Child Abuse, 1997).

Physical abuse is the most common cause of death to children, often committed by their own parents. By anyone's standard, this is a significant problem. The criminal justice community is at the center of efforts to combat what used to be considered a parent's prerogative. No longer is child abuse considered a family affair. From the criminal justice standpoint child abuse has gone from an insignificant part of the business of the legal system to a major focus of court activity (Sagatun & Edwards, 1995). Specialized units have been developed for investigating reports of child abuse in the courts, in police departments, and in social service agencies across the country.

Early studies suggest that females experience more child abuse overall than do males (U.S. Department of Health and Human Services, 1988). It is thought that the higher incidence of abuse to females was due to the fact that females were more susceptible to sexual abuse and to injury. For both abuse and neglect, the incidence of maltreatment increases with age, with the exception of fatalities. Child deaths are more numerous among the younger children.

Consistent with earlier findings, low income appears to be a significant risk factor for child maltreatment today. Children from families with annual incomes below $15,000 were over 22 times more likely to experience maltreatment than were children from families whose incomes exceeded $30,000. They were also 18 times more likely to be sexually abused, almost 56 times more likely to be educationally neglected, and over 22 times more likely to be seriously injured (Kharfen, 1996). Families with four or more children showed higher rates of physical abuse and physical neglect.

In 1995, over 3 million children were reported for child abuse and neglect to child protective service agencies in the United States, according to the National Committee to Prevent Child Abuse. Their numbers suggest that 14 out of every 1,000 U.S. children were substantiated as victims of child maltreatment (Lung & Daro, 1996). These numbers should not be accepted as the full extent of the problem. We know that not all cases are reported. In 1986, for example, approximately 22.6 children per 1,000 experienced abuse or neglect, yet only half of the incidents were reported to child protective service agencies (Sedlak, 1990). Since the National Committee to Prevent Child Abuse began its annual survey on the numbers of children reported to child protective services, there has been a steady growth of reports. Between 1977 and 1987 the total number of reports nationwide increased by 45 percent. Experts agree that a greater awareness of child abuse is responsible for the large increase in reports to child services. Every U.S. state has a law against abusing a child. Each state now has a reporting statute that requires certain persons to make reports of suspected child abuse. The reporting statutes define child abuse and identify groups of people who are mandated reporters. In most states the Department of Social Services, Department of Protective Services, Social and Rehabilitative Services, or Bureau of Children and Family Services is the agency designated to receive the reports. Some states now have gone a step beyond by requiring social service agencies to report the substantiated cases to law enforcement for possible criminal action.

Another important source of information on the incidence of child abuse and neglect is the U.S. Department of Health and Human Services, which administers the National Incidence Study (NIS), also called the Study of National Incidence and Prevalence of Child Abuse. The NIS attempts to estimate the actual number of abused and neglected children in the United States, including cases not reported to child protective services. According to the third National Incidence Study of Child Abuse and Neglect, over 2.8 million children have been abused or neglected in 1993, double the number of children who were abused in 1986 (Sedlak & Broadhurst, 1996).

Sexual abuse of children is an area of great controversy. Experts disagree on the prevalence of child sexual abuse, yet it is the fastest-growing form of reported child abuse. Sexual abuse of children is an issue of power and control, not love and intimacy. Between 1980 and 1986 the rate of sexual abuse to children more than tripled, according to the Study of National Incidence and Prevalence of Child Abuse and Neglect (U.S. Department of Health and Human Services, 1988). From 1986 to 1996, a decline in the proportion of reported cases involving child sexual abuse has been noted; most recently, they comprised only 7 percent of all cases (Wang & Daro, 1998). Unfortunately, recent studies indicate that the average age of the sexually abused child is on a downward trend since the 1970s (Lloyd, 1991). Preschool-aged children are being victimized more frequently than 20 years ago, which may account for fewer reported cases, since cases of sexual abuse to preschool children are extremely difficult to investigate and confirm. Seldom is there physical evidence, and young children have difficulty in explaining the nature of their abuse. Only the most serious cases involving young children, where significant physical injury is documented, can go forward for prosecution.

Reports indicate consistently that females are the most frequent victims of sexual abuse. The actual incidence varies, however. A recent survey indicated that girls are sexually abused three times more often than boys are (MacFarlane et al., 1986). According to the Center Against Sexual Abuse, 38 percent of girls and 16 percent of boys are sexually abused before the age of 18. Most agree that at least one of every five girls will be sexually abused by age 18 (Russell, 1984). Surveys to adults found that one-fifth to one-half of American women were sexually abused as children, most of them by an older male relative.

Experts agree that most sexual abuse of children is not reported (MacFarlane et al., 1986). This coincides with the controversy on the prevalence of sexual abuse to boys. It is estimated that between 50,000 and 90,000 boys are sexually abused every year. Mic Hunter and other clinicians who work with sexual abuse victims dispute the actual incidence, which may be as prevalent as sexual abuse to females (Mathews et al., 1990). Investigators of child sexual abuse note that cases involving male victims have steadily increased since the 1980s. National studies indicate that at least 25 percent of the victims of child sexual abuse are boys.

As pointed out by Kim Menard, the majority of research on sexual abuse to children concerns only males as perpetrators. She reminds us through her study that although it is difficult to determine the pedophilic rate among women, they do commit sexual child abuse (Menard, 1997). The review of current literature indicates that the degree of female child sexual abuse perpetration ranges from a low of 1 percent to a high of 32.5 percent.

The media has brought attention to cases of sexual abuse in day care settings. Recent reports of cultlike abuse have shocked the nation. However, only 2 percent of confirmed child sexual abuse cases reported to child protection agencies are reports of abuse in day care and foster care (Lung & Daro, 1996).

Elder Abuse

In this book we focus on "domestic" elder abuse, that is perpetrated by family members or others who are known through a caregiving role in the victim's home. Abuse may have relatively little impact on the elderly, or it may threaten their lives. Physical abuse ranges from a slap that knocks off an elder's glasses, to kicking and punching that might result in death. Financial exploitation may be as simple as theft from the elder's wallet, to the appropriation of one's home.

It is difficult to be precise on the extent of elder abuse (Figure 1–6) because very few scientifically valid studies of this population have been conducted (Pillemer &

Figure 1–6   The exact incidence of elder abuse is not known and difficult to determine. *(Photo courtesy of the Administration on Aging.)*

Suitor, 1990). Approximately 5 to 10 percent of older Americans are abuse victims. The exact incidence of elder abuse is not known and difficult to determine. Pillemer and Finkelhor organized the first large randomized survey of elder domestic abuse in 1988 (Pillemer & Finkelhor, 1988). Excluding self-abuse, they concluded that no more than 1.1 million elders were victims. In what was a surprising result, the study found that most perpetrators of elderly abuse were spouses who abused in almost equal amounts regardless of gender. Implications of elderly spouse abuse have not yet been fully researched. Is elderly spouse abuse a continuation of an abusive relationship that began when the couples were younger? It is suspected that some elderly spouse abuse begins with the strains of caregiving for a partner who is deteriorating physically or mentally. A majority of abuse victims are female. This is not surprising since they comprise the majority of the elder population.

The elder population is extremely vulnerable to domestic abuse because of lifestyle and infirmity. Despite the decline in the overall rate of elder crime victimization (U.S. Department of Justice, 1994), elders' fear of crime victimization is greater than that of any other group in society. Often, older Americans will attempt to limit their potential for victimization by altering their lifestyles. They sometimes withdraw from society by staying at home and not participating in activities after dark. Fear of being victimized may provide the catalyst for elders to isolate themselves more than is medically necessary, thereby increasing the possibility of domestic elder abuse.

Nationwide, the reporting of domestic elder abuse has increased 94 percent between 1986 and 1992 (Tatara, 1993). Experts agree that neglect is the most common form of domestic elder abuse. Physical abuse accounted for 15.7 percent in 1994, while financial/material exploitation represented 12.3 percent of the substantiated reports (National Center on Elder Abuse, 1997a). Physical abuse appears to be on the decrease, yet may be the most difficult to substantiate. Physicians and other health care professionals play an important role in the identification of elder abuse; they provided 21.6 percent of all domestic elder abuse reports in 1994 (National Center on Elder Abuse, 1997b). Family members and relatives of victims made 14.9 percent of all reported cases in the same year, and friends, business institutions, and elder abuse victims also made reports. Elders are susceptible to substantial injury during the performance of routine tasks such as cooking, or even walking when their eyesight is impaired. When injuries do occur, they tend to be more serious: Bones break more easily and bruising is more likely to occur. As violent crime victims, the elderly are more likely than other age groups to sustain serious injury (Bachman, 1992). It is no wonder that the elderly fear injury. Further complicating the issue is that some elders require restraint because of dementia; such restraint will often leave marks and bruises. When restraints cause suffering, pain, or are used for punitive reasons, the use is considered abusive.

The increase in domestic reporting is probably the result of recently legislated mandated reporting laws. All states have legislation that in some way addresses elder abuse; some are mandatory reporting laws, adult protective services laws, domestic violence laws, or specific elder abuse and neglect laws. As of 1994, all states but eight designated certain types of professionals as mandatory reporters of domestic elder abuse (Figure 1–7). They are required by law to report suspected cases of abuse, neglect, and exploitation. An agency is designated by law to investigate the reports. The investigating agency differs from state to state and may be a law enforcement or social service agency. The majority of elder abuse reports are substantiated after investigations.

Perpetrators of domestic abuse are equally likely to be male or female. In 1994, 50.6 percent of abusers were male and 49.3 percent were female (National Center on Elder Abuse, 1997a). What we don't know is the percentage of perpetrators who were abused as children by the elders to whom they are giving care. Are the victims acting out the consummate role reversal, treating their parents as they had been treated? Mark Lach, chief of geriatrics at New York Hospital, reported that childhood and family abuse might be linked to elder abuse and neglect, noting that abusers of the elderly are usually adult children or spouses of the victim (Lach, 1997). The most frequent elder abuser is the elder's adult child. Adult children may be responsible for providing caring for their parent(s) regardless of the quality of relationship they enjoyed in earlier years. Caring for an elderly person is made even more difficult with the added strains of a poor relationship. Additionally, codependence develops when the adult child receives room and board in exchange for caregiving to an elderly parent. The adult child may be reluctant or unable to provide the level of care necessary, but dependent on the elder for living arrangements. Conversely, the elder victims are often reluctant to report domestic abuse from a family member for fear of retaliation or isolation.

Figure 1–7 Physicians and other health care professionals play an important role in the identification of elder abuse. *(Photo courtesy of the Administration on Aging.)*

The majority of elders aged 65 and above who are not institutionalized are living in a family setting, according to U.S. Census reports. This population is most vulnerable to abuse that is domestic. The situation will become more desperate as demographics on aging change. According to the U.S. Senate Special Committee on Aging, the 65 and older population is expected to double between the years 1989 and 2030. By the year 2040, the elderly will outnumber the young, with more than one in four Americans age 65 or older (Usdansky, 1992). With an increase in the older population, police can anticipate more domestic elder abuse cases, and we must be prepared to respond.

CONCLUSIONS

Domestic violence includes every imaginable form of violence that can occur as long as there is a domestic relationship between perpetrator and victim. Thinking of domestic violence as a group of crimes linked together into a general category is helpful for remembering just what domestic violence is. The individual crimes that we refer to as domestic violence are usually crimes without being placed into the category of domestic. Defining the crimes as domestic in a legislative act allows each state to encourage law enforcement officers to enforce the laws regardless of the relationship between the people. Sometimes mandatory arrest or preferred arrest policies are included, spelling out the expectations that the state has with regard to police action. Some states include inducements for full enforcement. These topics are addressed later in the book.

Once in a while, a particular crime, such as the violation of a civil domestic restraining order, becomes a crime that is specific only to domestic violence. An "Act to Prevent Domestic Violence" is one way that the legislation in each state defines the specific crimes that will be placed into the domestic category. Further, such acts define what relationships will be considered. The relationships generally include all intimate partners, regardless of gender or marriage. Additionally, people who are related through marriage or blood are considered domestic partners.

The scope of domestic violence seems overwhelming when reading the statistics. It is important to note that not all statistics are what they appear to be. There are many reasons why a particular study or research project concludes with figures that are less than perfect. It really doesn't matter for the purposes of studying the issues. It is clear that we do not know exactly the extent of domestic violence! Experts agree that domestic violence crimes are largely underreported. Skeptics suggest that the numbers are inflated. So we should expect that the figures might not be exact. What they tell us, more importantly, is that there is a problem of violence in the United States. The violence has invaded many homes. There are many children who are sexually and physically abused and neglected every day. We know that people are killing their children, partners, and elders. In adult intimate relationships, many people are being dominated or controlled, physically, emotionally, or sexually, and even harmed financially. We have to face the horrible truth, even if we don't know the exact numbers. If you look around, you will see it.

𝒦 EY 𝒯ERMS

Abuse prevention acts	Financial exploitation
Battering	Neglect
Child abuse	Physical abuse
Domestic partner abuse	Psychological abuse
Domestic violence	Sexual abuse
Elder abuse	Spouse abuse
Emotional abuse	Wife abuse

𝒬UESTIONS 𝒻OR 𝓡EVIEW

1. Define *domestic violence*.

2. Domestic abuse is a classification containing many crimes that are committed against the person. List examples of these crimes.

3. What are abuse prevention acts?

4. What relationships constitute a domestic relationship?

5. List the various types of domestic abuse.

6. When is a woman at the greatest threat of being beaten or abused?

7. What is the major explanation for violence perpetrated by women on men in a domestic relationship?

8. What is the main cause of death among children? Name one significant risk factor for child abuse.

9. What is the primary reason that sexual abuse of children occurs?

10. Which group in society most fears crime victimization? What is the most common form of abuse to this group?

𝓡EFERENCES

American Society of Criminology. 1977. *Critical Criminal Justice Issues: Task Force Reports.* NCJ 158837. Washington, DC: National Institute of Justice.

Bachman, Ronet. 1992. *Elderly Victims.* Washington, DC: U.S. Department of Justice, Bureau of Justice Statistics.

Brody, Jane E. 1992. "When Love Turns Violent: The Roots of Abuse." *New York Times*, Health, March 18, p. 124.

Champion, Dean J. 1997. *The Roxbury Dictionary of Criminal Justice: Key Terms and Major Court Cases.* Los Angeles: Roxbury Publishing Company.

Coleman, Vallerie E. 1996. "Lesbian Battering: The Relationship between Personality and the Perpetration of Violence." Pp. 77–101 in *Domestic Partner Abuse*, L. K. Hamberger and Claire Renzetti (eds.). New York: Springer Publishing Company.

Collins, Karen S., Cathy Schoen, Susan Joseph, Lisa Duchon, Elisabeth Simantov, and Michele Yellowitz. 1999. "Health Concerns across a Woman's Lifespan." *http://www.cmwf.org/programs/women/ksc_whsurvey99_332.asp*. 1999.

Copeland, Louis and Leslie R. Wolfe. 1995. "A Radical Feminist View of Rape." In *Rape on Campus*, Scott Barbour (ed.). San Diego, CA: Greenhaven Press.

Follingstad, Diane R., Shannon Wright, Shirley Lloyd, and Jeri A. Sebastian. 1991. "Sex Differences in Motivations and Effects in Dating Violence." *Family Relations* 40(1):51–58.

Gardner, R. 1989. "Method of Conflict Resolution and Characteristics of Abuse and Victimization in Heterosexual, Lesbian, and Gay Male Couples." University of Georgia, Dissertation Abstracts International.

Golden, Renny. 1997. *Disposable Children: America's Welfare System*. New York: Wadsworth Publishing Company.

Goode, Erica. 1996. "Domestic Violence Is a Serious Problem for Women." Pp. 22–27 in *Domestic Violence*, Bruno Leone (ed.). San Diego, CA: Greenhaven Press.

Hamberger, L. K. 1990. *Effects of the Mandatory Arrest Law on Domestic Violence Perpetrator Counseling*. Kenosha, WI: Wisconsin Equal Justice Task Force.

Hamberger, L. K. and Theresa Potente. 1996. "Counseling Heterosexual Women Arrested for Domestic Violence." Pp. 53–75 in *Domestic Partner Abuse*, L. K. Hamberger and Claire Renzetti (eds.). New York: Springer Publishing Company.

Hattendorf, Joanne and Toni R. Tollerund. 1997. "Domestic Violence: Counseling Strategies That Minimize the Impact of Secondary Victimization." *Perspectives in Psychiatric Care* 33(1):10–14.

Heide, Kathleen M. 1992. *Why Kids Kill Parents: Child Abuse and Adolescent Homicide*. Columbus, OH: Ohio State University Press.

Helfer, Ray E. and Ruth S. Kempe (eds.). 1988. *The Battered Child*, 4th ed. Chicago: University of Chicago Press.

Hirschel, David J. et. al. 1992. *Charlotte Spouse Assault Replication Project, 1987–1989*. ICPSR 6114. Washington, DC: U.S. Department of Justice.

Kharfen, Michael. 1996. "Survey Shows Dramatic Increase in Child Abuse and Neglect, 1986–1993." *www.dhhs.gov*. 1998.

Klein, Andrew R. 1993. "Spousal/Partner Assault: A Protocol for the Sentencing and Supervision of Offenders." In *Domestic Violence: The Challenge for Law Enforcement*. Quincy, MA: Commonwealth of Massachusetts.

Lach, Mark. 1997. *A Coordinated Approach to Reducing Family Violence: Conference Highlights*. Washington, DC: National Institute of Justice and the American Medical Association.

Lehrman, Fredrica. 1997. *Domestic Violence Practice and Procedure*. Washington, DC: West Group.

Letellier, Patrick. 1996. "Gay and Bisexual Male Domestic Violence Victimization: Challenges to Feminist Theory." Pp. 1–22 in *Domestic Partner Abuse*, L. K. Hamberger and Claire Renzetti (eds.). New York: Springer Publishing Company.

Lloyd, D. 1991. *What Do We Know about Child Sexual Abuse Today?* Washington, DC: U.S. Department of Health and Human Services.

Lung, C. T. and Deborah Daro. 1996. *Current Trends in Child Abuse Reporting and Fatalities: The Results of the 1995 Annual Fifty State Survey*. Washington, DC: National Committee to Prevent Child Abuse.

MacFarlane, Kee, Jill Waterman, Shawn Conerly, Linda Damon, Michael Durfee, and Suzanne Long. 1986. *Sexual Abuse of Young Children: Evaluation and Treatment.* New York: Guilford Press.

Mathews, Ruth, Jane Mathews, and Kate Speltz. 1990. "Female Sexual Offenders." Pp. 275–93 in *The Sexually Abused Male: Prevalence, Impact, and Treatment,* Mic Hunter (ed.). New York: Lexington Books.

Menard, Kim. 1997."Female Sexual Offenders: A Review of the Literature with Research and Policy Implications." *Academy of Criminal Justice Sciences Annual Conference,* Albuquerque, NM, March. Unpublished.

National Center on Elder Abuse. 1997a. *Elder Abuse in Domestic Settings,* Vol. 2. Washington, DC: NCEA.

_____. 1997b. *Elder Abuse in Domestic Settings,* Vol. 3. Washington, DC: NCEA.

National Committee to Prevent Child Abuse. 1997. *1996 Annual Fifty State Survey.* Chicago: NCPCA.

Perkins, Craig and Patsy Klaus. 1996. *National Crime Victimization Survey: Criminal Victimization 1994.* NCJ 158022. Washington, DC: U.S. Department of Justice.

Pillemer, Karl and David Finkelhor. 1988. "The Prevalence of Elder Abuse: A Random Sample Survey." *Gerontologist* 28(1):51.

Pillemer, Karl and Jill Suitor. 1990. *Treatment of Family Violence.* New York: John Wiley & Sons.

Russell, Jeffrey B. 1984. *Witchcraft in the Middle Ages.* Ithaca, NY: Cornell University Press.

Sagatun, Inger J. and Leonard P. Edwards. 1995. *Child Abuse and the Legal System.* Chicago: Nelson-Hall Publishers.

Sedlak, Andrea J. 1990. *Technical Amendments to the Study Findings—National Incidence and Prevalence of Child Abuse and Neglect: 1988.* Washington, DC: National Center on Child Abuse and Neglect.

Sedlak, Andrea and Diane Broadhurst. 1996. *Executive Summary of the Third National Incidence Study of Child Abuse and Neglect.* Washington, DC: U.S. Department of Health and Human Services, Administration for Children and Families; and the National Center on Child Abuse and Neglect.

Sherman, Lawrence W. and Richard A. Berk. 1994. "The Specific Deterrent Effects of Arrest for Domestic Assault." *American Sociological Review* 49:261–72.

Sherman, Lawrence and Dennis Rogan. 1992. P. 46 in *Policing Domestic Violence: Experiments and Dilemmas.* New York: Free Press.

Sonkin, Daniel J. and Michael Durphy. 1997. *Learning to Live Without Violence: A Handbook for Men,* 5th ed. Volcano, CA: Volcano Press.

Steinmetz, Suzanne K. 1978. "The Battered Husband Syndrome." *Victimology* 2:499–509.

Straus, Murray A. 1996. "Domestic Violence Is a Problem for Men." Pp. 50–64 in *Domestic Violence,* Bruno Leone (ed.). San Diego, CA: Greenhaven Press.

Straus, Murray A. and Richard J. Gelles. 1986. "Societal Change and Change in Family Violence from 1975–1985." *Journal of Marriage and the Family* 48:465–79.

Straus, Murray A., Richard J. Gelles, and Suzanne K. Steinmetz. 1980. P. 222 in *Behind Closed Doors: Violence in the American Family.* Garden City, NY: Anchor Press/Doubleday.

Tatara, Toshio. 1993. *Summaries of the Statistical Data on Elder Abuse in Domestic Settings for FY90 and FY91.* Washington, DC: National Aging Resource Center of Elder Abuse.

U.S. Department of Health and Human Services. 1988. *Study of National Incidence and Prevalence of Child Abuse and Neglect.* Washington, DC: DHHS.

U. S. Department of Justice. 1994. National Crime Victimization Survey: Elderly Crime Victims. NCJ 147186. Washington, DC: DOJ.

Usdansky, Margaret L. 1992. "Nation of Youth Growing Long in the Tooth." *USA Today*, News, p. 10a.

Walker, Lenore E. 1984. *The Battered Woman Syndrome*. New York: Springer Publishing Company.

Wang, Ching-Tung and Deborah Daro. 1998. *Current Trends in Child Abuse Reporting and Fatalities: The Results of the 1997 Annual Fifty State Survey*. Working Paper 808. Chicago: National Committee to Prevent Child Abuse.

Whitcomb, Debra. 1992. *When the Victim Is a Child*, 2nd ed. Washington, DC: U.S. Department of Justice.

A Global View of Family Social and Legal Relations

INTRODUCTION

> For too long, the collective consciousness of contemporary Western society has promoted an idyllic image of the family as a safe haven in an otherwise turbulent, violent, and unsafe world. Closer examination of the nuclear family, however, provides considerable evidence that this unit of social organization is actually a fertile environment for deadly aggression. (Struve, 1990)

As we pointed out in Chapter 1, family violence is seen in numerous forms. Although they are often discussed separately, it must be remembered that all forms of domestic violence are interrelated. They occur within the family unit. Violence within families is a pervasive and long-standing problem, although it was not considered as such until quite recently. Even without an exact count of the numbers of victims, it certainly can be said that it affects millions of women, men, and children across the United States and around the world (Figure 2–1). It is not simply a family problem; the effects of the fight go beyond the individual family experiencing the hostility.

The contemporary field of domestic violence is the study of a *social problem*. Society is a collection of many groups. Patterns of behavior guide our interactions and reflect the goal of the group. We study human social behavior and interaction in sociology, psychology, and anthropology: the social sciences. They are the branches of learning that deal with the institutions and functions of human society. Family violence is studied through all of these perspectives, each using different approaches of examining human behavior.

Figure 2–1   Domestic violence affects millions of women, men, and children across the United States and around the world. *(Photo courtesy of the Administration on Aging.)*

In addition to the groups that make up a society are the institutions that interact. These institutions of government, families, and education are concerned with accomplishing goals within the society. The family is an important institution within the scheme of human stability. Its members follow rules and are bound by acceptable standards of behavior. Codified into a body of law are the principles of the past and of the present. Reflecting changes in human behavior are changing laws that document rights and responsibilities in marital relations. Examining these guideposts of human behavior is one way to understand the positioning of people today.

The social sciences use various approaches to examine social events, and often they consider the same circumstance from different points of view. Historians, for example, trace the development of families over time. Economists look at the labor pool, major lines of communication, and easily accessible consumer markets that would influence households. Both approaches have netted interesting information for the modern family. In this chapter, the historical progress of relationships is presented through legal definitions of the roles within the family.

There is very little social historical work available that will shed light on the condition of the family in ancient and medieval times. The legal sanctions on wife assault inform us about the expected code of behavior by husbands. Some evidence of the expectations of wives is also evidenced in legal history. This brief historical account will show that family structures and social status of these members have dictated the manner in which people are treated and how the expectations of family have evolved.

Like people themselves, social relationships change over time. Awareness of the problems associated with family violence today has brought us to a point where it is a recognized indicator of a dysfunctional family. That was hardly the case throughout history. In the past, violence against intimates has been tolerated as accepted social conduct and alternatively condemned as deviant behavior. Isolated initiatives to control interpersonal violence can be traced back as far as the Roman era, when patriarchy defined the relationships between the husband and his wife and children (Belknap, 1992).

Wife battering and child abuse are the oldest forms of what we currently refer to as domestic violence. Comparing the history of social relations over time is like looking at oranges and apples. Socially accepted views on property in ancient times are very different from those of today. Women were considered inferior to men, intellectually and physically. Punishment of errant wives was in the best interest of the husband, whose status has developed from a property owner to a life partner. The purpose of this chapter is to provide insight into the legal developments of family relationships. A kernel of truth may be found in all explanations for crime, and the social–legal historical perspective is only one of many factors in a larger picture.

EARLY SOCIAL–LEGAL HISTORY

Domination of men over women and children, or patriarchy, has a strong historical foundation. Some experts suggest that this inequality between the sexes is the foundation for the assumption of male superiority and the foundation for domestic violence. By providing husbands with the right to punish wayward wives, the system gives a rationale to male brutality against women. Others advise that the social order was just that, an order to life's relations for purposes of survival.

According to the civil law of Rome, the male head of the family had full rights and powers over his wife, children, and any descendants who sprang from him through male lineage only. This power was at one time exercised over the lives and deaths of both women and children. Women, children, and slaves were property that could be sold or bought. Any harm committed against a woman was viewed as an offense against the father if she was unmarried, or as an offense to the husband, but not to the victim.

The husband originally had the right to kill his wife if she engaged in adultery; this right was later limited to the father. Consequently, it was the male "owner" who sought vengeance or compensation for his loss. A female could not be an aggrieved

---

More about It: Patriarchy

Patriarchy is traced to the Latin term *patria potestas*, which refers to the paternal authority. It is the social system where men govern. This imbalance of power translates into the lack of legal standing for adult women and is evidenced throughout most of history throughout the world.

party, nor was she held responsible for her actions. It was therefore the responsibility of the husband or father to punish the woman whose actions were injurious to others. This lack of legal standing prohibited women from appealing to the courts for relief when their punishment was excessive or without cause.

The Ancient and Medieval World

The earliest known body of law is the Code of Hammurabi, eighteenth century B.C. All matters of living were governed extensively through the code. It contains lengthy and specific arrangements between husbands and wives, who entered into marriage by a contract, usually arranged by the father of the bride. Provisions were made to allow a woman to request entry into a convent to live as a nun, and such a request could not be denied (Horne, 1915).

As objects of possession, women were both controlled and protected by their male relatives. The code of ancient Babylon allowed a man to leave (divorce) his wife by telling her to go and returning to her the dowry that she brought (if they had no children together) (King, 1998). When there were children, he was required to provide her with a means of support in raising the children. If she wanted to leave, however, his permission was necessary. If he did not want to release her from the marriage, he could keep her as a servant in his home and take a new wife.

Adoption was a legal arrangement often used to provide care for parents during their old age, according to the Code of Hammurabi (Horne, 1915). Vestal virgins frequently adopted daughters to care for them in their "elder" years, since they were not supposed to have children.

The Roman Empire

Illustrations of acceptable physical punishment by husbands against their wives are evidenced in the early Roman Empire. Although the law sometimes placed obligations on both the husband and wife, the purpose was clearly to assure that the husband had control over his property. Early Roman law treated women and children as the property of the husband.

Back Then...

In 753 B.C., Romulus, who is credited with the founding of Rome, formalized the first law of marriage. In part the law stipulated: "This law obligated both the married women, as having no other refuge, to conform themselves entirely to the temper of their husbands and the husbands to rule their wives as necessary and inseparable possessions" (O'Faolain & Martines, 1973).

Under the laws of Romulus, the wife could not divorce her husband (Lefkowitz & Fant, 1992). He was granted rights of divorce when the woman had used drugs or magic, and for adultery. Other reasons were stipulated as acceptable motives for the male seeking divorce, but he would forfeit part of his estate for doing so.

The legitimate punishment of errant Roman wives during the first and second centuries A.D. is recorded through the following accounts (Lefkowitz & Fant, 1992):

- Egnatius Metellus took a cudgel and beat his wife to death because she had drunk some wine. He was not charged with a crime as she had violated the laws of sobriety.

- Quintus Angistius Vetus divorced his wife after he had seen her having a private conversation with a common freedwoman in public.

The Christian Era

Christianity embraced the subordination of wives over their husbands, and scriptures commanded women to be silent, obedient, and accepting of their husbands' authority. A passage from the New Testament, Ephesians 5:22–24, specifically states the role of a married woman according to the Church: "Wives should regard their husbands as they regard the Lord, since as Christ is head of the Church and saves the whole body, so is a husband the head of his wife; and as the Church submits to Christ, so should wives to their husbands, in everything" (*Jerusalem Bible*, 1996).

The notion that male supremacy was supported unconditionally by the Christian faith is further supported by the actions of Constantine the Great, the first Christian Roman emperor, later canonized as a saint. Constantine was the first emperor to order the execution of his own wife. In A.D. 298, Constantine married Maximillian's infant daughter, later having her scalded to death, in a cauldron of water brought to a slow boil over a wood fire, because he suspected her of adultery (Davis, 1971).

Back Then...

Corporal punishment of an errant wife was a widely accepted practice. A Christian scholar generated the *Rules of Marriage* in the late fifteenth century. They specified: "When you see your wife commit an offense, don't rush at her with insults and violent blows...Scold her sharply, bully and terrify her. And if this doesn't work...take up a stick and beat her soundly, for it is better to punish the body and correct the soul than to damage the soul and spare the body....Then readily beat her, not in rage but out of charity and concern for her soul, so that the beating will redound to your merit and her good" (Davidson, 1978).

The Russian Example

According to historian Natalia Pushkareva, women held positions of power and status in Russia prior to the advent of Christianity. The treaty between Byzantium and Rus in 911 specifically mentions women's property. A woman's legal entitlement to a portion of property that was to be retained in the event of her husband's death is unique for the period. The relative status of men and women during the tenth to fifteenth centuries was clear in the scriptures of the Russian Orthodox Church. Not only were men allowed to control their wives, they were expected to! Men who allowed themselves to be ruled by wives were scorned.

Evidence of legalized battering can be found in the Russian domestic codes during the sixteenth century, when the status of women declined in society. They provided that wives were to be soundly thrashed, but suggested that the beating not be on the face or ear, since it might disadvantage the husband if his spouse were to become blind or deaf. Careful placement of the whip was the provision to control his possession, without damaging his property (Masters, 1964). The restrictions on wife beating were instructions on restraint for practical purposes, not out of concern for the victim. Russian Orthodox teaching devoted particular attention to the elderly, unlike other unlike areas of Western Europe during the tenth to fifteenth centuries (Pushkareva, 1997). Multigenerational families included elders and treated them with respect.

British Common Law

Patriarchy is not the only social arrangement between married people, but it has been the dominant one in Western civilizations. Under common law, women and children were no longer viewed as property, but the results were the same. The order was based on the belief that when two are joined in marriage, they become one, socially and legally. The rights of the woman are then subordinate to those of the male, unlike the woman who remained single.

Historian Laurel Thatcher Ulrich offers this comment on the legal status of women under common law. It was authored by William Blackstone in *Commentaries on the Laws of England* (Ulrich, 1991) and explains the concept of this patriarchal order: "By marriage, the husband and wife are one person in law; that is, the very being or legal existence of the women is suspended during the marriage, or at least is

---

Back Then...

"Whoever is ruled by his wife, may he be the worst damned! Such men become soft, shameless, silly, unfree, and inarticulate." Further, the church warned that to give a woman freedom was like his committing suicide for a man. Disorder and destruction would be the inevitable results (Pushkareva, 1997).

B a c k   T h e n ...

According to Lunn, the earliest case of domestic violence heard in the British court was in 1395. Margaret Neffield and witnesses testified that her husband attacked her with a dagger, causing several wounds and broken bones. The court was not satisfied that this constituted grounds for a judicial separation, and Mrs. Neffield was ordered to return to living with her husband (Lunn, 1991).

---

incorporated and consolidated into that of the husband; under whose wing, protection, and cover, she performs everything."

Sir William Blackstone also coined the phrase *rule of thumb* in 1768 when he codified British common law. This rule asserted that a husband had the right to beat his wife as long as the stick was no thicker than his thumb. Husbands had the right and even a duty to chastise their wives (Pagelow, 1984). The rule is thought to be a compassionate replacement for the law that allowed a husband to beat his wife "with any reasonable instrument" (Dutton, 1998).

French Law

It was a dangerous thing to question the inferiority of women presumed by the Declaration of the Rights of Man. Olympe de Gouges wrote a *Declaration of the Rights of Women* in 1791 and was quickly arrested and tried for treason. On November 3, 1793, she was executed by the guillotine (Levy et al., 1979). In the early nineteenth century Napoleon Bonaparte formalized the civil code in France, subjugating women as legal minors for their entire lives. Under the Napoleonic Code wives could be beaten, punched, and permanently disfigured for minor disobedience or for "scolding" (Pagelow, 1984). The French code of chivalry allowed the husband to knock her to the earth, strike her in the face with his fist and break her nose so that she would always be blemished and ashamed (Dobash & Dobash, 1978).

The Napoleonic Code influenced French, Swiss, Italian, and German law (Dutton, 1998). Court relief in the form of divorce was a rare intervention for battered victims. It came only when the beatings reached the level of attempted murder.

MARITAL RELATIONS IN EARLY AMERICA

Patriarchy continued in the colonies as the ideal family structure. The British immigrants reestablished their customs of inheritance by the eldest son, called *primogeniture*. Land was retained within the family through a legal proscription against the sale or grant of land outside the lineage, which is referred to as *entail*.

B a c k   T h e n ...

In France as well as in Russia, we see social stigma attached to men who did not properly control their wives according to social custom.

"The unfortunate male was dressed up, seated backwards on a donkey, draped with kitchen paraphernalia, and punched in the genitals" (Dutton, 1998).

Physical force and chastisement of one's wife was clearly accepted under English common law, the legal foundation in the colonies. The rule of thumb is thought to have influenced the American system. Although there is no evidence that the rule was ever evoked in America (Pleck, 1989), it existed as a common law restriction on the size of the weapon to be used in wife chastisement.

Puritan Restrictions

As early as 1599, Puritan ministers in England spoke out against wife beating. Bringing this objection to America, the Puritans were the first to prohibit domestic violence through legislation. Puritan laws provided penalties for wife beating, consisting of fines, whipping, or both. Since wife beating was considered a social problem that involved the community, enforcement included "holy watching" by neighbors.

The Next One Hundred Years

After 1776 and the American Revolution, Americans formed their own laws which tolerated wife beating (Davidson, 1977). In instances when the practice exceeded restrictions that were set down by law, wife beating was rarely brought before the courts. Between 1633 and 1802, only 12 cases of domestic violence were prosecuted in the Plymouth Colony (Pleck, 1989).

Some early American legislation on domestic violence control included corporal punishment and fines as penalties for wife beating. Some courts exacted promissory notes from perpetrators who beat their wives, with the understanding that the offender would forfeit the money if reconvicted. In 1824 the Supreme Court of Mississippi

---

B a c k   T h e n ...

In 1642 the American Puritan legal criminal code provided the following: "Everie marryed woman shall be free from bodilie correction or stripes by her husband, unlesse it be in his own defense upon her assault" (Sherman & Rogan, 1992).

---

upheld the husband's right of chastisement in cases of "great emergency," saying that husbands should not be subjected to "vexatious" prosecutions for assault and battery (Dobash & Dobash, 1979). This period of nonprotection for victims of domestic violence lasted from the late 1770s to the 1850s.

Not coincidentally, at this time in history women were fighting for equitable laws including the right to vote. The first women's rights convention took place in New York in 1848. Elizabeth Cady Stanton drafted the 1848 Seneca Falls declaration, in which she proclaimed that all men *and women* were created equal. Citizenship was granted to blacks in the Fourteenth Amendment to the U.S. Constitution in 1868, and the right to vote was granted by the Fifteenth Amendment in 1870, but women were not included. Not until 1920 and the passage of the Nineteenth Amendment to the Constitution were women afforded the rights of citizenship.

African American Families

The West African peoples were stripped of family ties and kinship connections under slavery in Colonial America (Figure 2–2). Additionally, black women lacked the paternalist protection of the domestic sphere and were subjected to the sexual and economic desires of their owners. There was no legal recourse for the violence against black women during slavery. Any stability attained by kinship was transitory since neither church nor law sanctioned slave marriage. Slaves could be bought and sold, families separated at the whim of the master.

Interracial marriage was also forbidden. Early colonial statutes made it a criminal act to marry outside one's race or to conduct such a marriage ceremony. The Virginia Statute on Racial Intermarriage (1705) stated: *"Be it enacted,...*That whatsoever English or other white man or woman, being free, shall intermarry with a Negro or mulatto man or woman, bond or free, shall by judgment of the county court be committed to prison and there remain during the space of six months, without bail..." (Wortman, 1985).

Figure 2–2   The West African peoples were stripped of family ties and kinship connections under slavery in Colonial America. Neither church nor law sanctioned slave marriage. *(Photo courtesy of the Administration on Aging.)*

Sharon Angella Allard maintains that the historical legal view of women ignores the significant differences that exist between white and black victims of domestic violence (Balos & Fellows, 1994). In her view, the women of color are excluded from legal protections due to perceptions that they are stronger than other victims of patriarchy. They have been characterized as immoral and undeserving of refuge from the sexual predators who have stalked them. Since colonial times the black slave woman was a contradiction to the stereotypical passive white victim.

During the reconstruction period following the Civil War, the African-American couple slowly was afforded the legal right to marry. South Carolina was among the first states to regulate and recognize the marriage between persons of color (1866). In part, the statute provided the following permissions (Wortman, 1985):

I. The relation of husband and wife amongst persons of color is established.

II. Those who now live as such, are declared to be husband and wife.

Native American Families

Gender roles and marital customs among Native Americans were different from those in the English patriarchal system. Family membership and descent were traced through the mother's side in most Native American cultures (Williamsburg Foundation, 1998). The matriarchal system allowed for divorce. The traditional Navajo society was matriarchal, matrilocal, and matrilineal (Feinman, 1992). Indian children, however, were later required to attend boarding schools where they were taught Anglo values. The matriarchal system eroded and was replaced with colonists' views of patriarchy. As the women's traditional roles were devalued, abuse of children and women became prevalent.

A Brief Change

By 1870, wife beating had taken on an aura of social unacceptability and was once again declared illegal in most states of the United States. This change coincided with a growing concern over child maltreatment. Women were given legal standing in some isolated cases. Judges in Alabama were the first to recognize that white women should be afforded the same legal protections as other victims.

More about It: Matriarchy

A social system in which the mother is head of the family and descent is traced through the mother's side of the family. In the Native American tradition family name, bloodline, and inheritance came from the mother. This system was eroded with the infusion of values from the Anglo system of patriarchy.

B a c k   T h e n . . .

"The privilege, ancient though it be, to beat [one's wife] with a stick, to pull her hair, choke her, spit in her face or kick her about the floor, or to inflict upon her like indignities, is not now acknowledged by our law....[I]n person, the wife is entitled to the same protection of the law that the husband can invoke for himself....All stand upon the same footing before the law as citizens of Alabama, possessing equal civil and political rights and public privileges" (*Fulgham v. State*, 1871).

One Hundred Years of Secrecy

Not long after *Fulgham*, the Supreme Court considered whether females could be prohibited from practicing law. In 1873 the Court decided in *Bradwell v. Illinois* that the laws of Illinois did not abridge any of the privileges and immunities of citizens of the United States by legislating what offices and positions should be filled by men only. The legal and social positioning of women for that time period was evidenced in the concurring opinion. *Concurring with the opinion of the Court, Justice Bradley* said, in part: "The constitution of the family organization, which is founded in the divine ordinance, as well as the nature of things, indicates the domestic sphere as that which properly belongs to the domain and functions of womanhood....So firmly fixed was this sentiment in the founders of common law that it became a maxim of that system of jurisprudence that a woman had no legal existence separate from her husband, who was regarded as her head and representative in the social state" (*Bradwell v. Illinois*, 1873).

Court denials of a husband's "right" to batter his wife continued slowly. Responses differed between the states, and women had little success in prosecutions for wife beating (Gordon, 1989). Although wife battering had become socially repugnant in the United States, it continued behind closed doors. States created innovative laws to allow the practice of battering. Until recently, some states allowed arrest of a husband only if he inflicted injury that required stitches, the "stitch rule." In North Carolina, the "curtain rule" allowed police to "interfere" with a husband's actions toward his wife only after permanent injury had been inflicted on her (Belknap, 1992).

In 1882 Maryland became the first state to pass a law that made wife beating a crime, punishable by 40 lashes or a year in jail (Davidson, 1977). Oregon passed similar legislation in 1906. By the beginning of the twentieth century domestic violence as a legally sanctioned crime disappeared. Unfortunately, the brief reform period ended around 1914. By World War I, the concern for wife beating had faded again. Over the next half-century, the courts rarely intervened in domestic affairs, even when laws existed to prohibit the behavior. Social attention fluctuated, and no significant changes occurred with respect to domestic abuse. It was not until the 1960s that violence

---

Back Then ...

Acknowledging the secretive practice and justifying a husband's right to batter, the North Carolina Supreme Court held: "If no permanent injury has been inflicted, nor malice, cruelty nor dangerous violence shown by the husband, it is better to draw the curtain, shut out the public gaze, and leave the parties to forget and forgive" (*State v. Oliver*, 1874).

---

toward intimates again became a subject of concern and an object of government interference. By this time, effective legal remedies to prevent domestic violence ran from seriously lacking to nonexistent.

WOMAN BATTERING

Wife battering reemerged along with child abuse as a social issue in the 1960s. The dominant view held that marital violence was a "private affair." Domestic violence continued behind closed doors, although not sanctioned by law. Intervention was rare, occurring in cases where the victim had been killed or severely maimed. Forms of spousal violence prohibited by criminal law usually amounted to misdemeanors; unless police witnessed the violence, they had no powers of arrest. Most domestic violence assaults fell within this category. Police officers were trained to respond to the crisis of domestic violence by separating the parties for a "cooling-down period." It was a common practice for officers to "counsel" the parties. In extreme cases the victim would be referred to the court to file a private complaint. The complaints were not taken seriously, however, and resulted in fewer prosecutions than for any other crime.

The lack of effective legal remedies for the victim hindered progress, including police action. New legislation was needed to address the contemporary concerns of domestic violence that began to surface. A major complaint focused on the ineffective law enforcement response. The critique of the system is well founded, given that law enforcement could not legally intervene in family disputes. Isolated attempts to protect victims of abuse were contrary to the prevailing legal and social atmosphere.

Although a few examples of effective law enforcement intervention did occur, police noncompliance was a far more frequent occurrence. Faced with domestic violence situations, police officers often failed to effect an arrest, even when the law demanded it. During the 1970s, reformers sought changes that might ensure effective intervention. The debates centered on what type of intervention would be most appropriate, as well as the form that it might take. Civil actions against police departments and mandatory arrest of the perpetrator were tactics devised to force compliance.

Case in Point: No Provision for an Arrest

In 1974 a Massachusetts state trooper was sent to a domestic call at a home in his patrol area. The trooper had responded to the same house many times before. Each time the wife had accused the husband of beating her. This time she let the trooper in the door crying that her husband had hit her. Wearing only his underwear and drinking a beer, the husband yelled at his wife, "You called the police!! You called the police!! Just wait till he leaves; I'll get you good this time." To the officer he said, "I know my rights: You can't do anything to me—now get out of my house!"

In the 1970s, there was no provision to arrest a man on an allegation of domestic violence when the officer did not see the beating occur, even though it appeared as though the woman had been beaten. The officer had no power of arrest. Knowing that the woman would be beaten for having made the call to the police, the trooper took action that he should not have had to take. He threw the husband out of the door into the snow on his front steps. There he was promptly arrested for public drunkenness, a misdemeanor that amounted to a breach of the peace, for which the officer did have the power of arrest.

Deterrence of future battering was a major impetus for the swift arrest of the perpetrator. Still, problems surfaced regarding victims' reluctance to follow through with complaints of domestic violence. Was law enforcement the appropriate agency to control domestic violence? If not, what other measures could be taken to protect victims of abuse? With many questions and few answers, the critics debated these issues. The first national study of domestic violence, *Behind Closed Doors*, reported that spouses strike partners in one out of every six households (Straus et al., 1980). That now-famous study on family violence found that there was little difference in the rate of violence between husbands and wives.

The first controlled, randomized test of the effectiveness of arrest for domestic violence occurred in Minneapolis in 1980, with the results published in 1984 (Sherman & Schmidt, 1993). The findings of the study to assess the effects of various police responses, including arrest, suggested that the arrest of the perpetrator produced the least amount of repeat violence for the same victims within a six-month period. Subsequent domestic violence was reduced by nearly 50 percent when the suspect was arrested, as opposed to other interventions, such as ordering one of the parties out of the residence or counseling the couple. Richard Berk and Lawrence Sherman, who conducted the research, made three recommendations regarding the study: first, that police should probably employ arrest in most cases of minor domestic violence; second, that the experiment should be replicated to see whether it would hold up in other cities with many different kinds of people; and third, that mandatory arrest laws not be adopted, if only because they would put an end to further research and replications (Sherman & Rogan, 1992).

However, it was only a matter of months after the results emerged before mandatory arrest procedures in instances of domestic assault were adopted across the nation. The move has been called "unusual, if not unprecedented in the social sciences," and was cheered by feminists and battered women's advocacy groups (Gelles, 1993). The Minneapolis domestic violence experiment paved the way for six replications and extensions of the experiment. Known collectively as the Spouse Assault Replication Program, the research was undertaken in a variety of U.S. police departments. The results of the replications were inconsistent; in some instances, there was no deterrent effect due to arrest of the perpetrator. Only certain types of offenders were deterred by arrest, and in some cases, the arrest escalated violence (Garner et al., 1995).

Lawrence Sherman and others involved in the Minneapolis experiment now advocate repeal of mandatory arrest policies in favor of varied responses based on the individual cases (Sherman & Rogan, 1992). Others are suggesting that law enforcement alone is insufficient to combat the problems of domestic violence (Buzawa & Buzawa, 1996), necessitating a more systemwide approach. The coordinated approach includes implementation of policies that train personnel and develop guidelines and protocols for enforcing laws related to domestic violence as well as accountability measures that ensure enforcement of the law by all officers in the department. Adding to the law enforcement component are strategies to coordinate with other criminal justice agencies and victim service providers. Probation departments have instituted enhanced victim safety measurements and vigorously enforced protection orders. Prosecutors and advocates seek to keep victims better informed about their cases and the whereabouts of the perpetrators.

A recent review of the Spouse Assault Replication Program suggests that the results were flawed, indicating that arrest generally is the superior method of deterring future violence. The National Center on Women and Family Law conducted a recent study on mandatory arrest laws and policies. It concluded that these policies do result in an increase in arrests, enable more victims to be put in contact with helping agencies, and communicate to the entire community that domestic violence is a crime. The National Institute of Justice is sponsoring new research to evaluate the effects of an integrated response to domestic violence. Through grants funded by Title IV, the Violence Against Women Act, the need for research to assess the effectiveness of arrest in the context of a systemwide, coordinated approach to domestic violence will be conducted in the near future.

WHAT ABOUT THE CHILDREN?

Experts agree that children have always been abused and neglected (Sagatun & Edwards, 1995). *Patria potestas*, the Roman civil law espousing patriarchy, denied legal standing to children as well as women. Generally, children have been regarded as second-class citizens, and their treatment has historically been harsh. Physical abuse, neglect, and sexual abuse were considered socially acceptable behavior in ancient times (Sagatun & Edwards, 1995). Therefore, there is an absence of legal challenges to the status of children as property.

Ancient Times

Infants were the property of their fathers and had no rights of their own. Their fathers could even kill them for a number of "practical" reasons. Physical deformity, questionable health, and illegitimacy were rationales for infanticide, since destroying children who were bound to be a burden was viewed as promoting the general welfare of society (Iverson & Segal, 1990). Female children were a strain on the financial resources of a father, another justification for infanticide. Early Greek philosophers condoned infanticide, the killing of a newborn. Aristotle even recommended a law prohibiting crippled children to be raised.

The Code of Hammurabi provided that the father had full control of his children until they married. This right transferred to the mother in the absence of the father and included the right even to sell the children (King, 1998). Only incest was forbidden. The male perpetrator of incest with his daughter was exiled.

The Christian Era

Under Judaism and Christianity the children's right to live was protected, regardless of the quality of life. During the fourth century, the right to live for a child was established through the Christian faith. The commandment "Thou shalt not kill" was linked with the practice of infanticide. A similar trend is evidenced in the experience of the Russian Orthodox Church. Bearing children was the major task of women during the tenth century, defining the woman's role. Severe penalties were prescribed for committing infanticide, terminating pregnancies, or practicing birth control. Abortion was considered similar to that of murder—and the punishment varied with the stage of pregnancy. Aborting an embryo brought five years of fasting as punishment, seven years if it was completely formed (Pushkareva, 1997).

Social restrictions against sexual relations with children differed from today's standards also. With the exception of incest, it was permissible to loan children to guests or to hire them out for sexual use (Radbill, 1987). Pushkareva offers evidence that father–daughter incest continued to be practiced well into seventeenth-century Russia. She states that fathers had absolute authority over their daughters. Overall, child rearing was strict, and parents were encouraged to beat children frequently. Young boys and girls were also forbidden to complain about family beatings and would be flogged publicly if they brought family business out into the open.

Marriage in Russia could legally take place at age 12 for girls and 15 for boys. Since people often died very young during the seventeenth century, the restriction was not enforced. Only 7 percent of urban Muscovites during that period were over the age of 25 (Pushkareva, 1997).

English Law

Chancery courts in medieval Britain were granted control over the property rights of children, extending to their general welfare. These courts utilized the concept of *parens patriae*, which referred to the right of the king to act in the best interests of the child. There is little evidence that the courts used this power to protect children from abuse or neglect. As early as 1535, the English Poor Laws allowed for children who were identified as neglected or delinquent to be put to work or be placed in poorhouses (Sanders, 1945). The provisions are not considered by history as protections, but rather, as attempts to maintain strict control over children who were resistant to parental punishment.

Apprenticeship was another form used to remove children from their homes and place them into the care of adults who would train them in various skills. Some apprenticeships were forced until the child was 21 years old. Child labor practices included long hours, with physical punishment often leading to deformities. English records as late as 1829 cite the cause of death for infants as including babies drowned in pits full of water, cisterns, wells, ponds, and even pans of water (Radbill, 1987). Babies were also starved by their nurses, or killed by burning or scalding. A common form of death for children was overlaying or lying upon a child. This form of suffocation by carelessness accounted for 20 deaths in one English city in 1920, according to Samuel Radbill.

CHILDREN IN EARLY AMERICA

Early attempts to protect children are questionable by contemporary standards of justice. Often, the methods of government intervention amounted to control rather than opportunities for relief for the child. The colonists brought the English notions of juvenile protection to the United States. Here they instituted poor laws (Bremmer, 1970) and continued to practice forced apprenticeship. The range of acceptable punishment for errant children stopped with permanent disfigurement; laws against physical child abuse were nonexistent. Early law actually held parents responsible for the actions of their children, giving them the authority to punish harshly. Historian and psychoanalyst Lloyd de Mause wrote an article in 1975 in which he clearly describes the unfortunate role of the child: "A child's life prior to modern times was uniformly bleak....A search of historical sources shows that until the last century children were...offered beatings and whippings, with instruments usually associated with torture chambers. In fact, the history of childhood is a nightmare from which we have only recently begun to awaken....The further back in history we went, the lower the level of childcare we found, and the more likely children were to have been killed, abandoned, whipped, sexually abused and terrorized by their caretakers" (Pagelow, 1984).

During the Victorian era, infanticide was the most covered-up crime according to Marlene Stein Wortman. In Philadelphia alone, between 1861 and 1901, an annual average of 55 dead infants were found on the streets (Wortman, 1985), their cause of death listed as "unknown." During that same period, only one trial led to a first-degree murder verdict. Changes in the attitudes toward children came about slowly. Two significant reform periods to protect children took place during the first half of the nineteenth century. These were the Refuge Movement and the Child Saver Movement.

The Refuge Movement

The first refuge statute was passed in New York State in 1882, permitting the commitment of neglected and dependent children in a house of refuge (Pfohl, 1977). This led to the New York House of Refuge, which became the first in the country. Other states soon followed New York's lead, however. With strict prison-type organization, the houses were not meant to be therapeutic. Delinquent and runaway children, as well as those who were neglected or incorrigible, were sent to the same institutions. Discipline was harsh, and the conditions often met with rebellion. Many children who had been removed from their homes eventually returned to society as criminals. Critics soon charged that poverty and a cheap labor source were the reasons for removal of the children and placement in the houses of refuge.

In 1838 juvenile authorities were granted even greater power through the case of *Ex Parte Crouse*. Reaffirming the concept of *parens patriae*, the right to claim guardianship, a Pennsylvania court ignored the father's plea for custody of his daughter. Her mother had placed the girl in a house of refuge because she was unmanageable. A higher court denied the father's claim that parental control is exclusive, natural, and proper. The decision that was applied only to Pennsylvania was noticed by the other states that followed suit. The state had been given the right to restrain and protect children despite the wishes of parents.

The Child Saver Movement

Linda Gordon, historian and scholar, asserts that policy response to domestic violence emerged in the late 1870s with the "discovery" of family violence (Gordon, 1989). Social service agencies were confronted with problems of wife battering when their child welfare clients cited abuse as a major issue. The incidence of violence was linked to alcohol abuse and poverty. Identified as a problem confined to the low classes, the social service response to family violence was judgmental and prejudicial, with poverty as the common element of its clients. There was a lack of effective legal remedies for the domestic violence victim.

Societies for the Prevention of Cruelty to Children

The late 1870s witnessed a national movement to protect children who were abused or neglected. The child savers of the late nineteenth century established Societies for the Prevention of Cruelty to Children (SPCCs). According to Linda Gordon, the SPCC workers acted as quasi-law enforcement officers: they conducted investigations, home searches and seizures, and threatened families with arrest for noncompliance of their directives. To further their stated mission of enforcement of existing laws against child abuse, they conscripted police officers to make arrests and to act as supervisors in their cases. Both New York and Boston SPCCs acknowledged that sufficient laws existed at the time to protect children, but no one had been held responsible for their enforcement.

Due to their increased professionalism and police reluctance toward enforcement, the problems of child abuse were largely left with the social service agencies after 1920. Police officers did not perceive child abuse enforcement as part of their role, or were simply too busy with other duties to enforce child abuse statutes. The Social Security Act of 1930 somewhat improved intervention on behalf of children in need, because it mandated child welfare services for neglected or dependent children. Today, legal intervention has improved through specialized child abuse investigation units within police departments. Unfortunately, enforcement of child abuse protections is still not a priority with many police agencies.

DOMESTIC VIOLENCE: A GLOBAL CONCERN

The legal history presented on domestic relations develops from early European examples based on patriarchal social relations. Have things changed elsewhere in the world? Is domestic violence an international social problem? Are the concerns for social equality confined to the United States? The resounding answer is that America is not alone, either in its problem or in the search for change.

No comprehensive summary records the magnitude of family violence internationally. Piecemeal information is available; it documents concerns about the extent of family violence that has prompted action on a global basis. According to Lori Heise, research indicates that one-fourth to more than half of women report having been physically or psychologically abused by their partners in many countries (Heise, 1994).

It appears as though the movement to protect women and children from family violence has occurred internationally at roughly the same time as our own feminist movement in the United States. Comparisons between the United States and some countries are possible due to limited reports of research efforts on wife abuse. With few exceptions, violence to women has been legislated against with no mention of the other forms of domestic violence that were presented in Chapter 1. New Zealand is unique in its domestic violence legislation that is without specific reference to women or girls (UNICEF, 1997).

The United Nations

The United Nations General Assembly adopted the Declaration on the Elimination of Violence against Women in 1993. It emphasizes violence against women as a violation of human rights and recommends strategies to be employed by member states and specialized agencies to eliminate it (UN publication: Note for speakers, 1995). The fourth UN World Conference on Women then took place in Beijing, China, in 1995. Highlighting the problems of violence against women, the conference signified a worldwide effort toward ending domestic violence.

The United Nations active movement toward eliminating female violence appears to have prompted action toward that goal. One initiative that resulted was the forming of WAVE (*Women Against Violence Europe*). National membership of WAVE now stands at 15 organizations. By 1997, laws against domestic violence had been enacted in at least 44 countries around the world, including the United States (UNICEF, 1997). Of these, 17 have made marital rape a criminal offense, and 27 have passed sexual harassment laws. Austria joined the list in 1997 when the government implemented similar legislation (Schmid, 1997).

Prevalence Rates in Selected Countries around the World

Australia.   Domestic violence is the most common form of assault in Australia, according to the *Women's Resource Information and Support Centre, Women Against Violence Europe* (Women's Resource Information and Research Centre, 1998). Based on regional research, the Center estimates that each year in Victoria, between 30 and 40 women and children are killed by their husbands, boyfriends, ex-partners, fathers, and sons. One of seven married women is subjected to domestic violence.

In the News: Women and the United Nations

In June 1998, approximately 250 representatives of 150 nongovernmental organizations, social movements, and indigenous peoples groups met in Ottawa, Canada, to review and affirm the commitment to the principles of the Vienna Human Rights Conference of 1993. Among the key issues were these:

- The human rights of women and of the girl-child are an inalienable, integral, and indivisible part of universal human rights.

- The promotion and protection of all human rights and fundamental freedoms must be considered as a primary objective of the United Nations in accordance with its purposes and principles.

- All human rights—civil, cultural, economic, political, and social—are universal, indivisible, interdependent, and interrelated.

Source: Women's International Network News (1998).

In the News: Vatican City

Although Christianity was once the catalyst for social injustices against women, the Roman Catholic Church has taken a stand of family peace. In contrast to the scripture of the Bible, Pope John Paul II condemned violence against women and children in 1998 and made a plea for justice during a special New Year's Mass to mark the Roman Catholic Church's World Day of Peace (CNN Interactive, 1998). The news report quotes the Pope as saying: "The abuse of women and children is one of the most widespread violations of human rights, which has become an instrument of terror: Women taken hostage and children savagely massacred....Practical steps are needed to put an end to the increase in these forms of violence."

Austria.   Since 1978 the Austrian Women's Shelter Network has coordinated 19 shelters throughout the country, according to Birgit Schmid (Schmid, 1997). She reports that the *Centre Against Violence Against Women* in Vienna is the only institution in that country which conducts research, training, and documentation of domestic violence. It also provides training courses for the police and associated professions on domestic violence.

Britain.   Erin Pizzey founded the first refuge for victims of domestic violence in 1971. She first published *Scream Quietly or the Neighbors Will Hear* in 1974 (Pizzey, 1977). It is the earliest book about domestic violence from the battered women's perspective Her clients in Chiswick, England, grew to over 200 by the end of the decade. Her conclusion that some people actually choose violent relationships has been met with hostility (Pizzey, 1982). She noticed that some women seemed to be using the shelter when the level of violence got too much; afterward they returned to their violent men for another few weeks, returning to the shelter when the violence escalated. In her subsequent book, *Prone to Violence*, she talks about *why* people are violent and her experiences working with problem families.

According to the research of Diane Dwyer, violence against women in Great Britain occurs at roughly the same rate as in the United States (Dwyer, 1994). Her review of available literature indicated that at least 20 to 25 percent of reported assaults against women are committed in their homes. Similar frustrations with law enforcement protection are noted. Poor record keeping and historically poor police response are among the problems officials are confronting there. The rate of prosecution for domestic violence is extremely low, according to Dwyer, only 2.2 percent of cases in one study. Reluctant victims and the system's unwillingness to utilize a hostile witness provide immediate excuses for the lack of prosecution in cases of domestic abuse.

Canada.   Canadian authorities have concluded that the most dangerous place for a disabled girl or woman is in her own home (Webb, 1998). A 1987 survey of women with disabilities, carried out by DAWN Toronto and funded by the Ministry of Community and Social Services, discovered:

- 67 percent of those surveyed had been physically or sexually assaulted as children, compared with 44 percent of nondisabled women.
- Almost half of disabled women surveyed reported that they had been sexually abused as children, compared with 34 percent of nondisabled women.
- 33 percent of disabled women reported that they were assaulted during their adult years, mostly by husbands; 22 percent of nondisabled women reported similar abuse.
- 31 percent of disabled women reported being sexually assaulted as adults, compared with 23 percent of nondisabled women.

The Kennedy and Dutton survey (1989) in Alberta discovered that the Canadian incidence rates for minor wife assault were almost identical with the United States (Dutton, 1998). Dutton further reported that as the acts became more violent, the rates of incidence fell sharply below that of the United States. Still, he suggests that approximately 1,550,000 men in Canada are assaultive to women in any given year, presenting an incredible problem for law enforcement.

An Internet fact sheet on the prevalence of domestic violence against women in Canada gives these statistics (Violence Against Women, 1998):

- One in seven women will be battered by their male partners during their adult life.
- Severe repeated violence occurs within 1 in 14 marriages.
- An average of two women a week die at the hands of a current husband or partner.
- In all Canadian-reported sexual assaults, more than 90 percent are against women.

China.   No legal protection from domestic violence exists in China's southern Fujian Province, where family violence occurs in more than one-fourth of households, according to a recently released survey (Family Violence Prevention Fund, 1998). In the Chinese province, incidents of domestic violence are considered "family quarrels," and neither the court nor police tend to interfere. Parental battering of children in Chinese families in Hong Kong was found to be a common occurrence according to a recent study (So-Kum-Tang, 1998). The author cites the prevalence rate of 526 per 1,000 children for minor violence and 461 per 1,000 children for severe violence (Figure 2–3).

A comparative report on sexual abuse in Taiwan found that victimization was more common in preadolescence and adolescence, as in the United States (Chen, 1996). At least one-third of the abusers were known to the victims in this study. The

Figure 2–3   Comparison of severe child abuse rates (per 1,000 children) in Hong Kong and the United States. *(Data from So-Kum-Tang, 1998.)*

rate of victimization for females was found to be 34.6 percent and 2.6 percent for males (Figure 2–4).

India.   Violence against women in this country takes on an added twist with commerce due to the customs of India. More than 5,000 women are killed each year because their in-laws consider their dowries inadequate (UNICEF, 1997), often setting the women afire. In a country where hundreds and perhaps thousands of newborn girls are murdered each year simply because they are female, little value is given to adult women (Anderson & Moore, 1993). Of 1,250 women questioned, one survey concluded that more than half had killed baby daughters. Women are often sold to the highest bidder or given into marriage through dowries. Those who survive their husbands are so stigmatized that they seldom remarry.

Ireland.   Mental cruelty, physical cruelty, or sexual violence victimized approximately 18 percent of the women in Ireland in 1995, according to the Rathmines Refuge in Dublin (Women's Aid, 1998). The *Women's Aid* national helpline in Ireland reported receiving over 10,000 calls in that year. The Domestic Violence Sexual Assault Investigative Unit received an average of 6,000 calls per year due to domestic violence situations in the Greater Dublin area. The organizational newsletter noted problems that are similar to those in the United States: Victim provocation, behavior, and alcohol are frequent excuses for domestic assault.

Figure 2–4   Comparison of child sexual assault rates in the United States and in Taiwan. *(Data from Chen, 1996.)*

Korea.   The rate of family violence is believed to be much higher in Korean society than in the United States (Dutton, 1998). Dutton reports that a 1992 study by Kim and Cho estimated the rate of wife assault to be 37.5 percent compared to 12.4 percent in the United States at that time.

Poland.   The movement to protect battered women in Poland is fairly new. The Women's Rights Center in Warsaw was founded in 1994 (Nowakovska, 1997). This is an organization that addresses violence against women within a broad context of gender equality and discrimination. The majority, 98 percent, of perpetrators of domestic violence are male (Polish Ministry of Justice, 1996). According to the same report, 81 percent of the victims are married to their abusers. Although 78 percent of perpetrators (12,087) in 1996 were found guilty and given jail sentences, none of them actually served time! As in the United States, there are options for community service and suspended sentences in lieu of jail.

The 1998 Penal Code in Poland prohibiting domestic violence is gender neutral, and it includes violence against children. Article 184-1 states: "Whoever abuses physically or psychologically a member of a family, an intimate relation, a physically or mentally disabled person, or a juvenile may be found guilty and sentenced from 3 months to 5 years in jail. If the abuser acts with cruelty, the penalty is from 1 to 10 years."

The Women's Rights Center reported that research conducted by the Public Opinion Research Center in 1993 and 1996 suggests that more than half of Polish women personally know someone who is a victim of domestic violence (Figure 2–5; Polish Ministry of Justice, 1996). One in twenty Polish women are believed to live in an abusive environment.

South Africa.   Violence against women in South Africa is similar to international complaints of patriarchal social inequality. Compounded with the issues of apartheid and community instability, resources to confront the problems are scarce (Dangor et al., 1998). The authors report that the violence is often underreported and unrecognized. Without national studies, they report prevalence estimated from various sources:

In the News: Latin American Countries

The first law against domestic violence in Latin America was passed in Puerto Rico in 1989 (Cordova, 1997). In the past few years, 15 countries in Latin America and the Caribbean have also passed laws to prevent violence against women and children, Luis Cordova reports. Acceptances of violence as an integral part of the exercise of authority in the family and police reluctance to act are blamed for the widespread problem.

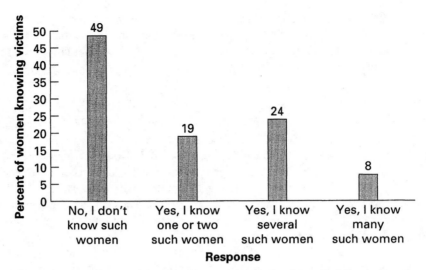

Figure 2–5   Over half of Polish women reported personally knowing a victim of domestic violence, according to the Polish Ministry of Justice in 1996.

- In Cape Town, the Rape Crisis Centre estimated that their partners beat one out of six women regularly.
- Preliminary studies reveal that 50 percent to 60 percent of marital relationships involve violence and abuse.
- In the Dangor study, 46 percent of respondents reported that they were personal victims of physical or sexual abuse.

A dowry system, *lobola*, is used among some African groups, further complicating the status of women whose customs involve payment for their marriage. The practice is seen to devalue the woman who has been "bought" and forced into arranged marriages by tradition and custom.

According to previous estimates (Richter, 1988), there are over 9,000 street children in South Africa (Dangor et al., 1998). These are children between the ages of 7 and 16 who have been abandoned by their families, schools, and immediate communities and who live on the streets. Incest and battering of children are emerging as recent concerns.

Sweden.   Since the late 1970s, Swedish activists have raised the issue of male violence against women. Their first battered women's shelters were opened in Stockholm and Gothenburg in 1978 (Beausang, 1997). One study indicated that police were reluctant to proceed with any action; only 33 percent of victims ever spoke with a prosecutor (Elman & Eduards, 1991). That same study suggested that Swedish shelters provided the best response to victims.

In the News: Spain

A 60-year-old Spanish woman was doused with petrol and burned alive by her husband after she had spoken on television about his repeatedly abusing her, according to news reports (BBC News Online: World, 1998). BBC News reported that the killing sparked widespread protests about the level of domestic violence in Spain, where their partners in 1997 killed more than 60 women. Husbands or boyfriends attacked at least 1,900 other women during the same period. The Spanish government announced new measures to combat domestic violence following the protests. The initiatives included greater police powers and heavier penalties against the perpetrators.

ROKS is the national organization in Sweden that has coordinated 123 shelters or crisis lines in all parts of the country. The organization reports that in 1997, 19,093 cases of women battering were reported to the police, equal to 35 percent of all cases of physical abuse in that country. Approximately 30 women are beaten to death every year, and most acts of violence against women are committed at home by men they know. (National Organization of Battered Women's Shelters in Sweden, 1998).

Turkey.   Until January 1998, Turkish victims of domestic violence were required to document complaints of abuse by a physician who could confirm that the physical damage lasted at least 10 days. Under new legislation, any person witnessing a domestic violence incident can file a complaint, and judges can forbid batterers from contacting their victims (Family Violence Prevention Fund, 1998).

Third World Countries.   The Fourth UN World Conference on Women keynotes documented epidemic proportions of domestic victims in third world countries (UN publication: Note for speakers, 1995): "In Bangladesh, the killing of women by their husbands accounts for 50 percent of all murders. In a study of 80 battered women in San José, Costa Rica, 49 percent reported being beaten during pregnancy. In Papua New Guinea, 67 percent of rural women and 56 percent of urban women have been victims of spousal abuse, according to a national survey conducted by the Papua New Guinea Law Reform Commission."

CONCLUSIONS

In this chapter, the social–legal historical perspective does not consider the existence of violence perpetrated against males, or within same sex-relationships. The predominant explanation for domestic violence is the evidence of female inferiority created by the patriarchal system of oppression against women throughout the ages. Women and children have been legally subordinated to men, first as property and, in the cases of females, as inferior partners in marriage.

In the United States, the changes in social and legal standing of women are documented. We do not, however, live in a vacuum! There is a larger world around us with many similar problems of legislated and social inequality. Our histories may be lineal in many respects. The patriarchal social system remains today as the primary explanation for violence against women in countries around the world. The United Nations, a collective group whose interest is in humane treatment for all human beings, has recently acted as one in this case, coming forth with a stand against female oppression. Other organizations have emerged that seek legislative changes to assure equal rights and treatment of women in their countries. Education on family violence and increased resources for its victims are international concerns.

Still, Erin Pizzey, renowned author and a pioneer in the field, cautions against the view that men are the only perpetrators of domestic violence (Pizzey, 1998). She suggests that a "gender war" has been declared against men based on mistaken beliefs about family assaults. The suffering of men who are physically and sexually abused and stripped of their right to have access to their children goes unnoticed, she maintains. In 1971, men, women, and children came to her door, the first shelter for victims of domestic violence in the world. Pizzey maintains that the female victims were often as violent as the men from whom they sought refuge. Other explanations for the violence that invades so many homes will be put forth in future chapters.

Violence against children is illustrated in this view with similar explanations. The presumed superiority of men over children due to the patriarchal system is at the root of current problems. Children, to an even larger extent than adult females, are viewed as the property of parents, most notably the father. Discipline can take any form and is usually viewed to be within the acceptable limitations of parental authority. Only recently has the idea been introduced into society that children should be protected against abuse from their families.

KEY TERMS

Curtain rule
Dowries
Entail
Incest
Infanticide
Lobola
Parens patriae

Patria potestas
Patriarchy
Primogeniture
Rule of thumb
Social–legal history
Stitch rule

QUESTIONS for REVIEW

1. What events led up to the formation of the Nineteenth Amendment?

2. Explain *Fulgham v. State* (1871).

3. What did the First National Study of Domestic Violence conclude?

4. Explain the Minneapolis experiment and its findings.

5. What were the Societies for the Prevention of Cruelty to Children (SPCCs), and what did they do to protect children?

6. Throughout the chapter, various countries and time periods are discussed. Compare the prevalence rate of any one (perhaps your own ethnicity?) to that of the United States.

7. Compare the treatment of children between two time periods. Have things changed in today's approach?

REFERENCES

Anderson, John W. and Molly Moore. 1993. "The Burden of Womanhood: Third World, Second Class." *Washington Post*, February 14, p. A01.

Balos, Beverly and Mary L. Fellows. 1994. *Law and Violence against Women: Cases and Materials on Systems of Oppression*. Durham, NC: Carolina Academic Press.

BBC News Online:World. 1998. "Spain Moves to Curb Domestic Violence." January 16. *www.news.bbc.co.uk/low/english/world/newsid_48088.stm*. 1998.

Beausang, Angela. 1997. "Sweden ROKS." *www.xpoint.at/users/aoef/WAVENEWS.html*. 1998.

Belknap, Joanne. 1992. "Perceptions of Woman Battering." Pp. 181–201 in *The Changing Roles of Women in the Criminal Justice System*, 2nd ed., Imogene L. Moyer (ed.). Prospect Heights, IL: Waveland Press.

Bremmer, Robert. 1970. *Children and Youth in America*. Cambridge, MA: Harvard University Press.

Buzawa, Eve S. and Carl G. Buzawa. 1996. *Domestic Violence: The Criminal Justice Response*, 2nd ed. Thousand Oaks, CA: Sage Publications.

Chen, Roda. 1996. "Risk Factors of Sexual Abuse among College Students in Taiwan." *Journal of Interpersonal Violence* 11(1):79–93.

CNN Interactive. 1998. "Pope Targets Plight of Women, Children at New Year's Mass." *www.cnn.com\/WORLD/9801/pope/*. 1998.

Cordova, Luis. 1997. "Rights—Women: Latin American Laws on Domestic Violence." *www.ips.fi/koulut/199750/8.htm*. 1998.

Dangor, Zubeda, Lee A. Hoff, et al. 1998. "Woman Abuse in South Africa: An Exploratory Study." *Violence Against Women* 4(2):125–49.

Davidson, Terry. 1977. "Wife Beating: A Recurring Phenomenon Throughout History." Pp. 19–57 in *Battered Women: A Psychosocialological Study of Domestic Violence*, Maria Roy (ed.). New York: Van Nostrand Reinhold.

_____. 1978. *Conjugal Crime*. New York: Hawthorn Books.

Davis, Elizabeth G. 1971. *The First Sex*. New York: Penguin Books.

Dobash, Emerson and Russell P. Dobash. 1978. "Wives: The 'Appropriate' Victims of Marital Violence." *Victimology* 2:426–39.

_____. 1979. Violence against Wives: A Case against the Patriarchy. New York: Free Press.

Dutton, Donald G. 1998. *The Domestic Assault of Women: Psychological and Criminal Justice Perspectives*, 3rd ed. Vancouver, British Columbia: UBC Press.

Dwyer, Diane C. 1994. "A Descriptive Analysis of the British Criminal Justice System's Response to the Victims of Domestic Violence." *Academy of Criminal Justices Sciences Annual Conference*, Chicago. Unpublished.

Elman, Amy and Maud Eduards. 1991. "Unprotected Swedish Welfare State: A Survey of Battered Women and the Assistance They Received." *Women Studies International Forum* 14(5):413–21.

Family Violence Prevention Fund. 1998. "World Round-Up." February. *http://www.igc.org/materials/speakup/02_13_98.htm*. 1999.

Feinman, C. 1992. "Woman Battering on the Navajo Reservation." *International Review of Victimology* 2(2):137–46.

Garner, J., J. Fagan, and C. Maxwell. 1995. "Published Findings from the Spouse Assault Replication Program: A Critical Review." *Journal of Quantitative Criminology* 11(1):3–28.

Gelles, Richard. 1993. "Constraints against Family Violence: How Well Do They Work?" *American Behavioral Scientist* 36(5):575–86.

Gordon, Linda. 1989. *Heroes of Their Own Lives: The Politics and History of Family Violence*. New York: Penguin Books.

Heise, Lori. 1994. "Violence against Women: The Hidden Health Burden." *women3rdworld.miningco.com/library/weekly/aa010898.htm*. 1998.

Horne, Charles F. 1915. "Ancient History Sourcebook: Code of Hammurabi." *www.fordham.edu/halsall/ancient/hamcode.html*. 1998.

Iverson, Timothy J. and Marilyn Segal. 1990. *Child Abuse and Neglect: An Information and Reference Guide*. New York: Garland Press.

Jerusalem Bible, The. 1996. New York: Doubleday.

King, L. W. (transl.) 1998. "Hammurabi's Code of Laws." *www.fordham.edu/halsall/ancient/hamcode.html*. 1998.

Kennedy, L. W. and D. G. Dutton. 1989. "The Incidence of Wife Assault in Alberta." *Canadian Journal of Behavioral Science* 21(1):40–54.

Lefkowitz, Mary R. and Maureen B. Fant. 1992. "Women's Life in Greece and Rome: A Source Book in Translation." *www.uky.edu/ArtsSciences/Classics/wlgr/wlgr-copyright.html*. 1998.

Levy, Darline, H. Applewhite, and M. Johnson (eds.). 1979. "Declaration of the Rights of Woman and Female Citizen." Pp. 92–96 in *Women in Revolutionary Paris, 1785–1795*. Urbana, IL: University of Illinois Press.

Lunn, T. 1991. "Til Death Do Us Part." *Social Work Today* 29(8):16–17.

Masters, Robert E. L. 1964. "Misogyny and Sexual Conflict." Pp. 3–52 in *The Anti-sex: The Belief in the Natural Inferiority of Women: Studies in Male Frustration and Sexual Conflict*, Robert E. L. Masters and Eduard Lea (eds.). New York: Julian Press.

National Organization of Battered Women's Shelters in Sweden. 1998. "About ROKS." *www.roks.se/english.htm*. 1998.

Nowakovska, Urszula. 1997. "Poland." *www.xpoint.at/users/aoef/WAVENEWS.html*. 1998.

O'Faolain, Julia and Lauro Martines. 1973. *Not in God's Image*. New York: Harper & Row.

Pagelow, Mildred D. 1984. *Family Violence*. New York: Praeger Publishers.

Pfohl, S. 1977. "The 'Discovery' of Child Abuse." *Social Problems* 24:431–33.

Pizzey, Erin. 1977. *Scream Quietly or the Neighbors Will Hear*. Hillside, NJ: Enslow Publishers.

_____. 1982. "Prone to Violence." *www.massey.ac.nz/~KBirks/gender/viol/ptv/ptv.htm*. 1998.

_____. 1998. "VAWA II Must Be Stopped." *www.acfc.org/vawa/pizzey-vawa.htm. 1998.*

Pleck, Elizabeth. 1989. "Criminal Approaches to Family Violence, 1640–1980." *Family Violence* 11:19–57.

Polish Ministry of Justice. 1996. "Violence against Women." *free.ngo.pl/temida/violstat.htm*. 1998.

Pushkareva, Natalia. 1997. In *Women in Russian History: From the Tenth to the Twentieth Century*, Eve Levin (ed./transl.). Armonk, NY: M.E. Sharpe.

Radbill, Samuel X. 1987. "Children in a World of Violence: A History of Child Abuse." Pp. 3–22 in *The Battered Child*, 4th ed., Ray E. Helfer and Ruth S. Kempe (eds.). Chicago: University of Chicago Press.

Richter, L. 1988. "Street Children: The Nature and Scope of the Problem in Southern Africa." *Child Care Worker* 6:11–14.

Sagatun, Inger J. and Leonard P. Edwards. 1995. *Child Abuse and the Legal System*. Chicago: Nelson-Hall Publishers.

Sanders, Wiley B. 1945. *Some Early Beginnings of the Children's Court Movement in England*. New York: National Council on Crime and Delinquency.

Schmid, Birgit. 1997. "Austria." *www.xpoint.at/users/aoef/WAVENEWS.html*. 1998.

Sherman, Lawrence and Dennis Rogan. 1992. P. 46 in *Policing Domestic Violence: Experiments and Dilemmas*. New York: Free Press.

Sherman, Lawrence and Jannell Schmidt. 1993. "Does Arrest Deter Domestic Violence?" *American Behavioral Scientist* 36(5):601–9.

So-Kum-Tang, Catherine. 1998. "The Rate of Physical Child Abuse in Chinese Families: A Community Survey in Hong Kong." *Child Abuse and Neglect* 22(5):381–91.

Straus, Murray A., Richard J. Gelles, and Suzanne K. Steinmetz. 1980. P. 222 in *Behind Closed Doors: Violence in the American Family*. Garden City, NY: Anchor Press/Doubleday.

Struve, Jim. 1990. "Dancing with Patriarchy: The Politics of Sexual Abuse." Pp. 3–45 in *The Sexually Abused Male*, Vol. I, Mic Hunter (ed.). New York: Lexington Books.

Ulrich, Laurel T. 1991. P. 7 in *Good Wives: Image and Reality in the Lives of Women in Northern New England, 1650—1750*. New York: Vintage Books.

UN publication: Note for speakers. 1995. "The Advancement of women." *women3rdworld.miningco.com/library/weekly/aa010898.htmhttp*. 1998.

UNICEF. 1997. "Women: Progress and Disparity." *www.unicef.org/pon97/p48a.htm*. 1998.

Violence Against Women, Services E.C. 1998. "Statistics to Consider...." *www.info.london.on.ca/vawsec/stats.html*. 1998.

Webb, Tracy. 1998. "Abuse of the Disabled." *www.vaxxine.com/nrpsweb/disabled.htm*. 1998.

Williamsburg Foundation. 1998. "Redefining Family." *www.history.org/life/family*. 1998.

Women's Aid. 1998. *www.ilinxmedia.com/waiddub/waidmyths.html*. 1998.

Women's International Network News. 1998. "Vienna Human Rights Conference Five Years Later: Declaration and Programme of Action." *Women's International Network* 24(4):13.

Women's Resource Information and Support Centre. 1998. "Women's Resource Information and Support Centre." *wrisc.ballarat.net.au*. 1998.

Wortman, Marlene S. (ed.). 1985. Discussion of the *Virginia Statute on Racial Intermarriage*. Pp. 70, 136, 269 in *Women in American Law: From Colonial Times to the New Deal*, Vol. 1. New York: Holmes & Meier Publishers.

Cases

Fulgham v. State, 46 AL 146-47 (1871).
State v. Oliver, 70 NC 60 (1874).
Ex Parte Crouse, 4 Wharton 9, PA 11 (1838).
Bradwell v. Illinois, 16 Wallace 130 (1873).

Part Two

Theories on Causation and Victimization

It is not enough to know that domestic violence occurs in numerous forms and that various populations are victimized. Why does it happen? What is being done to stop the perpetrators and to help the victims? Who are the perpetrators of these crimes? What happens to the victims? These are among the questions that are answered in Part Two.

In Chapter 3, "Theories on Family Violence," we examine the development of contemporary criminological theories and argue for the recognition that domestic violence crimes appropriately are studied from within similar theoretical perspectives. Why do people beat and sometimes kill the people they are intimate with or related to? Why do parents and dating partners commit rape? The questions are too complex to answer using any one theory alone. We consider the issues from a biological, sociological, and psychological perspectives. Contemporary theoretical models have emerged that involve a combination of the older theories that guide us toward the need for future research.

In Chapter 4, "From Theory to Practice," we look at how theoretical approaches have influenced the responses of policy makers and of society toward the perpetrator of domestic violence. Is there more than one type of abuser? Does it make a difference whether the relationship is between heterosexual or homosexual partners? What are the common characteristics of abusive men? Do women commit domestic violence crimes? Interventions to stop battering are explained and teen-dating violence is examined. We present many common characteristics of physical and sexual offenders and delve into the research that often guides policy decision making.

Chapter 5, "Survivors and the Consequences of Victimization," is an essential component in any discussion of domestic violence. For too long the victim has been ignored by the criminal justice system. What movement brought victimization to the forefront of today's examination? What is the children's rights movement? Have we learned anything about childhood abuse and its consequences? Do child victims grow up to become offenders? What has the battered women's movement contributed? Can theories on victimization help us to understand why victims sometimes stay in an abusive relationship? Since victims often do leave, however, what effects of long-term victimization must they overcome to be termed survivors?

Theories on Family Violence

INTRODUCTION

> To try to deny to ourselves and others that we feel anger is a distortion of reality which is likely to cause trouble; and to suppress issues precludes the possibility of resolving them. (Straus et al., 1980, p. 171).

Anger is not the *cause* of domestic violence. You can see it, though—it is there. Anger is brought out by a real or supposed injury to others or to us. When the back of your neck feels red and hot with anger, what do *you* do? The outward manifestation of that feeling is violence; it is evidenced due to a lack of self-control. Do you clench your teeth? Do you yell? Do you walk away? Do you punch a wall? Do you punch the one you love? Are all of these options allowed for the release of that anger—*that monster inside us all?* When feeling vulnerable and powerless, just how far are you willing to go?

All people are faced with situations that cause them to be angry, many times over the course of our lives. A teacher, our boss, a friend, or a motorist who cuts you off on the highway: All can arouse anger, that is, a passion or emotion. Love is also a passion or emotion. Few people will hit their teacher, yell at the boss, or rape a friend. Why do so many people feel free to abuse their lover, their child, or their parent? A simple answer is that we do it because we can. But can we get away with it? Most believe that the answer is not so straightforward.

No one really knows why people commit domestic crimes. We try to understand for many reasons. As a society, we don't want to be helpless, or hopeless. As individuals, the more we find out about others and the world around us, the better we know ourselves.

For every form of crime that is committed, there are many possible explanations; some of them make sense, some less so. Since we began to view domestic violence as criminal behavior, old theories were applied and new ones developed. There is a lack of consensus on the causes of family violence. The older theories often provide the cornerstone for new perspectives. For that reason, we focus first on the classical, biological, psychological, and sociological explanations.

Abuse within the family is not a simple matter, and we cannot expect simple solutions. Criminology, the study of crime causation, has long accepted that there is no single explanation for law breaking. Since the 1970s, there has been an incredible amount of research into domestic violence, resulting in theories too numerous to include in this introductory text. The most popular theories are multidimensional and draw from the old "schools" of thought, forming a new school. Some of the more contemporary ideas are included in the latter part of the chapter.

The social–legal historical viewpoint outlined in Chapter 2 is often placed under a broader umbrella as a political–historical approach. As stated earlier, it is useful as a description of the cause of wife and child abuse. Its limitation is that it excludes other theoretical explanations and other forms of violence. Still, this sociocultural anthropology view fits well within the broader understanding of family violence as one of the multidisciplinary descriptions within the social sciences. *Theories* that consider the *family, social system*, and others focus on *individual characteristics*. These theories generally define the other major categories under which familial violence occurs.

Been There... Done That!

Why should criminal justice students have to study theory? Criminological theories are only excuses that criminals use to "get off" after being caught! This has nothing to do with criminal justice! Statements such as these are typical of those from my criminal justice students over the years. Many would rather take any other three courses if they could escape being subjected to theory.

The question remains: Why should criminal justice students study theory? To *recognize the monster among us or inside us*, if for no other reason. After having interviewed over 100 abusers, I arrested clergy, professional persons, men, women, and children. They were old and young, educated and illiterate. Most didn't look bad or different. Some would have seemed like nice people if I hadn't known what they had done. What made them criminal was the *act* that they had committed. In domestic violence, the perpetrators are our neighbors and our friends, some of them "nice" people. "Why" becomes the operative word. When you study theory, it becomes possible to understand—not excuse—this criminal behavior.

Society Viewed at a Macro or Micro Level

There are two ways to study society: on a macro or a micro level. These terms do not refer to a particular theory, just the general approach that is used by theorists. As you proceed through this theoretical chapter, try to determine the level that describes the concept.

The social sciences approach acknowledges that social interactions are not random acts. Members of the family unit act purposefully to accomplish the goals of society. The learned patterns of behavior that are passed down from generation to generation are based on shared values and are shaped by the accepted rules of the group. This larger view of society and the influences that determine behavior is considered an examination on the *macro* level of society.

When inferences are made from individuals and applied to society at large, the study is being done on the *micro* level. From this perspective, an act that occurs between individuals is applied to the whole of society to form a theory. Typically, these involve psychological or individualist theories that are examined on the micro level of society. Most, although certainly not all, domestic abuse theory comes from this view. It allows generalizations to be made about groups of people while understanding that the individual results may be different. What happens in domestic violence is considered predictable, yet the result varies from one person to another based on intervening circumstances.

Think of each theoretical school described in this chapter as your own school. Although you can make a general statement about your college or university, you know that there are individuals within your institution that make it unique. Your generalization will not fit to describe each person but could be a fairly accurate statement about your institution.

THE CLASSICAL SCHOOL

Classical criminology is based on the idea that individuals choose to engage in crime. Cesare Beccaria (1738–1794) is called the father of classical criminology. He suggested that people possess a will that is free and therefore have the ability to reason. He suggested that to control behavior it would be necessary to spell out specifically through written law what was considered criminal behavior as well as the punishment associated with the act. Since people are *hedonistic* or pleasure-seeking, the threat of humiliation, pain, or disgrace would influence the will of the person, according to Beccaria.

Punishment is an important aspect of the classical approach to crime control because of its deterrent effects (Figure 3–1). To be effective, the punishment must fit the crime and be administered in a swift manner. It cannot be excessive or arbitrary in order to influence offenders into conformity.

Figure 3–1 Punishment is an important aspect of the classical approach to crime control because of its deterrent effect. *(Photo courtesy of Mark C. Ide.)*

Jeremy Bentham (1748–1833) popularized Beccaria's ideas through a "moral calculus" theory. He determined the extent of punishment necessary to deter the criminal. Believing that deterrence was the only acceptable reason for government punishment to be administered, he suggested that only minimal force could be used to encourage lesser crimes.

Since control and punishment are central to this theory, it is sometimes called the *legalistic* approach. You will note in upcoming chapters that the recent trend to criminalize domestic violence is often justified by the need to control family offenders. Arresting family lawbreakers is considered a form of punishment and a deterrent to future domestic violent acts. Applying penalties for family violence brings into the public forum acts that have traditionally been considered private. This is a huge departure from the way that society has conceived crime. In one generation, we have tried to change the perception that private violence is a public wrong. This was not possible until domestic violence was established as a social problem, and is still highly controversial.

Since the time of Beccaria and Bentham, government interference into the actions of individuals has been justified by the overriding needs of society. Recent research into the consequences of domestic violence has suggested that it is a pattern of behavior detrimental to a large number of citizens. Without regulation, family violence victims would be without the protection of the government.

The classical school was the dominant perspective in crime control for approximately 100 years. It established criminal procedures that continued in existence and sustained law enforcement practices after the theory was no longer debated. Neoclassical theory is a more current application of the principles contained in classical thought. It includes an economic perspective and an updated view of the behavioral sciences within the context of deterrence.

It is fair to say that contemporary classical thought is a restatement of the classical theories suggested by Beccaria and Bentham. They reaffirm the concept of punishment and have been categorized as separate approaches to combat domestic violence as well as other crimes. Social influences are believed to have an effect on the ability of the individual to exercise free will in the updated awareness of control and punishment.

Rational Choice Theory

Free or rational choice theory states that criminal behavior is more than just a response to social pressures or upbringing—it is also a choice (National Institute of Justice, 1994). Under this perspective, offenders calculate the relative costs and benefits of behavior and choose to commit domestic crimes. The National Institute of Justice report points out that offender choices are not necessarily rational but draw on previously established beliefs about their opportunities to commit personal violence and the likelihood of benefiting from their actions. The focus in this theory is to determine the effectiveness of interventions in order to decide how best to reduce the benefits of crime and increase the cost of criminal action.

Deterrence Theory

As with earlier statements on deterrence, today's theory is based on the idea that punishment must be swift and certain in order to deter crime. The deterrent effect of punishment can be specific or general in nature. Theorists suggest that we don't understand how effective deterrence is, and why it works or fails. They seek to update the concept with a greater understanding of community reinforcements and the role of official sanctions (National Institute of Justice, 1994).

When people are targeted in prevention efforts for a particular crime, the deterrence is considered specific. Larry Siegel suggests that efforts to reduce domestic violence through mandatory arrest policies exemplify specific deterrence (Siegel, 1995). Recidivism is reduced in some instances of domestic violence and appears greatest for those who have a greater stake in conformity. Those who are unemployed or otherwise lacking in social ties respond with repeated and often escalated violence (Figure 3–2).

When nonoffenders are affected by the punishment of offenders and choose not to risk apprehension, deterrence is general. If during an argument a person walks away muttering "you're not worth it" and holds himself or herself back when he or she might otherwise have swung out in his anger, that is an example of the general deterrence effect. One way that experts measure the deterrent effect of legislation is to examine the level of domestic crime to determine if the rate has gone down or risen. Only recently have studies attempted to determine the effects of legal sanctions, both criminal and civil, on the recurrence of domestic violence. We still do not know whether legal sanctions can control it effectively.

Figure 3–2   There is a risk of escalating future domestic violence when the offender arrested is unemployed or otherwise lacking in social ties. *(Photo courtesy of Mark C. Ide.)*

Critique of the Classical School

Classicism is a clear statement of law and punishment. All people are presumed equal and have the same opportunities to avoid crime. The assumption that all are equal is a target of criticisms of the legalist approach. Opponents claim that the law is unequally applied with bias toward minorities and the disadvantaged.

The Classical School has often been referred to as simplistic because it does not look to explain why people commit crimes; it seeks to control those who do. Domestic violence policy in the last decade has been based on efforts to control behaviors, and we have not yet determined if this has had the desired impact on recidivism. Classicism is reactive rather than proactive or preventive: It may not adequately protect the victim of abuse. The criminal justice system has a dual responsibility of protection as well as punishment. If deterrence is the goal of punishment, we must find out if legal sanctions deter the violence.

It can also be criticized because strict adherence to the theory leaves no room for mitigating circumstances or defenses. You do the crime, you do the time! Even Beccaria had to admit that some populations were incapable of exercising free will due to age or mental limitations, such as children and the insane! Classical theory was ultimately replaced in popularity with the Positive School.

THE POSITIVE SCHOOL

Positive theories are located in a broad school of thought where it becomes important to identify the cause of crime through scientific advances. The implication is that once the cause is isolated, a cure can be found to alter the behavior. *Cure* is a broad term in this sense; it could be a physical cure, a change in circumstances, or elimination of poverty. There are many possibilities.

The Positive School recognizes that the causes of crime are recognized from biological, psychological, and sociological viewpoints. The theories are not mutually exclusive and often overlap. It is not unusual for theorists to combine ideas to give direction toward solving new problems or merely to take a fresh look at old problems. Where classical thought is legalistic, the positive school is scientific. Continued research and the application of scientific principles are critical in this ever-changing body of thought.

BIOLOGICAL THEORIES

Biological theories are the most controversial and have limited application to family violence. Under this model violent or criminal behavior is beyond the control of the individual and caused by the person's biology. Once believed to result from a constant conflict between good and evil spirits, the triumph of evil was characterized by physical distinctiveness. Evilness was thought to reside in persons with red hair, according to Greek and Roman myth. Being ugly was an indictment of a bad person, one predisposed to commit crime.

Publication of Charles Darwin's theory of evolution in *On the Origin of Species* in 1859 influenced theorists who sought explanations for deviant conduct. An Italian psychiatrist, Cesare Lombroso (1835–1909), was the first to develop a theory based entirely on physical characteristics of the offender. His views on the "born criminal" suggested that offenders were less evolved than noncriminals. He concluded that it was possible to identify them through their atavistic or apelike tendencies. Although the atavistic explanation has repeatedly been refuted since then, it established the process of scientific inquiry that characterizes the positive school.

Early critics introduced social and cultural influences that affect biological tendencies as control mechanisms. The later theories forwarded by Lombroso included a variety of causes in addition to physical factors, many of which considered environmental variables (Vold & Bernard, 1986). At first controversial, U.S. society reacted favorably to biological determination, due to its scientific nature (Hofstadter, 1965).

Eugenics

The *eugenics movement* is an example of the reaction to this theoretical explanation for crime. Known as the "science of good breeding," the term *eugenics* was coined by Darwin's cousin, Francis Galton in 1883 (Hofstadter, 1965). Most people are aware of the role of eugenics in Hitler's attempts to "cleanse" the races; few realize its influence on the American way of behaving at the turn of the century. Richard Hofstadter wrote that eugenics had reached the dimensions of a fad by 1915 and proved to be the most enduring aspect of social Darwinism in the United States. Proponents of eugenics believed in the "survival of the fittest." Due to concern with the social significance of heredity and the expanding slums that were on the increase, the American Breeders' Association and the Eugenics Record Office were created (Hofstadter, 1965). Persons with mental health problems, immigrants, or those with low IQs were among the populations considered biologically inferior. The eugenics movement has rightly been charged with perpetuating racism due to its including persons of color among the unfit.

The movement advocated for the forced sterilization of both men and women who were considered socially and biologically inferior. In 1907 Indiana became the first state to adopt a sterilization law, and by 1915, twelve states had passed similar measures (Hofstadter, 1965). This approach became an accepted method of controlling the poor, who it was believed were held down by biological inadequacy. Eugenics reached its pinnacle in the 1927 Supreme Court case, *Buck v. Bell.* Considering the constitutionality of forced sterilization laws, Justice Oliver Holmes wrote in the opinion for the Court: "It is better for all the world if, instead of waiting to execute degenerate offspring for crime or to let them starve for their imbecility, society can prevent those who are manifestly unfit from continuing their kind. The principle that sustains compulsory vaccination is broad enough to cover cutting the Fallopian tubes" (*Jacobson v. Massachusetts*, 197 U.S. 11). "Three generations of imbeciles are enough" (p. 208).

The practice of forced sterilization was maintained in the United States well into the 1970s (Lilly et al., 1989). Although it is rarely discussed, criminal justice had continued to use chemical and physical castration and sterilization as forms of punishment as well as a means to control deviant conduct. Its popularity as an alternative to traditional forms of punishment has been rekindled due to scientific evidence suggestive of a link between violence and biological factors.

Among other areas, modern biological theories link violence to hormones and to neurological dysfunction. These two areas are considered the most promising of contemporary biological research into the causes of violent conduct. They differ from other biological explanations because the conditions are considered measurable and alterable. Although not broadly accepted, there has been a recent surge of interest in the use of biological influences toward explaining criminal behavior (Wright & Miller, 1998).

Critics of the application of biological theories point to the eugenics movement and diverge from two perspectives, moral and constitutional, although the two views are closely related. Moral critics refer to the biological intervention strategies as the *medicalization of repression* (Katz, 1984). It has been noted that the people targeted for these medical procedures are often poor and undereducated. Frequent complaints suggest that black and minority populations have been abused by government practices of coerced sterilization. An example is the recent acknowledgment of widespread abuse carried out by the Indian Health Services and other health care providers to Native American women. In 1975 alone, 25,000 Native American women were permanently

B e e n   T h e r e ... D o n e   T h a t !

In 1984, I investigated a case of incest. The father and daughter were found guilty of the crime. The father was sentenced to 20 years in prison; his adult daughter was placed on probation under the condition that she submit to being sterilized. She agreed. *What do you think about that?*

sterilized after being coerced, misinformed, or threatened, according to a study by the Government Accounting Office (Define, 1997). Sterilization of women as a condition of probation has continued with few complaints.

Prior to the 1980s, surgical castration as a method of reducing sex offenders' recidivism was practiced. Since then courts have struck down the measure under both "cruel and unusual" arguments and on "equal protection" grounds (Bund, 1997). In the past few years, five states have enacted legislation that permits *chemical* castration under certain circumstances. Fred Berlin, founder of the Sexual Disorders Clinic at Johns Hopkins University, fueled the debate by noting that molesters may have a recidivism rate as high as 65 percent (Van Biema, 1996). In response to the alarming rates of child molestation, California was the first to pass the legislation in 1996 to allow chemical castration of paroled sex offenders. Montana, Florida, Georgia, and Louisiana quickly followed the example in 1997. Texas passed a similar law in 1998.

M o r e   a b o u t   I t :   C h e m i c a l   C a s t r a t i o n

Jennifer Bund explains chemical castration in a preprint article from the *University of Pittsburgh Law Review* (Bund, 1997). From her analysis, the following information is provided. Medroxyprogesterone acetate treatment, better known by the trade name Depo-Provera, is a synthetic hormone. It lowers the blood serum testosterone levels in males by restricting the release of luteinizing hormones from the pituitary gland. The reduction of testosterone triggers a corresponding reduction in sexual interest and therefore is believed to reduce recidivism. It is also believed to effectively reduce the frequency of erotic imagery and to normally cause a temporary form of impotence (interference with erections) which also helps to reduce recidivism. The drug takes effect quickly, and positive results usually appear within six months of treatment. The side effects associated with Depo-Provera include weight gain, muscle weakness, fatigue, and increased blood pressure. Once treatment is discontinued, the side effects disappear.

Biochemical Imbalance Theories

A number of biochemical theories, including glandular and hormonal imbalances, as well as vitamin and diet deficiencies, have been suggested as possible causes of criminal behavior (Vold & Bernard, 1986). The raging hormones of women and the excess of testosterone in men have alternatively been accepted and rejected during this century. The most pervasive theory is a perceived link between testosterone and male aggressiveness. Vold and Bernard point toward research conducted in the 1980s which found that violent males had a significantly higher level of testosterone in their systems.

Neurological Theories

In the study of brain activity, numerous attempts have been made to link abnormal patterns to violent action (Figure 3–3). Antisocial behavior that afflicts approximately 5 percent of males has been linked to a brain dysfunction indicated by neuropsychological tests, according to recent research (Moffitt, 1997). This study, which attempted to show the connection between brain abnormalities and criminality, concluded that test scores were not helpful in predicting delinquent behavior. However, dysfunction may influence the personal relationships in a small subgroup of men and may have applicability in explaining some forms of domestic violence.

Chemical compounds that influence brain functions have been studied in relation to aggression as well (Siegel, 1995). Of particular interest are the endogenous opiates the brain produces that are similar to opium and morphine. Some theorists suggest that a "thrill" obtained through crime may cause production of these addictive chemicals, according to Siegel. Alderman suggests that excessive endorphin production may explain in part the reasons for self-inflicted violence (SIV; Alderman, 1997). She maintains that the majority of SIV patients have histories of abuse as children. Feelings of inadequacy, coupled with an inability to cope with life stresses, may influence people to seek pleasure through the pain of self-abuse.

Figure 3–3   Naturally produced chemical compounds that influence brain functions have been studied in relation to aggression. Endogenous opiates are an example that may occur with the "thrill" of crime.

Critique of the Biological Theories

The danger of early biological explanations for behavior was the tendency to view abnormalities as undesirable and unalterable. Belief that crime was caused by a person's biology and exhibited through physical characteristics, including racial differences, led us to adopt drastic measures in response. We should know about the danger in order to resist the impulse of looking for the easy cure or quick fix to the problems in society. Current controversy on the application of biological theory is aimed at medical procedures that are being used to control the sexual impulses of convicted offenders. Debates on the constitutionality of sterilization and castration as a method of controlling criminal behavior are likely to continue well into the next decade.

SOCIOLOGICAL THEORIES

Adolph Quetelet (1796–1874), a Belgian theorist, is called the "first social criminologist" according to Vold and Bernard (1986). Among the first to establish a relationship between crime and poverty, he suggested that the great inequality between the wealthy and the poor contributed to lawbreaking. Hundreds of studies on crime and the effects of unemployment have been conducted since that time.

For a short period after the introduction of biological theory, some sociological perspectives incorporated biological views. Belief in natural selection was evidenced through the broadly acclaimed works of Herbert Spencer. Between 1870 and 1890, Spencer had a profound influence on arguments within the United States regarding the nature of humankind. Against criticism, he claimed that government aid to the weak was in opposition to the natural order. The unfit should be eliminated, he suggested, and programs to aid the poor were contrary to natural selection of the species. Opposed to compulsory poor laws and other state measures, he did not argue against private charity to the unfit: "If they are not sufficiently complete to live, they die, and it is best that they should die," said Spencer (p. 41) (Hofstadter, 1965).

Despite Spencerism, the sociological explanations have gained credibility in the twentieth century. They provide the bulk of theory on the causes of criminal conduct. This theory is concerned with an interaction between social change and human behavior influenced by economics and culture. Sociological points of view have contributed enormously to the understanding of domestic abuses.

Social Structure and Cultural Theories

Social structure theories attribute domestic violence to the structures and cultural norms that legitimize deviance. Batterer intervention strategies are based on women's experience of these social and cultural factors. They use education and skills building

Gender-Role Theory

This uncomplicated explanation for domestic violence blames the traditional social-ization of children into gender-roles conducive to wife battering (Walker, 1979). In this perspective, children are oriented early in life as victims or perpetrators, accord-ing to their gender. Girls are taught to be passive and yielding to the "stronger" male sex. Proponents of gender-role theory suggest that society dictates the role of women in marriage, in child responsibilities, and toward domestic duties, all of which makes them vulnerable to abuse. Self-reliance or aggressiveness are male attributes that are unbecoming of females in the traditional sense.

According to gender-role theory, the expectation that girls should be physically and sexually pleasing to men makes them susceptible to sexual abuse. In relationships, girls are taught to be submissive while boys are expected to be the sexual aggressors. On the other hand, boys are taught that men must be in control at all times. They must exhibit strength and develop leadership qualities. Men are therefore socialized that their position is to be protected at all costs, including violence.

The tenets of this theory are believed to contribute to sexual violence of young women in dating relationships. Emotionally immature young women socialized in their roles are vulnerable to sexual victimization through aggression and dominance of young men. Py Bateman suggests that reports from adolescent date rape victims are rare in this culture that condones sexual violence toward women (Bateman, 1998). Conversely, young men may respond to peer pressure to be sexually aggressive through the same model. A major source of socialization for this model is the media. Television is blamed for depicting male and female roles in a limited and superficial characterization of male aggression and female passivity.

Critique of the Sociological Theories

Most of the criticism on the sociological theories is that they fail to explain why peo-ple who come in contact with crime do not themselves become deviant. The majori-ty of people do not commit domestic violence crime, even though they are socialized through similar media. Not all men are violent, nor all women victims. Nor do soci-ological theories explain why victims of sexual or physical violence do not perpetrate against others.

PSYCHOLOGICAL THEORIES

Yet another distinct category among the major schools of thought, psychological the-ory is itself diverse in the ways that it looks at people. Under the rubric of psycholog-ical theory, many theories examine the influence and impact of individual pathology, culture, socialization, and learning.

to resocialize battering males, emphasizing equality in intimate relationships (Healey & Smith, 1998).

Culture of Violence Theory.   The culture of violence theory looks at the broad acceptance of violence in our society and concludes that its acceptance is the foundation for violence within the family. In this view, theorists point out the perverseness of violence as entertainment and the means for settling disputes at the personal and national levels. The implied approval for violence is acknowledged and legitimizes the use of violence to settle family disputes as well. This theory claims that violence occurs at all levels of society as an accepted means to resolve difficulty, arguing that a restructuring of the cultural variables of society is needed in order to bring change. In other words, to stop wife abuse, it is necessary to alter man's reliance on violence as a means of resolving conflict.

Social Disorganization Theory.   The disorganization of community life causes a lack of social control in this theory. Considered in part the result of high mobility, a breakdown in formal and informal controls that might otherwise mitigate family conflict encourages criminal conduct. Poverty in transitional neighborhoods is believed to contribute to the lawlessness that results. People whose emphasis is necessarily on survival lack concern for community matters and fail to benefit from common sources of control such as family, school, and social service agencies.

Strain Theory.   Another type of social structure theory is the one referred to as *strain theory*. This is the struggle between desires and the ability to fulfill them. When social and economic goals are outside the reach due to poverty, strain occurs. The United States is a competitive and property-oriented country. Most people want material possessions, some of which are necessary, such as a car or a home. Beyond the basics are television sets, radios, and computers. For many the opportunity to go to college is outside their economic means. Strain theory suggests that a sense of futility develops when one is unable to achieve financial success or security. In some circumstances, this will lead to crime. As you will note in many of the multidimensional models, it is also believed to contribute to domestic violence crime.

Gamache points out that women of color experience battering in a different context than that of others in society (Gamache, 1998). Her position is in part explained through the strain theory. The "stick by your man" stance is an example of the protective response toward male partners whose dominance and abuse may be tolerated due to a shared sense of mistrust. A perception of a lack of power or ability to have significant impact on the culture has led many black men to make excessive demands on their partners for respect, according to Evelyn White (White, 1998). She suggests that this cause of domestic violence in the black community is based on the reality that black men face bleak futures regardless of how hard they may work to overcome the poverty that embraces them.

Social Learning Theories

According to *social learning theory*, people are not born with violent tendencies. They learn them through their environment and life experiences. Deviance is learned in the same manner as normative behavior. The process of learning is through communication with others and includes motives, drives, attitudes, and rationalizations on the commission of crime. When aggressive action brings desired results, violence becomes an acceptable means to an end. The primary source of learning occurs in intimate personal groups of family and peer, according to this view.

The frequency and duration of the violence in one's environment will influence the learning experience. Since people process life events in different ways, it can be said that *your perception is your reality*. The manner in which a person perceives a situation from his or her own viewpoint will affect the response. This becomes the reality under which the person will operate in the future and perceive similar events. This perspective provides a popular explanation for many forms of family violence and forms the basis for numerous variations. The continuum of family violence from the social learning perspective is illustrated through the behavior modeling theory and the intergenerational transmission theory.

Behavior Modeling Theory.   Albert Bandura (1925–present) pioneered the field of *behavior modeling theory*. His studies on family life showed that children who use aggressive tactics have parents who use similar behaviors when dealing with others. Children are most affected by the influence of family members in this view. Bandura is most famous for his modeling therapy, according to George Boeree, who states that the original research involved herpephobics, people with a neurotic fear of snakes (Boeree, 1998). Using real snakes in his original therapy, an actor would go through a slow and painful approach to the snake. Eventually, he removed the snake and draped it over his neck. The client was then invited to try it him or herself. Many clients were able to grow through the routine and sit with the snake around their neck.

Environmental experiences are another source of influence, according to social learning theory. Children who reside in crime-prone and violent areas are more likely to act out violently. Violent television shows and movies provide a third source of modeling for children. Since violence is often portrayed as acceptable behavior, children begin to view violent acts as normal behavior, which has no consequences for the actors.

Intergenerational Transmission Theory.   A frequently used explanation for domestic violence is the intergenerational transmission theory. Abusive behavior is handed down from generation to generation as an appropriate way to deal with conflict: **violence begets violence**. This does not suggest that battering tendencies are inherited; rather, they are experienced. People who observe violence in the home as children are more likely to resort to battering in their own relationships later in life. Simply put, if a child is abused, he or she learns that it is an acceptable if not normal way to achieve his or her goal. The child becomes an abusing adult—toward a spouse and often toward his or her own children. A cycle of abuse occurs across generations.

Cycle of Violence Theory.   There is substantial evidence that a generational *cycle of violence* occurs in domestic assaults. The theorist most often cited for application of the transmission of violence theory to domestic abuse is Lenore Walker. In *The Battered Woman*, she described three separate phases of an abuse cycle represented in a pattern that is repeated time and again in a battering relationship (Walker, 1979):

Phase I, *tension building*, is characterized by poor communication and minor incidents of abuse. In this phase, women are compliant and attempt to minimize problems in the relationship. The male feels increased tension and takes more control through dominance, causing the victim to withdraw. *Acute battering* is referred to as phase II. Here the batterer who is highly abusive evidences a loss of control. The woman suffers stress and injury. Phase III is often referred to as the *honeymoon phase*, when kindness and loving behavior emanate from the contrite batterer. As the tension drops between the perpetrator and victim, a renewed love is experienced. He is often apologetic and attentive to his partner. She at first has mixed feelings, then feels guilty and responsible for the outburst. He continues to manipulate the relationship through promises of change.

It is not unusual during the final phase for the batterer to shower gifts and flowers on the woman. The cycle usually repeats itself, however, and the violence is believed to escalate over time. Being victimized more than once increases the risk of subsequent assault (Straus et al., 1980). Early critics of the theory claimed that the female victim must "like it" or she would leave. It is therefore important to separate the idealized version that the victim has of the relationship from the reality. For many women caught in this repetitive cycle, an early hope for the continuation of kind and loving behavior is reason to hold onto the men with whom they fell in love. Often, the women cling to the idealized version of the men they love, not to the violence that they endure.

The theory was tested regarding children who were raised in violent homes. Would they become more violent in their personal relationships as adults? Research determined that to be the case (Straus et al., 1980).

Social Control Theories

Control theorists suggest that crime and delinquency are likely to occur unless people conform to social demands. Social constraints are the mechanisms that control anti-social behavior. When constraints are weakened or absent, delinquent behavior emerges. The three main bonds that link people to socially acceptable behavior are attachment, belief in shared values, and involvement in law-abiding activities (National Institute of Justice, 1994).

Attachment Theory.   According to *attachment theory*, the relationship that develops between the infant and his or her primary caregiver affects relationships later in life. Attachment theorists believe that attachment bonds may produce secure, anxious, or disoriented children (Garrett & Libbey, 1997). Children who are secure in their attachments are easily comforted and move freely from caregiver to stranger. The anxious children will resist comfort given to them, or may resist separation from the caregiver, at the same time displaying distrust of the caregiver. A disoriented child displays erratic and confused behavior based on an inability to determine which behaviors gain favorable attention from the caregiver. Garrett and Libbey further explain that whichever attachment patterns develop in childhood will be the type that is expected and recreated in adulthood. Children raised by neglectful parents then develop insecure attachments that they display in their own parenting later in life. Attentive parenting, as illustrated in Figure 3–4, is necessary to develop secure attachments with children.

Individual Pathology and Male Batterers.   Some theorists concede that a small number of domestic violence perpetrators exhibit behaviors similar to persons suffering with personality disorders (Tifft, 1993). These people are highly

Figure 3–4   Adults are expected to form relationships with children based on their own childhood relationships with adults.

resistant to counseling and other forms of intervention, which is suggestive of psychopathological sickness. Court intervention with supervised therapy is the most likely option for those whose behavior can be dangerous, if not lethal.

Donald Dutton has been working with assaultive men since 1978, both as a clinician and as a researcher. He suggests that approximately 2 percent of the population would qualify as habitual woman batterers (Dutton & Golant, 1995). In addition to that, many of his clients met the criteria for antisocial behavior; he defined them as having shallow emotional responsiveness. They are often violent with others in addition to their partners. Psychopathic batterers are frequently arrested for nonviolent crimes such as forgery, passing bad checks, or confidence rackets.

Dutton points out that his colleague Robert Hare, author of *Without Conscience: The Disturbing World of the Psychopaths among Us*, found brain abnormalities among psychopaths. Magnetic resonance imaging (MRI) brain scans performed on psychopaths lacked the huge color patterns radiating from the brain stem to the temporal lobes that were present in normal persons. Instead, a small amount of bright color in the stem area toward the back of the brain was the only indication of brain activity. Without evidence that psychopathy is the direct result of social or environmental factors, Hare theorizes that the condition is genetic.

Psychologist Neil Jacobson describes a subgroup of psychopathic men whom he calls *vagal reactors* (Dutton & Golant, 1995). Approximately 20 percent of all batterers and half of all antisocial personalities fall within this category, he maintains. These men become calm internally when engaged in heated arguments with their wives. Subjects actually showed a decline in heart rate during arguments with a spouse. The violence committed against a wife is for the purpose of dominating her; it is both controlling and controlled.

Critique of the Psychological Theories

The different models based on learning are the most frequently cited explanations for domestic violence and its continuation. However, they do not explain why all people do not commit personal violence after witnessing violence or victimization. It also does not adequately address personalities that are extremely successful in other aspects of their lives.

THE CONFLICT SCHOOL

In the conflict model, law is seen as the means by which the ruling class maintains its control. The lawmakers are presumed to legitimize their positions of superiority by dominating minorities and the lower classes. Poverty and unemployment resides at the core of crime in this approach. Conflict scholars also question the rule-making process itself and conclude that regulations exist because those in power determine how the rules are made and enforced. Since struggles over power are a normal part of any society, this school does not seek to understand the cause of crime. Rather, it argues that the larger the society, the greater the likelihood that groups will fail to agree on conduct norms.

Within this school, critics have argued for a more substantial role and consideration of gender in theoretical research. John Hagan is one that has called for the development of a research base considering power and dominance in the context of family, work, and criminal justice (Voigt et al., 1994). Feminist scholars agree on this need to examine gender-specific authority relations, charging that violence against women by men has been ignored. The patriarchal theory on woman battering emerged as one challenge to gender assumptions.

Patriarchal Theory

The most widely used perspective on woman battering is *patriarchal theory*, also referred to as the *feminist approach*. As with other radical views that spring from a revolution, the feminist model questions the way that women have been viewed in society and the lack of legal options for those that are victimized. The majority of violence against women occurs in their homes, formally a place of legal sanction for the abusers. This theory has greatly influenced the perception of domestic violence and criminal justice practice.

The major tenets of patriarchal theory are as follows:

- Gender relationships are considered a fundamental component of social life. The experiences of gender are therefore emphasized. Both men and women are part of the analysis, with the greater emphasis placed on the differences within the context of society and viewed from within power relations.

- The power of men by virtue of their privileged status is the means by which women are controlled. Men are the traditional lawmakers and property owners who have excluded female participation and justified abuse in order to maintain power. Therefore, power and control are the key elements that establish and maintain the subordination of women in society, legitimating the positioning of the genders.

- Ending the subordination of women by means of changing the social structure remains the major goal of the movement. This process would include, but is not limited to, equal access and protection through law.

In its most extreme form, the perspective holds that all men will be abusive. Catharine MacKinnon represents this radical feminist position (MacKinnon, 1993). She and colleagues seek to redefine the law from what is considered a male hierarchical system to a gender-equality standpoint. Perceived as initiating a war between the sexes, this is a controversial position that tends to alienate persons due to the hostility it embraces. Critics claim that its confrontational stance is self-defeating.

In a more moderate form, the position is a comparison between men and women within the context of power relations. The theory does not seek to take power away from men, but rather, to equalize it and share it between both genders. The status of women in society is related to the frequency of wife beating, according to this view. Wife abuse is explained through the exploration of the social structure of society and the analysis of power that has historically been identified in male dominance.

Research from the feminist perspective looks at the historical evidence of the subordination of women, as was outlined in the social–legal historical perspective from Chapter 2. Inferences are made from the legal status of women and translated into reasons why men batter (Figure 3–5). Case examples are another source of evidence that illustrates the patriarchal viewpoint.

Figure 3–5 This chart depicting the integrated feminist cognitive–behavioral strategy illustrates the dynamics of an abusive relationship. *(Courtesy of House of Ruth, Baltimore, Maryland.)*

Example of an Integrated Feminist/Cognitive-Behavioral Strategy

Gender Inequality

Feminist criminality has also been ignored in criminology. Some authors maintain that female offenders have been considered inferior and their crimes insignificant (Vito & Holmes, 1994). Perhaps that is why there are no concise theoretical explanations that examine why some women abuse their children and lovers. Child abuse advocates point to the devaluation of children in our society. Since women are the primary offenders against children, that may in part explain the absence of research in this area.

The chivalry hypothesis holds that women are likely to be protected by the criminal justice system and given more lenient treatment than men when they commit the same crimes (Vito & Holmes, 1994). In communities where mandatory arrest policies on domestic violence have been rigorously applied, the number of female offenders has risen dramatically. Since studies on domestic abuse often originate from law enforcement records, the process would alter the resulting data. Additional research is needed to determine the actual extent and causes of abuse by women.

Critique of the Conflict School

Implicating all men in the crimes of an individual rapist or physical abuser seems extreme to critics. Although the majority of victims of domestic abuse are women, the feminist explanation is considered an extreme indictment against all men. The theory fails to make clear why violence is sometimes perpetrated by women and happens within same-sex relationships. On the other hand, it is impossible to dismiss the value of the perspective. Case examples and the historical analysis point to patterns of behavior that have the effect of dominating women. The good ol' boy network perpetuates the inequality of the sexes while devaluing feminine qualities. Since equal protection is a cornerstone of the U.S. legal philosophy, it is difficult to explain why a group of individuals has been denied access due to gender.

MULTIDIMENSIONAL MODELS

Multidimensional models that combine different theoretical perspectives are among the most popular today to explain why personal violence occurs in specific or newly recognized forms of abuse. Contemporary multidimensional theorists often do not make any distinction between biological, psychological, and sociological views since they interchange frequently in discussions on the causes of domestic violence.

According to Garrett and Libbey, *ecological theories* were formulated to take into account beliefs that child abuse and neglect result from multiple factors rather than a parent's personality disorder alone (Garrett & Libbey, 1997). They suggest that the factors be divided into four systems: individual, family, community, and culture. Significant influences in these systems are peers, school, workplace, economic factors, childrearing history, child characteristics, parent characteristics, marital relationship, social support, and sociocultural environment.

Ecological theorists include influences on the family such as community violence and isolation from the community, according to Garrett and Libbey. Employment, economic, and relational stressors that may contribute to abuse and neglect are not addressed through community support due to the isolation from the community, and subsequent abuse can lead to further isolation and a code of silence.

Individual-Based Theories

Individual-based theories ascribe domestic violence to psychological problems such as personality disorders, the batterer's childhood experiences, or biological disposition. Early theories on child abuse and neglect presumed a personality disorder of the parent (Garrett & Libbey, 1997). Studies in recent years have refuted that general thesis, since less than 10 percent of abusive parents were found to be emotionally maladjusted. Multiple factor theories have sought to determine the causes of abuse and neglect to children. Psychotherapeutic, cognitive–behavioral, and attachment abuse interventions are used to target individual problems and help the batterer control violent behaviors (Healey & Smith, 1998). The underlying psychological cause of the violence is targeted in the psychodynamic approach to therapy. A cognitive behavioral approach is taken when the batterer is taught new patterns of nonviolent thinking and behavior. If the perpetrator has difficulty in establishing healthy relationships, attempts are made to facilitate secure attachments between batterers and loved ones.

Resiliency Theory.   We know that most children do not grow up to be abusive parents. Many abused and neglected children are not violent toward their own later in life. Why is this so? The resiliency theory examines the learning process and attempts to identify the intervening factors that might overcome the effects of abuse. Resiliency theory explains not why abuse occurs, but why it does not. Its focus on the victims of childhood abuse might offer explanations on ways to interrupt the "cycle of violence" by reinforcement of positive influences (Garrett & Libbey, 1997).

Individual Pathology and Gay Offenders.   David Island and Patrick Letellier suggest that all batterers have a mental disorder, although they may not necessarily be insane or psychotic (Island & Letellier, 1991). In their discussion on gay battering, the authors claim that socialization and cultural theories take the responsibility for battering away from the individual and serve to blame only society for behaviors that are abnormal and criminal. Noting that the research from Hamberger and Hastings (1988) confirmed their position that abusers suffer from a disordered personality, they applied this thesis to men who beat their male lovers (Island & Letellier, 1991). They further assert that accountability through the criminal justice system is the best intervention, an approach that is highly reminiscent of the classical arguments.

Social–Psychological Model of Lesbian and Gay Abuse.   Social isolation creates an environment where battering in same-sex couples can occur, according to this integrated model (Merrill, 1996). Gregory Merrill draws on the conclusions of Zemsky (Zemsky, 1990) and Gilbert (Gilbert et al., 1990) for his claim that domestic violence must be understood as both a social and a psychological phenomenon. Rather than viewing domestic theories as mutually exclusive of the other, the combination can enhance same-sex theories of violence and apply to heterosexual theory as well.

The model uses a broad application of social learning theory to explain that people who abuse have learned to do so through direct instruction, modeling, and reinforcement. Unequal power relations (real or perceived) contribute to the likelihood that abusive behaviors will be tolerated, an idea born through the feminist contribution. A third dimension is the recognition that domestic abuse is a personal choice: An abuser acts out with violence instead of using alternative conflict resolution.

Family-Based Theories

Violent behaviors are caused by the family structure and family interactions rather than by an individual within the family, according to these theories. *Family systems theory* is one example. Conflict within an intimate relationship is blamed on the lack of communication between the partners. Complicating the issue is the deeply intertwined mutual dependency that develops in some relationships. Self-imposed social isolation in addition to rigid expectations of loyalty and privacy make this a difficult situation for families when battering is introduced as a means of control (Tifft, 1993).

Family Systems Theory.   Family systems theory focuses primarily on the family and seeks to identify the problems that are a consequence of dysfunctional relationships among family members. The role that each family member takes in contributing to the abuse or neglect is considered. In situations of incest where the father is the perpetrator, for example, the possibility that the mother's reluctant intervention may appear to be tacit approval would be explored as a contributing factor in the repeated occurrence of abuse (Garrett & Libbey, 1997).

Self-Efficacy Theory.   Athena Garret and Heather Libbey state that the ecological theory also incorporates self-efficacy theory (Garrett & Libbey, 1997). This theory addresses how personal characteristics of the child and the parent influence family functioning. Primary is an investigation into the expectations of parents' effectiveness, which is believed to affect their motivation and behavior. If parents believe that they are unable to change their behavior, they are not likely to seek help in discontinuing abusing conduct, even though they know it is wrong.

Husband Abuse.   Despite numerous reports that women are equally likely to perpetrate violence against their husbands (Straus, 1996), no specific theory has been forwarded to explain the causes. In *Abused Men: The Hidden Side of Domestic Violence*, Philip Cook reached a similar conclusion (Cook, 1997). Official estimates of husband abuse range from 6 percent to 10 percent of family violence. According to Cook, the National Institute of Health was among those that found an equal or greater rate of offending by women.

Even though a model has not been forthcoming, four factors stand out as leading to husband abuse. The first is ineffective communication between spouses. Straus and colleagues found that husbands are more likely to be beaten in households where spouses do not share major decision making (Straus et al., 1980). A correlation was established between the amount of shared decision making and husband abuse. In families where couples made major decisions together, a lower rate of either husband or wife abuse was evidenced.

Second is a struggle over control and power in the relationship or perception of a lesser power. Although this was not the contention of L. Kevin Hamberger and Theresa Potente, they do suggest that sociopolitically based male offender treatment be applied to female offenders who evidence issues of power and control (Hamberger & Potente, 1996).

Third, husband abuse is evidenced as a form of social disorganization. A lack of adequate financial resources and social bonds leaves a relationship vulnerable to husband battering. Wife-to-husband violence was three times greater in households with the lowest family income, according to the Straus survey (Straus et al., 1980). They further found a relationship between problems reported by the individuals and the level of violence. The greater the family stress, the higher the likelihood of family violence. Inadequate financial resources do not necessarily suggest poverty; life stresses seem to produce an increase in wife beating and in husband beating in all income brackets.

Finally, wife-to-husband violence is in part explained through social structure theory. The decision to slap, hit, push, or punch a husband or boyfriend is made with the knowledge that the likelihood of apprehension or social censure is slim. These forms of violence against men appear acceptable and are perpetuated by the media. In one national survey, 27.6 percent of the couples felt that slapping a spouse was either necessary, normal, or good (Dibble & Straus, 1980).

Theories on Sibling Abuse.   Social offender theories focus on *power and control* within the context of social and cultural views. Many explanations look at what the adults do or fail to do in their parental role. *Imitation and ineffective parenting* are examples. No single explanation has evolved to explain sibling abuse; rather, a combination of conditions has been identified under which a child is born and conditioned into violent behavior.

Power and Control Model.   Rethinking the traditional social and cultural theories in adult maltreatment, Vernon Wiehe maintains that abuse of power generally occurs when a sibling attempts to compensate for a lack or loss of power (Straus et al., 1980). The abusers perceive an imbalance between themselves and younger siblings who they believe are favored due to academic or social successes or by virtue of their age or gender. Frequently, the abuse of power occurs along gender lines, with males abusing females. Gender-role socialization that favors male aggressiveness and female passivity contributes to the condition.

One method to assert control over sisters is through the use of physical and verbal force. Left unchecked by parents, the use of force may escalate. The highest level of violence occurs in homes where a boy has only brothers (Straus et al., 1980). What are some of the factors that contribute to rivalry gone awry?

Imitation and Reaction.   Research has indicated when parents are abusive toward each other, there is a high likelihood that they will abuse their children. It is possible that the victims treat younger children as they are themselves treated, in particular during the time they are babysitting their siblings. Erin Pizzey noted that children react differently to abusive situations according to their gender (Pizzey, 1977). Boys tended to become aggressive, and girls often reacted by withdrawal. This lends credibility to the suggestion that boys exposed to parental domestic violence offend violently more often than girls do.

Ineffective Parenting

1. *Overwhelmed parents.* Parents who are coping with problems that are over-whelming lack the ability or energy to intervene in sibling abuse. In this category of causes, Wiehe considers two major impediments to healthy parenting that can contribute to the problem. The first is drug and alcohol abuse, and the second is stress-related issues. Numerous studies on family violence indicate that abusers are frequently involved in alcohol or drug abuse. The author suggests that a relationship also exists between the parents' abuse of drugs and alcohol and their children's engagement in abusive behaving.

   His second point is more complicated and suggests that sibling incest may occur in homes where parents are absent either physically or psychologically. Fathers who are disinterested in parenting and mothers who are distant to their children promote an atmosphere where children may turn to each other for comfort, nurturance, and support with a risk of sexualizing as they enter adolescence. Alternatively, offenders may model their parents' aggressive behavior from what they observe in their parents' relationship.

2. *Inappropriate expectations.* Parents often expect an older sibling to care for younger children in their absence. Some children may not be old enough to handle the responsibility, according to Wiehe, or if old enough, they may lack the skills and knowledge to serve in a parental role. He suggests that parents be sensitive to complaints from children left in this vulnerable position.

3. *Lack of parenting skills.* Sometimes parents are ineffective in controlling sibling abuse because they don't know how or what to do.

Community Theory

Community relationships are thought to have an impact on behaviors, particularly in high-risk communities that experience cultural conflict. Disorganization of community life promotes community instability and limited participation in the formal and informal controls over delinquent and criminal conduct. *Network theory* addresses these concerns by exploring how people are recruited into criminal careers and how or why they stay in or leave them (National Institute of Justice, 1994). Peer relationships have an influence on behavior in disorganized and conflicting communities, and the extent of these influences is unclear. Additionally, network theory looks at offending rates that differ due to gender.

Culture Theory

One example of this viewpoint is suggested by Shawn Sullivan to explain domestic violence against black women by black men (Sullivan, 1996). Some young men are taught by their fathers or older brothers to refer to black women as "ho's" (whores), she suggests. The lack of respect coupled with the prevalence of violence as an acceptable means of resolving disputes put black women at risk for domestic assault.

The Social Causes of Dating Violence.   According to Denise Gamache, violence in dating relationships is reinforced by cultural beliefs that legitimize power and control over others (Gamache, 1998). She suggests a feminist model where cultural norms make domination appear normal and where challenges are perceived as a threat to the natural order. Although both young women and men report inflicting physical abuse, research has shown females to be the likely recipients of severe physical abuse and of sexual violence. Male battering in dating relationships is also likely to continue into the marriage.

Critique of the Multidimensional Theories

The approach that the multidimensional theories have in common is that they do not restrict themselves to any one major school of thought. In this way they retain the flexibility to consider causes and effects of family violence from a broader perspective. Some researchers even question the fact that most people do not commit family crimes—in fact, the majority of children do not grow up to be abusive parents. This positive approach has potential.

   With the expansion of theoretical approaches, however, comes confusion. Determining what works and what does not work is more difficult than ever. The lack of consensus on the cause of domestic abuse makes the response vary between jurisdictions. Conflicting approaches to deal with the problems result. Although it is not necessary that all agree, it would be helpful to have a clearer picture of how to combat the violence that is so pervasive.

CONCLUSIONS

There is no excuse for expressing violence against a loved one. Yet it happens frequently. Why does domestic abuse occur? To answer this question, theories examining society from a macro or micro level have been provided in this chapter. Depending on the perspective, either societal norms or individual behaviors are at the core of the explanation.

Traditional criminological theories have been discussed with their application to domestic crime. To the student of criminology, the terms are familiar. The basics from the classical, positive, and critical schools are the foundation for the multidisciplinary models that have emerged in recent times. The classical school with its legalist approach is the one that most criminal justice students find memorable. It is, after all, the model that criminal justice practice depends on. Suggesting that a formula for control is possible with the right combination, it supports punishment as a deterrent to crime. It becomes untenable when the deterrent effect of criminal justice intervention is questioned with respect to domestic violence.

Positive theory contains the most diverse options for examining family abuse. Scientific research questions and reexamines the possibilities from biological, sociological, and psychological viewpoints. Because the early biological explanations rest on racist and sexist foundations, they have been discredited. Modern theories such as the biochemical imbalance and neurological theories are offered from the study of medical conditions rather than physical characteristics.

When first developed, the sociological theories were unique because they explored the idea that a relationship exists between poverty and crime. From there it is possible to conceive that other influences, such as cultural norms and social structures, may have a cause-and-effect relationship to domestic violence. The disorganization of community ties leaves a family vulnerable, according to the social disorganization theory. Finally, socialization into gender roles is at the core of the gender-role theory which maintains that men and women act differently according to expectations from both outside and internal sources.

The psychological theory has developed a number of views that have been applied in the search to understand domestic violence. The collection of social learning theories is most often used to explain family abuse. Its popularity may be due to the intuitive appeal that learning suggests. We are not born violent, it points out. If we can learn to become this way, can't we unlearn the behaviors? Therapeutic practices often focus on education and behavior modification in an attempt to alter behavior.

Attachment theorists claim that our future may be determined from infancy through the early childhood years, depending on the strength or absence of bonds that develop between the child and parent. Neglectful parenting beginning at birth may orient the person into negative patterns of behavior and cause irreparable damage to the psyche. But what about the few people in the population who cannot feel remorse or guilt? Psychopathic theorists claim that there may be a biological indication that these people cannot alter their criminal tendencies. These men are violent both with a spouse and with others. Their detachment to the pain and suffering that they cause is remarkable.

The conflict school contributes the patriarchal and gender inequality theories. While both question the power and control of those in power to make and enforce the laws, they come to opposite conclusions. The feminist model contends that women are subjugated by law that has not protected women as victims of abuse by men. The offenders are protected by a society that seeks to ensure the domination of men. The gender inequality model suggests that women are treated differently in the criminal justice system, but that the difference is to their benefit.

After the major schools have been examined, the explanations still seem inadequate to address the problems of family violence for all people at all times. Multidimensional models concede that we need to try new ways to find out why domestic violence is occurring in epidemic proportions in our society. They combine the concepts developed in the major schools and suggest how they apply to situations of abuse. Views from both an individual perspective and the family structure are considered in this body of theory.

No one claims to have the answer—theorists continue to consider the problems and seek to develop ways to address them. Social programs and counseling methods have developed from the ideas covered here. We have gained great insight into the characteristics of batterers from the research that has developed. In the next chapter we look at the practices and applications of these concepts.

*K*EY *T*ERMS

Biological theory

Classical school

Culture theory

Deterrence theory

Ecological theory

Eugenics

Family systems theory

Gender-role theory

Hedonistic

Individual pathology

Multidimensional theories

Patriarchal theory

Positive school

Psychological theory

Rational choice theory

Resiliency theory

Self-efficacy theory

Social-psychological model

Social structure and cultural theories

Sociological theory

QUESTIONS for REVIEW

1. Which school of thought do you believe best explains why people commit domestic violence?

2. What role does Cesare Beccaria play in the study of criminology?

3. Explain the advantages and disadvantages of the deterrence theory.

4. Discuss and describe the eugenics movement.

5. What impact did Adolf Quetelet have on criminology?

6. Explain the gender-role theory.

7. Describe the cycle of violence.

8. In your opinion, which theory best explains the reasons that domestic violence occurs?

REFERENCES

Alderman, Tracy. 1997. *The Scarred Soul*. Oakland, CA: New Harbinger Publications.

Bateman, Py. 1998. "The Context of Date Rape." Pp. 95–99 in *Dating Violence: Young Women in Danger*, 2nd ed., Barrie Levy (ed.). Seattle, WA: Seal Press.

Boeree, George C. 1998. "Albert Bandura." *www.ship.edu/~cgboeree/bandura.html*. 1998.

Bund, Jennifer M., *University of Pittsburgh Law Review* (preprint article). 1997. "Did You Say Chemical Castration?" *www.pitt.edu/~lawrev/preprints/bund.htm*. 1998.

Cook, Philip W. 1997. *Abused Men: The Hidden Side of Domestic Violence*. Westport, CT: Praeger Publishers.

Define, Michael S., University of Maine School of law student. 1997. "Coerced Sterilization of Native American Women." *http://brooks.simplenet.com/mike.html*. 1998.

Dibble, U. and M. Straus. 1980. "Some Social Structure Determinants of Inconsistency between Attitudes and Behavior: The Case of Family Violence." *Journal of Marriage and the Family* 42:73–79.

Dutton, Donald G. and Susan K. Golant. 1995. *The Batterer: A Psychological Profile*. New York: Basic Books.

Gamache, Denise. 1998. "Domination and Control: The Social Context of Dating Violence." Pp. 69–83 in *Dating Violence: Young Women in Danger*, 2nd ed., Barrie Levy (ed.). Seattle, WA: Seal Press.

Garrett, Athena and Heather Libbey. 1997. "Theory and Research on the Outcomes and Consequences of Child Abuse and Neglect." *Child Abuse Intervention Strategic Planning Meeting*, Washington, DC. Washington, DC: National Institute of Justice.

Gilbert, L., P. B. Poorman, and S. Simmons. 1990. "Guidelines for Mental Health Systems Response to Lesbian Battering." In *Confronting Lesbian Battering: A Manual for the Battered Women's Movement*. St. Paul, MN: Minnesota Coalition for Battered Women.

Hamberger, L. K. and J. E. Hastings. 1988. "Characteristics of Male Spouse Abusers Consistent With Personality Disorders." *Hospital and Community Psychiatry* 39:763–70.

Hamberger, L. K. and Theresa Potente. 1996. "Counseling Heterosexual Women Arrested for Domestic Violence." Pp. 53–75 in *Domestic Partner Abuse*, L. K. Hamberger and Claire Renzetti (eds.). New York: Springer Publishing Company.

Healey, Kerry M. and Christine Smith. 1998. *Batterer Programs: What Criminal Justice Agencies Need to Know*. NCJ 171683. Washington, DC: U.S. Department of Justice.

Hofstadter, Richard. 1965. *Social Darwinism in American Thought*, 11th ed. Boston: Beacon Press.

Island, David and Patrick Letellier. 1991. *Men Who Beat the Men Who Love Them: Battered Gay Men and Domestic Violence*. Binghamton, NY: Harrington Park Press.

Katz, J. 1984. "Medicalization of Repression: Eugenics and Crime." *Contemporary Crisis* 8(3):227–41.

Lilly, J. R., F. T. Cullen, and R. A. Ball. 1989. "Search for the Criminal 'Man.'" Pp. 17–46 in *Criminological Theory: Context and Consequences*. Newbury Park, CA: Sage Publications.

MacKinnon, Catharine A. 1993. *Only Words*. Cambridge, MA: Harvard University Press.

Merrill, Gregory S. 1996. "Ruling the Exceptions: Same-Sex Battering and Domestic Violence Theory." Pp. 9–33 in *Violence in Gay and Lesbian Domestic Partnerships*, Claire M. Renzetti and Charles H. Miley (eds.). Binghamton, NY: Harrington Park Press.

Moffitt, T. E. 1997. "Neuropsychology, Antisocial Behavior, and Neighborhood Context." Pp. 116–70 in *Violence and Childhood in the Inner City*, Joan McCord (ed.). New York: Cambridge University Press.

National Institute of Justice. 1994. "Breaking the Cycle." *NIJ Research Report* 91.

Pizzey, Erin. 1977. *Scream Quietly or the Neighbors Will Hear*. Hillside, NJ: Enslow Publishers.

Siegel, Larry J. 1995. *Criminology*, 5th ed. New York: West Publishing Company.

Straus, Murray A. 1996. "Domestic Violence Is a Problem for Men." Pp. 50–64 in *Domestic Violence*, Bruno Leone (ed.). San Diego, CA: Greenhaven Press.

Straus, Murray A., Richard J. Gelles, and Suzanne K. Steinmetz. 1980. *Behind Closed Doors: Violence in the American Family*. Garden City, NY: Anchor Press/Doubleday.

Sullivan, Shawn. 1996. "Domestic Violence Is a Serious Problem for Black Women." Pp. 37–40 in *Domestic Violence*, Karin L. Swisher (ed.). San Diego, CA: Greenhaven Press.

Tifft, Larry L. 1993. *Battering of Women: The Failure of Intervention and the Case for Prevention*. Boulder, CO: Westview Press.

Van Biema, David. 1996. "A Cheap Shot at Pedophilia?" *Time*, September 6. *http://www.pathfinder.com/time/magazine/archive/1996/dom/960909/crime.html*. 1998.

Vito, Gennaro F. and Ronald M. Holmes. 1994. *Criminology: Theory, Research, and Policy*. Belmont, CA: Wadsworth Publishing Company.

Voigt, Lydia, William E. Thornton, Jr., Leo Barrile, and Jerrol Seaman. 1994. *Criminology and Justice*. New York: McGraw-Hill.

Vold, George B. and Thomas J. Bernard. 1986. *Theoretical Criminology*, 3rd ed. New York: Oxford University Press.

Walker, Lenore E. 1979. *The Battered Woman*. New York: Springer Publishing Company.

White, Evelyn C. 1998. "The Abused Black Woman: Challenging a Legacy of Pain." Pp. 84–93 in *Dating Violence: Young Women in Danger*, 2nd ed., Barrie Levy (ed.). Seattle, WA: Seal Press.

Wright, R. A. and J. M. Miller. 1998. "Taboo Until Today? The Coverage of Biological Arguments in Criminology Textbooks, 1961 to 1970 and 1987 to 1996." *Journal of Criminal Justice 26(1):1–19*.

Zemsky, B. 1990. "Lesbian Battering: Considerations for Intervention." In *Confronting Lesbian Battering: A Manual for the Battered Women's Movement.* St. Paul, MN: Minnesota Coalition for Battered Women.

Cases

Buck v. Bell, 274 U.S. 200 (1927).

Jacobson v. Massachusetts, 197 U.S. 11 (1905).

From Theory to Practice

INTRODUCTION

> The difference between domestic violence and most other fields is that the theoretical debate affects the practice of the professionals that deal with the problems. (Healey & Smith, 1998)

After reading Chapter 3 on the theories that have been developed to explain crime in the domestic relationship, you may be inclined to sit back and let the academics, researchers, and theorists battle it out among themselves. The many theories can be confusing and at times overwhelming. So who cares about their arguments? Not you, right? *Wrong!* The closer we look at domestic abusers, the more significant their differences appear. As we recognize numerous forms of family violence, no single theory seems to fit all the categories. Yet batterer programs and criminal justice practices have been based on these models! The intervention may not be appropriate—it may even make things worse. If we are to make an impact on the problem, it becomes important to understand the offenders and the available strategies, in addition to the theories that drive them. In the first part of the chapter we focus on the perpetrators of domestic battering. In the second half we examine domestic rape and sexual assault.

The dispute between the family systems model and the feminist position is one example. It is often a heated and uncompromising debate. The patriarchal theory assumes that the major cause of domestic violence is the social order, where men are the offenders and women are the victims. It stresses the empowerment of women and the criminal prosecution of assaultive men. Men's power over and control of women is believed to occur through psychological and emotional abuse as well as physical assault and rape. Aggressive law enforcement action, including mandatory arrest policies, has become a typical response. Therapy involving couples is strongly discouraged in this model because it encourages the victim to discuss openly issues that may later be used by the batterer. The terms *educational* and *psychoeducational* are associated with interventions based on this perspective.

On the other hand, the family systems theory assumes that the major cause of family assaults are inadequate interpersonal skills and a dysfunctional relationship. The anger and frustration that results is believed to lead to violence. Batterer intervention emphasizes building communications skills and may involve the use of couples counseling with the aim of family preservation (Healey & Smith, 1998). Power inequality is only one of the problems that is addressed through joint counseling. According to this perspective, both partners may contribute to the escalation of conflict, and either partner may resort to violence. No one is considered the perpetrator or the victim, even if only one person is physically violent. Intervention that is termed *couples therapy* is usually associated with the family systems approach.

As of 1996, twenty states had developed standards or guidelines against the use of couples counseling in batterer treatment (Healey & Smith, 1998). Family systems interventions are therefore less common than the other models and have limited application for criminal justice professionals who are looking for alternatives. Individually based models represent the third major theoretical intervention approach. This category includes the psychological theories that attribute domestic violence to personality disorders, the batterer's social environment during childhood, biological disposition, or attachment disorders. The term *group process* is usually associated with the psychotherapeutic interventions that target individual problems and/or build cognitive skills to help the batterer control violent behaviors (Healey et al., 1998). When treatment for domestic violence is suggested from the psychotherapeutic viewpoint, cognitive and behavior modification are often mentioned.

Can these positions reconcile the major theoretical assumptions that appear to be mutually exclusive? A review of the literature suggests that the answer to this question becomes vitally important to the criminal justice community.

HIGH-RISK VIOLENCE

Murray Straus questions the appropriateness of applying criminal justice sanctions to all family disputes. Acknowledging that the police and courts are not equipped to understand the unique circumstances of each family that can lead to violence, he argues that they also cannot be expected to determine what the best interest of either the victim, the offender, or the family might be. Additionally, numerous reports have indicated that in approximately half of the cases, women are the first to commit a physical assault. If men are arrested "only" for slapping their wives a few times, shouldn't women receive equal treatment? "If even half of the domestic assaults came to the attention of the police, the courts would have to deal with literally millions of such incidents and would be overwhelmed" (Straus, 1993).

It is necessary to distinguish between high-risk violence and the more usual marital violence, according to Straus. The high-risk offenders assault their partners on an average of 60 times per year, whereas the partners of battered women in the general population engaged in an average of five assaults a year. He suggests the following checklist to help identify high-risk cases (Straus, 1993):

Criterion A

- Suspect initiated three or more instances of violence in the preceding year

Criterion B

- Threatened partner with a weapon in hand or verbally threatened to kill the partner
- Medical treatment needed by the victim (regardless of whether it was obtained)
- Physical abuse of a child
- Physical abuse when a child
- Severe violence between parents
- Drunk more than five times in the past year
- Drug abuse in the past year
- Extreme dominance or attempts to achieve such dominance
- Thinks there are some situations when it is okay for a man to hit his wife
- Physically forced sex on the partner
- Extensive or repeated destruction of property
- Threats or actual killing or injuring of a pet
- History of psychological problems
- Assault of a nonfamily person or other violent crime
- Extreme jealousy and surveillance or restriction of partner
- Police involved in domestic assault incident in preceding 12 months

Straus maintains that after identifying those most at risk for severe or repeated battering, programs to treat male batterers would be appropriate. The intervention is consistent with the feminist model. Since almost 90 percent of couples fall in the low-risk category, however, these might be more suited to the family theory approach of couples counseling, he suggests.

The idea that dangerousness might be predicted and appropriate interventions be made is an appealing one. In jurisdictions that do not mandate arrest as a police response, Straus's idea holds the greatest potential. Its usefulness is toward predictions of future occurrences. Since the information is most important to the victims, it should be shared with them. Victims can assess their own potential for severe attacks if they know the signs to look for. For that reason, therapists and domestic violence shelters frequently use a variation of the Straus list on predicting the dangerousness of the offender. Keep in mind that it is not necessary to satisfy all the elements for a prediction of dangerousness to be made.

According to the guidelines established by EMERGE, the first program in the United States to treat male batterers, concrete and direct questions must be asked of the batterer to determine dangerousness (Figure 4–1). Examples of the questions include: "And what happens when you lose your temper?" and "What about grabbing or shaking?" "Have you hit her?" "When you hit her, was it a slap or a punch?"

BATTERER PROGRAMS

In a recent report to the National Institute of Justice, Kerry Healey and Christine Smith point out another compelling reason for the reconciliation of theory with practice. They contend that the requirement that batterers attend intervention programs as a condition of probation, or as part of a pretrial or diversion, is fast becoming a part of the response to domestic violence in many jurisdictions (Healey et al., 1998). Although that may be the practice, they suggest that judges and probation officers often lack basic information about program goals and methods. Since deterring future violence is the objective of criminal justice, it may be the reward for astute attention to the program goals and careful selection.

Program Procedures

Batterer programs typically consist of five stages: intake and assessment, orientation, victim orientation, program, and ending the program. A flowchart from the Domestic Abuse Intervention Project shows the process that an accused batterer will follow if he or she is referred to a court-mandated program (Figure 4–2).

Intake and Assessment.   The intake interview may take place at the courthouse after the perpetrator has been seen by a probation officer. In some jurisdictions, a representative from the program attends the civil court hearings. After the judge has issued an order, the staff member will meet with the perpetrator and explain the program. In other jurisdictions it is the responsibility of the batterer to initiate the contact and arrange for the assessment interview. During the intake process, the interviewer seeks information on the pattern and severity of the abuse toward current and past partners, children, and others. Not all batterers are accepted at this stage. Much depends on whether the offender has substance abuse or mental illness problems that

Figure 4–1   The three major intervention programs are EMERGE, the Duluth curriculum, and the AMEND model. *(Adapted from Healy et al., 1998.)*

Duluth Curriculum: based on feminist theory; issues of power and control as primary targets.

Program structure: 2 or 3 sessions on each of eight themes: nonviolence; non-threatening behavior; respect; support and trust; honesty and accountability; sexual respect; partnership; negotiation and fairness.

EMERGE: blend of feminist educational approach with more in-depth and intensive group work.

Program structure: 48-week program divided into two stages: 8 weeks of orientation and 40 weeks of group work. About one-third of the batterers require additional time in the program.

Orientation topics include: defining domestic violence; negative vs. positive "self talk"; effects of violence on women; psychological, sexual and economic abuse; abusive vs. respectful communication; effects of partner abuse on children.

Groups meet weekly for 2 hours. Sessions typically include:
1. A short check-in to recount any conflicts during the week; a long check-in for new members to detail the last abusive episode and focus on batterer responsibility
2. Longer discussions concerning issues raised during check-in that focuses on alternatives to violence
3. Development of individualized goals based on current and past abuse

The Amend Model: blend of feminist educational approach with more in-depth and intensive group work.

Program structure: Variable—from 36 weeks to 5 years for the most difficult cases. AMEND takes a "multimodal" approach centered on group therapy, but it may also include some individual counseling or couples work.

Approach: AMEND's philosophy has seven tenets:
1. Belief in the feminist "power and control" theory of battering is central.
2. Intervention with batterers cannot be value-neutral—violence is a crime.
3. Counseling aims to teach behavior change to stop violence and abuse and addresses the psychological features of the batterer's problem.
4. Violence and abuse are choices, and the victims are not responsible for the violence.
5. Ending violence is a long-term process, from 1 to 5 years.
6. Ending violence is complex and requires "multimodal" intervention.
7. Treatment of batterers requires special skills and training.

Figure 4–2   The domestic abuse intervention project chart shows the typical process for bat-terers: Duluth model. *(Courtesy of Springer Publishing Company, Inc., New York 10012. Used by permission.)*

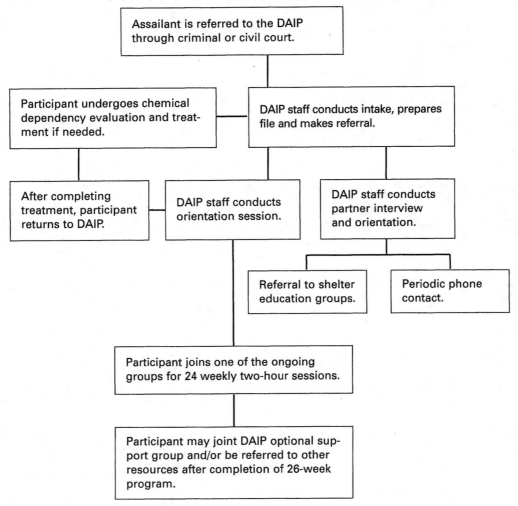

might make him or her more suitable to a different program that can address those needs. Many programs will not admit a person who denies being violent or appears likely to disrupt the group.

Orientation.   During the orientation session, the new clients meet and are told the rules and goals of the program. One purpose of the orientation is to estab-lish rapport between the participants and the counselors. Since a majority of clients are court ordered to attend the session, it is an effort to reduce their defensiveness. It is important to find out as much as possible about the abuse that was perpetrated so that effective intervention can occur. Counselors meet one-on-one in addition to the group meeting in order to assess how the program can best benefit each person.

Victim Orientation.   Many programs offer an opportunity for the person who was battered to meet with the staff. Some states require that partners be notified at various points of intervention. The purpose of meeting with the victims is threefold. First, it allows a counselor the opportunity to explain the program goals and philosophy. Second, it is an opportunity to get the victim's assessment of the abuse in the relationship. Third, safety issues and protection options can be discussed so that the battered person is aware of the resources available if services are needed. Shelter locations and orders for protection are among the topics that may be discussed.

Program.   Anger management skills training in a group setting are common components of batterers' programs. Education on power and control issues and the development of critical thinking skills are emphasized to help batterers understand and change their behavior. Some programs offer in-depth counseling that is designed to force the batterer to accept responsibility for his or her actions. Others focus on the relationship between the batterer and the victim to promote respect and positive behavior.

The group sessions may involve role-playing based on personal experiences to teach appropriate ways to deal with family situations that batterers find frustrating. They may discuss situations that have caused men or women to batter and apply alternatives to violence. Videos and stories about abuse from the victim's perspective are designed to sensitize the perpetrators about the effects of abuse on their partners.

Ending the Program.   A client may be terminated prior to completion of the program for a number of reasons. Among them are revocation of probation, alcohol and drug abuse, disrupting the sessions; failure to take responsibility for abusive acts, and not attending group sessions regularly. Successful completion of the program may involve an exit project, such as a letter on how the client was affected by the process. Some programs offer follow-up at specified time periods after a client has been discharged from the program.

Specialized versus Attachment Theory Intervention

The trend toward specialized treatment came with the recognition that the batterer's socioeconomic status, racial or ethnic identity, country of origin, and sexual orientation can affect intervention, according to Healey and Smith. In response to concerns regarding diversity, *culturally competent interventions* were developed to draw on the strength of the offender's family or community social systems (Healey & Smith, 1998). Programs for men of African descent, recent Asian immigrants, and Latinos who speak Spanish are examples of culturally based intervention programs. Recognizing ethnic and racial differences in curriculum planning is central to the specialized approach. African-American groups enable men to focus on what they did instead of social injustice or racism, Asian programs counter the social acceptability of private violence; and the concept of "machismo" is challenged in strategies used with Latino groups.

Attachment theory provides the basis for the opposite approach seen in the Compassion Workshop, based in Silver Spring, Maryland (Healey & Smith, 1998). Several types of offenders, including male and female heterosexual batterers, gay and lesbian perpetrators, victims, and child abusers, work together to develop trust, intimacy, and commitment. The positive development of emotions is meant to overcome the anger rooted in powerlessness and worthlessness, which they believe triggers offender behavior. This approach is considered controversial.

Can Interventions Stop Battering?

As stated earlier, referral to batterer treatment programs is fast becoming the usual procedure for the courts. How well do these programs work at lowering recidivism? According to Healy and Smith, the majority of studies that have attempted to evaluate batterer treatment programs have netted inclusive results. Methodological problems such as sample size and unreliable sources of follow-up have caused uncertainty. A few evaluations have found modest but statistically significant reductions in recidivism among men participating in batterer interventions. A 40 percent recidivism rate was found after five years in a study of the graduates of Duluth's domestic abuse intervention project (Pence & Paymar, 1993). At issue are the criteria for evaluating a batterers' program. Although it would be the goal of every project to end domestic violence, practitioners wonder if that is a realistic expectation.

Promoting the safety of the victims is an important consideration, for example. When the Duluth program measured victims' perception of increased safety due to their partners' participating, they were pleased with the results. The majority of women stated that they felt safer during the program. Further, the victims reported increased safety when the community was actively involved in the coordination of services to both protect the woman and provide alternatives to the perpetrator. It takes a community effort to affect domestic violence. Those options included mandating jail when the men reoffended.

These findings point to the success of a coordinated community approach to combat domestic violence that involves the courts, the police, the community, and the batterers' programs. Other studies concluded that educational programs were successful at transmitting information but not deterring violent behavior. If deterrence is not a likely outcome of an intervention, suggests Healy, then punishment, education, behavioral monitoring, or social change must be explicitly advanced (Healey et al., 1998).

CHARACTERISTICS OF DOMESTIC VIOLENCE ABUSERS

The theories on the causes of family violence still do not tell us very much about the individual batterer. What type of person commits violence in a domestic relationship? What behaviors indicate an abusive partner?

The majority of domestic violence victims are females who were physically assaulted by an intimate partner, according to the National Violence Against Women Survey (Tjaden & Thoennes, 1998). An intimate partner in the 1998 survey was defined as a current or former spouse, opposite-sex cohabiting partner, same-sex cohabiting partner, date, or boyfriend or girlfriend (Figure 4–3).

The National Violence Against Women Survey confirmed that intimate partners were the most frequent perpetrators of adult rape and physical assault against women (Tjaden & Thoennes, 1998). Seventy-six percent of the women who were raped and/or physically assaulted since the age of 18 reported being assaulted by a current or former husband, cohabiting partner, or date, compared to 17.9 percent of the

Figure 4–3   Victims by gender of perpetrator and gender of victim. *(Data from Tjaden and Thoennes, 1998.)*

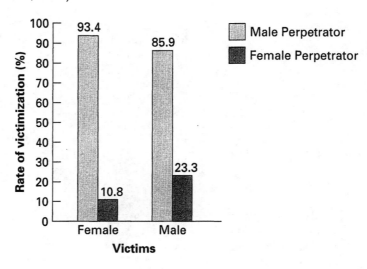

men. Relatives other than the spouse accounted for assaults toward 8.6 percent of women and 6.8 percent of men (Figure 4–4).

Descriptions of the Batterer

These descriptors have developed from studies on the battering male. Although illustrating the characteristics of an abusive male, they are listed here because they have been applied to the identification of perpetrators in homosexual and lesbian relationships, elder and child battering, and female offenders. Abusive behaviors in the lesser-known categories are discussed separately in the chapter.

Controlling Behaviors. A tendency for the abuser to dominate the victim has been noted in the various forms of domestic violence (Ramsey-Klawsnik, 1997). Sometimes the control is due to jealously; the perpetrator often seeks control over the victim's time, dress, and behavior. Controlling behaviors show contempt and a general lack of respect for the partner.

Excessive name-calling and "put-downs" are techniques used to attack the confidence of the victim and assure future dominance. Calling a partner a "bitch" or similar derogatory terms devalues the person. An abuser may refer to the other as a "pig," "lousy housekeeper," "bad mother," or "lousy father." The use of derogatory language in addressing one's partner may start as the intimates develop a familiarity with each other. Such a pattern is not legally prohibited. It signifies emotional abuse, however, which often accompanies physical battering.

Fear and Intimidation. Fear and intimidation is achieved through violence or the perception of impending violence. Victims of repetitive abuse recall a particular

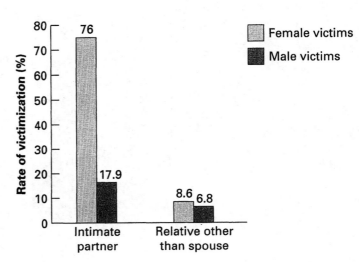

Figure   4–4
Victims by relationship. *(Data from Tjaden and Thoennes, 1998.)*

B e e n   T h e r e . . . D o n e   T h a t !

Penny knew that her husband did not like her to have friends over to the house. He made it quite clear. But she was a self-employed woman who was confident about herself and of the friends that meant so much to her. During the early years of their marriage she continued to invite them. Over time she drifted away from them—it became too difficult, she stated. She thought she was going mad and couldn't face them with the confusion that she felt. Things that she did, she couldn't remember doing or didn't ever know. For example, the plates were kept in the cupboard to the right of the sink. Then they were on the left side. They always were, said her spouse. The clothes she wore were in her bedroom closet, or were they kept in the hall closet? Dog food was always in the cellar—why was it in the garage? Years later, she realized that she was not going crazy at all—it was her husband who had tried to convince her otherwise. He frequently moved things and insisted that she was "losing it." He loved her; she had believed it.

"look" from the offender that serves as a warning signal of an explosion that is about to occur. A raised fist or hand in a threatening gesture serves the same purpose.

Discharging or displaying a firearm in or around the house or at pets is a severe form of intimidation. It is the ultimate display of power. Even the presentation of a weapon raises the level of acceptable violence that is difficult to decrease. Any direct or indirect threat that involves a gun or other weapon should not be taken lightly, due to the desperation that it signifies.

Killing or mutilating a pet is meant to convey the message, *"you could be next."* For the many victims and potential victims of domestic homicide it is no idle threat.

Of particular concern to professionals is the abuser who is legitimately carrying a firearm for work, business, or pleasure.

Manipulation.   Abusers have been characterized as the masters of manipulation. After an abusive attack, it is not unusual for the offender to beg for

---

B e e n   T h e r e . . . D o n e   T h a t !

Marilyn was a middle-aged professional woman in a 10-year relationship. The reality that her lesbian partner was leaving did not sink in until Betty came home to pack her belongings, bringing her new companion for support. Marilyn burst into the room waving a gun. Stating that she could not stand it any longer, she threatened to kill herself and *maybe* take someone with her. Fortunately, the two women were able to get out of the house and call the police. After hours of negotiation, the STOP team was able to remove Marilyn to safety without anyone being hurt.

Been There...Done That!

Penny recounted coming home in the near dark one evening to find the severed head of her horse in the walkway. She recoiled in horror, asking herself, "Why would he do such a horrible thing?" Many years later, Walter still shoots at trees around the parimeter of her country home that he has been restricted from entering through a permanent court order.

forgiveness. Gifts and flowers may accompany the statements that they will never "do it" again.

Another destructive behavior is the unrealistic demand for proof of love or loyalty characteristic in abusive dating relationships. Coercion into sexual relations as a condition of a continued relationship can be extremely dangerous for the victim during a dating relationship. Manipulation is almost always a tactic to keep the victim *in* the abusive relationship. When the abuser fears that the partner will leave, desperate attempts to retain control through pity (making the victim feel that she is needed) or fear (that she will be hunted down and brought back) are not unusual. Leaving the relationship is the most dangerous time for the victim (Feld & Straus, 1990)!

Excessive Rule Making.   When a partner makes rules that the other must follow, it signifies an unequal relationship based on dominance. One way to recognize this pattern is to notice when a penalty or punishment is attached to the failure to fulfill expectations. A healthy request does not begin with the phrase "you had better..." and it is not followed with the statement, "or else...." Taking back a gift or present because "you are not a good girl" indicates an anticipation of rule following by the abuser. It implies that some form of punishment will result for unfulfilled expectations.

Isolation.   The role of geographical isolation is explained by Neil Websdale in *Rural Woman Battering and the Justice System*. Women who live in secluded areas with no public transportation report not having had any friends for years (Websdale, 1998). He suggests that the choice to reside in isolated areas of the country may stem from

Been There...Done That!

The marital relationship of Frank and Martha was described by witnesses as mutually combative. Frank was a police officer. His wife called the station to report that during an argument, he had held a gun to the head of their child. Officers who responded confiscated all of his weapons and arrested him for assault and battery with a dangerous weapon. He was suspended without pay and denied access to any guns pending a full investigation.

B e e n   T h e r e ... D o n e   T h a t !

The relationship was over—moving out was the next step. Debbie explained that she had returned home one day to an ominous setting that convinced her that moving day had come! He had "set up" the house to appear as though he had committed suicide, she stated. The gun drawer was left open, with an empty holster and an open box of ammunition. The house alarm was not set. All indications were that he was somewhere in the house, possibly dead or dying, maybe lying in wait for her. She made an excruciating search through every closet, behind every door, and throughout the cellar before she realized he was not there at all. Then another fear set in: He would be back, and he had a loaded weapon on him! What would happen then?

---

their batterers' calculated decision. Control tactics include removing the phone receiver (when the batterer goes to work), disabling or destroying motor vehicles to limit the victim's mobility, closely monitoring the odometer reader on motor vehicles, and locking the thermostat in the winter (as a form of torture).

Demands for constant attention to the exclusion of friends and family are one form of isolating the victim. Although it may be attractive in the beginning of a relationship, it becomes a form of isolation when the abuser insists on being the only focus of the victim's life. Extreme forms include demands that the victim not work, or denial of transportation to leave the home. These accomplish economic and physical isolation that cuts the victim off from resources or protection from abuse.

Abusive Men

Remember that the majority of domestic violence perpetrators are men, according to government studies that use arrest as a criterion. The average abuser brought to court for restraining orders or to police attention for a domestic disturbance call is 32 years old, with two-thirds being in their mid-20s (Burnley et al., 1996). They often have low self-esteem and are overly dependent on the victim. Most are extremely jealous and possessive. Almost always the abuser blames others for his actions, and denies or minimizes the effects of his violence on his victims. Abusers often present a very different posture in public than they do in the privacy of their own homes. Although they may be charming on the outside, they can terrorize their partner behind closed doors!

Personality risk factors in male batterers include:

- Aggressive and hostile personality
- Antisocial personality
- Depression
- Emotionally dependency
- Insecurity
- Low impulse control
- Low empathy
- Narcissism
- Poor communication and social skills

Next we look at some specific red-flag identification characteristics in these men.

1. *Men who abuse alcohol and other drugs.* There is substantial evidence of a link between alcohol use and domestic violence. Between 1980 and 1988, the results of 23 studies on batterers indicated that 24 to 86 percent had prior histories of drug and/or alcohol abuse (Burnley et al., 1996). Some experts suggest that perpetrators drink alcohol in order to become violent (Gelles, 1974). Aggression has also been linked with psychoactive drugs such as barbiturates, amphetamines, opiates, phencyclidine, cocaine, and alcohol–cocaine combinations (Fagan, 1990). The need to achieve personal power and control though woman abuse may be similar to the origins for substance abuse (Gondolf, 1995).

2. *Men who have explosive tempers.* Daniel Sonkin and Michael Durphy state that abusive men often confuse anger and violence (Sonkin & Durphy, 1997). Violence is just one expression of anger; they insist that it is a behavior that can be controlled.

Experts caution against a one-size-fits-all description of the male batterer, however. In a review of the different types of men who abuse their spouses, colleagues Holtzworth-Monroe and Stuart categorize three types of violent men (Holtzworth-Monroe, 1994):

1. *Family-only offenders.* The perpetrators in this category may have a history of exposure to aggression in their family of origin. Relative to nonviolent men, they are poor communicators and lack social skills. They rank as less deviant than the other two categories of men in areas of impulsivity, substance abuse, and criminal behavior. They would rarely require personality disorder treatment, according to Holtzworth-Monroe and Stuart.

2. *Dysphoric or borderline offenders.* These men are believed to have had a history of child abuse and parental rejection. Delinquent behavior has been an early indicator of problems for these men. They are marked by negative attitudes toward women and positive attitudes toward violence, coupled with low remorse. Additionally, this group has a high dependency on their partners and poor social and communication skills.

3. *Generally violent or antisocial offenders.* The batterer in this category is the most aggressive. He is profoundly deficient in communicating and social skills. Believed to have been abused as a child, he comes from a violent family of origin. This abuser has developed antisocial behavior and views violence as an appropriate response to any provocation due to his socialization. Treatment for personality disorder is suggested for this type of offender.

Abusive Women

One of the most heated arguments in the field of domestic violence is over the nonexistence of the *battering woman*. Is there such a phenomenon? Are women likely to be

.the physical aggressors in an intimate relationship? Some evidence suggests that women perpetrate minor violence in domestic relationships at an equal rate to men (Straus et al., 1980). Lesbian battering is believed to be occurring as often as heterosexual domestic violence (Renzetti & Miley, 1996). Young women are suspected to be the instigators of violence in the majority of dating relationships, according to numerous studies (Sugarman & Hotaling, 1998). Physical abuse against children as likely to be committed by mothers as by fathers (U.S. Department of Health and Human Services, 1996). Domestic battery in elderly couples may be perpetrated more often by the woman (Wolf, 1996). On the surface it appears as though women are as capable as men of being violent *and* acting out the tendency.

Critics argue that there is no such thing as a battered husband syndrome. Government studies indicate that extremely small percentages (approximately 6 to 10 percent) of perpetrators are women. In the majority of these cases, the female is responding to long-term wife battering (Hattendorf & Tollerund, 1997). In every report that documents women as offenders, a disclaimer is attached: *Most are believed to be self-defending victims.* What does this mean? Self-defending victims are women who use physical aggression to prevent further injury; they are not batterers but victims. They are believed to be women who act in self-defense against the men that are abusing them. If there is a typology that can describe a woman prone to violence, it has not been forthcoming. There is no argument among professionals that women receive severe injuries from male battering and that this type of battering is in no way comparable with women's battering of men.

Perpetrators in Gay Male Relationships

It is difficult to provide an accurate portrayal of the batterer in a gay relationship because so little research has focused on violence in this type of domestic relationship. Although no government studies depict the extent of male gay battering, the rate is estimated to be as high, if not greater than, violence in the heterosexual community (Island & Letellier, 1991). Island and Letellier argue that it is not a gender issue and advocate a psychological framework that emphasizes battering treatment.

B e e n   T h e r e . . . D o n e   T h a t !

Leaving the restaurant, I was amazed at what was happening in the parking lot. It was noontime, broad daylight. A man was lying on the ground in a ball; a slight woman was standing over him and furiously kicking. He cried out in pain as she kicked him in the stomach, the back, and on the head! Obviously he was drunk, but hey! As she was dragged away, I asked the officer if he was going to arrest her. He said, "No—Fred would be so embarrassed if I did that!" Wait a minute, I thought—something is terribly wrong here. Even if violence by women *is* rare, it should not be ignored.

In *Men Who Beat the Men Who Love Them*, authors David Island and Patrick Letellier describe the following characteristics of violent gay males:

1. *Gay batterers are those who are unclear on the concept of masculinity.* For gay men the concept of masculinity is confused because being gay itself is considered unmasculine in our culture. Negative stereotypes about how men should behave are adopted by these males in their attempt to control others so that they are not controlled. Island and Letellier reject the overgeneralization of gender-role stereotyping and patriarchal rhetoric, however. They insist that the majority of men in the United States cannot be identified as aggressive, sexist patriarchs.

2. *They choose to abuse their lovers.* Most men do not batter; those gay men who engage in family violence do so by choice. The authors call it the "cowards' choice."

3. *Their violence is criminal.* Committing an act against a gay lover is no less a crime than in any other domestic relationship. It cannot be explained away as a "lovers' quarrel" or minimized because of the sexual orientation.

4. *The conduct is a learned dysfunctional behavior.* Since battering is a learned condition; it is treatable. Gay abusers should be classified by the psychological community as dysfunctional and afforded opportunities for treatment.

Lesbian Domestic Offenders

The feminist model of power and control is often used to describe the context of battering within a lesbian relationship. In discussing lesbian teen abuse, authors Levy and Lobel state that the same elements of hierarchy, power, ownership, entitlement, and control exist in lesbian as in nonlesbian relationships (Levy & Lobel, 1998). An added isolation for these young women exists due to their sexual orientation and resulting homophobia. Like most teens, they have difficulty trusting adults; additionally, they have few supportive peer relationships. Young lesbians are at risk of being trapped in abusive relationships with no role models and no resources (Figure 4–5).

Preliminary studies show that 22 to 46 percent of all lesbians have been in a physically violent same-sex relationship, according to Claire Renzetti and Charles Miley (Renzetti & Miley, 1996). The forms of violence include physical, sexual, and emotional abuse. The editors of *Violence in Gay and Lesbian Domestic Partnerships* suggest that lesbian battering is often dismissed by myths of mutual battering and notions that women can't really harm each other. This dismissal puts the victims of domestic violence at risk for future harm and emboldens the perpetrators.

Juvenile Bullying

Violence between siblings is underreported and underdocumented. Most instances of this type of family violence are attributed to sibling rivalry, but its effects *can* be serious.

Figure 4–5   Advocates for Abused and Battered Lesbians display this logo at *http://www.aabl.org/site.html. (Copyright © 1997 Kirsten Odegard. Used by permission.)*

Adults and children commit the same types of abuse that were described in Chapter 1: physical, sexual, and emotional abuse. The acts involve punching, hitting, kicking, biting, and rape. Critics have argued that most aggression between siblings is not serious and should not be considered abuse; proponents suggest otherwise. In the classic book on family violence, *Behind Closed Doors*, its authors contend that sibling abuse occurs more often than violence by parents on children or violence by spouses on each other (Straus et al., 1980).

Sibling abuse goes beyond child play and contains strong elements of violence. It is not an isolated act but a cycle of behavior that looks very much like spouse abuse. The child who is violent is often male and larger than his siblings. According to Vernon Wiehe, it looks like the stronger beating up the weak (Wiehe, 1997). The size of the child is deceiving, however, as the abuse is a way to compensate for a lack of power or perceived loss of power. He may feel jealous toward siblings who appear to please the parents through better academic achievement, looks, or even personality. Given the opportunity to express feelings of inadequacy, he may direct them at the siblings.

Researchers suggest that abused children learn to be abusive through modeling and instrumental learning according to the social learning theory. This may explain why juveniles who are abused, physically or sexually, sometimes perpetrate against others. However, critics using the cycle of violence theory as an intervention point out that only 20 to 30 percent of child abuse and neglect victims become involved in abusive and criminal behavior as adults (Garrett & Libbey, 1997).

Teen Dating Violence

David Sugarman and Gerald Hotaling refer to dating or courtship physical violence as a problem of *pandemic* proportions (Sugarman & Hotaling, 1998). They report estimates of individuals who have experienced violence in a dating relationship to be between a high of 60 percent and a low of 9 percent. Major studies on the gender of the offender suggest that women have higher levels than men of both inflicting and sustaining physical dating violence.

Risk Factors.   In an analysis of the risk markers for dating violence, Sugarman and Hotaling looked into major intrapsychic categories that are believed to influence this form of physical violence (Sugarman & Hotaling, 1998):

1. The authors suggest that *attitudes toward intimate violence* in premarital and marital relationships do affect whether there is abuse in dating. The studies generally do not examine whether these attitudes toward violence were more predictive of being victimized or of being a perpetrator of violence, however.

2. Research into the *gender-role attitude* of partners has netted conflicting results according to Sugarman and Hotaling, who examined nine major studies. Five studies did not offer evidence of a relationship between traditional gender-role attitudes and assaultive behavior. Two did uncover the expected violence, and two others found that gender-role orientation was predictive of dating physical aggression by women but not for men.

3. The third intrapsychic category involves the influence of *personality variables* for predicting assaultive behavior. The most consistent finding was an association between lowered self-concept and being a victim of dating violence. Some studies found no relationship between self-concept and assaultive behavior; one found that women who scored higher on an aggressiveness scale were more likely to inflict violence on their partners.

In contrast, Walter DeKeseredy and Martin Schwartz are openly annoyed at the contention that "women do it too" when it comes to discussions on intimate violence (DeKeseredy & Schwartz, 1998). They point out that there is a scarcity of solid empirical information about the men who claim to be battered by women. In their analysis of dating violence, they delved into the question of why women use violence during courtship. A common motive for violence was self-defense, they found; a majority of women did not initiate an attack. Moreover, women using defensive violence experienced higher rates of severe victimization, including physical and sexual assault after they had used defensive violence.

Perpetrators of Child Abuse

The vast majority of child abusers are parents (77 percent) or other relatives of the victim (11 percent) according to the U.S. Department of Health and Human Services (1998). They estimate that approximately 75 percent of the neglect and medical cases were associated with female perpetrators. Only 2 percent of the perpetrators were in caretaking relationships outside the family, such as child-care providers, foster parents, and facility staff members. This information is consistent with the findings of the *Third National Incidence Study* (U.S. Department of Health and Human Services, 1996). It reports that the majority of all child abuse was at the hands of birth parents, 72 percent of those who were physically abused and 91 percent of those who were neglected. Birth parents committed the emotional abuse in 81 percent of cases. Fathers and mothers were found equally likely to abuse their children. When the abuse was physical, the mother was more apt to be the offender (60 percent versus 48 percent). When a parent substitute was the offender, the perpetrator was often a father substitute.

Family Characteristics That Contribute to Child Abuse. Research indicates that many factors contribute to child abuse and neglect. Just as no single theory can explain why child abuse occurs, no single contributing factor can be isolated that provides a solution. The family characteristics serve to profile those that are at greatest risk of abusive behavior and victimization. They provide opportunities for social intervention and program development. Where child abuse and neglect are suspected, these categories might serve as "red flags" to the professionals who serve needy populations that have been identified.

1. *Family size.* The incidence of child maltreatment has been linked to the size of the family; the larger the family, the greater the incidence of victimization. Families with four or more children experienced a higher prevalence of abuse and neglect than did families with one to three children, according to the National Incidence Study of Child Abuse and Neglect (Sedlak & Broadhurst, 1996).

2. *Income.* Children in households with an annual income below $15,000 a year were over 25 times more likely to experience abuse or neglect compared to families with annual incomes above $30,000. Higher rates of sexual and physical assaults have been documented in low-income households (Kilpatrick & Saunders, 1997). The *Third National Incidence Study* reported that children from the lowest-income families were 18 times more likely to be sexually abused, almost 56 times more likely to be educationally neglected, and over 22 times more likely to be injured seriously through maltreatment.

3. *Single-parent households.* In single-parent households, children had a 63 percent greater chance of being victimized by physical abuse than did those who lived in two-parent families, according to the *Third National Incidence Study*. They were physically neglected at an 87 percent higher rate than those in two-parent households. Their risk of being seriously injured or harmed from abuse or neglect was 80 percent higher. Their risk of being educationally neglected was higher also, more than three times greater than for the children from two-family households.

4. *Alcohol and drug abuse.* Associations among alcohol abuse, physical abuse, cocaine abuse, and sexual maltreatment have been documented (Famularo et al., 1992).

It should be noted that these studies have been based on known victims who have been officially reported to child protective services. The source of the statistics itself limits our knowledge to those who are more likely to be reported to child protective services those who have come to the attention of mandated reporters of child abuse. Despite this limitation, the *Third National Incidence Study* contributes greatly to an understanding of the circumstances where child abuse and neglect are more likely to occur. All the risk factors have one thing in common: poverty. Single-parent families with low income are limited in their choice of housing location. The stresses of providing the necessities of life for these families appear to influence parenting, including the education of the children.

Poverty is the most common contributing factor in families where neglect is suspected. Since neglect is also the most common form of abuse and cause of death for children, this is a significant concern. Higher levels of stress in the lives of caretakers are thought to be a contributing factor to child abuse as well. Yet Helfer and Kempe warn that for mothers, the incidence of abuse is high regardless of stressful events. They point out that most people who experience stress do not physically abuse their children (Helfer & Kempe, 1988).

Perpetrators of Elder Abuse

Compared to the other forms of family violence, there is relatively little information about domestic abuses toward the elderly. The extent of spouse abuse is believed to be lower than other forms of violence in the family (Pillemer & Finkelhor, 1998). Adult children are often in the caretaking role, and they are represented as the most frequent abusers of the elderly (Tatara, 1996).

Ramsey-Klawsnik describes three general categories under which elders are abused (Ramsey-Klawsnik, 1997).

1. *The stress-precipitated abuser.* This form of abuse to an elder is intentional, yet it is caused by stress and abuse and is not necessarily the intended result. It is used to describe the situation where abuse is related to stress, low resources, or impairments. Caring for an elder can be an extremely difficult situation for a family member who is already overburdened with his or her own family responsibilities. This abuser might benefit from and be willing to accept services.

2. *The greedy abuser.* The second category is related to greed and lack of concern for the elder. This abuser intentionally denies care and services; may cause physical or sexual harm; or takes money and possessions directly from the elder. The purpose is to control and acquire whatever financial resources the elder may possess. He or she should be removed from the caretaking

role. Criminal intervention may be necessary, particularly in cases of financial exploitation.

3. *The intentional harm perpetrator*. The third category is the most dangerous abuser, having the intention to harm through power and control over the victim. Protection for these elders may be through empowerment. Prosecution for severe harm caused the elder should be considered.

Mutual Battering: Challenging Criminal Justice

The idea of *mutual battering* in domestic violence is one of great controversy and presents enormous challenges to the criminal justice community. In the heterosexual community, it implies that both men and women initiate physical and emotional violence to resolve conflicts in the relationship. We typically think of domestic abuse as gender specific: a male batterer and a female victim. In mutual battering, both parties are believed to be equally involved in initiating the violence, although not necessarily at the same time. Mutual battering as an explanation for domestic abuse blurs this picture of who is the victim and who is the perpetrator. The victim and offender roles may not exist in this relationship or may change as one or the other becomes the aggressor.

The challenge for the criminal justice community is in assigning blame. One party must be responsible and held accountable in the criminal justice paradigm. Some police officers respond by arresting both the male and female in the domestic violence dispute to avoid having to sort it out. This practice of mutual arrest is strongly discouraged by the courts. Not only does it confuse the court as to how to proceed, it often results in neither party's being prosecuted. Victims are not being protected and batterers are empowered. In addition, this tactic serves to punish the victims of domestic violence because they are being put before the court as if they were the abusers.

Dismissing domestic abuse as "mutual battering" causes concern to those confronting problems of violence within homosexual and lesbian communities. Abuse among same-sex couples can be confusing to law enforcement officers; traditionally, they have looked at gender and physical size when determining who is at fault in a domestic dispute. A clearer picture of who is in need can be made when one person is obviously dominant in a relationship due to stature or gender. When the relationship involves two persons of the same gender, the determination becomes more difficult. Critics argue that police officers dismiss claims of same-sex battering as "mutual," rather than taking the time to access the situation adequately. The failure to assign any blame by viewing the situation as mutual is detrimental to the victim.

Experts are beginning to acknowledge the dilemma and offer direction on how to proceed. In a domestic dispute, *determine the primary physical aggressor!* Healy and colleagues explain this criterion (Healey et al., 1998):

1. *Do not assume that the physically larger partner is always the primary aggressor.* Care must be taken to question the couple and any witnesses closely before making an arrest.

2. *Be aware that bruises may take hours to appear, whereas signs of defensive violence, such as scratching or biting, are immediate.* Question the partners separately and determine how the visible marks were made, and why. Did the victim bite an arm that was holding him or her down, for example?

3. *Determine if there has been a history of abuse.* Batterers tend to recommit. It is more likely that the perpetrator of violence in the past has perpetrated again. Ask if there has been a recent escalation in the violence, and why.

4. *Victims may feel free to express their anger about the violence to police.* Anger or the expression of anger should not be mistaken for primary aggressive behavior.

5. *Do not allow yourself to be provoked into arresting both partners.* An angry victim's conduct is not a justification for arresting. Failure to "shut up" is not criminal behavior or indicative of who the batterer is.

6. *Determine who the initial aggressor was.* When signs of injury are exhibited by both parties, consider the possibility of self-defense and examine the relative level of injury or force involved.

STAGES OF VIOLENCE

Most researchers agree that domestic battering is a pattern of behavior that follows somewhat predictable stages. As noted earlier in this chapter, the frequency of the abuse differs depending on the relationship. In severe cases, the battering incidents may be as frequent as 60 times a year, while the average abuse cycle occurs only about five times a year (Straus, 1993). The length of time in each stage also can vary from hours to weeks. Education groups for men who batter frequently use the *power and control wheel* developed by the Duluth model to illustrate the elements of a battering relationship (Figure 4–6). The tactics used by the batterer are similar to those used to sustain many other forms of group domination (Pence & Paymar, 1993). According to the authors of *Education Groups for Men Who Batter*, even though the men may feel out of control when battering, the actions are intentional. At the core of the cycle is the element of power and control—all actions are for the purpose of dominating and controlling the spouse. Each cog in the wheel represents a form of behavior that in total makes up the abusive conduct. This represents the feminist idea of the battering relationship.

DOMESTIC RAPE AND SEXUAL ASSAULT

Relatively little has changed in the characterization of rapists over the last decade. What is new is the application of this knowledge to our understanding of rape within a domestic relationship. As with every other family violence crime, a relationship between the victim and the perpetrator is not a factor in the determination of rape. It

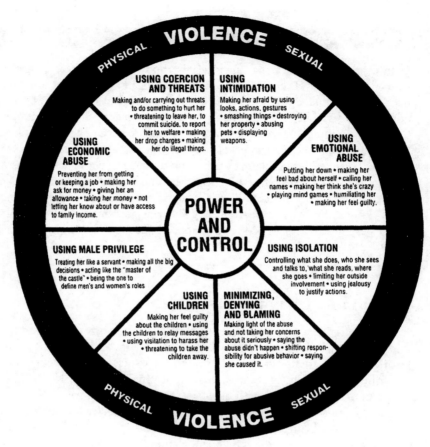

Figure 4–6   Power and control wheel: Duluth model. *(Courtesy of Springer Publishing Company, Inc., New York 10012. Used by permission.)*

becomes an element only when the considered criminal charge is incest. Follow the criminal elements defined in your jurisdiction to determine if this crime has been committed. Consent is a legal consideration in cases that involve adults only. Consent is not an issue when rape is committed against a child.

Sexual offenders are best described initially through their diversity. Although sexual offenders are usually male, the offender sometimes is reported to be a female. They may be juveniles or elders and every age in between. Perpetrators are found in every race and ethnic background; they may be gay or straight, religious and nonreligious; professionals or criminals already found guilty for some other crime. A relatively unknown category is the sexual abuse of the elderly. The largest category of suspected offenders against elders is thought to consist of sons who were sexually abusing their elderly mothers (Ramsey-Klawsnik, 1991).

B e e n   T h e r e ... D o n e   T h a t !

In an otherwise peaceful and quiet neighborhood, shocking facts emerged due to one woman's complaint of childhood abuse. The investigation found that every member of the nuclear and extended family, boys and girls, had been sexually molested: not by neighbors, not by strangers, but by family. The list of victims was long enough that we made charts to keep them clear. A hot curling iron and scissors were among the mutilation tools that rendered at least one woman unable to bear children as an adult. Boys were dressed up and photographed. Little children were made to have sex with one another while an adult watched. Wives said that they were raped by these same men and didn't know that the children were being assaulted also. The abuse was traced as high as the oldest living male—he was 72 when I arrested him. The youngest arrested was a 15-year-old boy. Other perpetrators were too young to consider taking them through the criminal justice system as offenders.

Common Characteristics of a Rapist

Sexual offenders who perpetrate in domestic relationships can readily be compared to stranger rapists. No personality or physical characteristics make them stand out from others. They are not identified through their social status, occupation, race, or ethnic group. Rapists may be *power* or *anger* motivated (Bradway, 1990). Those who commit the crime of rape do so with purpose. It may be to confirm their own manhood or to express their manhood to the victims, as in the power rapist category. Anger rapists are considered extremely dangerous because they may obtain pleasure from inflicting pain and seek to degrade the female victims.

Marital Rape and Male Offenders

Authors David Finkelhor and Kersti Yllo graphically point out in *License to Rape: Sexual Abuse of Wives* that rape is not a trivial family quarrel over sex, with the man getting his way. It is a brutally forced act, designed to humiliate and harm the woman. In their study on the topic, one-fourth of the wives spoke of forced anal intercourse; a fifth stated that they were forced to perform oral sex; almost one-fourth of the women were raped in the presence of others, usually their children; and the majority reported brutal vaginal intercourse. These authors illustrated three types of marital rape (Finkelhor & Yllo, 1985):

1. *Battering rape.* Battered women are believed to be at high risk for marital rape. The type of man who beats his wife is also more likely to rape her.

2. *Force-only rape.* In relationships that have little or no other violence, force-only rape is linked with the power to control the frequency of sexual relations within the marriage. The assaults are typically after the women has refused

sex and is characterized by physical brutality of slapping, hitting, and holding the woman down despite her pleas for him to stop. The goal of the rapist is sexual conquest, by any force necessary.

3. *Obsessive rape.* This form of rape was characterized by the bizarre, strange, and perverse sexual interests and fantasies of the husband, often inflicting pain on the woman. An example provided by victims included being tied up and having objects inserted, as well as being burned, bitten, or beaten during the act. Taking pictures of the wife was a common part of the abuse, according to Finkelhor and Yllo.

Had any of these forms of violence been perpetrated by a stranger, there is little doubt that the offender would be prosecuted if caught.

Female Sex Offenders

It is difficult to determine the exact prevalence of sexual abuse perpetrated by women since there are few studies that look strictly at that offender population. In her review of the literature on child sexual abuse, Kim Menard found a range of 1 percent to 32.5 percent of perpetrators who were women (Menard, 1997). She suggests the disparity in female perpetration rates that exist among studies may be due to the criterion when defining abuse (rape versus sexual conduct) as well as the source of the data (convicted offenders versus self-reports). In part this may be due to the absence of terminology in government studies that include female-perpetrated sex crimes. As late as 1994, the Uniform Crime Reporting System still defined rape for female victims only.

The most comprehensive estimates on the prevalence of female sexual abuse have been compiled by David Finkelhor and Diana Russell (1984), cited by Mic Hunter (Mathews et al., 1990). They found that 24 percent of sexually abused males and 13 percent of sexually abused females were victimized by females either acting alone or with an accomplice. In approximately 2 percent of the cases of male sexual

---

B e e n   T h e r e ... D o n e   T h a t !

One by one, the prosecutors laughed at my request to bring forward a rape case that involved a female perpetrator in her 30s and a 15-year-old boy. Comments like, "I should have been so lucky," and "Are you kidding. That is every boy's dream," to "We would never win a case like that in court!" were among the responses. Never mind that the crime of statutory rape was committed or that the youngster suffered great emotional and psychological harm from the relationship. Forget that she threatened to kill the child that she bore from him if he cut off the relationship! I suggest that we need to know more about these infrequent but occurring instances of sexual abuse by women.

victimization and 54 percent of the cases of female victimization by females, the female offender was acting in the company of others.

What we do know about female sexual offenders has largely been derived from small samples of adjudicated adults (Atkinson, 1996). In a review of the literature on the population, Atkinson identifies three typologies:

1. *Teacher or lover sex offender.* This offender initiates the sexual abuse of an adolescent from a position of power obtained through either age or status, including that of mother, aunt, or guardian. The offender would probably be a person who had suffered severe emotional and verbal abuse as a child, but not necessarily sexual abuse. The offender views her victim as an equal, thus denying the seriousness of the offense. A minority of this population has been found to be developmentally delayed.

2. *Male-coerced sex offender.* Male-coerced offenders, who induce or are forced into sexual abuse by a male, are the most frequent type reported in adult clinical research. She is typically passive and nonassertive, which may have resulted from childhood sexual and physical abuse. A frequent offender in this category is the daughter of a male aggressor.

3. *Predisposed sex offender.* Without male accomplices, the offender in this group usually perpetrates against her own children. Seventy-five percent of these offenders are believed to have been victims of incest.

Ruth Mathews and colleagues suggest another category in addition to the above (Mathews et al., 1990):

4. *Experimenter or exploiter.* This is a juvenile female offender who tends to be 16 years old or younger and generally chooses a young male child (6 years old or younger). Typically, this is a one-time event that is characterized by detachment, no intimacy, and low emotionality. The offender is very anxious and naive about sexual relationships and fearful of advances from peers.

Sexual Abuse against Children

The majority of sexual perpetrators against children are male, although females are also believed to commit these crimes, which are forbidden by law in every state. Research confirms that a substantial minority of adult males are aroused by children (Faller, 1993). However, it confirmed that most men with these feelings do not act on them. Comparable research has not been conducted on women. People whose primary sexual object of desire is a child are referred to as *pedophiles*. Not only do they prefer children, they tend to have a particular age and gender as their primary target. They often carry pictures of children in nonsexualized poses just as adults carry photographs of their adult loved ones. Pedophiles frequently have multiple victims and actively seek opportunities where they have access to children. They may have adult sexual partners also, but this is often a guise to gain access to the partner's children.

Been There... Done That!

Jay was a willing suspect and confessed during my interrogation of him to having sexually abused his own children and countless others. He knew that what he did was legally wrong, but he professed that he "loved" children. It was important to him that he not "hurt" the children, and he explained that he thought he did more good for them by showing his love. He was totally unaware of the emotional, physical, and psychological effects on his victims. His actions were not benign, regardless of his claim; he was adjudicated as a sexually dangerous person.

There are organizations that exist for the sole purpose of promoting sexual relations between adults and children. The North American Man–Boy Love Association (NAMBLA) and the René Guyon Society are among those that dispute the claim that sexual abuse is bad because of its effects on children. They challenge the right of society to make sex between children and adults illegal.

Interventions for child sexual abuse often involve a combination of theoretical approaches. The family systems model is among those; it assumes that dysfunctional relationships among family members contribute to the continuation of sexual abuse. A mother's reluctance to intervene, for example, may appear as tacit approval or collusion for the deviant action. Critics fear that this approach blames others for the sexual abuse and absolves the offender of responsibility. Although that may be a theoretical or treatment concern, it does not influence the legal responsibility for the criminal action.

Garrett and Libbey point to two programs that utilize the family approach (Garrett & Libbey, 1997): the Family Center in Somerville, Massachusetts, and the Ina Maka Family in Seattle, Washington. Program intervention is designed to prevent the breakup of the family by helping clients develop positive self-esteem, anger management skills, healthy family communication, and parenting skills. Group and individual therapies are frequent components of programs that treat sexual abusers. You will remember that these interventions are characteristic of the individual or psychotherapeutic approach. In additional to ongoing therapy, a recent method used to control sexual predators is chemical castration. This option was discussed in Chapter 3.

Juvenile Incest Offenders

In 1993, approximately 20 to 25 percent of sexual abuse of girls and 50 percent of sexual abuse of boys were perpetrated by adolescents. Frequently, sexual offenders report that they began offending in their adolescent years. An early target may be a younger sibling. Vernon Wiehe explains sibling sexual abusing (Wiehe, 1997) through a model that had been developed to describe adult–child sexual abuse (Finkelhor, 1984). It includes four conditions under which sexual abuse of siblings is more likely to occur:

1. *Motivation.* Sexual abuse perpetrated by a child does not happen without the motivation to sexually abuse. For example, the child may feel more comfortable relating to a younger sibling due to his or her own poor self-worth and self-esteem or arrested psychological development. The older sibling may be physiologically aroused by children.

2. *Weakened internal inhibitors.* If the motivation is present, the sibling must also overcome the internal inhibitors in order to act on the impulses. Prior victimization is one factor that may contribute to the willingness to perpetrate against others. Having been victimized, the child may abuse because he or she has learned that this is acceptable, or may act out of rage due to his or her own experiences of being abused.

3. *External inhibitors.* This third precondition, according to Wiehe, refers to the failure of parents to intervene in the protection of their children. If a parent is physically or psychologically absent due to death, divorce, illness, or extended absence from the home, the likelihood of sexual abuse increases. Sexual victimization often occurs when the parents are absent and the perpetrator is left in charge, babysitting the younger children in the family.

4. *Victim resistance.* The perpetrator of child abuse must be able to overcome the resistance of the potential victim. Lack of sexual information and emotional insecurity of the victims are characteristics that make them vulnerable to abuse by an older child. Physical harm and threats of harm may break down younger children's resistance.

Experts caution against viewing the child sexual abuser from a purely intrapsychic or psychological perspective. Although the child may have personality and development dysfunction, there is no single cause that can address these complex problems adequately. Sexual crimes committed by juveniles are not perpetrated for sexual gratification alone; they mirror the abusive use of power and control evidenced in the sexual crimes committed by adults.

Date Rape Offenders

Unlike the picture presented for physical dating violence, sexual aggression is almost exclusively male perpetrated, according to Py Bateman (Bateman, 1998). She states that although reports of date rape are rare, it is significant to note that many adolescents don't recognize the pressures that lead to unwanted sex as rape. Experts agree that the crime is grossly underreported. A number of studies indicate that both men and women often share the belief that women are responsible for both stimulating and satisfying men's sexual urges, a factor that might contribute to a victim's unwillingness to view the event as criminal. Cultural pressures on young men lead them to insist on sexual relations, using whatever psychological or physical force is necessary.

CONCLUSIONS

The chapter began with the major theoretical models that influence batterer intervention programs: the feminist model, family systems model, and individual-based models. Although they appear to be diametrically opposed, one suggestion for their reconciliation would be an approach based on frequency and severity of the domestic violence assaults.

Batterer programs and typical procedures are explained. The lengths of time in the programs vary, but the structure is similar in the major models that were presented. This is not meant to imply that all batterer programs are the same. Many grassroot efforts have emerged that do not easily fit into the major model descriptions. They include specialized or culturally competent interventions and models based on the attachment theory. It was noted that efforts to evaluate the effectiveness of batterer intervention programs have brought mixed results. It appears that a greater emphasis needs to be placed on identifying the goals that are desired from intervention programs. Are we trying to stop it totally? Is victim protection the major purpose? Does recidivism matter? These are all questions that need to be explored.

The characteristic descriptions of domestic violence batterers based on gender give an idea of the type of person who commits these crimes. Controlling tactics and methods of intimidation are part of the domestic violence cycle. Aside from their social and personality deficiencies, we found that the majority of offenders are males who perpetrate against females. The typology typically used to describe heterosexual offenders differs when homosexual relationships are included in the discussion. Criminal justice professionals need to be sensitized to all forms of family violence, regardless of pre-existing notions about gender and perpetration. Age is no longer a factor when we put juvenile offenders into the mix. Actions that constitute domestic violence must be considered as such despite age, gender, or sexual orientation. A crime is a crime.

Presenting information about female perpetrators is not meant to minimize the severity of abuse toward women victims. The offenses are usually minor and far less frequent than those committed by men. Ignoring acts because the offender is a female is unfair to the victim, whoever he or she may be.

Child abuse and neglect was the next category covered. The most difficult part of this analysis was in paring down the information. The dynamics of child abuse, both sexual and physical, are so complicated that I would encourage the reader to explore this topic at greater length in addition to reading Chapter 9 of this book. Elder abuse is covered in greater depth in Chapter 10. The abuser of this form of violence has access to the elder as well as financial motivations, no matter how insignificant those resources may appear to be to outsiders. It is sad to think that some people's final years can be so full of pain.

One of the most promising directions for law enforcement is in the concept of the *primary physical aggressor*. If you missed that part, go back to the section on mutual battering. It can be difficult for professionals to distinguish between acts of primary and mutual battering; this is one method that tries to define what the officer should be looking for. Of course, it is still a difficult process, and the primary aggressor may also change within a relationship. Focus on the facts at hand and don't rush to make a judgment. To better understand the dynamics of battering, three models through the stages of abuse are offered: cognitive, feminist, and integrated.

The second half of the chapter focused on domestic rape and sexual assault. Offender characteristics and typology give insight to the behaviors of the sexual rapist. As in battering, the vast majority of sexual offenders are men, although some women are known to offend. Children are frequent victims of sexual abuse and rape by both adults and other juveniles. Elders are also victimized through domestic rape.

KEY TERMS

Attachment theory
Family systems model
Individual-based models
Marital rape
Mutual battering

NAMBLA
Patriarchal theory
Power and control wheel
Self-defending victims
Specialized treatment

QUESTIONS for REVIEW

1. Describe the five stages that are involved with batterer programs.

2. According to the National Violence Against Women Survey, who are the majority of domestic violence victims?

3. What behaviors or actions would a batterer exhibit?

4. Describe the average male batterer and his personality.

5. What results did Island and Letellier find in their study about men who batter men?

6. List and describe factors that contribute to child abuse and neglect.

7. Ramsey-Klawsnik describes three general categories in which elders are abused. Detail these categories.

8. Explain why it might be difficult to determine the primary abuser in a case where there is mutual battering.

9. Define marital rape and describe the three types according to Finkelhor and Yllo.

10. What conditions make sexual abuse among siblings likely to occur?

REFERENCES

Atkinson, J. L. 1996. "Female Sex Offenders: A Literature Review." *Forum* 8(2):39–42.

Bateman, Py. 1998. "The Context of Date Rape." Pp. 95–99 in *Dating Violence: Young Women in Danger*, 2nd ed., Barrie Levy (ed.). Seattle, WA: Seal Press.

Bradway, William C. 1990. "Stages of a Sexual Assault." *Law and Order*. September, 119–24.

Burnley, Jane et al. (eds.). 1996. *National Victim Assistance Academy Textbook*. Washington, DC: Office for Victims of Crime.

DeKeseredy, Walter S. and Martin D. Schwartz. 1998. *Woman Abuse on Campus: Results from the Canadian National Survey*. Thousand Oaks, CA: Sage Publications.

Fagan, J. 1990. "Intoxication and Aggression." Pp. 241–320 in *Drugs and Crime*, M. Tonry and J. Q. Wilson (eds.). Chicago: University of Chicago Press.

Faller, Kathleen C. 1993. *Child Sexual Abuse: Intervention and Treatment Issues*. Washington, DC: National Center on Child Abuse and Neglect.

Famularo, R., R. Kinscherff, and T. Fenton. 1992. "Parental Substance Abuse and the Nature of Child Maltreatment." *Child Abuse and Neglect: The International Journal* 16(4):475–83.

Feld, S. L. and M. A. Straus. 1990. "Escalation and Resistance from Wife Assault in Marriage." Pp. 489–505 in *Physical Violence in American Families: Risk Factors and Adaptations to Violence in 8,145 Families*, M. A. Straus and R. J. Gelles, (eds.). New Brunswick, NJ: Transaction Publishers.

Finkelhor, David. 1984. *Child Sexual Abuse: New Theory and Research*. New York: Free Press.

Finkelhor, David and Kersti Yllo. 1985. *License to Rape: Sexual Abuse of Wives*. New York: Holt, Rinehart and Winston.

Garrett, Athena and Heather Libbey. 1997."Theory and Research on the Outcomes and Consequences of Child Abuse and Neglect." *Child Abuse Intervention Strategic Planning Meeting*, Washington, DC. Washington, DC: National Institute of Justice.

Gelles, Richard. 1974. *The Violent Home: A Study of Physical Aggression between Husbands and Wives*. Beverly Hills, CA: Sage Publications.

Gondolf, E. W. 1995. "Alcohol Abuse, Wife Assault, and Power Needs." *Social Service Review* 69:275–83.

Hattendorf, Joanne and Toni R. Tollerund. 1997. "Domestic Violence: Counseling Strategies That Minimize the Impact of Secondary Victimization." *Perspectives in Psychiatric Care* 33(1):10–14.

Healey, Kerry M. and Christine Smith. 1998. *Batterer Programs: What Criminal Justice Agencies Need to Know*. NCJ 171683. Washington, DC: U.S. Department of Justice.

Healey, Kerry, Christine Smith, and Chris O'Sullivan. 1998. *Batterer Intervention: Program Approaches and Criminal Justice Strategies*. NCJ 168638. Washington, DC: U.S. Department of Justice.

Helfer, Ray E. and Ruth S. Kempe (eds.). 1988. *The Battered Child*, 4th ed. Chicago: University of Chicago Press.

Holtzworth-Monroe, A. and G. L. Stuart. 1994. "Typologies of Male Batterers: Three Subtypes and the Differences Among Them." *Psychological Bulletin* 116(3):476–97.

Island, David and Patrick Letellier. 1991. *Men Who Beat the Men Who Love Them: Battered Gay Men and Domestic Violence*. Binghamton, NY: Harrington Park Press.

Kilpatrick, Dean and Benjamin Saunders. 1997. *The Prevalence and Consequences of Child Victimization*. Washington, DC: U.S. Department of Justice, Office of Justice Programs.

Levy, Barrie and Kerry Lobel. 1998. "Lesbian Teens in Abusive Relationships." Pp. 203–8 in *Dating Violence: Young Women in Danger*, 2nd ed., Barrie Levy (ed.). Seattle, WA: Seal Press.

Mathews, Ruth, Jane Mathews, and Kate Speltz. 1990. "Female Sexual Offenders." Pp. 275–93 in *The Sexually Abused Male: Prevalence, Impact, and Treatment*, Mic Hunter (ed.). New York: Lexington Books.

Menard, Kim. 1997. "Female Sexual Offenders: A Review of the Literature with Research and Policy Implications." *Academy of Criminal Justice Sciences Annual Conference*, Albuquerque, NM, March. Unpublished.

Pence, Ellen and Michael Paymar. 1993. *Education Groups for Men Who Batter*. New York: Springer Publishing Company.

Pillemer, Karl and David Finkelhor. 1998. "The Prevalence of Elder Abuse: A Random Sample Survey." *Gerontologist* 28(1):51.

Ramsey-Klawsnik, Holly. 1991. "Elder Sexual Abuse: Preliminary Findings." *Journal of Elder Abuse and Neglect* 3(3):73–89.

_____. 1997. "Sessions I and II; III and IV, Workshop Handouts." Canton, MA: Massachusetts Executive Office of Elder Affairs.

Renzetti, Claire M. and Charles H. Miley (eds.). 1996. *Violence in Gay and Lesbian Domestic Partnerships*. Binghamton, NY: Harrington Park Press.

Sedlak, Andrea and Diane Broadhurst. 1996. *Executive Summary of the Third National Incidence Study of Child Abuse and Neglect*. Washington, DC: U.S. Department of Health and Human Services, Administration for Children and Families; and the National Center on Child Abuse and Neglect.

Sonkin, Daniel J. and Michael Durphy. 1997. *Learning to Live without Violence: A Handbook for Men*, 5th ed. Volcano, CA: Volcano Press.

Straus, Murray A. 1993. "Identifying Offenders in Criminal Justice Research on Domestic Assault." *American Behavioral Scientist* 36(5):587–99.

Straus, Murray A., Richard J. Gelles, and Suzanne K. Steinmetz. 1980. *Behind Closed Doors: Violence in the American Family*. Garden City, NY: Anchor Press/Doubleday.

Sugarman, David B. and Gerald T. Hotaling. 1998. "Dating Violence: A Review of Contextual and Risk Factors." Pp. 100–118 in *Dating Violence: Young Women in Danger*, 2nd ed., Barrie Levy (ed.). Seattle, WA: Seal Press.

Tatara, Toshio. 1996. *Elder Abuse in Domestic Settings*. Washington, DC: National Center on Elder Abuse.

Tjaden, Patricia and Nancy Thoennes. 1998. *Prevalence, Incidence, and Consequences of the Violence Against Women: Findings from the National Violence Against Women Survey*. NCJ 172837. Washington, DC: U.S. Department of Justice.

U.S. Department of Health and Human Services. 1996. *Study of the National Incidence and Prevalence of Child Abuse and Neglect*. FS-13. Washington, DC: DHHS.

_____. 1998. *Child Maltreatment 1996: Reports from the States to the National Child Abuse and Neglect Data System*. Washington, DC: DHHS.

Websdale, Neil. 1998. *Rural Woman Battering and the Justice System: An Ethnography*. Thousand Oaks, CA: Sage Publications.

Wiehe, Vernon R. 1997. *Sibling Abuse: Hidden Physical, Emotional, and Sexual Trauma*, 2nd ed. Thousand Oaks, CA: Sage Publications.

Wolf, Rosalie S. 1996. "Understanding Elder Abuse and Neglect." *Aging* (367):4–17.

chapter

5

Survivors
and the Consequences
of Victimization

INTRODUCTION

> I make my husband's coffee just the way he likes it—not too hot, not too cold—not too strong, not too weak. I make his coffee just the way that he likes it. *It better be....* A public service announcement from the Connecticut Public Welfare.

In Chapter 4, the perpetrator was the major focus. The causes and consequences of domestic crime were developed through the offender characterizations. This reflects the majority of criminological theory: the focus of crime prevention and control originates with attempts to understand the offenders. Appropriate interventions to end their deviant behavior are the primary task achieved through deterrence as well as social policy. Where do the victims fit in?

For those who are unfamiliar with the criminal justice process, it is surprising to learn that victims have relatively few rights. Constitutional provisions protect the accused, and crimes are considered to be committed against the state, not against the individual. Victims do not control whether a case is heard in the criminal system. The decision to proceed with a trial is made by the district attorney or prosecutor's office. The severity of the crime against the state and the likelihood that a trial would result in a finding of guilty are among the many factors that go into that decision-making process. Least important of all is whether the victim wants the satisfaction of having the perpetrator punished or compensation arranged for wrongs that were committed.

It was not always like that. Before the modern concept of a criminal justice system the victim and his or her family were responsible for assuring that justice was done.

This was accomplished through retribution or restitution. *Retribution* is a philosophy which says that offenders should be punished for purposes of revenge. A perpetrator was expected to suffer to the degree of harm that his or her actions caused. *Restitution*, on the other hand, is a financial compensation arranged to make whole the person who was victimized. The person who suffered loss due to deviant conduct was often responsible for carrying out the punishment and benefiting from any restitution.

In most societies, individual concerns became secondary to the impact of crime and its effect on the public order. Law enforcement developed into a gatekeeper for societal norms rather than a protector against individual injustices. Ultimately, the victim was relegated to the role of a witness to the behaviors committed against society at large. Even retribution and restitution were to compensate a wronged state due to criminal transgressions. The social science approach of conducting research and expanding theory on the causes of criminal behavior ultimately was responsible for bringing the victim back into focus. That criminological specialty concerned with the role of the victim is called *victimology*.

VICTIMOLOGY

In one of the earliest attempts to explain mental illness and symptoms of hysteria in women from the psychological perspective, Sigmund Freud published his *seduction theory* in 1887 (Adams, 1992). The cause for the majority of these afflictions, he claimed, was that they were victimized through sexual abuse. Freud had found that the majority of his wealthy female clients had been raped by male family members. Faced with professional scorn, Freud recanted the seduction theory in 1890, saying that women were not actual victims of sexual abuse but that they fantasized such abuse. He replaced his seduction theory with the Oedipal complex and notions of penis envy.

Interest into the role of the victim in the commission of crimes was reborn during the 1940s. The first major theorist who contributed to the popularization of this approach was Hans von Hentig. In 1948 he wrote a major study entitled *The Criminal and His Victim*. Hans von Hentig emphasized the *victim's vulnerability* to crime. Those most likely to be victimized were categorized (Von Hentig, 1948):

- The young
- The female
- The old
- The mentally deranged
- Immigrants
- Minorities
- Dull normals
- The depressed
- The acquisitive
- The wanton
- The lonesome and the heartbroken
- The tormentor
- The blocked, exempted, or fighting

The trend to involve victims in the study of crime has continued since Von Hentig. Although there are many who have added significantly to the field, a major contribution was made by Benjamin Mendelsohn. He earned the title "father of victimology" with his typologies on victim–offender relationships. Mendelsohn assigned a *victim responsibility* rating: It is the relative amount that victims caused their victimization. In his view on the responsibility of victims, Mendelsohn classified them in a range from "completely innocent" to "as guilty as the offender" (Meadows, 1998).

Victim characteristics and behaviors became a primary focus that was believed to facilitate criminal behavior in the view called *victim precipitation*. It involves the degree to which the victim is responsible for his or her own victimization. Marvin Wolfgang pioneered this approach when he used homicide data to develop a theory on victim involvement to homicide (Wolfgang, 1975). He concluded that victims were more likely to die at the hands of someone they knew rather than those of a complete stranger. The precipitator was the person who had thrown the first blow or otherwise escalated the violence in a personal relationship that lead to his or her being killed. Hence the victim of a spousal homicide was believed to have played a significant part in his or her own demise. The idea that a murder victim may in a way cause his or her own death is controversial.

Wolfgang paved the way to the notorious study of Menachem Amir. In *Patterns in Forcible Rape*, Amir concluded that the victims of forcible rape shared responsibility for their victimization (Amir, 1971). The manner in which a woman dressed, her use of "bad" language, and her alcohol consumption were among the unconscious expressions of her desire to be raped, according to Amir. The reaction to this thesis was anything but positive!

The study of victimology came under harsh criticism from victim advocates and women's groups. The inclusion of women victims did not involve the standpoint of the victim. Critics charged that the opposite was happening. Where crimes involved relationships, the tendency toward victim blaming was evident, particularly crimes where there was an intimate relationship. Theoretical interventions for battered women focused on the pathology of the victim—the "Why doesn't she leave" question—rather than asking, "Why does he batter?" Changes that have occurred attempt to shift the focus of responsibility from the victim to the offenders.

THE VICTIM MOVEMENT

From the theoretical attempts to understand crime, including the debate on relative responsibility and victim precipitation, sprang genuine concern about the people that were being victimized. Practitioners engaging in providing services and treatment began to speak up about what they saw happening. In the middle to late 1960s, several grassroots movements were initiated simultaneously in response to urgent victim needs. The first to gain respect became known as the *children's rights movement.* Another significant effort is the *battered women's movement.* The interest groups have common threads:

1. Identification of the victims through research on the prevalence and severity of the abuse
2. Heightened concerns over the cause of victimization specific to each group
3. The development of intervention strategies, including legal reform
4. Protection and prevention efforts that are sensitive to the identified victims
5. Attempts to reduce future occurrences through services and education

Most of the victim reform effort was concerned with family violence. A model of the "ideal" relationship was conceived, against which relationships were to be judged as healthy or not. The equality wheel depicted in Figure 5–1 illustrates the ultimate relationship goal of equality.

THE CHILDREN'S RIGHTS MOVEMENT

Looking back to Chapter 2 and the historical legal status of children, it is not difficult to imagine the need for change. Violence against children in every conceivable form— physical, emotional, through neglect, and by sexual exploitation—had become a normal secret. It was alternately encouraged and tolerated. Beating and abusing children was the privilege of parents. Society did not want to know what was happening under the guise of parenting. Nor did it want to interfere with the legal rights of parents to do what they want with their offspring. As the "chattel property" of parents, a child had no rights whatsoever.

Identifying the victims of child physical abuse is relatively easy: they present visible bruises, broken bones, bite marks, and burns. They are buried in little coffins. Lesser known victimization is committed by poisoning and through neglect. Sexual exploitation from inappropriate touching to intercourse and forced prostitution is not unheard of by the practitioners involved in child advocacy. The professionals who patched the wounds saw what was happening to the future generation; they spoke out about what they were treating behind their closed doors. Raising the public consciousness to the plight of children who were victimized was the first step in the movement. Admitting to the lack of responses to these helpless victims was more difficult. Allocating resources to protect them is still a daunting challenge.

Criminal justice intervention remains inconsistent. When partner domestic violence reports are filed and law enforcement is called, they may not be aware of the need to protect children. Officers seldom consider their authority to intervene in cases of battering when a child is present or realize the harm that can occur through witnessing violence committed against a parent. Indirect harm through witnessing is a criminal

Figure 5–1   Healthy relationships are built on a core of equality as indicated by this equality wheel. *[(From Education Groups for Men Who Batter (1993, copyrighted), Ellen Pence and Michael Paymar, Springer Publishing Company, Inc., New York 10012. Used by permission.]*

justice concern, as well as abuse and neglect where the child is the intended victim. In every domestic violence case, particular attention should be given to the presence of any children in the household. Domestic violence is criminal behavior that affects the children as well as the adult being victimized.

Child Witness or Victim?

There is a strong link between spouse abuse and child abuse. Approximately 50 percent of men who abuse their wives also abuse their children. Battered women were found to be six times more likely than nonbattered women to have children reported for child abuse (Stark & Flitcraft, 1988). Mothers who are victims of domestic battering also are at higher risk for physically abusing their children (Walker, 1984). Children from abusive homes are more likely to abuse their own offspring in adulthood (Davidson, 1995).

Inflicted injuries take many forms, depending on the source and weapon used in the abuse. The physical characteristics of violence committed against a child are discussed in Chapter 9 and will not receive full attention here. It is important to know at this point, however, that the action or inaction that results in abuse or neglect against a child is referred to as *direct abuse*. When the child is witness to domestic violence, this is often called *indirect abuse*.

The effects of indirect abuse have been a topic of recent concern to child advocates. What happens when children reside in a home where parental battering occurs? Reports from battered women show that the majority of children do witness domestic violence; some actually see their mothers being beaten and raped. They hear their parent screaming and crying; they see the effects of blood, bruises, or broken windows and furniture. The American Medical Association (AMA) is among the professional organizations that have documented the harm to children who witness their mothers' abuse. Authors Balos and Fellows cite this statement from the AMA (Balos and Fellows, 1994): "Infants exposed to violence are often characterized by 'poor health, poor sleeping habits, and excessive screaming' (all of which could contribute to further abuse of the mother). Studies have found that preschoolers showed signs of 'terror, as evidenced by the children's yelling, irritable behavior, hiding, shaking, and stuttering.'...By the time children in violent homes reach adolescence, the violence typically becomes more commonplace, yet children in this age group are often more guarded and secretive about the circumstances at home, and often deny problems. These children often use aggression as a predominant form of problem solving, projecting blame on others and exhibiting a high correlation of anxiety behaviors."

Research indicates that exposing children to violence of one parent against another is one of the most severe forms of psychological abuse that can occur (Saunders, 1994). Fear that a parent could be killed and guilt because the children are unable to stop the violence can cause severe psychological trauma to the witnesses. They are likely to exhibit many forms of aggressive or withdrawn behavior. Hyperactivity and an increased tendency to be argumentative are examples of some external behaviors that have been noted in males who witness (Hilton, 1992). Girls often react by becoming withdrawn, passive, and anxious (Pizzey, 1977). Some authors suggest that children who witness domestic battering can be affected in the same way as children who are physically and sexually abused (National Committee to Prevent Child Abuse, 1996).

In addition to the short term, there is evidence of a long-range impact on families and to society when children are exposed to violence in the home. Children who have been witness to domestic violence are more likely to condone violence and less likely to know how to cope when violence occurs (Wolfe et al., 1986). Men who witness their parents physically attack each other are believed to be more likely to hit their own wives (Straus et al., 1980). An estimated 30 percent of those who witness violence become perpetrators of violence (Gelles & Conte, 1990).

Juvenile violence has been linked strongly with both direct and indirect victimization. Thornberry found in his analysis of the relationship between family violence and youth violence that children exposed to multiple forms were at the greatest risk of being violent themselves. In other words, when children were abused both directly and indirectly, youth violence was twice the rate of those from nonviolent families (Thornberry, 1994).

Additionally, those who witness violence have a greater chance of being involved in criminal activity as juveniles, and later as adults (Windom, 1998). Cathy Windom reports that while the majority of indirect abuse victims do not commit family or other forms of violence as adults, many suffer long after the abuse occurs. Victims are at greater risk for many other problems throughout their lives, including participation in violent crime as adults. Due to the added risks of victimization in domestic settings, advocates are seeking additional rights for children in custody and marital torts. Fair consideration of children in the legal system is deemed an important intervention when assessing visitation and custody rights of parents.

Childhood Abuse and Criminal Behavior

In addition to the psychological and behavioral effects that children may experience due to their exposure to domestic violence, there is concern about later criminalization due to direct abuse. Links to criminal and violent behaviors have been established for children who experience any form of abuse. For the victims of multiple abuse, the risk becomes greater. According to Windom, maltreatment during childhood does increase the likelihood of arrest, as a juvenile by 53 percent, as an adult by 38 percent, and for a violent crime by 38 percent (Windom, 1998).

Children who were sexually abused were 28 times more likely than a control group of nonabused children to be arrested for prostitution as an adult (Windom and Ames, 1994). Neglected children are at higher risk for committing sexual offenses as adults, more so than children who were sexually abused (U.S. General Accounting Office, 1996). Even though spanking is a pervasive form of child punishment, its victims are thought to be at a higher risk of being depressed and thinking about suicide, as well as being violent (Giles-Sims et al., 1995). Teenagers who are hit by their fathers are believed to act out higher levels of violence in later years (Helfer & Kempe, 1988).

Childhood Abuse and Social Consequences

Recent reports indicate that victimization of children also has grave social consequences. One study conducted by the National Institute of Justice indicates that neglected children suffered from impaired language development and had lower intellectual and social competence (Garrett & Libbey, 1997b). Sexual assault victims frequently experience a decline in school grades or participation in after-school activities. A form of role reversal is noted in homes where violence occurs. As the result of developmental and emotional needs not being met, Elbow found a symbiotic and ambivalent relationship between children and violent parents (Elbow, 1982). This causes a blurring of appropriate age and appropriate development.

An increase in somatic symptoms such as colds, sore throats, bed-wetting, insomnia, and fitful sleep are experienced by children in abusive homes (Pagelow, 1984). These symptoms clear up after the child is removed to a safe place, such as a shelter. Kilpatrick and Saunders report that preliminary findings indicate that personal victimization is a risk factor for mental health problems as well as abuse of drugs and alcohol. Approximately 30 percent of sexual assault victims and 23 percent of those physically abused develop post-traumatic stress disorder (Kilpatrick & Saunders, 1997). This figure is compared to nonvictims, where less than 11 percent develop the disorder.

Satanic Activities.   Due to recently increasing concerns about satanic beliefs and practices among adolescents, some researchers are looking at a possible connection between child abuse and satanic involvement. One study involving adolescent boys who admitted to voluntary involvement in group satanic activities were all found to have been physically and/or sexually abused (Belitz and Schacht, 1995). The common reaction for boys is, however, anger rather than satanic involvement, which is an expression of the rage as well as of pervasive feelings of inadequacy and powerlessness. The harm to a victim does not cause satanic involvement but may be an avenue for some adolescents to gain the power and control that they lack due to victimization. Additionally, cult membership is not illegal; it is the criminal activity that a member may engage in that will bring him or her to the attention of law enforcement.

The Consequences of Abuse to a Child

The majority of children who are victimized through domestic violence do not commit criminal acts as adults, according to Windom (Windom, 1998). What happens is an increased likeliness. The harm to a child who is victimized is not universal and cannot be predicted with any certainty. Many conditions might affect the response, both from the child victim and later in life as an adult. Forms and frequency of abuse, age, and mental condition of the child, as well as his or her personality, will all play a role on how the victim reacts. The consequences of abuse will vary according to multiple factors (Garrett & Libbey, 1997a):

1. *Characteristics of the child.* The age, emotional and cognitive development, gender, race/ethnicity, personality, and strengths or resiliency of the child all play a part in determining the effects of maltreatment.

2. *Type of trauma.* Two types of trauma have to do with the severity and intensity of the abuse. Type I, referred to as *acute trauma*, is a single event; type II, a chronic or repetitive abuse over time, is usually more difficult for the child to overcome.

3. *Type of abuse or neglect.* All forms of maltreatment to a child—physical, sexual, psychological/emotional abuse or witnessing domestic violence—carry the possibility of long-term effects on the psychological and social adaptation of the victim.

4. *Co-occurrences of types of abuse and neglect.* When multiple abuses occur simultaneously, the risk of maladaptive behavior is heightened as a result. Frequently, emotional/psychological abuse occurs when any other form of abuse is perpetrated.

5. *Relationship.* Child relationships affect the resiliency of the victim and his or her ability to overcome adverse effects of abuse. All relationships that the child has with the victimizer, the nonoffending parent, other family members, other adults, and peers will affect the consequences of abuse and/or neglect.

Consequences of Sexual Abuse.   A child who is being sexually assaulted typically will not report the abuse when it first occurs. Children often do not even realize that it is abusive. There is usually an *engagement* phase before the perpetrator initiates sexual contact. During this time, a relationship is being established between the victim and the offender. By the time any sexual conduct takes place, the child trusts the adult. Next is a *progression* phase: The abuser may begin with common activities that require the child to undress. Swimming is one example. This is done to desensitize the child about removing clothing in the presence of the perpetrator. From then on, a range of sexual abuses may be attempted, ranging from indecent touching to intercourse. The final phase is *suppression.* Somehow the offender must ensure the secrecy of the events that have occurred.

Summit's characterization, referred to as the sexual abuse accommodation syndrome, includes five phases common to the experiences of the child who has been sexually victimized: secrecy; helplessness; entrapment and accommodation; delayed, conflicted, and unconvincing disclosure; and retraction (Summit, 1982).

Secrecy.   Child sexual abuse is almost always cloaked in secrecy. Frequently, the perpetrator will threaten the child not to tell anyone. Secrecy is secured in various ways, depending on the age of the child and the relationship to the perpetrator. If a child tries to tell an adult about the behavior, the attempt is usually met with disbelief and minimization. Additionally, the child abuser picks his or her victims carefully; he or she already knows the vulnerability of the child and how to guarantee silence before the abuse occurs.

Rewards and incentives for secrecy are common. For example, a young child may be bribed with toys, a bicycle, or dolls. Affection and attachment for needy youngsters is sometimes enough to win compliance. Adolescents may be given permission to use the family car; buying expensive clothing and jewelry is not uncommon. The fact that the victims are rewarded for incestual secrecy does not mean that they are being "paid" for the act. This becomes confusing when the victim is an adolescent, particularly if the child has been taught manipulative behavior through abuse. In time the victim knows that secrecy has a price, comes to expect gifts and rewards, and may even demand them.

Shame and guilt come as the child begins to realize what is happening to him or her. When the violator is a family member, the child may have been cajoled into the sexual activity, being told "this is normal," "everyone does this," or "this is called love." Although the child probably does not like the activity, he or she has no reason to doubt what he or she has been told. At some point the realization that the activity is *not* right creeps in, regardless of what the children have been told, and they feel guilt and shame for their participation.

The victim knows that a price is paid for the silence; it takes on importance to a young person. Victims wonder what the cost of breaking that silence would be. Keep in mind that these are children: They don't reason as adults. They might not be able to ride the bike they love, or wear that pretty dress. Often, the offender will warn the child that if he or she tells anyone, the offender would go to jail and the child would never see him or her again. To a young child, that idea is devastating. In relatively few cases, the family abuser will threaten to kill the child, other family members, or even pets. Threats do not have to be elaborate or particularly believable to adults for it to have a severe impact on a child. The perspective of the child is therefore important.

A bond exists in the relationship, even though it is deviant behavior. The child may fear losing his or her parent's love if he or she told anyone. The victim is favored in the family—although others don't know, it is his or her secret.

Helplessness.   *Intrusiveness* characterizes sexual assaults against children. Frequently, it occurs in their own bedroom, making that place no longer safe for them. The intrusion causes anxiety and insecurity, another part of the victimization process. Children may feign sleep during the assault, even though a sibling may be in the next bed or a parent in the next room. Rarely will a child cry out.

Entrapment and Accommodation.   *Self-hate* develops over time as the child exaggerates his or her own responsibility in the abuse. "No one will believe you," victims are often told. Older children, frequently adolescents, can be blackmailed through sexually explicit photographs that the abuser states will "prove" that they consented. Remember: Consent is *not* a legal issue when sex occurs between a child and an adult, but children don't know that! In most jurisdictions, a child *cannot* consent to sexual intercourse.

A promise may be involved not to sexually assault siblings. It is not unusual for a victim to come forward with a complaint of sexual abuse at the time that she or he believes that the offender is breaking that promise. A child who has been victimized over time comes to accommodate his or her abuse, yet often will not tolerate it happening to a younger sibling.

Delayed, Conflicted, and Unconvincing Disclosure.   Sexual abuse that is ongoing is frequently kept secret within the family. The victim usually remains silent until he or she enters adolescence. A family fight or punishment that the teenager disagrees with may trigger disclosure. A younger sibling being targeted for abuse may also spark the victim to tell someone. They may tell a friend or a teacher. The reaction is usually one of disbelief and denial. If a nonoffending parent is the first told, the reaction will probably affect what happens next.

Retraction.   Whatever a child says about incest, he or she is likely to recant at some point. This is problematic for criminal justice, and it must be anticipated if prosecution is to occur. The victim needs support and reassurance through a prosecution for incest. The investigation needs to actively seek any form of corroboration available in anticipation that the victim will at some point deny the abuse. If a case for sexual abuse rests solely on the word of a child (without evidence) and the truthfulness of the victim comes into question through a denial, a successful prosecution is impossible.

Conclusions on the Children's Rights Movement

Due to the struggle, we now recognize that children can be harmed physically, sexually, and through neglect. In addition, they are abused psychologically through witnessing violence. The awareness of the consequences of these forms has led to legislative reforms discussed in Chapter 6.

As increased attention was given to the victims of child abuse, activists sought similar recognition of the abuses perpetrated against women. One of the major theories that explained battering in intimate relationships is based on the perception that violence begets violence, known as the *intergenerational transmission of violence*. The research conducted relative to child abuse both supported and connected the effort to understand violence against women. Although the two movements are separate, they are so interconnected that it is impossible to study one without the other.

THE BATTERED WOMEN'S MOVEMENT

The National Coalition Against Domestic Violence (NCADV) defines the battering of intimate partners as a political issue of sexism (Battered/Formerly Battered Women's Task Force, 1992). Over 25 years have passed since the beginnings of the alliance to gain equal rights and end oppression against women. The vast majority of survivors of domestic violence are women. Their battering is considered one part of the oppression that patriarchy maintains. The movement seeks social change of the cultural values that enable oppressors to control and maintain the power as it has been in the past. It seeks to empower all women and children and to restructure and redistribute the social power. Ending physical and sexual abuse perpetrated against women and children is a significant effort in the movement, but it is seen in a larger context of economic and sexist oppression.

The movement has accomplished major victories since its inception and it is still strong today:

1. The victims have been identified: They are 95 percent to 98 percent female.

2. Heightened public awareness has been achieved, although the causes and consequences are still hotly debated.

3. Intervention strategies have been established through a range of services: shelter, information services, and hotlines. Complaints of insufficient funds to implement additional needed services and to maintain existing ones are constant. Major organizations, including the American Medical Association and American Bar Association, have acknowledged the high number of instances of domestic violence against women and sought reform to address needs. Legal reform has been accomplished in every state in the United States. Federal legislative reform has brought unprecedented change. Refer to Chapter 6 for an in-depth discussion of recent legislative reform.

4. Protection and prevention efforts now include civil and criminal actions that were never before available to domestic violence victims.

5. Batterers' programs have become the most frequent response from the courts to domestic battering. Education is occurring at this level on television and in classrooms across the country.

One unintended consequence of the battered women's movement has been increased awareness of violence committed against lesbian and gay partners, and males. Violence in dating relationships was discovered as well. The implications of personal violence in these additional populations are included in the discussions that follow.

Woman Battering: Health and Safety Issues

Women who are victimized through domestic violence may suffer emotionally and physically. Financial hardships occur when the victim is forced to seek alternate living arrangements and when caring for her children. Recent studies indicate that as many as 1 in 10 battered women seek professional medical treatment due to their injuries (Greenfeld et al., 1998). Women are the majority of emergency room patients who seek treatment for intentional injuries caused by an intimate. How have professionals sought to address the problems? Some initiatives include emergency hotlines. Another alternative is for the victim to seek emergency shelter.

Injury.   In addition to loss of life, the risk of serious injury due to domestic violence is severe. The National Research Council reports (Chalk & King, 1998): "Family violence has been identified as a contributing factor for a broad array of fatal and nonfatal injuries and health disorders, including pregnancy and birth complications, sudden infant death syndrome, brain trauma, fractures, sexually transmitted diseases, HIV infection, depression, dissociation, psychosis, and other stress-related physical and mental disorders.... Estimates on the impact of family violence on the public health and health care system indicate that family violence accounts for 39,000 physician visits each year; 28,700 emergency room visits; 21,000 hospitalizations; and 99,800 hospital days."

The American Medical Association declared in 1992 that physical and sexual violence against women had reached "epidemic proportions" and recommended that physicians routinely screen all women patients for domestic abuse. Approximately 30 percent of women who seek hospital emergency room treatment had injuries caused by battering (Schaffler, 1994). Pregnancy has been identified as a risk factor associated with domestic battering. Studies of battered women in shelters have indicated that between 40 and 60 percent of the women were abused during pregnancy (McFarlane, 1998). One study found that 17 percent of the women receiving prenatal care at public clinics in Houston and Baltimore had been physically or sexually abused (Flitcraft, 1992).

In a survey of women who were not residents of battered women shelters, McFarlane and colleagues reported that one out of every 12 women interviewed reported battering during the current pregnancy (McFarlane, 1998). One-third of the pregnant women had sought medical attention for injuries sustained from the abuse, and 29 percent reported that the abuse had increased with knowledge of present pregnancy. A strong indicator of violence during pregnancy was the pattern of battering beforehand. The majority of pregnant women (87.5 percent) had been battered prior to becoming pregnant. McFarlane cautions that the risks of violence during teen pregnancy are also severe. Twenty-six percent of pregnant teens reported physical battering in one study alone.

Hotlines and Shelters.   The first hotline for battered women started in St. Paul, Minnesota, in 1971. Since then national and local hotlines have been established to provide callers with crisis intervention, details on local resources, and information about domestic violence. The National Domestic Hotline reports nearly 10,000 calls each month (National Domestic Hotline, 1999).

The first shelter in the United States opened for battered women in St. Paul, Minnesota, in 1974. Over 2,000 shelters and service programs exist today. Due to the magnitude of the problem of domestic violence, however, shelters are inadequate to meet the needs of all survivors. In many areas, shelters turn away four women (and their children) for every woman they can accept (National Coalition Against

Domestic Violence, 1998). Women with adolescent male children are frequently denied access to shelters, due to possible disruptions and fear that their presence produces. Lesbians, gay men, and male victims are also denied shelter. Adequate resources for those who qualify are insufficient to meet the demands.

Homelessness.   The relationship between domestic violence and homelessness was examined in a recent report (National Coalition for the Homeless, 1998). Long waiting lists for assisted housing and the lack of affordable housing force many women and their children to choose between abuse at home or life on the streets, according to the report. The following studies are cited that demonstrate the contribution of domestic violence to homelessness:

- A 1990 Ford Foundation study found that 50 percent of homeless women and children were fleeing abuse.
- In Missouri, 24 percent of the sheltered homeless population are victims of domestic abuse.
- Shelter providers in Virginia report that 35 percent of their clients are homeless because of family violence, and more than 2,000 women seeking shelter from domestic violence facilities were turned away.
- A 1995 study of homelessness in Nebraska found that victims of domestic violence represent 25 percent of the homeless population.
- In Minnesota, the most common reason for women to enter a shelter is domestic violence. Homeless women surveyed indicated their main reason for leaving housing was to flee abuse.

Safety Planning.   An increased risk of severe and fatal injury to survivors of domestic battering has been linked to the final stage of the relationship, when the batterer knows that the relationship is being ended. Advocates suggest that domestic violence victims take additional precautions to protect themselves during this period. When the batterer has been court ordered out of the home, the following steps are recommended:

- Consider changing the locks in the house or apartment, even if you have asked the abuser to surrender all keys.
- If you live on the first floor or have an apartment with porch windows, consider ways to secure those windows with metal casement key locks or screw-in window locks.
- If you have no phone, consider having one installed as soon as possible; change your current phone number if you do have one.
- Keep the phone number of the police handy, as well as the number of the local shelter.

- Keep all important papers in one place where you can grab them on the way out if you are forced to flee. These include birth certificates, marriage license, social security cards, health cards, checkbooks, and savings accounts.
- Leave extra keys to the apartment and car with a friend or relative who knows the situation.
- Consider talking with your neighbors to ask for their cooperation. A system or code such as lights flicking on and off or banging on the floor or ceiling could indicate that you need the help of the police if they are willing to call. Many neighbors do not want to interfere, so asking them in advance gives them permission to help.

Learned Helplessness Theory

One of the early examples of theory that came from the victim movement was that of *learned helplessness*. In suggesting this alternative, Lenore Walker made clear that the most popular explanation at that time (1978) was that battered women were believed to be masochistic (Walker, 1995). Refuting the assumption that women sought out men who would fill their need to be beaten, she claimed another psychological rationale. Employing the social-learning perspective, Walker theorized that women accept their powerlessness in domestic battering situations due to gender-role socialization that induces a false belief that they cannot escape from the situation. The feeling of powerlessness may be reinforced by the "happy family" cultural stereotype as well, she suggested. Victim isolation from friends, family, and other victims allows the reality of the situation to be minimized while victims accept responsibility for the battering incidents. In this explanation, battering produces a psychological paralysis that maintains the victim status of their victimization. Economic and social factors contribute to their victimization and to its continuance in this view.

The battered woman syndrome describes the cyclical nature of battering over time. Domestic abuse is not a single explosive incident of hitting; it is the building of tensions that contribute to the ever-existing nature of the abusive relationship. Victim denials and accommodation of the batterer add to the victimization, which is psychological and emotional as well as physical and/or sexual.

SURVIVORS OF DOMESTIC BATTERING

A recent trend in the study of domestic violence is toward changing the characterization of the battered victim to that of a survivor. Kathleen Ferraro typifies this movement. Citing the Campbell study of 1994, she clarifies the incredible obstacles that are overcome by almost half of battered women who are ultimately successful in leaving their abusers (Ferraro, 1997). Her stages of engagement and disengagement offer insight into the intimacy characteristics of marital relationships and the difficulties of dealing with dependent men who threaten, harass, and often assault women as they try to leave. An adaptation of her theory in Figure 5–2 illustrates that the final desperate attempt to get away may lead to homicide.

CONSEQUENCES OF FAMILY VIOLENCE

Larry Tifft places woman battering in an organization structure consisting of two parts: The initial stages and later stages (Tifft, 1993). He differentiates between pushing, shoving, and slaps that are perceived by others as violent outbursts but are in fact not real violence. Only when both partners understand that the violence is intended does battering occur. It is repetitive, uncontrolled, unacceptable behaviors that are disruptive to the victim's feelings or sense of self (Figure 5–3).

Figure 5–2   Surviving violence. *(Adapted from Ferraro, 1997).*

Phase I: Physical and emotional attraction brings the partners together. During the first six months of the relationship there is no battering. She enjoys time alone with her partner and does not see his desire for social exclusivity as oppression but as mutual affection.

Phase II: The first act of physical violence is met with disbelief. The woman rationalizes the assault and denies the uncharacteristic victimization. The perpetrator blames her through some imagined provocation. It is unlikely that the violence will be deterred by the minor sanctions of criminal justice action unless it occurs in the early stages and in certain types of battering relationships. Societal pressures frequently force the woman into "making the best of it".

Phase III: A change in the severity or frequency of the abuse may trigger a transition into this stage. Defensive violence is one tactic that may be used to ward off attacks. The woman may attempt to leave the emotional and economic bond that had developed. Threats or psychological torture make early attempts difficult and often they return. About one-half of those who leave are successful in this attempt toward survival.

Phase IV: Convinced by threats from constant surveillance and punishments, women believe that they cannot get away. Failed attempts to leave reinforce the perception. This stage is horror filled and may bring about depression and posttraumatic stress syndrome. Suicide may be contemplated. A severe altercation may lead to homicide as the final stage in what becomes a "kill or be killed" scenario.

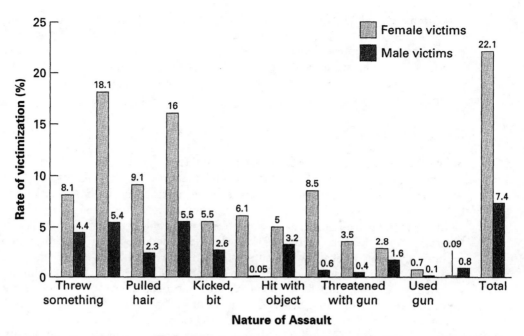

Figure 5–3   Percentage of persons physically assaulted by an intimate partner in lifetime. *(Data from Tjaden and Thoennes, 1998).*

Battering in this context *steals your soul.* It is both physical and spiritual pain that causes the survivor to grieve in the initial stages. Both people will typically pretend that the first real violent episode did not occur. As the violence escalates in frequency or severity, a loss of affection surfaces. For normality to be reestablished, both partners must cooperate; this causes an extension of pain for the woman, according to Tifft. She cannot deny the abuse and will be unable to dismiss the injury. The framework of the family becomes distorted as guilt, ambiguity, and insecurity dominate every interaction. Hostility, anger, depression, and fear increase within the relationship. The continued focus on her pain distorts the survivor's vision, suggests Tifft. Her own strategies for survival narrow as she tries to cope with the contradiction of being in love with a partner who both loves and hurts her. As the situation worsens, the survivor comes to the realization that the battering has become a permanent part of their relationship, and she refuses to take the blame that her batterer heaps on her.

The later stage that Tifft describes involves the methods that the family has adopted to alter life according to the abuse. Children may withdraw from school activities to get home and protect their mom. The family becomes socially isolated to accommodate the presence of the batterer. Overwhelmed by the atmosphere of violence, the mother may become less able to care for the children as all of her attention becomes focused on the abuser. Sexual violence may also occur as the batterer becomes more jealous of what he has already lost. The battering may stop temporarily due to his being arrested or the survivor's seeking refuge at a shelter. Typically they reunite, and he resumes his pattern of battering. The survivor who hangs on to her love for him will have a difficult time in severing the relationship. It may take numerous attempts at separations and rejoinings before the survivors are permanently able to "freeze out" the batterer.

Female Victims

Suman Kakar suggests that victims have both internal and external factors that explain why they tolerate violence (Kakar, 1998). The internal traits that victims possess may be natural or due to the experiences of the battering relationship, however. Examples are timidity and low self-esteem. Feelings of helplessness can be acquired when the victims feel trapped and unable to escape. Some researchers suggest that through controlling tactics, the perpetrator "brainwashes" the victim, and a traumatic bonding occurs, according to Kakar. Overly optimistic victims may feel that they love the offender and hope that they can change the abuser's behavior. External factors that influence the victim can be summed up through economic dependence on the perpetrator. Women often remain economically dependent on the man while they care for children in the home; they may delay their education and forgo employment outside the home.

In *Battering of Women: The Failure of Intervention and the Case for Prevention*, Larry Tifft likens battered women to the "peoples of invaded nations...perceived by the general culture as the cause of their own invasion, torture, and anguish" (5). After 15 years of empirical research focused on the characteristics of women who have been battered, few risk markers have been identified (Tifft, 1993). When low self-esteem, codependency, or lack of assertiveness is suggested, says Tifft, it blames the victims and draws attention away from the real problem. Rather than viewing women who are battered as in need of therapy, advocacy, justice, and support are the needed responses.

Lesbian couples are believed to have the highest rate of domestic victimization (Coleman, 1996). Societal notions on the role of women have contributed to the reluctance of lesbian victims to identify the abuse. Lesbians fear reporting domestic violence battering due to the double victimization that is likely to occur. Women are expected to be nonviolent in this culture that attributes battering primarily to males. Accusations of violence by a female toward another female may be met with disbelief.

Effects of Rape.   Women who have been raped by an intimate partner experience profound disbelief and shock that the person professing to care about them would so humiliate and frighten them (Finkelhor & Yllo, 1985). Anger, hatred, and feelings of betrayal are familiar among survivors of marital rape. Finkelhor and Yllo state: "For most of the women the rape experience has continued to have an emotional impact years and even decades later. Among the more common long-term effects were the inability to trust men, an aversion to intimacy and sex, and a lingering acute fear of being assaulted again."

Male Victims

Sexual and physical crimes committed against men and boys are believed to be under-reported. Male victimization is barely acknowledged in our culture. Since the male identity includes expectations of problem solving and self-protection, battered men often do not perceive their victimization as abuse. Vast amounts of research into the effects and consequence of women's abuse have been conducted in the last decade, but relatively little is known about male victimization.

In *The Sexually Abused Male*, Jim Struve applies the dynamics of patriarchy and the learned helplessness theory to the sexual victimization of boys (Struve, 1990). Sexual entitlement, the belief that sex is the privilege of dominant adult males, blurs the boundaries between adult and child in this patriarchal view. The legal, economic, and social dependency on parents leaves no feasible alternative for children when their safety is threatened, and they learn to accommodate. Cultural dictates on sexual secrecy and misinformation on sex serve to perpetuate the shroud of secrecy that envelops this form of male abuse. Struve suggests nine socialization factors that make it more difficult for male survivors to achieve recovery.

1. *Treatment.* Men are not as likely as women to seek treatment. This is a reluctance to see oneself as a victim—a female-associated persona.

2. *Minimization.* Males are reluctant to make a disclosure about sexual abuse for fear that it will not be seen as a victimization experience. If the victim is a self-identified homosexual, the abuse may be seen as the result of sexual choice.

3. *Shame.* The male victim typically focuses on why he failed to protect himself. Male survivors frequently report internalized anger, according to Struve, as well as their having failed at their manly responsibility of inflicting serious physical harm on the offender.

4. *Masculine identity.* The male survivor may overcompensate for the anxiety surrounding his inability to protect himself by using macho behaviors to project a strong male image. For the heterosexual male, fears that he will be "branded" as homosexual will plague him.

5. *Male intimacy.* Intense anxiety or anger is produced in settings with other males that might create intimacy. The victim typically will avoid relationships with other males, to avoid appearing weak or needy.

6. *Sexual identity.* A male that has been sexually assaulted may assume that his failure to protect himself equates with passivity, wrongly considered a female trait. Since the majority of perpetrators are also male, the self-perception of arousal or physical pleasure from a same-sex assault can lead to the false assumption of homosexuality.

7. *Power and control dynamics.* Low self-esteem is related to having been victimized sexually. It may lead to an exaggerated effort to control others.

8. *Externalization*. Victimizing others sexually is one way that victims externalize their feelings. Isolation surrounding his own victimization and patriarchal values place the victim at risk for offending against others.

9. *Compulsive behaviors*. Some male survivors mask their emotional anxiety and pain through compulsive behaviors. These may include alcohol and substance abusing, or rigid repetitive behaving patterns.

According to Urquiza and Capra, initial effects of the sexual abuse of boys are the presence of a variety of behavioral disturbances, such as aggression, delinquency, and noncompliance (Urquiza & Capra, 1990). Victims have problems with self-concept, self-esteem, guilt, and shame. In addition to gender confusion, children who have been sexually victimized have been identified as sexually aggressive. Researchers suggest that severe victimization may have a disinhibiting effect on children's sexual behavior. The most common long-term effect of male child victimization is depression (Urquiza & Capra, 1990).

As explained in Chapter 4, the physical abuse of men by women is a contentious issue. Male victims of physical battering must overcome the social barriers that do not recognize their abuse as legitimate. Philip Cook suggests that physical injury should not be the measure of an abusive relationship (Cook, 1997). He maintains that abused men do exist and in greater numbers than people realize. Battered men frequently stay in marital discord for reasons similar to those of women. Cook maintains that it is false to assume that economic resources offer greater escape possibilities for men; they are held responsible for financially supporting a former spouse and children regardless of abuse. Fear of losing contact with children also inhibits fathers from leaving abusive relationships: Women most often receive physical custody of children. Additionally, abused men feel powerless due to their inability to change the situation in the past.

One of the major differences between battered gay and bisexual men and battered women is that gay and bisexual men are often unable to see themselves as victims, simply because they are men (Letellier, 1996). Patrick Letellier suggests that unless there is a high level of physical harm or injury to their bodies, gay and bisexual men are likely to deny or minimize the violence that is perpetrated against them. Additional problems for these victims are the silence about same-sex battering and the risk of a homophobic response. These factors contribute to the tendency for gay and bisexual men not to report domestic violence.

Victims of violence are created by batterers, suggest Island and Letellier (Island & Letellier, 1991). They state that it is all too easy to lump together victims and offenders in the same psychological package. Why male victims stay is a much more difficult question to answer. Each gay victim has his own set of reasons for staying with his batterer. The cycle of violence theory and learned helplessness theory offer theoretical explanations. Fear, they contend, is the most powerful reason.

Dating Victims

Years after adult victimization was recognized, scholars began to look at violence during the courtship phase. Research has indicated that approximately one out of 10 high school students experience physical violence in dating relationships. For college students the figure rises to 22 percent, which is the same as violence in adult relationships (Gamache, 1998). Clearly, violence occurs in the context of both marital and dating partnerships. Yet, dating someone is different than being married. The two most stressful events of marriage, money management and childrearing, don't exist in the context of courtship. Problems associated with having a place to live and going to work are not involved. It sounds as though dating would be free of any factors that are associated with violence. Why does it happen?

Scholars are beginning to associate intimacy with violence, in both adult and dating relationships. James Makepeace, for example, suggests a developmental theory based on the need for intimacy between partners as his explanation for courtship violence (Makepeace, 1997). He states that intimacy is a fundamental individual need, and its attainment is both magnified and romanticized in our culture. The frustrations to satisfy that need begin early during the courtship stage. Youngsters often begin dating when they have not yet gained the maturity to handle the frustrations of satisfactory intimacy and may react in inappropriate ways. He cites jealousy as the most frequent reason for courtship violence, and hitting as a response to jealousy is often accepted by both males and females.

Makepeace reports that the majority of respondents (54 percent) first experienced violence in courtship between ages 16 and 18. The life experiences that are significant in predicting this violence include the family background, such as absent, emotionally distant, or harsh parents; school difficulties; difficulties in employment; and having begun dating at an early age. Consistent with studies on adult interpersonal violence, the use of drugs and alcohol is a consistent risk factor in abuse. Neither can be used as an excuse for perpetration, however.

For lesbian teens, an absence of role models may lead the adolescents to engage in destructive behaviors that they falsely assume are characteristic of the sexual choice that they have made (Levy & Lobel, 1998). Confusion about what is normal behavior makes this population especially vulnerable to abuse. The isolation due to the sexual identity adds to their low self-esteem and creates an intense bond with their lover. When the victim is unable to trust others, it is difficult to seek support if a partner becomes abusive.

Date Rape. Since the 1980s the term *date rape* has been used to describe rape of young women or adolescent girls perpetrated by casual or intimate dating partners. There is no crime called "date rape." This is a social term used to explain the context under which the crime is occurring; it brings attention to the fact that rape occurs within relationships. The legal term for date rape is simply *rape*. Studies on the prevalence of acquaintance rape have indicated shocking rates of occurrence. During the 1980s, early research of high school and college students reported rates of dating violence ranging from 12 to 65 percent (Levy, 1990). Women are five times more likely to experience rape in a dating relationship than from strangers (DeKeseredy & Schwartz, 1998).

In addition to the fear and depression that is common to rape victims, adolescent survivors suffer in ways that are unique (Gallers & Lawrence, 1998). In their review of the literature, Gallers and Lawrence explain that teenagers experience a sense of loss of personal integrity as well as trust of the world around them. Young people frequently feel invincible, and the personal violation shatters that myth, altering their reality. The self-esteem of a normally narcissistic adolescent may be damaged from an assault. Victims tend to internalize and falsely blame themselves for being with the offender in the first place. Sudden personality changes, such as a drop in school performance, withdrawal from usual school or social activities, and flagrant promiscuous behavior are among the symptoms that adolescent rape victims display. They may engage in self-destructive behavior such as drug or alcohol abuse or develop eating disorders such as bulimia or anorexia.

A concern now is the increasingly predatory nature of rape indicated by the use of *date rape drugs* by high school and college students. The most common is Rohypnol, often called "roofies" and "forget pill" (Figure 5–4). According to the Drug Enforcement Administration, this illegal drug is manufactured worldwide and brought in through Mexico. Its popularity among young people is due to the drug's low cost, usually below $5 per tablet. Placed into the drink of an unsuspecting victim, the drug is tasteless and odorless. Within 15 to 30 minutes, the effects include dizziness, drowsiness, confusion, and memory impairment. Another drug, gamma-hydroxybutyrate (GHB), is also being used to incapacitate victims in order to abuse them sexually. Its side effects are similar to those of Rohypnol. Most commonly found in liquid form, it is also colorless and odorless.

People who suspect that they have been drugged and sexually violated should have their urine and blood tested within 24 hours. All clothing and physical evidence should be kept and given to the police. It is important not to change, shower, or douche, so that a hospital protocol and rape examination may be made to secure evidence of the assault.

Figure 5–4   "Roofies" or Rohypnol tablets are white and are single—or cross-scored on one side with "ROCHE" and "1" or "2" encircled on the other.

EFFECTS OF VICTIMIZATION

Throughout this chapter, a number of different responses to personal violence have been offered. The reactions of victims may vary greatly. The severity and frequency of the abuse, the personal characteristics of the victim, and the form of abuse all contribute to the range of victim reactions. Presented here are some responses that have been identified from the psychological viewpoint. Although attributing mental health disorders to victims of domestic violence is hotly debated, these characterizations are interwoven into the literature on victimization. The disorders are not specific to any group or determined by race, ethnicity, gender, or age.

Borderline Personality Disorder

Described as a pervasive pattern of instability of mood, interpersonal relationships, and self-image, the borderline personality disorder affects functioning in numerous areas of life (Alderman, 1997). Examples include employment or school, social relationships, and/or personal well-being. Alderman explains that this disorder is a chronic, intense instability and chaos characterized by fluctuating extremes. She likens the personality disorder to the video game "Sonic the Hedgehog": "In the game, Sonic was safe from his enemies as long as he curled up in a tight ball and kept spinning. Once he stopped and stood up, he was vulnerable to the attacks of various creatures. As long as the people with borderline personality keep spinning, creating and repairing chaotic situations within their lives, they feel safe. When their lives get too calm or too stable, vulnerability, tension and anxiety emerge, causing them to seek new chaos. Stability sends these people spinning."

Posttraumatic Stress Disorder

Posttraumatic stress disorder (PTSD) is the diagnostic category most frequently used by psychotherapists to explain the trauma associated with rape, battering, and sexual abuse. Often, it is experienced as the result of one severely traumatic event; its application to domestic violence is limited. Kilpatrick and colleagues found that 57.1 percent of rape victims developed PTSD after the incident (Kilpatrick et al., 1987).

The *Diagnostic and Statistical Manual of Mental Disorders* (American Psychiatric Association, 1987) defines *posttraumatic stress disorder* as a type of anxiety disorder caused by trauma and prolonged stress. First applied to Vietnam veterans, it is also reported in victims of violence. The diagnostic criteria for this psychological condition are these:

1. That the person has experienced an event outside the range of usual human experience that would be distressing to almost everyone.

2. That the person reexperiences the trauma as evidenced by at least one of the following:

   a. Recurrent or intrusive recollections of the event

   b. Recurrent dreams of the event

    c. Sudden acting or feeling as if the traumatic event were recurring because some stimulus triggers an association [including a sense of reliving the experience, illusions, hallucinations, and dissociative (flashback) experiences]

    d. Intense psychological distress at exposure to events that resemble or symbolize the traumatic event

3. That the person has a numbing of responsiveness to, or reduced involvement with, the external world beginning sometime after the trauma, as shown by at least one of the following:

    a. Markedly diminished interest in one or more significant activities

    b. Feelings of detachment or estrangement from others

    c. Constricted affect

4. That the person shows persistent symptoms of increased arousal that were not present before the trauma:

    a. Hypervigilance

    b. Sleep disturbance

    c. Memory impairment or trouble concentrating

    d. Irritability or outbursts of anger

    e. Exaggerated startle response

    f. Intensification of symptoms (and physiological reactivity) by exposure to events that symbolize or resemble the traumatic event

5. That these symptoms last for at least one month.

Stockholm Syndrome

Characteristics common to hostage taking have been identified in nine groups examined by Graham (Graham & Rawlings, 1998). The bidirectional bonding between the captor and the hostage appears to occur between the abuser and physically and/or emotionally abused children, incest victims, battered women, and procured prostitutes, as well as cult members, concentration camp prisoners, prisoners of war, civilians in Chinese prisons, and people in hostage situations. Known as the Stockholm syndrome, the condition occurs as a survival strategy. Graham proposes that the following conditions precede the phenomenon:

- The victim perceives a threat to survival along with the belief that the captor is willing to carry out that threat.
- The captive perceives that some small kindness from the captor occurred within the context of terror of the situation.
- An isolation from perspectives other than those of the captor narrows the victim's perception of the events.
- The captive perceives an inability to escape.

Self-Inflicted Violence

Victims of abuse do not always resort to self-inflicted violence (SIV), states Alderman. Trauma is not believed to cause SIV but seems to be *related* to childhood victimization. She notes that the majority of people who engage in self-destructive practices have previously been victimized by physical, sexual, or emotional abuse (Alderman, 1997).

SIV involves acts done to oneself by oneself that are physically damaging and intentional but not suicidal. Cutting, burning, and hitting oneself are examples. Pulling out hair and excessive nail-biting are others. Razor blades and lit cigarettes are common tools in the practice. Equally important to the description is that these are repetitive and extremely private actions. SIV is not done to conform to cult requirements or as a fashion statement. It is a self-destructive coping mechanism and often the response to stress.

THE COST OF FAMILY VIOLENCE

In terms of personal pain and suffering, it is impossible to gauge the costs of family violence. The damaged lives and generations of troubled persons due to abuse are something that we have only recently begun to understand. A recent report estimated that 1.3 million adults received hospital emergency treatment for physical and sexual assaults in the one-year period before the survey (Tjaden & Thoennes, 1998). The figure includes personal assaults against males by strangers but not victimization against children.

Those who do not personally experience violence should realize that there is a cost to society as well. Researchers have attempted to assess the costs and place dollar amounts on them. The National Research Council has analyzed the data and estimated that family violence in the United States costs somewhere between $1.7 billion and $140 billion annually (Chalk & King, 1998). Included in the estimate are medical costs, foster care, and lost productivity due to victimization. Chalk and King explain that the variation among cost estimates stems from differences in the variables selected to generate the figures. One estimate included a high set of indirect costs associated with pain and suffering. The use of different prevalent rates of violence is a factor that also contributes to the wide range of cost. Regardless of the lack of an exact figure, it should be apparent that the problems of victimization are far from personal; it affects us all.

CONCLUSIONS

The key emphasis in this chapter is emphasis on understanding domestic violence from the viewpoint of the victim. This shift grew out of complaints concerning the criminological explanations that included victims but tended to assign to them a responsibility for personal violence. The *victim movement* was born during the 1960s to address the victim blaming that occurred. The two movements outlined here are the children's rights movement and the battered women's movement. Both have attempted to remedy the lack of attention to victimization and the consequences of victimization. Social and legal changes have been the focus of both. Of note is the interconnection between child abuse and women abuse. Men who batter their wives are more likely to abuse their children as well. The witnessing of domestic violence against women is now considered an abuse against the children. Childhood abuse is a problem that has both criminal and social consequences—its prevalence cannot be ignored.

The health and safety concerns of women who survive battering in an intimate relationship are predicated on research that documents the possibility of severe injury. The physical injury due to abuse of both children and women is a significant social problem. This chapter specifically addressed the risks of injury during pregnancy. Homelessness has been defined as a problem related to domestic violence.

For female and male victims of domestic battering and rape, the psychological effects can be devastating. Numerous mental and emotional problems associated with victimization at the hands of an intimate point to the need for increased sensitivity to all victims of abuse. Gender has been the primary victim characteristic in the past, but this does not mean that men do not experience forms of domestic violence or that women do not commit it.

A new domestic relationship has been established for the victims of dating violence. Recent studies point to an alarming rate of both physical and sexual abuse within the courtship context. In Chapter 4 we addressed the conflicting information on the perpetrators of dating violence, who are male and female in roughly equal numbers. The response to this information has been an outpouring of research into the causes and effects of premarital abuse. Most surprising is the seemingly nonchalant attitude of teens who are affected by this violence. Most distressing is the current predatory nature of drug use for the purpose of gaining control and sexually abusing young women.

KEY TERMS

Battered women's movement	Restitution
Borderline personality disorder	Retribution
Children's rights movement	Roofies
Direct abuse	Stockholm syndrome
Indirect abuse	Victimology
Learned helplessness	Victim precipitation

QUESTIONS fOR REVIEW

1. What role did Benjamin Mendelsohn play in the study of victimology?

2. Can the consequences of child abuse be predicted?

3. What is the sexual abuse accommodation syndrome?

4. Explain the accomplishments of the women's movement.

5. What are the socialization factors that make it more difficult for male survivors to achieve recovery?

6. Explain the dynamics of courtship violence.

7. Explain posttraumatic stress disorder.

8. What is the Stockholm syndrome?

9. Give examples of self-inflicted violence. Why does it happen?

$\mathcal{R}$EFERENCES

Adams, David. 1992. *Historical Timeline of Institutional Responses to Battered Women, 1850–1992.* Cambridge, MA: Emerge.

Alderman, Tracy. 1997. *The Scarred Soul.* Oakland, CA: New Harbinger Publications.

American Psychiatric Association. 1987. Pp. 146–48 in *The Diagnostic and Statistical Manual of Mental Disorders*, 3rd ed. Washington, DC: APA.

Amir, Menachem. 1971. *Patterns in Forcible Rape.* Chicago: University of Chicago Press.

Balos, Beverly and Mary L. Fellows. 1994. *Law and Violence against Women: Cases and Materials on Systems of Oppression.* Durham, NC: Carolina Academic Press.

Battered/Formerly Battered Women's Task Force. 1992. *A Current Analysis of the Battered Women's Movement.* Tucson, AZ: National Coalition Against Domestic Violence.

Belitz, Jerald and Anita Schacht. 1995. "Satanism as a Response to Abuse: The Dynamics and Treatment of Satanic Involvement in Male Youths." Pp. 82–95 in *Family Violence: Readings in the Social Sciences and Professions*, James Makepeace (ed.). New York: McGraw-Hill.

Chalk, Rosemary and Patricia A. King (eds.). 1998. *Violence in Families: Assessing Prevention and Treatment Programs.* Washington, DC: National Academy Press.

Coleman, Vallerie E. 1996. "Lesbian Battering: The Relationship between Personality and the Perpetration of Violence." Pp. 77–101 in *Domestic Partner Abuse*, L. K. Hamberger and Claire Renzetti (eds.). New York: Springer Publishing Company.

Cook, Philip W. 1997. *Abused Men: The Hidden Side of Domestic Violence.* Westport, CT: Praeger Publishers.

Davidson, Howard. 1995. "Child Abuse and Domestic Violence: Legal Connections and Controversies." *Family Law Quarterly* 29(2):357–75.

DeKeseredy, Walter S. and Martin D. Schwartz. 1998. *Woman Abuse on Campus: Results from the Canadian National Survey.* Thousand Oaks, CA: Sage Publications.

Elbow, M. 1982. "Children of Violent Marriages: The Forgotten Victims." *Social Casework:* October, 465–71.

Ferraro, Kathleen. 1997. "Battered Women: Strategies for Survival." Pp. 124–40 in *Violence between Intimate Partners: Patterns, Causes, and Effects*, Albert P. Cardarelli (ed.). Needham Heights, MA: Allyn & Bacon.

Finkelhor, David and Kersti Yllo. 1985. *License to Rape: Sexual Abuse of Wives.* New York: Holt, Rinehart and Winston.

Flitcraft, Anne. 1992. "Violence, Values and Gender." *Journal of the American Medical Association*, Vol. 267, No. 23, pp. 194–6, June.

Gallers, Johanna and Kathy Lawrence. 1998. "Overcoming Post-traumatic Stress Disorder in Adolescent Date Rape." Pp. 172–83 in *Dating Violence: Young Women in Danger*, 2nd ed., Barrie Levy (ed.). Seattle, WA: Seal Press.

Gamache, Denise. 1998. "Domination and Control: The Social Context of Dating Violence." Pp. 69–83 in *Dating Violence: Young Women in Danger*, 2nd ed., Barrie Levy (ed.). Seattle, WA: Seal Press.

Garrett, Athena and Heather Libbey. 1997a. "Common Outcomes of Abuse and Neglect." *Theory and Research on the Outcomes and Consequences of Child Abuse and Neglect*, Vol. 2. Washington, DC: National Institute of Justice.

———. 1997b."Theory and Research on the Outcomes and Consequences of Child Abuse and Neglect." *Child Abuse Intervention Strategic Planning Meeting*, Washington, DC. Washington, DC: National Institute of Justice.

Gelles, R. and J. Conte. 1990. "Domestic Violence and Sexual Abuse of Children: A Review of Research in the Eighties." *Journal of Marriage and the Family* 52:1045–58.

Giles-Sims, Jean, Murray A. Straus, and David B. Sugarman. 1995. "Child, Maternal, and Family Characteristics Associated with Spanking." Pp. 124–33 in *Family Violence: Readings in the Social Sciences and Professions*, James Makepeace (ed.). New York: McGraw-Hill.

Graham, Dee and Edna Rawlings. 1998. "Bonding with Abusive Dating Partners: Dynamics of Stockholm Syndrome." Pp. 119–35 in *Dating Violence: Young Women in Danger*, 2nd ed., Barrie Levy (ed.). Seattle, WA: Seal Press.

Greenfield, Lawrence, Michael Rand, Diane Craven, Patsy Klaus, Craig Perkins, Cheryl Ringel, Greg Warchol, Cathy Matson, and James Fox. 1998. *Violence by Intimates: Analysis of Crimes by Current or Former Spouses, Boyfriends, and Girlfriends*. NCJ 167237. Washington, DC: U.S. Department of Justice.

Helfer, Ray E. and Ruth S. Kempe (eds.). 1988. *The Battered Child*, 4th ed. Chicago: The University of Chicago Press.

Hilton, N. Z. 1992. "Battered Women's Concerns about Their Children Witnessing Wife Assault." *Journal of Interpersonal Violence* 7(1):77–86.

Island, David and Patrick Letellier. 1991. *Men Who Beat the Men Who Love Them: Battered Gay Men and Domestic Violence*. Binghamton, NY: Harrington Park Press.

Kakar, Suman. 1998. *Domestic Abuse: Public Police/Criminal Justice Approaches towards Child, Spousal and Elderly Abuse*. San Francisco: Austin & Winfield.

Kilpatrick, Dean and Benjamin Saunders. 1997. *The Prevalence and Consequences of Child Victimization*. Washington, DC: U.S. Department of Justice Office of Justice Programs.

Kilpatrick, D. G., B. E. Saunders, L. J. Veronen, C. L. Best, and J. M. Von. 1987. "Criminal Victimization: Lifetime Prevalence, Reporting to Police, and Psychological Impact." *Crime and Delinquency* 33:479–89.

Letellier, Patrick. 1996. "Gay and Bisexual Male Domestic Violence Victimization: Challenges to Feminist Theory." Pp. 1–22 in *Domestic Partner Abuse*, L. K. Hamberger and Claire Renzetti (eds.). New York: Springer Publishing Company.

Levy, B. 1990. "Abusive Teen Dating Relationships." *Response* 13(1):5.

Levy, Barrie and Kerry Lobel. 1998. "Lesbian Teens in Abusive Relationships." Pp. 203–8 in *Dating Violence: Young Women in Danger*, 2nd ed., Barrie Levy (ed.). Seattle, WA: Seal Press.

Meadows, Robert J. 1998. *Understanding Violence and Victimization*. Saddle River, NJ: Prentice Hall.

Makepeace, James M. 1997. "Courtship Violence as Process: A Developmental Theory." Pp. 29–47 in *Violence between Intimate Partners: Patterns, Causes, and Effects*, Albert Cardarelli (ed.). Needham Heights, MA: Allyn & Bacon.

McFarlane, Judith. 1998. "Violence during Teen Pregnancy: Health Consequences for Mother and Child." Pp. 137–41 in *Dating Violence: Young Women in Danger*, 2nd ed., Barrie Levy (ed.). Seattle, WA: Seal Press.

National Coalition Against Domestic Violence. 1998. "About the National Coalition Against Domestic Violence." *www.healthtouch.com/level 1/leaflets/ncadv/ncadv002.htm*. 1999.

National Coalition for the Homeless. 1998. "Domestic Violence and Homelessness." May. *http://nch.ari.net/domestic.html*. 1999.

National Committee to Prevent Child Abuse. 1996. *The Relationship between Domestic Violence and Child Abuse*. 20. Chicago: NCPCA.

National Domestic Hotline. 1999. "Hotline Services." *www.ndvh.org/ndvh5.html*. 1999.

Pagelow, Mildred D. 1984. *Family Violence*. New York: Praeger Publishers.

Pizzey, Erin. 1977. *Scream Quietly or the Neighbors Will Hear*. Hillside, NJ: Enslow Publishers.

Saunders, Daniel. 1994. "Child Custody Decisions in Families Experiencing Woman Abuse." *Social Work: Journal of the National Association of Social Workers* 39(1), pp. 51–59.

Schaffler, M. 1994. *Health Care Response to Domestic Violence Fact Sheet*. Minneapolis, MN: Trauma Foundation.

Stark, Evan and A. Flitcraft. 1988. "Women and Children at Risk: A Feminist Perspective on Child Abuse." *International Journal of Health Services* 18(1):97–118.

Straus, Murray A., Richard J. Gelles, and Suzanne K. Steinmetz. 1980. *Behind Closed Doors: Violence in the American Family*. Garden City, NY: Anchor Press/Doubleday.

Struve, Jim. 1990. "Dancing with Patriarchy: The Politics of Sexual Abuse." Pp. 3–45 in *The Sexually Abused Male*, Vol. I, Mic Hunter (ed.). New York: Lexington Books.

Summit, Roland. 1982. "Beyond Belief: The Reluctant Discovery of Incest." In *Women's Sexual Experience: Explorations of the Dark Continent*, Martha Kirkpatrick (ed.). New York: Plenum Press.

Thornberry, Terence. 1994. *Violent Families and Youth Violence*. FS 9421. Washington, DC: Office of Juvenile Justice and Delinquency Prevention.

Tifft, Larry L. 1993. *Battering of Women: The Failure of Intervention and the Case for Prevention*. Boulder, CO: Westview Press.

Tjaden, Patricia and Nancy Thoennes. 1998. *Prevalence, Incidence, and Consequences of the Violence Against Women: Findings from the National Violence Against Women Survey*. NCJ 172837. Washington, DC: U.S. Department of Justice.

Urquiza, Anthony and Maria Capra. 1990. "The Impact of Sexual Abuse: Initial and Long-Term Effects." Pp. 105–35 in *The Sexually Abused Male*, Mic Hunter (ed.). New York: Lexington Books.

U.S. General Accounting Office. 1996. *Cycle of Sexual Abuse: Research Inconclusive about Whether Child Victims Become Adult Abusers*. GAO/GGD-96-178. Gaithersburg, MD: U.S. General Accounting Office.

Von Hentig, Hans. 1948. *The Criminal and His Victim: Studies in the Socio-Biology of Crime*. New Haven, CT: Yale University Press.

Walker, Lenore E. 1984. *The Battered Woman Syndrome*. New York: Springer Publishing Company.

_____. 1995. "Battered Women and Learned Helplessness." Pp. 243–51 in *Family Violence: Readings in the Social Sciences and Professions*, James Makepeace (ed.). New York: McGraw-Hill.

Windom, Cathy S. 1998. "Victims of Childhood Sexual Abuse: Later Criminal Consequences." Pp. 62–67 in *Deviant Behavior 98/99*, 3rd ed., Lawrence M. Salinger (ed.). Guilford, CT: Dushkin/McGraw-Hill.

Windom, Cathy and M. Ames. 1994. "Criminal Consequences of Child Sexual Victimization." *Child Abuse and Neglect* 18:303–18.

Wolfe, D. A., S. K. Wilson, and P. Jaffe. 1986. "Child Witness to Violence between Parents: Critical Issues in Behavioral and Social Adjustment." *Journal of Abnormal Child Psychology* 14:95–104.

Wolfgang, Marvin. 1975. *Patterns in Criminal Homicide*. Montclair, NJ: Patterson Smith.

Part Three

Legal and Enforcement Responses

The criminal justice system is the focus of Part Three. What laws have been enacted to protect victims of abuse and to make the perpetrators responsible for their actions? How did the criminalization of domestic violence emerge in recent times? Why did law enforcement, rather than social service, become the primary tool to eradicate domestic abuses in our society? What should police officers *do* in cases of criminal domestic violence?

In Chapter 6, "Legal Responses," we examine federal and state legislative action that has poured forth in response to the problems of domestic abuses. Every state has criminalized partner violence, child abuse, and elder abuse, yet little consistency exists among the states. In this chapter we look at the criminal statutes that define and prohibit crimes against intimate and family members. We discuss the civil protections for victims in domestic violence and the remedies that may be available after victimization occurs. Antistalking legislation and gun control emerge as recent components to both federal and state efforts in combating domestic violence. For the first time in history, domestic violence has become a federal concern.

In Chapter 7, "The Role of the Police," we acknowledge the pivotal responsibility that police officers have in cases involving domestic violence. Here the nature of policing is examined along with the trends toward a problem-oriented approach that is consistent with the needs of the victim of family violence. This chapter sets forth the three law enforcement goals that specifically address domestic violence, yet are relevant to the overall organizational goals of policing. Common myths about domestic abusers and victims are discussed as well as the realities that police must acknowledge when responding to these crimes. It includes a discussion on obtaining truthful information for the determination of criminal responsibility in domestic situations involving an allegation of abuse.

In Chapter 8, "Law Enforcement Response," we address the ambivalence toward the role that police have been awarded regarding domestic violence. How do the police get involved in these cases? In this chapter, mandated arrest policies are examined in addition to alternative resources for police to consider. Civil protection codes and mental health codes appear to complicate the law enforcement response at first glance, but ultimately are tools for officers to use toward resolving conflict. The determination of probable cause is critical to any police action that may involve an arrest; therefore, the officer must collect evidence and interrogate suspects. Also discussed are the constitutional constraints that law enforcement must work within in order to gather information and evidence.

Legal Responses

INTRODUCTION

> The people reign in the American political world as the Deity does in the universe.
> They are the cause and the aim of all things; everything comes from them, everything
> is absorbed in them. Alexis De Tocqueville (Knopf, 1994)

In his classic description of equality in the American political system, Alexis De Tocqueville (1805–1859) expressed the spirit of our nation that has resurfaced. Claims that the U.S. criminal justice system has been way out of balance are being addressed. Small grassroot movements that began nearly four decades ago to right injustices for victims of crime have gained significant ground. Although insignificant when weighed against the rights of the government and that of the accused, enormous changes have occurred.

Historians will someday look back on the twentieth century and judge the society in which we live today. A progression will be evidenced during which tremendous gains toward equality and protection for crime victims will be noted. The domestic social problems that are identified throughout this book and the responses to them have been well documented. Legislative responses have come forward in both the criminal and civil arenas. Never before in the history of men and women have so many statutes been enacted toward the goal of equal protection.

Strong victims rights' laws make a difference, but a question remains as to whether victims' needs are being met. It is not enough to enact statutes unless they are given full force by the criminal justice community, which is positioned to give them meaning through enforcement. Since education has often been recognized as the most effective method of bringing about social change, that initial step is being taken now. Knowledge is power—in this case, it is the power for the present generation to be successful in implementing the vast amounts of legislative amendments that seek to protect victims' rights.

In this chapter we present a brief overview of the legal codes, which have come about so fast that it is difficult to keep up with them. For persons involved in protection of the public, we provide a starting point to use when examining particular state statutes.

COURT JURISDICTION

Before we can consider laws governing domestic violence and personal relations, it is necessary to understand the complexity of the U.S. court system and the positioning of domestic violence legislation. With the recent criminalization of domestic violence, the lines between criminal and civil actions are blurring. Protection and relief from domestic violence are both criminal and civil in nature. Domestic law is now located within both federal and state court jurisdictions.

A network of courts across the United States makes up the judicial system. The scope and power of authority for each court is called its *jurisdiction*. The constitutional or statutory parameters within which judicial power may be exercised limit the court to a geographical area and to specific subject matter. One group of courts in the system maintains federal jurisdiction: It tries crimes and hears controversies that have occurred anywhere in the nation that a federal law is alleged to have been violated. The U.S. Supreme Court interprets the U.S. Constitution. As you can see in Figure 6–1, the federal court system is made up of the U.S. Supreme Court, the U.S. Courts of Appeals, and the U.S. District Courts.

Within each state are one or more federal judicial districts, within each of which is a U.S. District Court. There is also a U.S. District Court in the District of Columbia. These are the trial courts with *general jurisdiction* over cases involving federal law violations, crimes committed on federal property, and for disputes between citizens of different states. General jurisdiction refers to the court's authority to hear any case put before it that does not belong exclusively to another court. The authority to consider a case in the first instance, and to try it and pass judgment on the law and facts, begins in these courts of *original jurisdiction*.

District Court is also the name given to many lower courts of the states and in the Commonwealth of Puerto Rico. These general jurisdiction courts are sometimes called superior or circuit courts. State courts of general jurisdiction have the authority to try all cases, both civil and criminal. When a court is given limited original jurisdiction, it may, for example, hear only misdemeanor cases. Lower courts may then bind over felony cases to the higher court. Large urban areas commonly have divisions that specialize in different kinds of cases, such as juvenile or family matters. The state court system is illustrated in Figure 6–2.

Codes governing domestic relations belong in a body of law that is called *civil law*. Contrasted with criminal law, these codes are concerned with civil or private rights

---

United States Supreme Court

This is the highest court in the nation. It has the power to choose the cases that it wishes to hear, through the writ of certiorari. Cases are presented through appeals from lower federal courts and from state supreme courts on the interpretation of federal law or of the Constitution itself. The opinions of the Courts provide precedent or guidelines for the states to follow. The decisions of the Court become case law. The states cannot take away any citizen rights afforded by the U.S. Constitution as interpreted by the U.S. Supreme Court.

United States Court of Appeals

These federal courts have jurisdiction over decisions of U.S. District Courts. The country is broken down into areas referred to as *circuits*. They hear appeal from the lower courts.

United States District Courts

Only when federal laws are alleged to have been violated will the case come before a U.S. District Court. These courts have original jurisdiction in all matters of federal criminal law. Domestic violence offenses committed after crossing a state line, for example, may be prosecuted here.

Figure 6–1   Federal court system.

and remedies. Family and probate courts typically have jurisdiction over divorce, custody, and guardianships. In some states these courts have a limited jurisdiction in civil and criminal domestic violence cases. Those with appellate jurisdiction review the judgments of these lower courts. Laws prohibiting domestic violence are within the subject matter of original jurisdiction courts. For example, a district or lower court has original jurisdiction to hear the facts and pass judgment on violations of criminal law.

Federal versus State Jurisdiction

Until recently, domestic violence was not within the federal jurisdiction. One early attempt to provide federal sanctions to those who battered was a bill introduced in the

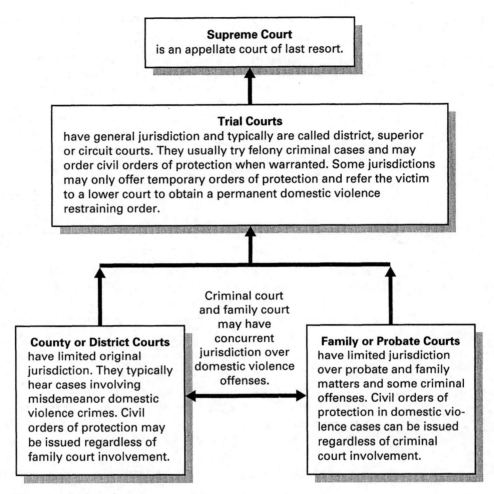

Figure 6-2   State court system.

U.S. Congress in 1906. This attempt to impose federal whipping of wife beaters was defeated. In January 1978, the U.S. Commission on Civil Rights sponsored a consultation to look at the issues of public policy concerning battered women. Many people presented evidence on the problem of domestic violence and the inadequate police response to its victims.

The first two federal efforts to assist victims of domestic violence failed in 1978 and 1979. They would have provided federal grants to states to be used for spouse abuse shelters. Legislative responsibility as well as police domestic abuse response were identified as areas of concern. Since family relations were under the exclusive jurisdiction of state courts, there was no protection against domestic violence committed on federal property. This meant that there was no federal law prohibiting spouse or child assault for families in the military and on tribal lands.

Domestic violence continued to be under the exclusive jurisdiction of the states until 1984. It was not until the passage of the Family Violence Prevention and Services Act and the Victims of Crime Act that Congress approved federal legislation to aid victims of domestic violence. The 1984 acts provided federal funding to help states provide shelters for domestic violence victims, education, research, and crime victim compensation.

The Violence Against Women Act of 1990 introduced for the first time in history legislation that called for the federal prosecution of a person who has traveled across state lines and intentionally injures or sexually abuses his or her spouse or intimate partner. Originally defeated, the bill was reintroduced on subsequent years until some provisions were incorporated into the Violent Crime Control and Law Enforcement Act of 1994, referred to as Title IV of VAWA.

The states continue to legislate and control criminal and civil actions relative to domestic violence for the majority of cases. Federal legislation is not meant to take away the jurisdiction of the states in these matters. Instead, it is a body of law that represents a joint effort between the federal and state governments to close the loopholes and provide more comprehensive protection for victims of family violence. To better understand the federal versus state court jurisdiction, refer to Figure 6–3. Travel between states is a common occurrence. The likelihood of escaping responsibility for domestic crime due to differing jurisdictions is now diminished due to the possibility of federal prosecution.

Civil versus Criminal Court in the State System

The allegation of a criminal law violation can be tried in a court of general jurisdiction at the state level. Provisions for civil protection orders when a domestic relationship exists are found in the state codes. An overlap between the criminal and civil law is inherent in domestic violence cases. Traditionally, family courts of limited jurisdiction handled relationship issues. For this reason, a person can obtain a civil order of protection in a family or probate court in addition to filing a petition for protection in the lower criminal courts. Moreover, some criminal offenses have been added to the jurisdiction of family court through state statutes. This is called *concurrent jurisdiction*. It occurs when different courts are each authorized to deal with the same subject matter within a similar geographical area.

Significant points that lead to the decision of whether a case belongs in the family or in a criminal court include:

- Type of offense
- Relationship of the victim to the offender
- Age of the perpetrator

State Court Jurisdiction

Domestic violence offenses have traditionally been state crimes. State statutes and civil codes protect citizens within their jurisdiction.

Federal Court Jurisdiction

New federal offenses make it unlawful to cross a state line to commit domestic violence crimes or to violate a protection order. Federal statutes prohibit domestic violence crimes on federal property.

The full faith and credit provision of VAWA requires that foreign orders of protection be recognized and enforced in every state as if they had originated in the jurisdiction of the offense. Some states have responded with their own statutes to implement the requirement; others rely on the federal mandate.

Federal Statutes may be used when

1. An interstate crime makes it difficult for local law enforcement to gather evidence.

2. Penalties for domestic violence, because of old statutes or early parole, don't fit the crime.

3. Release of the defendant on bond is an issue.

4. The offense occurs on federal property, such as tribal lands or military installations.

5. A civil rights violation that is gender motivated is alleged.

Figure 6–3   Federal versus state court jurisdiction in cases involving domestic violence.

It is up to the complainant or victim to make the choice when concurrent jurisdiction occurs. Making that choice in domestic violence cases does not exclude the possibility of dealing with both criminal and civil courts at the same time. For example, a person may file criminal charges in a trial court and obtain a civil restraining order in the family court. Figure 6–4 illustrates the determination and defines when concurrent jurisdiction exists.

Criminal Law.   Since 1984, all states, the District of Columbia, the Commonwealth of Puerto Rico, and the Virgin Islands have enacted some form of legislation specific to domestic violence. The first domestic abuse statutes applied only to adult married spouses of abusers, and only to women as victims. Today, the majority of statutes include domestic partners regardless of gender, age, or marital status. Case law has clarified disputes of gender, age, or marital status where the statutes have failed to do so adequately.

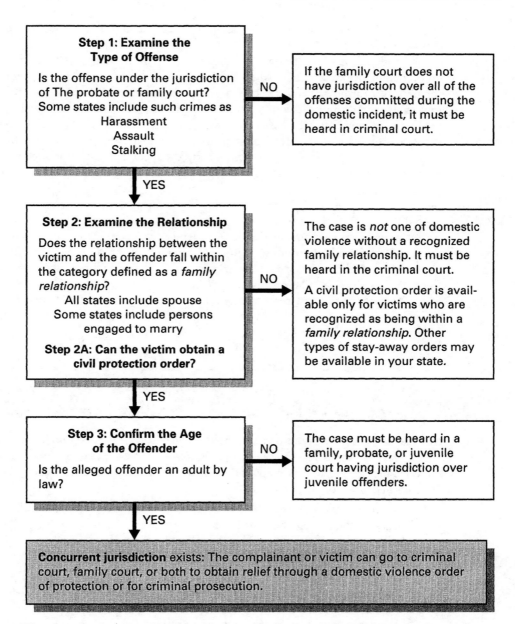

Step 1: Examine the Type of Offense

Is the offense under the jurisdiction of The probate or family court? Some states include such crimes as
Harassment
Assault
Stalking

NO →

If the family court does not have jurisdiction over all of the offenses committed during the domestic incident, it must be heard in criminal court.

↓ YES

Step 2: Examine the Relationship

Does the relationship between the victim and the offender fall within the category defined as a *family relationship*?
All states include spouse
Some states include persons engaged to marry

Step 2A: Can the victim obtain a civil protection order?

NO →

The case is *not* one of domestic violence without a recognized family relationship. It must be heard in the criminal court.

A civil protection order is available only for victims who are recognized as being within a *family relationship*. Other types of stay-away orders may be available in your state.

↓ YES

Step 3: Confirm the Age of the Offender

Is the alleged offender an adult by law?

NO →

The case must be heard in a family, probate, or juvenile court having jurisdiction over juvenile offenders.

↓ YES

Concurrent jurisdiction exists: The complainant or victim can go to criminal court, family court, or both to obtain relief through a domestic violence order of protection or for criminal prosecution.

Figure 6–4 Resolving concurrent jurisdiction. *(Adapted from the Capital District Women's Bar Association Legal Project, 1998.)*

A crime can be a positive or negative act in violation of law. Many crimes have originated from common law, while most have been created by statute. In many states, criminal violations have been codified. Each law describes the act that is forbidden, called the *elements of the crime*. Unless all legal elements of the crime are met, there is no crime.

Police action is not limited by the relationship of the victim to the offender. Law enforcement response occurs when any criminal violation comes to the attention of the police, regardless of any family relationship. For example, a drug addict may break into the home of his or her parents and steal money. The crimes charged would be breaking and entering, and larceny (or the appropriate statute in that state). The elements of the crime must still be satisfied and police powers of arrest for the crime remain the same. The penalty for committing the forbidden act, contained within the statute, does not change.

There is no such thing as a crime entitled *domestic violence*. The term refers to one or more illegal acts that are coupled with a domestic relationship and recognized though legislation. It can be confusing when specific crimes are identified as domestic through violence protection acts. This legislative classification does not exclude other crimes from being domestic; instead, it identifies those crimes that bring *additional* responsibilities and *specific commands* to law enforcement *for those crimes* when they occur within the relationship.

Domestic violence arrest laws authorize warrantless arrests when particular conditions are met and encourage or mandate police officers to arrest for certain crimes. Domestic violence arrest laws can be classified as mandatory, discretionary, or hybrid

More about It—Police Procedures and Abuse Prevention Law

Each state specifies the responsibilities of police within its abuse prevention law. Excerpts from the Massachusetts General Laws ch. 209A, §6, Abuse Prevention Law, show some of the specific procedures that are required when a Massachusetts police officer responds to a domestic abuse scene.

4.1 *The Officer's Responsibilities.* Whenever any officer has reason to believe that a family or household member has been abused, or is in danger of being abused, such officer shall use all reasonable means to prevent further abuse. The officer shall take but not be limited to the following action:

A. *Remain on the scene* where the abuse occurred or was (or is) in danger of occurring as long as the officer has reason to believe that at least one of the parties involved would be in immediate physical danger without the presence of an officer for a reasonable period to prevent abuse.

B. Give abuse victims immediate and adequate *notice of their rights* by handing them and reading a form detailing their rights. Where said person's native language is not English, the statement shall be provided in said person's native language whenever possible.

(Lehrman, 1997). The mandatory arrest statutes require that police officers make a warrantless arrest of an abuser when called to the scene of a complaint of domestic violence. The discretionary arrest statutes allow the police officer to make the decision on whether or not to arrest, but also authorize a warrantless arrest if necessary. A hybrid statute mandates an arrest in some circumstances and grants discretion to police officers under some other situations.

Civil Protection Orders.   The most significant legislative change for protection against domestic violence is the civil protection order. Civil protection orders are now available to adults in every state and in the District of Columbia (Hart, 1992). These orders are generally referred to as *restraining orders* since their intent is to restrain the perpetrator from further abusive behavior and to grant relief. To qualify for this type of order, an abuse must have occurred that places the victim in fear of imminent, serious physical harm. Violation of a civil protection order carries some penalty. The penalty for a violation is a criminal offense, usually a misdemeanor.

For an order to be valid, a magistrate, a clerk, or a judge authorized to issue such orders must sign it. It contains the name of the person who is under the order as well as the name of the complainant or victim. An attempt to serve the order on the offender must be made. In some cases, the offender cannot be located. Failure to accept service of the order does not invalidate its provisions. In some jurisdictions, provisions exist to obtain an emergency judicial order when the court is not in session. Referred to as the emergency judicial response system in Massachusetts, it places a judge on call to be reached by telephone when one is not available through the court. The judge can issue a temporary protection order over the phone and instruct the police officer to take protective measures. The victim must then go to the court on the next business day to obtain the order in writing.

As with any court order, the civil protection order restricts or instructs only one person to conform to the provisions within it. This is frequently misunderstood. For example, an order that directs Barney to stay away from Betty means that Barney alone is responsible for maintaining the distance between himself and the subject. If Betty calls Barney and invites him over to dinner, she is not in violation, because the order is not directed to her. But if Barney accepts, and comes to dinner when he is under order to stay away, he is in violation of a court order and alone must face the consequences. In many states, Barney is subject to arrest for his actions—but not Betty! Violation of some of the provisions contained in a civil protection order may be a criminal offense. Each state has passed legislation describing the portions that are enforced though criminal action and the criminal penalties.

FEDERAL LEGISLATION

As indicated earlier, Title IV of the Violence Against Women Act of 1994 was incorporated into the Federal Crime Bill of 1994. Through this legislation the government

---

Case in Point: Violation of a Protection Order

Amy filed a petition for a civil protection order against her husband Fred. The final court order contained a "no contact" provision, stating that the defendant must stay away from the victim. Contact could be no closer than 200 yards. When in the lobby of a local movie theater, Amy saw Fred in line waiting to buy popcorn. She notified him that he was in violation of the court order since he was within the 200-yard limit, asking him to leave or she would call the police. He refused to leave the theater, and the local police were called. Since Massachusetts expressly instructs police officers to arrest for violations of restraining orders, Fred was placed under arrest.

---

committed substantial federal funds to support state and local prosecutions of domestic violence. It encourages states to adopt mandatory arrest policies for abusive partners and for the aggressive enforcement of domestic violence law. VAWA provides federal penalties for sex crimes as well as mandatory restitution and assistance to the victim of sexual offenses. Interstate domestic violence was also criminalized. It is now a federal offense to cross state lines for the purpose of engaging in conduct in violation of a domestic violence restraining or protection order.

To assist states in drafting their own domestic violence legislation, the National Council of Juvenile and Family Court Judges developed a *Model Code on Domestic and Family Violence* (McHardy, 1994). The model includes a range of crimes that should be considered domestic, from arson to trespass; suggests an enhanced penalty for second or subsequent crimes of family violence; and provides an expansive list of duties for law enforcement officers to aid victims of domestic abuse. Addressing a common concern for police officers who face opposing complaints in domestic violence calls, the model suggests that officers determine the *primary physical aggressor* in these cases. Stressing that police are not obligated to arrest both parties believed to have committed family violence, the council suggests that the officer consider these points in identifying primary physical aggressors:

- Prior complaints of domestic or family violence
- The relative severity of the injuries inflicted on each person
- The likelihood of future injury to each person
- Whether one of the persons acted in self-defense

Antistalking Legislation

The Interstate Stalking and Punishment Act of 1996 prohibits people from traveling across a state line with the intent to cause injury or to harass another person or placing such a person in reasonable fear of death or bodily injury. As of April 1998, the

Department of Defense has prosecuted nine stalkers under this law (National Institute of Justice, 1998). All the stalking defendants were men, and in six of the cases, the victim was a current or former intimate, or a dating partner. Most of the victims were female; one victim was male.

The legislation was developed as a result of a directive from the U.S. Departments of Commerce, Justice, and State; the judiciary; and related agencies under the *Appropriations Act* for fiscal year 1993. The act congressionally mandated the creation of a model antistalking code to assist states in developing their own anti-stalking laws (Bureau of Justice Assistance, 1996). Key elements in the model code that emerged included (National Institute of Justice, 1996):

- Conduct occurring against an individual or his or her family members
- Multiple incidents
- Conduct that involved following or threatening behavior, or both

Recently, legislation has been introduced to amend the antistalking law. Senator James S. Cafiero of New Jersey has called for an amendment that would allow the parents or guardian of a developmentally disabled child or adult to file a complaint on that person's behalf (Epstein, 1999).

Domestic Violence across State Lines

Interstate domestic violence and interstate violation of protection orders are two new federal offenses under VAWA. It is illegal to cause a spouse or intimate partner to travel for the purpose of committing violence. The law is gender neutral; it applies to both male and female victims and their intimate partners.

In 1995, the first successful federal prosecution for interstate domestic violence took place in the Southern District of West Virginia (Lehrman, 1997). Christopher Bailey battered his wife into a coma in their West Virginia home and then drove through Ohio and Kentucky for several days, abusing her throughout. During the travel, he often confined her in the trunk of the car.

Full faith and credit is mandated by VAWA. This means that a state must enforce a sister state's protection order, even where the enforcing state would not issue such an order itself. States have implemented this provision by including the language of full faith and credit in their own statutes and codes on domestic violence prevention.

Domestic Violence on Federal Enclaves

An important void was filled by the Violence Against Women Act of 1994 with respect to military installations. Since jurisdiction of federal court did not previously reach into domestic relations, the victims who resided within federal enclaves were not ensured legal recourse for domestic violence protection (Malinowski, 1990). When the victim was a child, there was no clause in military or federal law authorizing the removal of the child. Abusers were subjected only to military authority, which was without domestic violence law. Previously, a conflict of interest existed, in that military officials represented military personnel but not the spouses who were being abused. Without domestic violence jurisdiction, federal installations had not adequately addressed victim needs.

Indian reservations represent another area where federal protection failed to include domestic intervention and legal recourse for citizens. The *Indian Child Welfare Act* of 1978 was an early attempt to meet the needs of Native American children. Through this act, Congress declared its commitment to the establishment of foster or adoptive homes that would reflect the unique values of Native American culture and promote the security of Indian tribal families. Exclusive jurisdiction was recognized for Indian trial courts in proceedings that involved Indian child custody. It also provided for full faith and credit in every state to the judicial proceedings, records, and public acts of Indian courts. Emergency removal of a child from Indian land was retained by state authority to prevent imminent physical damage or harm to the child.

Although information on the prevalence of partner violence among the Native American population is scarce, it is believed to be slightly higher than in non-Native American families. In one rare study, Ronet Bachman found severe violence by Native American husbands to be 6 percent higher than that by whites (Bachman, 1992).

Gun Control

Proclaimed as one of the most significant advances to end domestic violence, the *Domestic Violence Offender Gun Ban* was passed as part of the Omnibus Consolidated Appropriations Act of 1997 (Feminist Majority Foundation, 1997). Hotly debated, opponents referred to the ban as excessive. *Newsweek* called it "one strike and you're out" (Reibstein et al., 1996). Arguments focused on the failure of the bill to exclude police and military personnel from its provisions.

This federal legislation amended the Gun Control Act of 1968 (GCA). It makes it illegal for any person convicted of a *misdemeanor or felony crime of domestic violence* to ship, transport, possess, or receive firearms or ammunition. Selling or disposing of a firearm or ammunition to any person knowing or having reasonable cause to believe that the recipient has been convicted of a misdemeanor is also unlawful.

A misdemeanor crime of domestic violence is defined in the act as an offense that (1) is a misdemeanor under federal or state law; and (2) has, as an element, the use or attempted use of physical force, or the threatened use of a deadly weapon, committed by a current or former spouse, parent, or guardian of the victim; by a person with whom the victim shares a child in common; by a person who is cohabiting with or has cohabited with the victim as a spouse, parent, or guardian; or by a person similarly situated to a spouse, parent, or guardian of the victim. The law became effective on September 30, 1996. Application of this legislation is retroactive. It prohibits people convicted of domestic violence offenses from purchasing a weapon or ammunition even if the offense occurred before the legislation became effective, regardless of whether a weapon was used during a domestic assault.

Specific concerns about the extent of domestic violence among police officer families prompted the legislative change that did not exempt them from the gun ban. The instance of domestic violence among families in the general population is estimated at 10 percent, contrasted with an estimated 40 percent of police officer families (Feminist Majority Foundation, 1997). The GCA was purposefully amended to prohibit all law enforcement officers and government employees convicted of domestic violence offenses—misdemeanor or felony—from carrying, owning, or possession *for any purpose*. This provision, known as the Lautenberg Amendment to Public Law 104-208, has caused considerable controversy among law enforcement officers, who without the ability to carry a weapon in the performance of their duties, might lose their jobs.

The debate was taken back to Congress with the filing of three House resolutions that seek to amend the provision that prohibits law enforcement officers from owning or possessing a firearm. In August 1998, the U.S. Court of Appeals for the District of Columbia Circuit ruled that the section of the law that prohibited a law enforcement officer or soldier from possessing a firearm if he or she had been convicted of a misdemeanor involving domestic violence was unconstitutional. The effects of this ruling are yet to be seen. The ruling affects only police officers and military personnel.

Apart from the federal initiative, numerous state and local police departments have instituted policies that conform to the Lautenberg gun ban. Recent state law also reflects the trend in nonexemption for police officers who batter a child or spouse. A clear trend has emerged that will include, not excuse, police officers who commit family violence crimes.

Privacy for Domestic Violence Victims

A concerted effort is being made at the federal level to offer protections to victims of domestic violence who fear that public information will be made available to an abuser or stalker. The *Driver Privacy Protection Act*, which became effective on September 13, 1997, is one example. Under this act, personal information can be disclosed only to certain categories of requestors. Personal information is defined as including a person's name, address, and driver license number. Redisclosure of personal information from RMV records to an authorized person will remain on record and retained for five years.

Another measure to protect victims of abuse from being located is the recent policy change announced by the Social Security Administration (Fischer, 1998). Because employers, banks, credit card companies, health care providers, and many other organizations have used the numbers routinely, it has been almost impossible for a domestic violence victim to change identity. For those who flee from an abuser, the difficulty in obtaining a new social security number was another insurmountable problem. The new rules require a victim to provide proof of current abuse simply by presenting a protection order or statements by law enforcement officers or other knowledgeable persons.

In the News: Instant Background Checks

As of December 1998, the Federal Bureau of Investigation began the new *National Instant Criminal Background Check System*. Within 14 days, the system had processed 372,565 background checks on people who sought to purchase firearms. There were 3,348 gun sales denied to those attempting to purchase weapons in violation of federal law during that period. Domestic violence offenders have lost the right to purchase weapons and ammunition, along with fugitives, the mentally ill, those dishonorably discharged from the military, illegal aliens, drug users, and those under domestic violence restraining orders.

The Instant Criminal Background Check System eliminates the need for the waiting or "cooling off" period that had been required under the Brady Bill. Sarah Brady, wife of James Brady for whom the gun control law is named, expressed concern over the removal of that safeguard. On the other hand, the National Rifle Association (NRA) has filed a federal suit against the new FBI background check system. The NRA claims that the system is a violation of a federal law prohibiting the establishment of a national registry of gun buyers.

Source: Family Violence Prevention Fund (1999).

Child Abuse Initiatives

Our national concern regarding the welfare and well-being of abused and neglected children initiated several federal and state laws that provide safeguards for young victims. The first major effort came from the *Child Abuse Prevention and Treatment Act* of 1974, which required states to assign an agency to receive and investigate reports of alleged child abuse and neglect. Social service departments are those most frequently designated to receive the reports. Some state laws have since expanded their reporting system with a reciprocal reporting to a designated criminal justice agency.

The act also created the *National Center for Missing and Exploited Children*. Pursuant to 42 U.S.C. §5771, and 5780, this nonprofit organization was established in 1984. It provides technical information on missing and exploited children, offers training programs to law enforcement and social service professionals, distributes photographs and descriptions of missing children nationwide, and coordinates child protection efforts with the private sector. NCMEC also maintains a 24-hour toll-free telephone line open for those who have information on missing and exploited children.

Reporting Laws.   While the government has mandated child abuse reporting within the states since 1974, it was not until the *Victims of Child Abuse Act* of 1990 that similar provisions were created for federal reporting laws. This act requires professionals to report on child abuse and neglect for cases arising under federal jurisdiction.

Child abuse and neglect that involves any Native American as perpetrator or victim that occurs on Indian reservations must be reported to the FBI under the *Indian Child Protection and Family Violence Prevention Act* of 1996.

Child Abuse Information.   Numerous sources have recently been created on issues concerning child protection. One of the earliest and most significant was the *First National Incidence Study* (NIS) in 1974. The NIS was congressionally mandated under Public Law 93-247 and represents the periodic efforts of the National Center on Child Abuse and Neglect to gather information and analyze the incidence of child abuse and neglect in the United States. It was repeated in 1984 and again in 1996. There are immense advantages to having a comparable source of data such as NIS. The most obvious is that it enables researchers to identify problem areas that require additional support and to contrast present figures with previous years. For example, the *Third National Incidence Study* (Sedlak & Broadhurst, 1996) reported that more children are now being abused and neglected than in 1986, and that their injuries are more serious. The report identified neglect as the most frequent maltreatment activity which needs greater attention from social service response agencies.

Parental Kidnapping,   The Census Bureau estimates that over half of marriages that have occurred since 1970 end in divorce and that over half of divorces involve couples with children under the age of 18. These statistics give rise among other things to concerns relative to parental kidnapping in cases where domestic violence is alleged. The U.S. Congress passed the *Missing Children's Assistance Act* in 1984 as Title IV of the Juvenile Justice and Delinquency Prevention Act. Through this initiative, Congress mandated a national response to the problem of missing and exploited children to be coordinated by the Office of Juvenile Justice and Delinquency Prevention (OJJDP) along with the National Center for Missing and Exploited Children. A major source of information on parental kidnapping comes under the direction of OJJDP from the National Center for Prosecution of Child Abuse, a nonprofit agency.

The center reports that a family member abducted over 354,000 children in 1988 alone. Noting that the majority of parental kidnappings involve minor violations, they suggest serious consequences for the child in terms of emotional turmoil, inadequate schooling, poor nutrition, and neglect. Often, the child snatching is driven by family violence, with up to one-third involving allegations of child abuse (Klain, 1995). All states and the District of Columbia have statutes that prohibit parental kidnapping. In addition, the *International Parental Kidnapping Crime Act* of 1995 makes it a federal offense for a parent to abduct a child from the United States to another country. It also criminalizes keeping a child who is in the United States away from a person with parental rights to custody. Provisions of the act allow that if a battered woman with custody is fleeing abuse from her current partner, she can invoke the defense that return of the child was not possible. She must, however, notify her children's father within 24 hours that the children are safe.

STATE INTERVENTION

The laws of this nation are created and shaped by society's beliefs. Codes in most states address the need for crisis intervention, counseling, and advocacy services for battered women and children (Hart, 1992). This means that funding is made available for such services to victims as emergency shelters, information and referrals, counseling, and legal advocacy. Due to the high demands for services and the lack of adequate funding, those available are usually strained. Legal assistance for victims of domestic violence comes through the victim assistance programs described below. State programs providing medical intervention, school and community educational programs, and provisions for housing and employment for victims of domestic violence are among the initiatives discussed in Chapter 12.

Victim Assistance

Victim assistance programs are located in law enforcement and prosecutors' offices. Staffed with a mixture of full-time, part-time, and volunteer workers, these state-run programs receive funding from various sources, including the federal government. The services that are offered vary widely, as well as the training that staff members receive. The majority of individuals who seek assistance are victims of domestic assault, according to the National Institute of Justice (NIJ) (McEwen, 1995). Advocates provide information about legal rights and on the criminal justice process. Assistance in applying for state victim compensation aid and referrals to social service agencies are also key services.

Antistalking Laws

In response to the murder of actress Rebecca Schaeffer, California became the first state to pass an antistalking law, in 1990 (California Penal Code 646.9). In a short period of time, all 50 states, the District of Columbia, Puerto Rico, and the Virgin Islands have followed suit, and there is also the federal legislation that was discussed earlier in the chapter. Nine states—Alaska, Connecticut, Florida, Iowa, Louisiana, Michigan, Minnesota, New Mexico, and Vermont—permit enhanced penalties in stalking cases involving victims who are minors.

Arrest without a Warrant.   According to the NIJ report, 24 state statutes consider stalking a felony crime. The power to arrest without a warrant for a felony is based on probable cause, and no warrant is required. In 13 other states, stalking may be either a felony or a misdemeanor, depending on the seriousness of the action and the use of a weapon or injury. For the 10 states that classify stalking as a misdemeanor, police are specifically authorized to arrest without a warrant, regardless of any domestic violence involvement. If stalking is perpetrated against an intimate or other legally recognized domestic partner, no warrant is necessary if sufficient probable cause exists. Police are authorized in 49 states to arrest, without a warrant, a person suspected of committing misdemeanor domestic violence, including stalking.

Cyberstalking.   State antistalking statutes vary widely (National Institute of Justice, 1998). Four states—Alaska, Michigan, Oklahoma, and Wyoming—specifically prohibit stalking through electronic means such as e-mail. These statutes have yet to be tested, however. They present enormous difficulty for law enforcement in the identification of perpetrators, determining the jurisdiction of the crime, and satisfying necessary elements of the crime of stalking. They may be unenforceable or fall to a constitutional challenge on vagueness. Still, they represent the states' attempt to include all possible modes of victim harassment. Cyberstalking provisions may be most helpful when considered in harassment cases or in addition to other acts that together satisfy the elements of state stalking statutes.

Stalking Protection Orders.   A problem identified in the NIJ report is the unavailability of stalking protection orders in most states. Civil orders of protection are available specifically for victims of stalking in only 23 states. The remaining states offer an order only as an element of a protection order issued against domestic violence or abuse.

Civil Orders of Protection

As you know, protection against domestic violence is found in various forms, including criminal law (with legal sanctions), civil orders (some provisions may include criminal/legal sanctions), and health state codes. Abuse protection acts authorize domestic violence policy. Each state has defined which relationships will be considered as domestic, set forth the forms of behavior prohibited as domestic violence and denote which criminal laws are considered as violations of abuse protection, and stipulate avenues of redress for victims of abuse.

Additional provisions may include financial resources for domestic violence, such as shelters or training. Codes mandate specific duties and responsibilities of law enforcement. They are far from being uniform, however. Since the first protection from abuse act was passed in Pennsylvania in 1977, each state has developed considerably different acts in both form and content. The acts continue to change constantly to meet the demands of recent domestic violence legislation. Some states specifically authorize protection orders for children, although most allow this protection only for adults.

The full enforcement of civil protection orders, regardless of the original jurisdiction, has been mandated under the federal VAWA, referred to as *full faith and credit*. Many states have conformed with the VAWA and legislated their own statutes that include interstate enforcement. The wording found in Massachusetts General Laws ch. 209A, §3.3G is representative:

A protective order issued in another jurisdiction shall be given full faith and credit in the Commonwealth. Therefore, officers shall make a warrantless arrest of any person the officer witnesses or has probable cause to believe has violated an emergency, temporary or permanent vacate, refrain from abuse, stay away, or no-contact order or judgment issued by another jurisdiction.

In assessing probable cause, an officer may presume the validity of the protection order issued by another jurisdiction when the officer has been provided with: (A) a copy of the order, by any source; and (B) a statement by the victim that such order remains in effect.

Victims who move from an issuing jurisdiction should be aware that their order has force in another county or state. They should be prepared to carry the actual order with them at all times if they fear continuing abuse.

Victim Criteria.   To obtain a civil protection order, the victim must meet the following criteria:

1. The victim and abuser must be related family or household members as defined by the specific state code. In all states, this includes people who were or had been legally married. Although marriage is generally a factor, relationships may include same-sex or living partners. The defined domestic relationships might be so broad as to include persons who had substantial dating relationships in the past. Intensity of the relationship rather than the length is significant. Know your state code!

2. Abusive or threatening behavior that is prohibited by criminal statutes or domestic violence protection acts must have been perpetrated against the victim who is filing for the protection or against a child that the adult is responsible for protecting. Generally, any act that is illegal, such as an assault where the relationship is domestic, is prohibited. Specific examples of prohibited behavior include attempting or causing physical harm, forced sexual relations, stalking, or threatening the victim.

3. The victim must make a written application for the order. The forms are available at the court and sometimes at police departments or shelters for battered women. Called a *petition*, it must include the name and address of the person seeking the protection (called the plaintiff); the name and address of the accused (the defendant); and the specific behavior that occurred, along with the date(s) of violence for which the petitioner seeks relief. Provisions exist to protect the victims of abuse through confidentiality of their residence, school, employment, and child-care information.

4. The petition must be filed before a state or federal court with jurisdiction over the subject matter where the abuse occurred or where the victim is likely to be at risk. In most states, the victim appears before a probate or family court judge. A few, however, specify concurrent jurisdiction with the district

court. Most of the states provide 24-hour access to the courts for the purpose of obtaining a protection order. Sometimes police officers may file the petition for the victim over the telephone when the court is not in session; the judge then issues a verbal order of protection. In Massachusetts, this is called the *emergency judicial system*, and is activated when an officer telephones an on-call judge during evening and weekend hours.

Elements of a Petition.   Many states allow the victim to proceed *pro se*, for himself or herself, and without the assistance of a lawyer. The victim of abuse must go to a court where he or she lives or where the abuse occurred to fill out the form requesting a civil protection order. The example form in Figure 6–5 is from Massachusetts. It shows typical questions that are asked on a request for protection, including but not limited to these:

- The name, address, phone number, and description of the victim
- The name, address (if known), and description of the defendant (perpetrator of the offense/s)
- The age of the victim, or name of the adult who is filing for the victim if she or he is a minor
- Any knowledge of weapons that the defendant may possess
- Any knowledge of prior or pending court action involving the victim and defendant
- The forms of relief requested

The majority of states provide temporary custody of minor children under the prevention of abuse order. These states will also include questions regarding any minor children that the parties may have in common. It is not unusual for a court to require a sworn affidavit about the circumstances of the abuse in addition to completing the required form. When victims need help to fill out the forms, it is usually available from a clerk of court or a victim witness advocate. Some jurisdictions provide assistance from battered women shelters or police departments.

Forms of Available Relief.   The provisions contained in a protection order are referred to as *relief*. Violation of a civil protection order may be a misdemeanor offense, a felony offense, or contempt of court. All protection orders authorize some form of relief for the victim of domestic violence. Commonly, they restrain the defendant from committing future acts of violence, grant exclusive possession of the victim's residence to the victim and/or evict the perpetrator, award temporary custody of common children, and provide child and spousal support along with stay-away or no-contact orders (Hart, 1992). Some jurisdictions mandate the defendant to forfeit property such as weapons, keys to a joint residence, checkbooks, and automobiles. Common forms of relief include, but are not limited to, these examples:

COMPLAINT FOR PROTECTION FROM ABUSE (G.L. c.209A) Page 1 of 2	COURT USE ONLY – DOCKET NO.	TRIAL COURT OF MASSACHUSETTS

A | BOSTON MUNICIPAL COURT   DISTRICT COURT   ☐ PROBATE & FAMILY COURT   ☐ SUPERIOR COURT   _____ DIVISION

B Name of Plaintiff (person seeking protection) | Name of Defendant (person accused of abuse)

C Plaintiff's Address. DO NOT complete if the Plaintiff is asking the Court to keep it confidential.   *See K. 4. below.*

Daytime Phone No. (_____)
If the Plaintiff left a former residence to avoid abuse, write that address here:

G
Def. Date of Birth | Defendant's Alias, if any

Defendant's Address | Day Phone (   )

Sex: ☐ M ☐ F

Social Security # | Place of Birth

Defendant's Mother's Maiden Name (first & last)

Defendant's Father's Name (first & last)

D
I ☐ am over the age of eighteen.
I ☐ am under the age of eighteen, and _____,
my _____ (relationship to Plaintiff) has filed this complaint for me.
The Defendant ☐ is ☐ is not under the age of eighteen.

H
The Defendant and Plaintiff:
☐ are currently married to each other
☐ were formerly married to each other
☐ are not married but we are related to each other by blood or marriage; specifically, the Defendant is my
_____
☐ are the parents of one or more children
☐ are not related but live in the same household
☐ were formerly members of the same household
☐ are or were in a dating or engagement relationship.

E
To my knowledge, the Defendant possesses the following guns, ammunition, firearms identification card, and/or license to carry:

F
Are there any prior or pending court actions in any state or country involving the Plaintiff and the Defendant for divorce, annulment, separate support, legal separation or abuse prevention? ☐ No ☐ Yes
If Yes, give Court, type of case, date, and (if available) docket no.

I
Does the Plaintiff have any children? ☐ No ☐ Yes If yes, the Plaintiff shall complete the appropriate parts of Page 2.

J
On or about (dates) _____ I suffered abuse when the Defendant:
attempted to cause me physical harm   ☐ placed me in fear of imminent serious physical harm
caused me physical harm   ☐ caused me to engage in sexual relations by force, threat of force or duress

K
THEREFORE, I ASK THE COURT TO ORDER:
1. the Defendant to stop abusing me by harming, threatening or attempting to harm me physically, or placing me in fear of imminent serious physical harm, or by using force, threat or duress to make me engage in sexual relations unwillingly.
☐ 2. the Defendant not to contact me, unless authorized to do so by the Court.
☐ 3. the Defendant to leave and remain away from my residence which is located at: _____

   If this is an apartment building or other multiple family dwelling, check here ☐
☐ 4. that my address be impounded to prevent its disclosure to the Defendant, the Defendant's attorney, or the public. *Attach Request for Address Impoundment form to this Complaint.*
☐ 5. the Defendant to leave and remain away from my workplace which is located at: _____

☐ 6. the Defendant to pay me $_____ in compensation for the following losses suffered as a direct result of the abuse: _____

   You may not obtain an Order from the Boston Municipal Court or a District or Superior Court covering the following item 7 if there is a prior or pending Order for support from the Probate and Family Court.
☐ 7. the Defendant, who has a legal obligation to do so, to pay temporary support for me.
☐ 8. the relief requested on page two of this Complaint pertaining to my minor child or children.
☐ 9. the following: _____

☐ 10. the relief I have requested, except for temporary support for me and/or my child(ren) and for compensation for losses suffered, without advance notice to the Defendant because there is a substantial likelihood of immediate danger of abuse. I understand that if the Court issues such a temporary Order, the Court will schedule a hearing within 10 court business days to determine whether such a temporary Order should be continued, and I must appear in Court on that day if I wish the Order to be continued.

DATE | PLAINTIFF'S SIGNATURE X | **Please complete affidavit on reverse of this page**

This is a request for a civil order to protect the Plaintiff from future abuse. The actions of the Defendant may also constitute a crime subject to criminal penalties. For information about filing a criminal complaint, you can talk with the District Attorney's Office for the location where the alleged abuse occurred.

FA 1 (9/95)   COURT COPY

Figure 6–5   Sample civil protection request form.

COMPLAINT FOR PROTECTION FROM ABUSE (G.L. c.209A) Page 2 of 2	COURT USE ONLY – DOCKET NO.	TRIAL COURT OF MASSACHUSETTS

ISSUES PERTAINING TO CHILDREN

A. RELATED PROCEEDINGS. Is there any proceeding that the Plaintiff knows of or has participated in which is pending or has been concluded in any Court in the Commonwealth or any other state or country involving the care or custody of the child or children of the parties? ☐ YES ☐ NO

If Yes, the Plaintiff shall complete and file with this Complaint an Affidavit Disclosing Care or Custody Proceedings as required by Trial Court Uniform Rule IV, and provide copies of documents required by the Rule. This Affidavit and related information are available from the office of the Clerk-Magistrate or Register of Probate of the Court.

B. RELATED PROCEEDINGS. Are there any prior or pending court actions in any state or country involving the Plaintiff and the Defendant for paternity: ☐ YES ☐ NO

C. CUSTODY.
The Plaintiff may not obtain an Order from the Boston Municipal Court or a District or Superior Court for custody if there is a prior or pending Order for custody from the Probate and Family Court or Juvenile Court.
☐ I request custody of the following minor child or children of the parties:

NAME	DATE OF BIRTH	NAME	DATE OF BIRTH

D. CONTACT WITH CHILDREN. I ask the Court to order the Defendant not to contact the following child or children unless authorized to do so by the Court:

NAME	NAME

The specific reasons for this request are: _____

_____

_____

If the Plaintiff alleges that the Defendant has abused the above-named child or children, a separate Complaint may be filed on behalf of each child.

E. VISITATION. If the Plaintiff is filing this Complaint in the Probate and Family Court, the Plaintiff may request a Visitation Order. Such Orders are not available in other Courts. Regarding visitation, I ask the Court to
☐ permit visitation.
☐ order no visitation between the Defendant and our minor child or children.
☐ permit visitation only at the following visitation center:_____
_____ to be paid for by _____ (name) .
☐ permit only visitation supervised by _____ (name)
at the following times:_____
_____ to be paid for by _____ (name) .
☐ order visitation only if a third party, _____ (name) , picks up and
drops off our minor child or children.

F. TEMPORARY SUPPORT.
The Plaintiff may not obtain an Order from the Boston Municipal Court or a District or Superior Court for temporary support if there is a prior or pending Order for support from the Probate and Family Court or Juvenile Court.

☐ I ask the Court to order the Defendant, who has a legal obligation to do so, to pay temporary support for any children in my custody.

DATE	PLAINTIFF'S SIGNATURE
	X

FA 1A (9/95)

COURT COPY

Figure 6–5   (cont'd)

1. *Restraining orders.* All states except Arkansas and Wisconsin have the restraining order provision as a general form of relief. As of 1996, Wisconsin requires the perpetrator of domestic violence to stay away from the residence of the victim for a 72-hour period following an arrest (National Council of Juvenile and Family Court Judges, 1997).

2. *Exclusive use of a residence or eviction of a perpetrator from the victim's household.* All states have some form of this provision. Some states provide for the defendant to continue to make payments for the home or apartment that defendant and victim once shared even though the perpetrator has been evicted under a prevention order.

3. *Custody or visitation.* Most states acknowledge the risk to children due to domestic violence. Those that address custody or visitation in the restraining order will specify the parent who will be granted custody. Protection orders are not meant to supersede probate and family court orders for custody and are usually temporary, pending a separate hearing to consider the best interests of the child. Arizona, Indiana, Nebraska, Oklahoma, Virginia, and Wisconsin do not address visitation or custody in the protection order. In such cases, a custody hearing may still take place apart from the protection order, through a family or probate court.

4. *Payment of child or spousal support.* Many states now authorize the payment of child or spousal support to be determined in the protection order.

Each state provides different lengths of time that the order is valid after a court order is issued, ranging from three months to over two years (Table 6–1). Additionally, only the person who is named as the defendant on a protection order can be held liable for its violation. Every provision must be adhered to for the defendant to be in compliance with the order. If one part of the order is violated, the order itself is being violated. It is not necessary that abuse recur for a violation to take place.

Limitations of protection orders.   Professionals warn that obtaining a protection or stay-away order has its limitations and should not replace taking safety precautions. Although orders do provide immediate relief for the victims of domestic violence, they may only be a temporary measure. Citing frequent revictimization within two years of the restraining order, some experts suggest that they offer a false sense of security (Klein, 1998). Most abusers in this study had a prior history of criminal offenses; most had histories of crimes of violence with men as well as women (Klein, 1998).

A frequent concern in the criminal justice community is that of victims who obtain a temporary restraining order and do not return to make the order permanent. One study specifically addressed this problem, citing why 40 percent of victims failed to return for permanent protection orders (Harrell & Smith, 1998). The authors concluded that the majority of women who sought protection orders had serious complaints of abuse, yet chose not to return for the permanent order. Their reasons included these explainations:

- Their abusers had stopped bothering them.
- Their abusers exerted pressure on them to drop their complaints.
- They feared retaliation if they persisted in their complaints.
- They had encountered problems in getting temporary orders served on the abusers, a prerequisite to the hearing for a permanent order.

Marital Rape Laws

Rape of a woman has always been illegal, but until recently a marital privilege existed that prohibited men from being prosecuted if the crime was committed against a spouse. In the wake of studies that indicated a high percentage of physically abused women who were also raped by their husbands, legislative reforms have occurred concerning this crime. The crime of rape is no longer specific to women: Legislation now includes the use of gender-neutral language that also recognizes male victims of rape.

According to the research of Jacquelyn Campbell (Russell, 1990):

- Approximately 51 percent of women who are physically abused by their husbands are also raped by them.
- The severity and frequency of aggression and of injuries are significantly higher for battered women in sexually abusive relationships.
- Victims of wife rape are at greater risk of being murdered by their husbands.

For domestic violence victims, the battle to achieve legal protections against rape by their husbands has been a difficult one. Some of the first changes occurred in 1981 in the Massachusetts and New Jersey Supreme Courts, which acknowledged rape within a marriage relationship. As of July 1993, marital rape became a crime in all 50 states, the District of Columbia, and on federal lands (National Clearinghouse on Marital and Date Rape, 1996).

Force is usually an element considered in the prosecution of rape by a spouse, and some exceptions to prosecution still exist. Men cannot be prosecuted in some states if their wife is temporarily or permanently physically or mentally unable to consent legally. In 1998, five states had no provision to charge a man who raped his wife who was incapacitated and in a coma, for example (National Clearinghouse on Marital and Date Rape, 1996).

Child Abuse Protection

In every state, police officers are permitted to take temporary emergency custody of a child in need of protection. Approximately half of the states authorize social service

TABLE 6-1

State Analysis of Civil Protection Orders

	Relationships								Remedies								Violation Penalty			Length of Order		
	Spouse or Former Spouse	Pregnant or Child in Common	Stepparent or Stepchildren	Parents and Children	Living Together	Related by Consanguinity	Dating, Engagement Relationship	Other	Restraining Order	Vacate Joint Residence	Custody	Child/Spousal Support	No Contact	Counseling	Attorney Fees or Cost	Other	Misdemeanor	Felony	Contempt	Six Months or Less	One Year	Two Years or More
Alabama	×			×	×	×			×	×	×	×			×	×	×		×		×	×
Alaska	×			×	×		×	×	×	×	×	×	×	×	×	×	×	×			×	
Arizona	×	×		×	×	×			×	×		×					×	×		×	×	
Arkansas	×			×	×	×			×	×	×	×					×	×			×	
California	×	×		×	×	×	×		×	×	×	×	×	×	×	×	×	×				×
Colorado	×			×	×	×	×	×	×	×	×	×					×	×		×		×
Connecticut	×	×		×	×	×			×	×	×		×				×	×		×	×	
Delaware	×	×		×	×[a]				×	×	×	×	×	×			×	×		×	×	
D.C.	×	×		×	×	×	×	×	×	×	×		×	×			×	×		×	×	
Florida	×	×		×	×	×		×	×	×	×	×	×	×			×	×			×	
Georgia	×	×	×	×	×			×	×	×	×	×	×	×			×	×		×	×	
Hawaii	×			×	×	×			×	×	×		×	×			×	×				×
Idaho	×	×		×	×				×	×	×		×	×	×	×	×	×			×	
Illinois	×	×		×	×	×	×	×	×	×	×	×	×	×	×	×	×	×		×		×
Indiana							×	×	×		×	×			×	×			×	
Iowa	×				×	×			×	×	×	×	×	×	×		×			×	×	
Kansas					×				×	×	×	×	×	×	×	×	×	×		×	×	
Kentucky	×	×	×	×		×			×	×	×	×	×	×	×		×	×		×	×	
Louisiana	×		×	×					×	×	×	×	×	×	×		×	×		×	×	
Maine	×	×			×	×			×	×	×	×	×	×	×	×	×	×		×		×
Maryland	×	×	×	×	×	×			×	×	×	×	×	×	×		×	×		×	×	
Massachusetts	×	×		×	×	×	×		×	×	×	×	×	×	×		×	×		×		×
Michigan			×	×	×		×		×	×							×	×		×	×	
Minnesota	×	×		×	×	×		×	×	×	×	×	×	×			×	×		×		×
Mississippi	×			×	×	×			×	×	×	×			×	×		×		×		×
Missouri	×	×			×	×			×	×	×	×	×	×	×	×	×	×			×	

TABLE 6-1 (Cont'd)

State	Relationships — Spouse or Former Spouse	Pregnant or Child in Common	Stepparent or Stepchildren	Parents and Children	Living Together	Related by Consanguinity	Dating, Engagement Relationship	Other	Remedies — Restraining Order	Vacate Joint Residence	Custody	Child/Spousal Support	No Contact	Counseling	Attorney Fees or Cost	Other	Violation Penalty — Misdemeanor	Felony	Contempt	Length of Order — Six Months or Less	One Year	Two Years or More
Montana	×		×				×	×	×	×	×			×		×	×				×	
Nebraska	×	×		×	×			×	×	×				×			×				×	
Nevada	×	×	×						×	×	×	×	×			×	×				×	
New Hampshire	×		×	×	×	×			×	×	×	×	×	×	×	×	×			×	×	
New Jersey	×	×			×		×		×	×	×	×	×	×			×			×	Not stated	
New Mexico	×	×	×	×		×	×	×	×	×	×	×	×			×	×			×	×	
New York	×	×		×		×			×	×	×	×	×	×	×	×				×	×	
N. Carolina	×	×			×ª				×	×	×	×			×	×	×			×	×	
N. Dakota	×	×		×	×	×	×	×	×	×	×	×	×	×	×	×	×		×	×	Not stated	
Ohio	×	×		×	×		×		×	×	×	×	×	×	×	×	×			×		×
Oklahoma	×	×		×	×		×		×	×	×				×	×	×				Continuous	
Oregon	×	×		×	×		×		×	×	×		×	×	×		×			×	×	
Pennsylvania	×	×		×	×		×		×	×	×	×	×	×	×					×	×	
Rhode Island	×	×		×	×	×	×		×	×	×		×	×			×			×	×	
S. Carolina	×	×		×	×ª	×		×	×	×	×	×	×	×	×	×	×			×	×	
S. Dakota	×	×			×	×		×	×	×	×	×	×	×	×		×	×		×		×
Tennessee	×	×		×			×		×	×	×	×	×			×	×			×	×	
Texas	×	×		×	×		×		×	×	×	×	×	×			×	×	×	×	×	
Utah	×	×			×	×			×	×	×	×	×			×	×				Continuous	
Vermont		Family			×			×	×	×	×		×				×		×		Fixed Period	
Virginia	×	×			×		×		×	×		×	×	×	×	×	×				×	
Washington	×	×		×	×	×	×		×	×	×		×	×	×	×	×	×	×	×	×	
W. Virginia	×	×	×	×	×	×		×	×	×	×	×	×	×			×			×	×	
Wisconsin	×	×		×		×			×	×		×		×			×					×
Wyoming	×	×		×	×				×	×	×	×	×	×			×	×		×		

ªOpposite sex only.

Sources: Data from Hart (1992), Family Violence Department (1997), and Lehrman (1997).

professionals and physicians to take custody when they have reason to believe that a child is in imminent danger. Emergency removal is a temporary measure, typically not to exceed 48 hours. A judicial review is then necessary to review the action and continue the separation if warranted.

Most state statutes also authorize emergency medical treatment of a child if the care is critically needed. When a parent refuses to allow medical care on behalf of a child whose life is in danger, a judicial review may be necessary once the child's condition is stabilized. Some states provide a religious exemption for parents who refuse medical assistance for their children. An example is the following, from Wyoming (Stat. Ann. §14-3-2029A): *"Religious exemption:* Treatment given in good faith by spiritual means alone, through prayer, by a duly accredited practitioner in accordance with the tenets and practices of a recognized church or religious denomination, is not child neglect for that reason alone."

Child Victims and Criminal Law.   State criminal codes and statutes treat children differently from adults. Crimes committed against children are specifically stated offenses, such as neglect and rape without force. The majority of states have extended the *statute of limitations* for child sexual abuse and other crimes against children. The statute of limitation refers to the time that is allowed by law in which a case may be prosecuted after the illegal act occurs. Murder is the only crime that all state statutes agree has no time limit. Limitations vary widely from state to state and among crimes. A few states have no time limitation for the prosecution of most sexual offenses against children.

Under the Child Abuse Protection and Treatment Act, as amended in 1990, children are allowed to submit victim impact statements "commensurate with their age and cognitive development." Hand-drawn pictures and letters from child victims may be allowed in some states. Special courtroom procedures are allowed in many states. The provisions are sensitive to the needs of children in the court process and do not require special statutes in order to be implemented (U.S. Department of Health and Human Services, 1998c). Examples of criminal justice provisions provided by the department that are specific to child victims and witnesses include

1. *Allowing the judge to close the courtroom during a child victim's testimony.* The purpose of these statutes is to reduce a child's fear of testifying and to protect the child from the embarrassment of talking about his or her victimization. News reporters and others not directly associated with the case would be excluded from the courtroom.
2. *Allowing leading questions to be asked of child witnesses.* Trial courts have the inherent authority to allow leading questions of witnesses on direct examination. Challenges to the practice of leading witnesses can occur during trial. A few state statutes grant specific entitlement for the prosecution to ask leading questions when the victim is a child.

3. *Allowing the use of anatomical dolls in child abuse trials.* A few states have specified that courts may allow use of anatomically correct dolls to aid a child's testimony.

A wide range of provisions has been adopted to make the child's participation in the criminal justice system less traumatic. Videotaped interviews or statements from child victims are allowed in 16 states; 27 states admit videotaped deposition in lieu of courtroom testimony (U.S. Department of Health and Human Services, 1998a). Thirty states have statutes that allow the use of closed-circuit television testimony of children under specific circumstances (U.S. Department of Health and Human Services, 1998b).

Domestic Violence and Child Custody.   The majority of states consider domestic violence as a factor when determining custody of children. The District of Columbia and at least 34 states have now enacted statutes that require the court to consider domestic violence in determining who will be awarded custody of minor children (Hart, 1992). This directly opposes the past preference for joint custody of minor children that has prevailed across the nation. Research has found that children who live under a joint custody order in high-conflict families are more likely to be emotionally troubled and behaviorally disturbed than those in sole custody (Hofford et al., 1995). Reflecting the growing movement to advocate for children's rights over parental rights, the trend is moving in the direction of denying custody and visitation to spouse and child batterers.

When allegations of abuse surface during custody hearings, the court may order an investigation. Child witnesses and expert testimony, considerations of the fitness of a parent who abuses his spouse, as well as the impact of family violence on the battered spouse's capacity to parent, add to the complexity of these hearings. In many states the court will appoint a *guardian ad litem* (GAL) or an attorney to speak for the child. The GAL may also be an attorney, a layperson, or a trained volunteer. The role of the GAL is different from that of the court-appointed attorney. The GAL represents the best interests of the child and speaks on his or her behalf. A court-appointed attorney, on the other hand, will advocate for the child's wishes.

Parental Kidnapping.   Allegations of child and spouse abuse are common in parental kidnapping. The American Prosecutors Research Institute reported the need for a case-by-case evaluation and well-trained staffs to detect false allegations. Although most prosecutors in that study believed that the accusations were credible, they were distrustful in situations involving custody disputes (Klain, 1995). The circumstances under which the abuse was divulged play a key role in how prosecutors and police treat the allegations. "Parental kidnapping refers to the taking, retention or concealment of a child or children by a parent or other family member, or his or her agent, in derogation of the custody or visitation rights of another parent, family

member or legal custodian. Parental kidnapping, parental abduction, custodial interference and family abduction are often used interchangeably" (Klain, 1995).

Less than half of parents abducting are the mothers; approximately 55 percent
are the fathers (Hart, 1992). Many states consider domestic violence a defense against
abandonment and concealment of a child, recognizing that a battered parent may flee
with the child. States that allow this defense typically require proof that the parent had
no alternative other than to kidnap the child.

Elder Abuse Legislation

Society has moved forward in legally protecting elders. All states agree that this population is in need of protection, since some elders may be unable to protect themselves. Although each state believes that intervention on behalf of elders is needed,
each state defines this population differently. States label persons covered under their
elder abuse laws as those who are 60 years of age or older, 65 years or older, disabled
adults, incapacitated adults, or dependent adults. Age is a significant factor in determining who is covered under each state's statute. However, age may not matter if the
person has physical or mental problems. In some states, for example, the same law
used to protect 18-year-old disabled persons from abuse would also apply to the
abused elderly, 60 years of age or more. An elder might also apply for protection
under more than one category or definition.

The majority of state statutes include disabled persons and others within elder
abuse laws (Tatara, 1995).

Definition of Elder	Percent of States Using the Definition
Elderly 60+	23
Elderly 65+	11
Disabled	47
Incapacitated	32
Dependent adult	30

Legal Definition of Elder Abuse.   Seven types of elder abuse have been
defined in state statutes: financial exploitation, misuse of restraints, neglect and abandonment, physical abuse, psychological abuse and emotional abuse, self-neglect, and
sexual abuse. States do not consistently include all these forms of abuse in their laws;
abuses are also defined differently from state to state. For those states that have more than
one elder abuse law, the definitions can vary within state borders. Due to repetitive and
overlapping laws, there is a total of 71 state laws covering elder abuse (Tatara, 1995).

Why do states have more than one law to deal with elder abuse? Some have tried
to draw a distinction between those contractually obligated to care for the elderly, such
as nursing homes, versus the family caregiver. Approximately 67 percent of states have
one law dealing with elder abuse in both places, while the remaining 33 percent have created two or more separate laws shaped around the place of abuse (Tatara, 1995).

Legal Remedies for Elder Victims.   Significant resources are committed to ensure the safety of the elder population. The most widely available among all the states are protective services, psychiatric/medical services evaluation, guardianships, and emergency protective services. States also provide such resources as food, clothing, shelter, and psychological assistance to their abused elders. States cannot give back to abuse victims their dignity or emotional and physical well-being. However, states issue various criminal and civil penalties against their perpetrators to punish the abuser and to try and compensate the victims.

Criminal Remedies. Criminal remedies are issued by courts to punish the perpetrator of a crime and to keep society safe. Twenty-nine state laws have deemed a violation of the elder abuse law as a misdemeanor; 32 state laws consider violations a felony (Tatara, 1995). Some states have classified elder abuse as both a felony and a misdemeanor.

Criminal law suits are rarely filed since the prosecutor has the burden of proving the abuser's guilt beyond a reasonable doubt (Hankin, 1996). Beyond a reasonable doubt means that a reasonable person could find the alleged abuser guilty after weighing all the evidence of the case and finding no other possible reasonable explanation (Black, 1990). This burden may be hard to overcome if the victim is physically and mentally impaired, as is often the case.

Civil Remedies. Civil lawsuits are brought against perpetrators to compensate the elder victim for the suffering endured as a result of the abuse. In the case of financial exploitation, where the entire purpose of the suit is to recover the money stolen, it is unlikely that money is still around to be recovered. It is also hard to prove to the court how much money was actually stolen when the person who stole it was the care-taker of the elder's financial matters in the first place. As in most types of lawsuits, it is hard to recover damages in a civil lawsuit since the elder victim is of the age where severe physical injury may lead to death. These are difficulties which, coupled with the fact that most elder victims are financially unable to pay high attorney fees, make many attorneys reluctant to take the case.

In previous court cases, if the elder died before the suit was filed or completed, those injuries sued upon were not recoverable. A recent act passed in California in 1992 (Elder Abuse and Dependent Adult Civil Protection Act) has reshaped elder abuse lawsuits and created a model for other states (Hankin, 1996). Under this act, an amount close to $250,000 could be recovered if it is proven by clear and convincing evidence that the abuse was intentional or reckless (Hankin, 1996). The attorney for the elder victim has to prove that it is more probable than not that the abuse was intentionally or recklessly inflicted (Black, 1990). Since there is now such a significant amount of money to recover, the attorney is more willing to represent this victim.

When police officers are located in those states that designate some agency other than law enforcement to receive reports of elder abuse, they need to be aware of their obligation under state law to redirect those reports to those other agencies.

States vary the form that these reports of elder abuse must take. Some states require a written report, while others require an oral report of elder abuse. Since circumstances are different among alleged cases of elder abuse, the states took this into consideration when allocating the time in which the reports had to be made to the designated agencies. For instance, some elders may be in imminent danger from the abuse and have to be removed immediately from the reach of abuser.

Approximately 46 percent of all the various laws on elder abuse require an "immediate" report of that abuse (Tatara, 1995). The states differ when it comes to designating an amount of time to be attached to the term *immediately*. Some states require a report within 48 hours; others require a report within 24 hours.

There has been a tremendous move in educating the public, especially police officers, on matters of domestic violence. To ensure the enforcement and strength of all elder abuse laws, this education must be continued and extended to all professions and courts that deal with such tragedy.

CONCLUSIONS

As a society, we have always been concerned with violent crime and sought to punish offenders. Now the horrible crimes that are committed behind closed doors are recognized as illegal behavior as well. Personal actions within a family do affect the members of that family, both inside and outside the home. In this chapter you have learned that for the first time in history, domestic violence is a federal offense. An egregious act of violence on family members is no longer tolerated in the military or on tribal lands. Those who seek to escape detection for family violence by traveling to distant states are now subject to additional penalties and federal prosecution.

In the News: Elder in Need of Services

A home health care nurse isolated a 94-year-old woman from her family and allegedly got her power of attorney by illegal means. After obtaining such power, the nurse continued her allegedly illegal acts by stealing nearly $1 million from the elder's bank account and investments and by selling her home for $98,000 by forging the elder's name. Complaints were made to police on many occasions by friends, family, and even neighbors for over two years. The police undertook a serious investigation only after a coincidence occurred whereby a law enforcer, who had bought the elder's house, saw that something was wrong with the entire situation. The police removed the elder woman from where she was found, in a two-bedroom apartment with a feeding tube.

Source: Wood (1998).

You have learned about abuse prevention laws that give additional guidance to law enforcement in how they should handle the cases involving victims of abuse in a domestic situation. Civil protection orders can be an effective emergency measure to assist these victims with or without criminal prosecution. They may be obtained in either civil or criminal courts as well. While the remedies available vary from state to state, in general they provide significant relief to victims of violence.

Antistalking legislation is another new area of criminal conduct that has been defined as illegal on both the state and federal levels. You will find more information about stalking in Chapter 11.

Recent gun control legislation is both controversial and encouraging. It will take time before the dust settles on the problem of police domestic offenders; meanwhile the concern has been raised. More is needed in the identification and treatment for batterers who wear the badge. It should not be a shield that offenders can hide behind if they are intent on terrorizing their family members. They must be held accountable to the same standard as that for the general population.

Advances in technology are evidenced in the ability to conduct instant background checks on people applying to buy weapons and ammunition. This is so new that it needs to be evaluated and scrutinized closely in the future. Will it even withstand a court challenge? This remains to be seen.

Unprecedented efforts are noted in government agencies that deal with personal information. It appears that there is a concerted effort to allow privacy of information in the Registry of Motor Vehicles and the Social Security Administration for victims of abuse. Reporting laws are being strengthened on both the state and federal levels as well, particularly for children and elders.

In this chapter, parental kidnapping was addressed. Both the federal and state governments have commitments to protecting children who are abducted contrary to custody and visitation orders. Skepticism is noted, however, when allegation of abuse surfaces during a custody hearing. It is in the best interest of the children to have access to both parents after a separation and divorce, provided that the environment is safe.

$\mathcal{K}$EY $\mathcal{T}$ERMS

Civil law
Concurrent jurisdiction
Driver Privacy Protection Act
General jurisdiction
Jurisdiction
Marital rape
National Center for Missing and
   Exploited Children

National Incidence Study
National instant criminal background
   check system
Parental kidnapping
Petition
Pro se
Relief

QUESTIONS for REVIEW

1. What is the body of law that contains the codes governing domestic relations? Which body of law carries protections and relief from domestic violence?

2. What does it mean when a court has general jurisdiction?

3. Which court system (state or federal) has jurisdiction over crimes of domestic violence? When did this change take place?

4. What does concurrent jurisdiction mean? What is its significance for domestic violence in the state court system?

5. What are some of the most common forms of relief found in an order of protection?

6. What happens if a person needs a protection order when the court is not in session?

7. Give examples of the professionals who are authorized to take emergency custody of a child in need of protection. Is there any limitation to what can be done for a child?

8. How are children treated differently in the criminal court system?

9. Name some of the resources and accommodations associated with elder safety and criminal prosecutions.

REFERENCES

Bachman, Ronet. 1992. *Death and Violence on the Reservation*. Westport, CT: Auburn House.

Black, Henry C. 1990. *Black's Law Dictionary*. St. Paul, MN: West Publishing Company.

Bureau of Justice Assistance. 1996. *Regional Seminar Series on Developing and Implementing Antistalking Codes*. Washington, DC: U.S. Department of Justice.

Capital District Women's Bar Association Legal Project. 1998. *Representing Victims of Domestic Violence in Family Court*. Albany, NY: Domestic Violence Legal Connection, Albany Law School.

Epstein, Richard. 1999. "Anti-stalking Law Needs Amendment." January 17. *www.bergen.com:80/home/dis017199901178.htm*.

Family Violence Prevention Fund. 1999. *Letter to News Flash* (E-mail). January 4.

Feminist Majority Foundation. 1997. "Police Family Violence Fact Sheet." *www.feminist.org/police/pfvfacts.html*. 1999.

Fischer, Craig. 1998. "Domestic Violence Victims to Get New Social Security Numbers." *Criminal Justice Newsletter*, September 1, 29(17):3.

Hankin, Marc. 1996. "Making the Perpetrators Pay: Collecting Damages for Elder Abuse, Neglect, and Exploitation." *Aging*, 367:66–70.

Harrell, Adele and Barbara Smith. 1998. "Effects of Restraining Orders on Domestic Violence Victims." *Legal Interventions in Family Violence: Research Findings and Policy Implications.* NCJ 171666. Washington, DC: U.S. Department of Justice.

Hart, B. J. 1992. State Codes on Domestic Violence: Analysis, Commentary and Recommendations. 43(4). Reno, NV: National Council of Juvenile and Family Court Judges.

Hofford, Merry, Christine Bailey, Jill Davis, and Barbara Hart. 1995. "Family Violence in Child Custody Statutes: An Analysis of State Codes and Legal Practice." *Family Law Quarterly* 29(2):197–227.

Klain, Eva. 1995. *Parental Kidnapping, Domestic Violence and Child Abuse: Changing Legal Responses to Related Violence.* Alexandria, VA: American Prosecutors Research Institute.

Klein, Andrew. 1998. "Re-abuse in a Population of Court-Restrained Male Batterers: Why Restraining Orders Don't Work." In *Legal Interventions in Family Violence: Research Findings and Policy Implications.* NCJ 171666. Washington, DC: U.S. Department of Justice.

Knopf, Alfred. 1994. P. 58 in *Alexis De Tocqueville: Democracy in America.* New York: Random House.

Lehrman, Fredrica L. 1997. Pp. 6–25 in *Domestic Violence Practice and Procedure.* Washington, DC: West Group.

Malinowski, Michael. 1990. "Federal Enclaves and Local Law: Carving Out a Domestic Violence Exception to Exclusive Legislation Jurisdiction." *Yale Law Journal* 100(189):189–208.

McEwen, Thomas. 1995. *Victim Assistance Programs: Whom They Service, What They Offer.* Washington, DC: National Institute of Justice.

McHardy, Louis, Executive Director. 1994. *Model Code on Domestic and Family Violence.* Reno, NV: National Council of Juvenile and Family Court Judges.

National Clearinghouse on Marital and Date Rape. 1996. *State Law Chart.* Berkeley, CA: NCMDR.

National Council of Juvenile and Family Court Judges. 1997. *Family Violence Legislative Update,* Vol. 3. Reno, NV: NCJFCJ.

National Institute of Justice. 1996. *Domestic Violence, Stalking, and Antistalking Legislation: An Annual Report to Congress under the Violence Against Women Act.* NCJ 160943. Washington, DC: U.S. Department of Justice.

——. 1998. *Stalking and Domestic Violence: The Third Annual Report to Congress under the Violence Against Women Act .* NCJ 172204. Washington, DC: U.S. Department of Justice.

Reibstein, Larry, John Engen, and Brad Stone. 1996. "One Strike and You're Out." *Newsweek,* December 23, 128(26):53.

Russell, Diana. 1990. *Rape in Marriage.* Bloomington, IN: Indiana University Press.

Sedlak, Andrea and Diane Broadhurst. 1996. *Executive Summary of the Third National Incidence Study of Child Abuse and Neglect.* Washington, DC: U.S. Department of Health and Human Services, Administration for Children and Families; and the National Center on Child Abuse and Neglect.

Tatara, Toshio. 1995. *An Analysis of State Laws Addressing Elder Abuse, Neglect, and Exploitation.* Washington, DC: National Center on Elder Abuse.

U.S. Department of Health and Human Services. 1998a. "Child Witnesses: Admissibility of Videotaped Depositions or Testimony." *Child Abuse and Neglect State Statutes Series* IV(21).

_____. 1998b. "Child Witnesses: The Use of Closed Circuit Television Testimony." *Child Abuse and Neglect State Statutes Series* IV(20).

_____. 1998c. "Special Procedures in Criminal Child Abuse Cases." *Child Abuse and Neglect State Statutes Series* IV(28).

Wood, Sylvia. 1998. "Nurse Charged in Swindle of Widow." *Times Union* (Albany, NY).

Cases

California Penal Code 646.9.
Massachusetts General Laws ch. 209A, §6.
Wyoming Stat. Ann. §14-3-2029A.
42 U.S.C. §§5771, 5780.

The Role of the Police

INTRODUCTION

> Each incident of family violence which comes to public attention, each child that is
> beaten or battered to death, each wife who dies at the hands of her husband after having
> called the police for help or tried to get aid from social agencies, results in demands that
> something be done to prevent such incidents from occurring. Feminists, child advocates,
> and others plead that something be done. The question is, what? (Straus, et al., 1980)

The purpose of this chapter is to examine the controversies surrounding law enforcement intervention for domestic violence. What is the police role? Increased demands
for enforcement of criminal justice statutes in family violence and the creation of legislation to address newly recognized forms have not settled the debate on the role for the
peace officer. If anything, they have fueled the controversy over appropriate intervention
strategies for intimate disputes. A lack of consensus has resulted in practices that vary
widely from state to state. Without a clear direction on how to handle these complex
problems, officers will often respond inappropriately.

THE NATURE OF POLICING

Contemporary studies aimed at understanding the macrocosm of policing have
developed specific categories and styles to describe what officers do. *Service style* and
enforcement style are examples of the labels that have been applied to modern policing

efforts. These terms have been beneficial in providing easily recognizable patterns of policing. Additionally, they serve to educate students on professional demands and associated problems.

At the same time, the labeling of police action over the years may have unnecessarily restricted the expected range of police action. Perceptions of policing styles should recognize the reality that every law enforcement department includes any and every type of imaginable response style. Officers themselves have preconceived notions about the job and often anticipate unrealistic drama. The media and television add to the public perception of policing as a nonstop crime-fighting business. The reality is much different, however. Crime fighters are called upon to respond to the mundane and to the domestic. Service-oriented departments also enforce laws. Road patrols may be faced with violence in rest stops and from people in vehicles pulled over to the side of the road. Service calls are a large part of police work. Writing reports and making application for warrants is more time consuming than response and service combined. In many jurisdictions, domestic violence disputes make up the majority of calls for police assistance. Understanding the range of police action is not as simple as applying a descriptive label.

As the needs of society have changed, so has the recognized role of the police officer. The changes are illustrated in Figure 7–1. Is the application of the term *multifaceted* a more realistic description of the police role or just another attempt to find a label that fits? Police are increasingly expected to do all and be all—the superhero of modern day. Visions of Robocop inspire expectations that can be unrealistic. As demands increase for police officers who can do it all, the strains on modern policing show more clearly. The tensions are particularly evident in cases of domestic violence (Dantzker, 1995). Demands on slim police resources make it difficult to commit necessary assets. A major problem in large cities is the volume of dispute calls and a possible lack of time to spend with them.

Been There... Done That!

The crime-fighter role is easily attributed to the Massachusetts State Police. Having responsibility for rural patrol within the department made me reassess the usefulness of my job! An urgent call came in about a loose bull, for example. Since I'd never been trained in roping a bull, it was not the easiest of calls to handle. But it was my job to respond. How about a call for a man who was running down a country road banging his head on each tree that he came upon? That man had been drinking gasoline; moreover, he had a plastic windpipe from a previous suicide attempt. Don't police get calls about cats stuck in trees and barking dogs? You bet they do. Highway patrol officers come across disabled vehicles and domestic disturbances in cars pulled off the highway. As a young officer, I dealt with some ambivalence with the belief that my job should really be crime fighting! Nonsense: The job is to do whatever is necessary, I finally concluded.

Figure 7-1   The police role timeline continuum illustrates the changing role of police officers. *(Adapted from Dantzker, 1995.)*

1700s–1820s	1820s–1850s	1850s–1920s	1920s–1960s	1960s–1980s	1990s
Colonial Times	Preindustrial America	Industrial America	Modernization	Crisis America	Today
Reactive crime fighter	Reactive crime fighter	Proactive crime fighter	Mobile proactive crime fighter	Proactive social servant	Multi-faceted

Key Highlights

Colonial: Results of English heritage: adoption of limited authority and local control; primary law enforcement institutions included the sheriff, constable, and the Watch

Preindustrial: London Metro Police Department was created in 1829, used as a model for Boston, New York, and Philadelphia—homes of first "modern" police agencies in the United States

Industrial: Industrial revolution, World War I, the need for a stable police role

Modernization: Technology; Wickersham Commission, O. W. Wilson, and the Federal Bureau of Investigation

Crisis: Landmark Supreme Court cases, civil unrest, rise in crime; Law Enforcement Assistance Administration; need for order maintenance, crime fighting, social service

Today: Multifaceted mobile police force expected to be everything to everyone

Note: This continuum was initially designed by Dantzker as a teaching aid for his police course. It is offered as one possible explanation for the role conflict in policing as well as a quick, historical reference for the development of policing in the United States.

Specialization for crime investigation is one way in which police are dealing with the pressures of increased expectations. Enhanced education and training for officers has provided experts who respond to a variety of crimes. Examples of special units include child abuse divisions, juvenile crime units, and domestic abuse units. The trend is not limited to crimes of domestic violence; similar directions are evidenced with accident reconstruction teams and multidiscipline arson investigation. Although not all departments take the approach of specialized units, some have incorporated civilian expertise to enhance the job of law enforcement. An example is the use of the forensic interviewer specialist in child abuse investigations.

Forensic Interviewing

Of all domestic cases, child abuse investigations are the most time consuming and difficult for police officers. Interviewing alleged victims is a task that requires a thorough knowledge of children's age and developmental levels. When someone uses words that a child doesn't understand, confusion and conflicting statements result. The questions cannot be leading, encouraging the child to respond with answers conforming to what the child thinks is expected. The depth of information that would lend credibility to the child's statement is different from the needs of the social service interview. Legal guidelines constrain the manner in which the juvenile can be questioned. A new specialty, *forensic interviewing*, emerged in the field to address the concerns of the criminal justice community. The American Professional Society on the Abuse of Children (APSAC) is among the many organizations that advocate specialized training for adults who investigate child abuse allegations. The trained interviewer may be a police officer or a civilian, depending on the resources of the community.

The Problem-Oriented Approach

Identifying problem areas and targeting specific populations is another response to deal with the increased demands for police service. Described as a proactive approach to reducing crime rather than random patrol efforts (Wilson, 1997), two forms are evidenced:

1. *Programs that respond to the needs of the community.* Striving to meet the needs of the young and the old and to provide positive contact with minority groups, the programs are varied. Known as *community policing*, Lawrence Sherman identifies four significant fields in the approach (Sherman, 1997).

   • *The neighborhood watch* uses volunteer surveillance of residential neighborhoods. Involving the residents is one way to make them aware of and enabled to do something about crime. It also serves to provide police with information on crimes occurring in the community. Maintaining that police have a duty to help citizens protect themselves against crime, John Dempsey argues that police *must* turn to the public for its active participation and support to improve the quality of life in neighborhoods (Dempsey, 1994).

More about It: The Community Policing Approach

Legislation requiring police to maintain a registry of sex offenders, and to make that information available to the public, typifies the movement toward increased public awareness concerning crime. Citizens may receive the names and current addresses of convicted sex offenders released from prison. Registry information is available from police departments, and in some cases, over the Internet. Title 11, Sections 4120 and 4121 of the Delaware Code, for example, requires the Delaware State Police to maintain a registry of sex offenders available to the public via the Internet.

More about It: The Problem-Oriented Approach

The Duluth Abuse Intervention Project began in 1981 for the residents of that city in Minnesota. Funded by several private foundations, it was a community effort to combat the frustrations of domestic violence. The goal was to set up consistent protocols coordinated with the police, the courts, and the human service agency. Working together, these agencies mandated arrest of the batterer if there was injury and probable cause that an assault had occurred. Equally important was the court-mandated education and counseling for those arrested. After 10 years in operation, Teri Randall reported the findings:

1. There were *more* arrests in domestic violence, which represented *less bias*. The arrest of physically abusive women increased from zero to 8 percent. The percentage of minorities arrested dropped to a level more in proportion with their population in the community.

2. Conviction rates in domestic assault cases increased significantly. Women were filing and following through on protection orders, which tripled.

3. Rehabilitation consisted of 2-hour discussion groups that met weekly for 26 weeks. Batterers were given the choice of attending counseling or going to jail.

In a follow-up study of the project, abusive behaviors that were reported fell from 23 to 4 calls in the three-month period after completing the program. A five-year follow-up found that 40 percent of the abusers were back in the system (Randall, 1991). If the study is accurate—that means over half—60 percent were not rearrested for abuse.

- A *community-based intelligence* approach justifies public meetings and informal police contact. Meeting with residents and offering an outlet for their concerns may reduce citizen isolation from law enforcement. Convincing the public that police are concerned about the problems specific to a community might ease tensions between the two.

- The *public information about crime* version empowers citizens to protect themselves by increased information. Here officers inform citizens about the crimes they know are occurring and what has been done about them.

- The *police legitimacy* approach assumes that the public confidence in police will improve when citizens are treated fairly. Enforcers are encouraged to improve cooperation from residents through informal contacts. All of these efforts to reduce crime through education and outreach strive to increase the quantity and quality of police–citizen contact.

2. *Programs that respond to specific problems.* Initiatives such as zero tolerance to gang activity and gun buy-back programs illustrate the *problem-oriented approach*. In recognition that communities have different needs, police are encouraged to identify problems, seek nontraditional solutions, and test them in the field.

However one explains what police are doing now or whatever term is used to describe law enforcement today, care must be taken that these descriptive phrases do not narrowly frame the job of policing.

Police Response Strategies

Intervention approaches vary widely. There is no consistency on how police combat the challenges of family violence (Figure 7–2). Discussions about the nature and extent of acceptable police intervention for family violence occupy theorists, researchers, academics, law enforcement, and communities alike. In part, response strategies have had difficulty in keeping up with the almost constant stream of newly recognized categories that have emerged since the 1960s. Additionally, definitions vary from discipline to discipline. Research has returned conflicting theories on criminalizing intimate abuse. In the past, police did not have the power to arrest a domestic offender for crimes committed in the abuser's home. Another part of the problem is the lack of agreement about policing personal relationships. Unique to this form of criminal behavior are equally passionate arguments ranging from one extreme to the other (Buzawa & Buzawa, 1996). Conflicts on policing practices are as varied as the debates about police themselves.

The Role of Police in Child Abuse.   Child abuse received great social attention with the "discovery" of the battered child syndrome in the early 1960s (Helfer & Kempe, 1988). The use of police powers in child maltreatment cases has

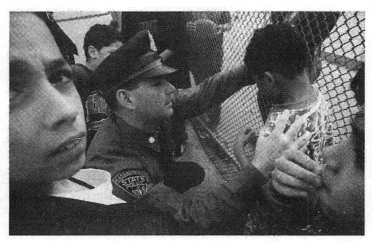

Figure 7–2 A state trooper helps a child in need. *(Photo courtesy of Mark C. Ide.)*

been surrounded with controversy since the earliest attempts at intervention. Initially police agencies were named to receive mandated child abuse reports simply because they had staff available 24 hours a day (Shepherd, 1988). Child protective agencies were also expected to respond to the abuse allegations, causing confusion on who should do what in the investigation. Despite the controversy, police administrators viewed child maltreatment as an important law enforcement concern. In a relatively short time police agencies responded through increased resources to confront the challenges.

By the 1970s, specialized police units were developed to investigate and prosecute physical and sexual abuse to children. The 1980s brought a movement toward the development of multidisciplinary teams and interagency cooperation. Thus child protective services and law enforcement have been brought together for the investigation of child abuse allegations, and this cooperation has led to an approach that is generally accepted.

Disputing the prevalence of child abuse, claims are made that inflated social statistics have invented a crisis where none exists. Parental and natural rights have been subverted to serve the interests of the state according to some, including Allan Carlson. He criticizes the current response as government interference through mandated reporting legislation that requires doctors, teachers, and social workers to report suspected cases of child abuse. "Sensing their opportunity, the Child Savers [have] returned" (Carlson, 1996).

Still other accusations reflect dissatisfaction with child abuse reporting statistics that may be inaccurate and inflate a problem, however real; with solutions considered phony; with poverty being confused as neglect; and with the failure of agency protection. Newspaper headlines such as "Experts Denounce Children's Agency" report the conflict (Swarns, 1997). Once the most widely published defender of family preservation, Richard J. Gelles now admits that our child welfare system is flawed. Preserving families can cost children's lives, he now says (Gelles, 1996).

Law enforcement investigators are concerned with deliberate false complaints of child sexual assault that have been estimated to occur in 14 percent of cases involving

Been There... Done That!

At the same time that domestic violence became a criminal justice concern, women and minority officers were making their way into the ranks. Fertile ground for specialization existed, especially for officers with special skills or education. The belief that women would be the best investigators for child abuse was a commonly held notion. One of my academy classmates was approached to take a position for child abuse investigation. Her response, it was rumored, went something like this: I hate those little buggers. No, thank you, if I wanted to be around kids, I would have some. Don't like them, don't want them—don't make me talk to kids! *Gender alone does not qualify someone as a child abuse expert. Being a man does not exclude one from doing a great job in this field.*

marital relations courts (Goldstein & Tyler, 1998). In a recent article from the *FBI Law Enforcement Bulletin*, these authors called such child sexual allegations *frustrations of inquiry*. The title is earned due to the difficulty in distinguishing a valid allegation from one that may be false. Untruthful accusations can occur from a misguided but honest belief that a child has been abused. These investigations are more difficult to solve and it is more difficult to discover the truth. The cases are time consuming and require specialized skills to uncover the evidence that will prove or disprove allegations made during marital crisis.

Day-care allegations involving satanic and ritual abuse have brought national media attention, but no physical evidence and no guilty defendants. Celebrated legal cases such as the McMartin preschool case (1983–1990) and the Little Rascals Day Care case (1990–1997) invoke disbelief. After 11 years on the FBI Behavioral Science Unit and hundreds of allegations involving satanic ritual abuse, Kenneth Lanning addressed the question: Why are victims alleging things that do not seem to be true? "Some of what the victims in these cases allege is physically impossible (victim cut up and put back together)…some is possible but improbable (human sacrifice, cannibalism, vampirism)…not only are no bodies found…there is no physical evidence that a murder took place…why?" (Lanning, 1992). Pathological distortion, traumatic memory, childhood fears and fantasy, and overzealous intervenors are among the possibilities, according to Lanning. Through all the controversy, one common element emerges—there are dangers in eliciting statements from children. The warnings have not abated.

The Role of Police in Adult Violence.   Clearly, police have the duty to respond to reports of domestic disputes (Figure 7–3). Early research has documented the relationship of family crisis to crime. In Marvin Wolfgang's 1958 study, 65 percent of 500 homicide victims were found to be relatives, close friends, paramours, or homosexual partners to the principal offender (Zahn, 1991). Only 12 percent were complete strangers. The realization that family crime could be deadly was born. The criminal justice community, under attack for being lax with perpetrators of domestic violence, began searching for a way to deal with intimate violence that was consistent with crime enforcement policy. Eager to find an answer that would suggest safety for those who responded to such calls, departments embraced the *family crisis model* (Bard, 1970). Officers were trained to negotiate with the parties and refer them to social services agencies in this mediation process.

Many departments desperate for an answer that would suggest action to the complex problem welcomed the idea that police *should* arrest for crimes of intimate violence. Social science researchers first reported preliminary results of the Minneapolis domestic violence experiment in an article that appeared in the *New York Times* on April 5, 1983. Ten days later, the same paper reported that Police Commissioner Ward had issued new orders requiring police officers to make arrests for domestic violence, citing the experiment as among the reasons for the new rules. A rush to establish mandatory and preferred arrest procedures resulted, a total

---

In the News: The McMartin Preschool Case

The earliest and largest child sexual abuse case in this country is the McMartin preschool case, which begin with an accusation in 1983 to a deadlocked jury in 1990. Today, it is a reminder of the dangers and difficulty of using children's testimony. It is thought to have been the catalyst for extensive research into determining child credibility.

The preschool was a respected institution that cared for the children of prominent local families in Manhattan Beach, California, when the first allegation was brought forth from the mother of a 2½ year-old-boy. Raymond Buckey was soon arrested and then released due to lack of evidence. The following year, police rearrested Ray along with his sister Peggy Ann, his mother Peggy, and grandmother Virginia, as well as three other teachers.

Dozens of children were interviewed and examined as the result of 200 letters sent by police to the parents of children in the day-care center. In part, the children reported bizarre satanic rituals, mutilating animals, touching dead bodies, and hidden underground passageways beneath the school. Over the course of the investigation, therapists evaluated approximately 400 children, with 350 children disclosing sexual abuse (Dickinson, 1985). Two hundred and nine (209) counts of child molestation were brought in connection with the case. In 1986, charges were dropped against five of the seven. Only Ray and his mother were tried. All of the interviews these videotaped, some of which were shown to jurors at trial.

The first trial of Ray and his mother, begun in April 1987, ended in April 1989 with acquittals on some counts and a deadlocked jury on others. Ray was tried a second time, and in 1990 another jury was deadlocked on all counts. Ray had spent five years in jail and Peggy had spent two before being released. Some jurors in the first trial stated that it was the videotaped statements from the children that had prevented them from finding the McMartins guilty, according to news reports (*Frontline*, 1998).

---

departure from the mediation approach that was prevalent. Arrest of the perpetrator when a probable cause exists emerged as the preferred response in most jurisdictions.

Reports indicate that some departments resist the laws requiring them to make arrests (Mignon & Holmes, 1995). Change is occurring slowly in others. Individual officers may not always comply with the mandates. At the same time, social scientists question and have reexamined the results of the Minneapolis domestic violence experiment.

Subsequent research has cast doubt on the use of arrest to deter domestic violence, noting that arrest may help some victims at the expense of others. Five replication studies uncovered mixed results. Arrest was found to escalate future violence for relationships involving unemployed and unmarried couples after an initial 30-day respite. In cases where the batterer had left the scene before the police arrived, a mailed summons to appear in court showed promise of decreasing repeat violence.

Figure 7–3   Arrest is the preferred
response for domestic violence crimes.

Evan Stark contends that due to the nature of domestic violence, mandatory arrest laws are the best intervention that we have (Stark & Sherman, 1994). He claims that the combination of arrest, aggressive prosecution, and imprisonment has lowered violence in a number of cities where that approach has been used. In the same article, Lawrence Sherman disagrees.

Back Then...

The *family crisis model* was developed from the classical study undertaken by Morton Bard in 1968 (Bard, 1969). Realizing that family disturbances constituted a major aspect of police work, the project tested an intensive training period for officers who would respond in the family crisis car. The month-long course was followed by weekly in-service training sessions. In an attempt to reduce injury to police officers who were dispatched, a mental health strategy of intervention was employed. At the same time, the participating officers also received generalized calls—rejection of an exclusively specialized role was a major goal. Emphasis was placed on the establishment of police agency relationships with other agencies in the helping system. Bard reported that the method did reduce injuries suffered by enforcers, and the community's attitude toward the police showed a marked improvement.

In a recent book, Philip Cook examines the dynamics of injury toward men (Cook, 1997). Urging us to avoid the temptation of determining who is the most deserving, he looks at the scant research surrounding male victimization. Female assailants against male partners show an increased use of deadly weapons, he reports, and of knives in particular. Although Cook does not minimize the violence against women, he also advocates the aggressive use of mandatory police arrest powers when men are the victims of physical assault. The police and the courts do not take assaults by women seriously, he charges.

Been There... Done That!

The years that Alice was married to William can only be described as a reign of terror. Her daughter moved out of the house at an early age to escape the frequent rape and other physical assaults that she had endured at the hands of her stepfather. I knew of the sexual assaults because of the investigation prompted by the adult Deborah. It was a frustrating experience—most of the incidents had been committed past the statute of limitations for Massachusetts. So heinous were the crimes, however, that Assistant District Attorney Anger, who was handling the case, filed new legislation to extend the period under which crimes against children could be prosecuted across the state. Little was known about the conditions under which the abuse had occurred.

Then the call from Deborah came: Would I do her a favor and come to the hospital to document her mother's injuries? The face that I photographed was so swollen, blackened, and bloody that one would swear she had barely survived a fatal car accident. It was not the first time that William had beat her bloody, and it would not be the last. Prosecution did occur, but the system was not equipped to offer any protection or advice.

Approximately 10 years later, I met Alice again. She has difficulty looking at me; the detached retina in one eye is a permanent condition, due to the numerous blows to her face. Hunched over, she finds it difficult to stand erect; hard objects that were used to beat her across the back took their toll. She walks with a cane; her legs had suffered many breaks. I remembered her telling how William would beat her to the ground and twist her legs backward around the kitchen table.

Now she is working as an advocate for battered women and felt able to tell me more of what had happened. Worse than the beating was the loss of her daughter, she related. She was still bitter about her inability to protect herself or her child, and their relationship was strained. Living in an isolated area of the state, she had taken solace in caring for her animals. Her precious dogs were found dead from gunshots from time to time. Anything of joy to her was broken over the years, including her spirit. My intervention was the first of many that were necessary for her to leave the situation. She had little strength left after the ordeal. What had changed? The *criminal justice response*. Once restraining orders were made available, she used that option. She could report the events to the police, even though it had taken years for anyone to listen. She survived, barely.

In a study to document domestic violence intervention from the victim perspective, Eve Buzawa and Austin found evidence of differential treatment by police toward male victims (Buzawa & Austin, 1993). None of the men who had been victimized were satisfied by the police handling of their assault, yet most of the female victims indicated that they were. Further complicating this consideration of the law enforcer's role is the discovery that police officers themselves have a high rate of domestic violence (Mignon & Holmes, 1995). More research is needed before conclusions can be drawn, but potential conflicts exist. What do you do if the perpetrator is another police officer? The answer is simple: The response is the same as with any other domestic dispute.

The Role of Police in Elder Abuse.   Protecting the elderly is a new concept without proven methods or consistent policies (Figure 7–4). Given the increasing population of elder citizenry, the need to establish acceptable police practices is imperative. This is the only form where few disputes on police intervention exist so far. A major difference between this population and the others is a perceived incompetence that may not be valid. Some victims who are in fact capable may appear unable to make decisions to protect themselves, and officers often proceed on that

Figure 7–4   The elder population deserves to be treated with respect. *(Photo courtesy of the Administration on Aging.)*

false assumption. Elders retain the right to participate in the decision making when offenses against them are being investigated.

There is no doubt that spouse abuse exists among the elderly, demonstrated in cases of abuse that have been on going for decades (Wolf et al., 1984). Remembering that spousal abuse perpetrators are as likely to be female as male (Straus et al., 1980), enforcers should keep the protection of the victim as their primary objective. For those who regard their responsibilities to children and grandchildren highly, the maltreatment of the elderly should be considered along lines similar to those of other forms of domestic abuse. Older persons have been identified as particularly vulnerable to financial exploitation, and care must be taken to determine if they willingly and knowingly parted with their resources or if they were duped.

LAW ENFORCEMENT GOALS

Public awareness of the various forms of violence has risen due to research efforts coupled with media coverage of the events. Their existence was not a revelation to the law enforcement community, however. Police frequently encountered intimate violence, and discussions within that community are long-standing. What has changed is the availability of information on the causes and effects of family violence as well as its estimated frequency. Consistent with the movement toward problem-oriented law enforcement response (Wilson, 1997) in addition to our historical tendency to criminalize objectionable behavior (Biggs et al., 1995), policing goals have developed.

The signs and symptoms of domestic violence in differing populations have been covered in previous chapters. The recognition of abuse and neglect plays a significant part in determining appropriate responses. What is criminal justice trying to accomplish? The primary goals for law enforcement in responding to domestic violence are: (1) to protect the victim, (2) to determine if a crime has been committed, and if so, (3) to provide a basis for successful prosecution for the crime(s).

Goal 1: Protect the Victim

When police are confronted with stranger violence, the victim is readily apparent. That is not the case with domestic offenses. Common myths prevail with expectations that the victim and the perpetrator can easily be identified. Myths about the reliability of the witness are usual. Here are some of these misconceptions.

Victims: Myth and Reality

- *Myth:* The victim of domestic violence is the passive one in the relationship.
- *Reality:* The couple may appear to be mutually combative at the time of intervention. They may both lash out at anyone trying to help them. To determine who is the primary aggressor, it is necessary to defuse the anger and interview both parties without prejudice. There is no proper way for a

victim to act. Victims may be either passive or aggressive. Victims often appear defensive. Determining who threw the first blow and why is one way to attach responsibility.

- *Myth:*   The police will find the victim more likable than the perpetrator.
- *Reality:*   Often, the victims of abuse will be interviewed when they are in crisis. Frustrations, anger, fear, and shame are just some of the emotions that they might be experiencing. The mix of emotions may cause the victim to yell and scream at the person attempting to intervene. It is conceivable that the victim will be the least "likable" of the people in a domestic violence situation. An objective interview will not be based on the sympathies of the interviewer toward any party.
- *Myth:*   The victim will be grateful for help.
- *Reality:*   Although some victims will be very grateful, that is not always the case. Past experience with ineffective interventions may cause a victim to resent interference. Recent studies have suggested that when the police arrest the perpetrator, it may lead to an increase in violence in some populations (Buzawa & Buzawa, 1996). Presumptive prosecution could render the victim without any control of future events after an initial intervention. For the person who is dependent on the abuser for economic or emotional support, criminal justice barging in is not welcome, and the one intervening should not expect gratitude.
- *Myth:*   The woman is always the victim.
- *Reality:*   Domestic abuse victims can be of either gender and of any age. The victim is the injured party; most often that is the woman, but not always. Determining the harm can be complex and at times goes beyond a simple physical assault. Injury may be due to defense posturing. The police officer is guided by legislation that dictates the manner and extent of law enforcement action in domestic violence. Your state may not recognize same-sex domestic violence or marital rape. Policy and law must guide the officer.

Perpetrator: Myth and Reality

- *Myth:*   Perpetrators of domestic violence are mean and nasty people.
- *Reality:*   For the "family-only" type of abuser (Rucinski, 1998), the face that is presented to the outside world is of charm and humor. These offenders are often skilled in control and manipulation. They may control themselves and attempt to manipulate officials as well. This perpetrator is just as likely to be the more calm and sweet-tempered of the two when faced with police officers. Alternatively, a generally aggressive abuser will be more apt to remain violent during intervention (Rucinski, 1998).
- *Myth:*   Abusers are lowlifes and uneducated people.

- *Reality:*   The perpetrator may be the pillar of the community and have a high level of education. Such abusers will attempt to explain away their behaviors, often in front of a passive victim. Abusers know that it is in their best interest to befriend the interviewer, and they do tend to act in their best interest.
- *Myth:*   "She asked for it."
- *Reality:*   The perpetrator may feel justified in using physical force due to a precipitating event. This does not excuse or justify violence other than for self-defense. It is a crime to use physical violence against another, regardless of the personal relationship that exists.
- *Myth:*   Only women can be raped.
- *Reality:*   A forced sex act can be perpetrated against a woman, a man, or a child. The operative word is *force*—a nonconsensual sex act committed with force is rape.

Witnesses: Myth and Reality

- *Myth:*   Witness information is the best evidence.
- *Reality:*   Witness statements are often the most unreliable of evidence and should be supported with additional proof whenever possible. This is as important in domestic violence as with any other crime. To decide if statements can be relied upon, it is imperative that the motives for offering information be explored. This is not to suggest that a witness will purposefully lie about what he or she has seen but that a witness's perception may be inaccurate or lacking. The witness should not be treated like a suspect; some people simply become nervous when confronted by police officers. Treating the witness with respect can improve his or her willingness to be helpful. Determine if there is a relationship between the witness and either party in a domestic dispute. Find out if there is any prejudice against one or the other on the part of the witness. How the witness came to have the information is another area worth exploring.
- *Myth:*   Witness statements will always be voluntary.
- *Reality:*   There are a number of barriers to obtaining accurate information from a witness. Reluctance to give a statement could be due to a fear of reprisal or hesitation in getting involved. A witness who is related or a friend may not want to get anyone in trouble. The witness may also be dependent emotionally or economically on one or both in the relationship, such as a child or elder.

Prevention Strategies.   Efforts aimed at preventing domestic violence can be grouped into three categories: prevention, protection, and response. Interagency coordination of services has surfaced as an ideal prevention approach. However, implementing strategies for new or better procedures may be hampered by competing agency goals. Police often need specific information on improving investigative techniques, and social agencies seek to determine trends for service direction. The need for greater involvement of police personnel has been identified as essential in attempting to develop an integrated community response to domestic violence (Holmes & Headley, 1995).

Community efforts are more responsive to particular needs but fail to provide consistency in police services across the nation. The police officers' role in prevention has taken on a new and expanded meaning because of their involvement in domestic disputes. The way that police officers respond to domestic dispute calls has an impact on future domestic violence. In a recent report to Congress, Lawrence Sherman argued that *the effects of police on crime are complex, and often surprising*. "Perceptions of police legitimacy is believed to strongly affect citizen willingness to obey the law. Reanalysis of the Milwaukee Domestic Violence Experiment found that repeat domestic violence was lowest among arrestees who thought police had treated them respectfully; a powerful effect on recidivism was associated with police who simply took the time to listen to the offender's side of the story. Police themselves, Sherman maintains, create a risk factor for crime simply by failing to treat citizens with respect!" (Sherman, 1997).

Criminal justice and other professionals are repeatedly in the position to identify high-risk households. The information needs to be passed on to the agencies that can respond with services once a genuine suspicion has been documented that a child is in need. Mandated reporting legislation requires police to report severe abuse and neglect to child protection services. Too often, officers are frustrated when a report is filed and no action occurs. Feelings of disappointment and frustration are at the root of an officer's future noncompliance in reporting. To enable follow-up on the initial actions, current practices should require a duplicate copy to be filed with the police department and used to document service agency culpability.

Additionally, departments themselves often fail to validate the time that officers spend for domestic investigations, which includes making referrals or filing mandated reports. A weekly or monthly activity report frequently requires officers to list the number of traffic tickets issued and arrests that they have made during a specified period. The practice serves a number of important functions. First, it makes officers accountable in a manner consistent with police department goals. Second, it identifies for the officers the work that will be recognized as *legitimate* use of their time. Since referrals are legally required of police, they must be identified as justifiable efforts and included in activity documentation. Changes must be accompanied by clearly defined incentives and rewards for the officers involved in crisis interventions (Bard, 1973).

The role of the police does not stop with simply making a report, however, and follow-up is suggested. Prevention of death and severe injury to children is a concern that cannot be delegated to a social service organization and forgotten. Frequent home visits can reduce child abuse and injury to children aged 0 to 2, according to the Sherman report, and law enforcement officers are some of the "other professionals" involved. In some cases it would be appropriate to contact parallel community services that might offer aid to the family and reduce the risk to the child. Home health aides, visiting nurses' associations, local crisis centers, YMCA, or family members could be included when appropriate. Supervisors who charge police personnel with identifying community services, establishing relationships with these agencies, and following through using available resources will arm officers with the tools needed for prevention.

Protection Efforts.   Increased protection for victims of violence is evidenced through a number of initiatives across the country that are the combined effort of government and civilian organizations; here are just a few examples.

Batterer Counseling. EMERGE, the first counseling program for men who batter, was founded in 1977. Similar programs have since been developed in an effort to modify the violent behavior evidenced by men who commit domestic violence. Gay men have joined counseling groups since the first was formed at MOVE in San Francisco in 1987.

Court Advocacy. The courts are an intimidating place for victims of crime. The forms necessary to request a civil protection or restraining order are confusing. On top of that, many victims cannot afford to hire an attorney to help with the process. The victim/witness assistance program was developed to address these needs. Typically referred to as an *advocate*, the victim/witness assistant does not work for the court, but for the victim. Fines collected from those who are convicted criminals pay their salaries. The men and women can be found in most courthouses across the nation. Advocates provide a variety of victim-related services that had been ignored previously. They will instruct the victim or witness on the procedure itself, telling the person when she or he is required for court appearances. Frequently accompanying victims into court, advocates also track the case and provide updates for the victim.

Due to increased demands for advocate services, some jurisdictions have difficulty in arranging for assistance in filing abuse complaints. Volunteers and paid professionals from battered women shelters may supplement the advocate services with their own staff. College internship programs can arrange for appropriate undergraduate and graduate students to provide services as well.

Protection Order Confidentiality. When filing for a court order of protection, the victim can request that his or her name, telephone number, and address not be made part of the public record. This is standard procedure for those who fear for their safety.

Victim Services. The first rape crisis center opened in 1971; by 1976, over 400 programs for battered women and rape victims existed. Support groups for lesbian battered women first emerged in Seattle in 1985.

Victim Shelters. The first battered women's shelter in the United States opened in St. Paul in 1973. Since then, the need for emergency shelters has been proven. The establishment of shelters for battered women has been supported partly through legislative funding. For those able to use this emergency measure, it provides a temporary safe haven from abuse. Only a handful of shelters exist for battered men. Most recently, a shelter for abused gay men has opened in California (Anon., 1998).

Voter Registration Confidentiality. Victims of domestic violence and of sexual assault may request that their names and addresses be kept confidential on certain public lists. A police chief must supply the victim with an affidavit saying that the person qualifies to have his or her name omitted from annual street lists and the annual register of voters. This allows victims to participate in the voting process without fearing that their vital information will be accessible to their attackers. A sample affidavit is shown in Figure 7–5.

Weapons Confiscation and Gun Ban. The Lautenberg Gun Ban was passed in 1996 as part of the Omnibus Spending Bill. It prohibits anyone convicted of a domestic violence misdemeanor crime from carrying a gun. Under its provisions, officers are obligated to seize the guns and gun permits from all persons convicted of misdemeanor domestic violence.

For High-Crime Hot Spots: Extra Police Patrols. Drug and gang task forces are two examples where police have provided extra patrols for prevention of crime. The practice is beneficial in preventing crime, according to Sherman. Providing additional police patrols to high-prone areas of domestic violence is as valid as it is for combating car theft, and domestic violence is much more prevalent.

Lawrence Sherman maintains that *the more focused the police strategy, the more likely it is to prevent crime.* "Merely increasing police force strength does not prevent crime. Adequate numbers of police utilized for directed patrols, proactive arrests and problem-solving at high-crime hot spots have shown substantial evidence of crime prevention" (Sherman, 1997). Conclusions drawn from the report to Congress include making on-scene arrests for domestic abusers who reside in neighborhoods where most households have an employed adult; and mailing arrest warrants to suspects who leave the domestic violence scene before police arrive (Sherman et al., 1998).

Response.   Does a person retain the right to personal protection by the government even when it involves violence perpetrated from within the family? That question has been answered with the legislative changes that put a duty to respond to domestic violence on the shoulders of law enforcement. The rights of the family no longer supersede the rights of the individual. Equal protection must be provided regardless of the victim's relationship to the perpetrator. Attitudes based on gender and age bias add another dimension to the complexity of domestic violence response. Appropriate police responses are now outlined through legislation, without regard to the age or the gender of the perpetrator.

In earlier chapters, theories that would help to explain why equal protection was not afforded were put forth. Patriarchy rooted in perceptions of male supremacy is

Voter Registration Confidentiality Law

SAMPLE AFFIDAVIT

In accordance with the provisions of Chapter 87 of the Acts of 1998, _____

I, _____ do solemnly swear that the party

named below is duly entitled to have certain information withheld from the public pursuant

to Massachusetts General Laws, C. 265, §24C.

_____ a resident of _____ in the
         (named party)   (city/town)

Commonwealth of Massachusetts.

Executed on _____, _____ in the
               (date)   (city/town)

Commonwealth of Massachusetts.

I declare under the penalty of perjury that the foregoing is true and correct.

_____ of _____
    (Signature of Colonel/designee)   (city/town)

Commonwealth of Massachusetts

Figure 7–5   Victims of domestic violence and sexual assault may ask that their addresses be kept confidential on certain public lists. This is a sample affidavit for voter registration confidentiality.

one common reason for historical noncompliance in providing police protection. From what began as the right of the husband or father to "police" his family developed a police liability for failure to respond to all domestic violence. What was once understood as a property issue has developed into a personal rights concern.

Exigency provides the legal reasoning that allows officers to enter and to arrest people in their homes. Excuses for lack of intervention can no longer be tolerated. The question remains how far our society is willing to commit police involvement in areas that include personal choice decisions where harm may result.

Goal 2: Determine If a Crime Has Been Committed

Using the standard of probable cause, determine if a crime has been committed. This *sounds* easy to someone who has never been in the position to determine culpability in an intimate dispute or family violence accusation. The reality here is that the determination takes time—facts must be gathered in a neutral and unbiased manner. The primary objective of interviewing is to gather *truthful* information (Figure 7–6). With this in mind, the interviewer must determine the best method of obtaining as much detail as possible in order to evaluate the truthfulness and objectivity of the person under scrutiny, whether he or she be a victim, a perpetrator, or a witness (Figure 7–7).

Interviewing the Adult.   The best method is to separate the parties and question them individually after a brief cooling-down period. The interviews should be outside the hearing range of the other, with equal levels of respect afforded to each. For crimes by intimates, the process may be a long one. Sufficient time to assess the

Figure 7–6   The primary objective of interviewing is to obtain truthful information. *(Photo courtesy of Mark C. Ide.)*

Figure 7-7   The interviewer must obtain as much detail as possible. *(Photo courtesy of Mark C. Ide.)*

situation involves skillful interviewing and the desire to be thorough. There is no quick resolution of a domestic dispute. The practice of "arrest everyone" punishes rather than protects the victim and is contrary to the first goal.

The three basic phases to the interview process are preparation, establishment of the psychological content, and the actual questioning. Obtaining information for the dispatcher or from officers on the scene satisfies the preparation stage. If the interview is staged at the convenience of the officer rather than a result of crisis intervention, additional preparation would include contacting agencies that have previously been involved. Record checks and witness interviews would also be considered part of the necessary preparation.

The second phase contains the extremely important element of *rapport*, which describes the relationship established between the interviewer and the interviewee. This relationship can be constructed or destroyed within seconds if the responder shows distaste, distrust, or condemnation of the person who is confronted. Evidenced bias such as asking the woman what she did to provoke an attack, or assuming that a blood-soaked man was the abuser are examples of what breaks down rapport and inhibits information that would benefit the officer and facilitate a resolution. Victim cooperation is consistently tied to officer attitudes. Look at the evidence and question both parties without prejudice. If a victim does not believe that he or she will get fair treatment from the officer, the person won't bother to try. If victims won't give information, you can't proceed.

The third phase is the actual questioning. In addition to questions about the incident under investigation, a *risk assessment* must be made. To determine the level of danger the batterer presents, the following key points should be addressed:

1. *Does the suspect believe the victim is attempting to end the relationship?* This is when the majority of killings take place. The most dangerous period for the victim is when the batterer realizes that this time the victim is really going through with the breakup.

2. *Does the suspect possess weapons?* This question must be asked in all situations. Guns, knives, nunchaku, and any other weapons should be confiscated if possible, even if they have not been used against the victim. If they have been used before, the danger for the victim is much greater. Threats to use weapons, even if they were not carried out, are just as serious as when a weapon has been displayed.

3. *Does the suspect abuse alcohol or drugs?* The batterer who is also a substance abuser is at increased risk of committing a dangerous or lethal assault.

4. *Were threats made?* Threats to kill the victim and/or the children and/or to commit suicide must be taken seriously. Batterers do not commonly kill themselves without first attempting to kill at least one family member.

5. *Has the suspect committed any previous sexual assaults against the victim?* Previous sexual assaults are indicators that the batterer is almost twice as likely to commit a dangerous act of violence against the victim.

6. *Has the suspect been following the victim?* Stalking, reading the victim's mail, listening in on phone calls, or other acts of surveillance should be considered an implied threat.

7. *What are the frequency and severity of the violence?* The best predictor of future violence is past violence. Frequent violence (two or three times per month or more) or severe violence (requiring hospitalization) places the victim in a high-risk category.

8. *Is the batterer depressed or suffering from mental health problems?* Some mental health problems are linked to increased propensity to commit a lethal assault. Look for delusional fears and for severe depression.

When the allegations involve child abuse or neglect, the investigator must talk with the caretaker(s). The Department of Health and Human Services (Pence & Wilson, 1992) suggests that the caretaker be asked for an explanation for any child injury. An assessment of the match between the injuries and the explanations offered by an adult caretaker might become critical during the investigation. To maximize the information, be careful not to acknowledge the impropriety of caretaker actions and to remain nonjudgmental.

Researchers using cognitive psychology have identified a specific technique for memory retrieval. Known as the *cognitive interview*, the procedure is believed to increase the amount of correct information obtained from a wide range of eyewitnesses without producing a higher percentage of inaccurate information (Geiselman & Fisher, 1985). This interview method involves a three-phase procedure. Rapport development, techniques for eliciting information, and finally clarification by the witness are incorporated into the structured plan to increase reported information. Originally developed for adult interviewing, the technique has been applied successfully for eliciting statements from children as well (Geiselman et al., 1992).

Interviewing the Child.   Some children are no strangers to juvenile, criminal, and family courts. As victims, perpetrators, and co-conspirators, they are routinely interviewed. Although courts are afforded wide discretion in modifying some trial practices to accommodate the special needs of children (Stearns, 1998), children's competency and credibility are usually an issue. State practice on how the judge may modify the trial varies, as does the determination of competency itself. Any interview of a child should be conducted in anticipation of future legal challenge on competency and credibility.

1. *Competency: Who makes the determination?* In 1974, the revised Federal Rules of Evidence abolished the competency rule for trials in federal courts, a trend that most but not all states follow (Sagatun & Edwards, 1995). Thirteen states presume that children over age 10 are competent, and 18 states require a demonstration that the child understands the nature and obligation of the oath to tell the truth. A judge conducts competency hearings in those states where no presumption exists or the age of the child dictates.

   The U.S. Supreme Court considered whether a judge could modify the procedures of a competency hearing to accommodate children for the first time in *Kentucky v. Stincer* (1987). The Court decided that a defendant being excluded from a hearing to determine competency did not violate the accused's right to confrontation. States are free to establish their own procedures based on this ruling.

   The language and definitions used to determine competency are often vague and general in nature. The Massachusetts General Laws (ch. 233, §20) illustrate this, stating that a person of "sufficient understanding" is competent to testify. A two-prong test is then used to determine (1) the child's general capacity and ability to remember and give expression and (2) whether the child understands the difference between truth and falsehood and his or her obligation to tell the truth (Stearns, 1998).

2. *Credibility: What is it?* For states that presume competence, juries are left to determine the *credibility* (believability) of the child witness. Other models decide through the competency hearing if the testimony will be allowed. Investigators must establish credibility before submitting a case for trial, and that process can be a difficult one. Because children differ from adults in their ability to remember and recount events accurately, controversy regarding child statements exists. Debate on the reliability of child statements escalated

with the failed McMartin preschool case in California during the late 1980s (*People v. Buckey*, 1984). The case prompted an outpouring of research into the cognitive and communicative abilities of children and their suggestibility to provide misleading or inaccurate information. A number of suggestions for effective interviewing and specific techniques when questioning children followed, putting greater responsibility on the investigator to ensure truthful statements.

Videotaping Child Interviews. As illustrated, videotaping can be destructive to a case. Some experts suggest that routinely videotaping investigative interviews with children is not in their best interests and is counterproductive to prosecution (Stern, 1992). Others advocate the tremendous advantages of the approach (Berliner, 1992). The controversy considers some of the points discussed below.

1. *Does this method provide an accurate documentation of the victim's account of the crime?* It depends on the technology used as well as the skill of the interviewer. Taping only provides verification of what happens during that session. It may not record when voices are too low to be heard. Common problems result from human error, such as failure to put a tape in the machine or to recharge the batteries so that the interview is only partially recorded.

    Taping will document when a child refuses to talk and serve to illustrate inconsistencies in a prior or subsequent statement. It does not guard against attacks about what was said before the interview began and how the child was prepared for the taping. Questions asked during the interview can and will be scrutinized in the future.

    Alternative methods of documenting the statement are available, such as audio taping, note taking, or having the interview witnessed by a third party. The National Center for Prosecution of Child Abuse suggests that video and audio taping of child interviews should be carefully considered and agreed upon by a multidisciplinary team (Marx, 1992). Due to concerns as to the suggestibility of children, taping can be an appropriate way to demonstrate that the process was not leading or suggestive to the child witness, assuming that the professional is trained properly to interview children. The Center for Child Protection has been using videotaping in conducting interviews with suspected victims of abuse since 1983. In part, they state: "Interviewers who are properly trained and who conduct themselves in a professionally responsible manner can benefit from this. The videotape can stand as a rebuttal to allegations that the interviewer coached, coerced, or intimidated a child into making abuse allegations" (Davies et al., 1996).

    Professionals who routinely interview children as to suspected abuse and neglect can attest to the fact that words alone cannot adequately describe the impact of abuse to a child. While revealing the details of abuse, the body language, facial expressions, and physical demonstrations by the victim can be as illuminating as the disclosure itself. The videotaping preserves this account and freezes the abuse within the time frame of disclosure. The child who testifies is often more mature and will present differently in the years after the abuse has been documented, when the case finally comes to trial.

2. *How can an investigator use a videotaped statement?* Tapes can provide a valuable training tool to sharpen interviewing skills (Davies et al., 1996). Routinely used as a training method for forensic interviewers, an interview can be scrutinized to improve techniques and develop appropriate questions for future interviewing.

   Children who divulge abuse during a videotaped interview provide the investigator with an important tool for interrogation that should not be overlooked. Although this point is unexamined by research, the practice is probably more frequent than suspected. Confrontation of the perpetrator should be a routine aspect of any child abuse investigation, and the statement can be introduced in any form. Using the videotape for someone in denial breaks down barriers and may elicit confessions.

   Only one case before the U.S. Supreme Court has considered the importance of proper documenting of pretrial interviewing of children. In *Idaho v. Wright* (1990) the Court excluded the hearsay statement of a child taken in an interview with Dr. Jambura. In part the Court stated: "The questions and answers were not recorded on videotape for preservation and perusal by the defense at or before trial; and blatantly leading questions were used in the interrogation."

3. *Can the prosecution use a videotaped interview of an abused child?* There are no statutes that restrict testimony of the child in domestic relations cases (Sagatun & Edwards, 1995). Since it would not be uncommon for a criminal case to be conducted simultaneously with a probate or juvenile case, the videotaped interview may be an option to avoid multiple interviews and unnecessarily traumatizing the victim. Alternatively, the interviewer could testify as to the contents of the interview in the probate, family, or juvenile court. Prior to a criminal trial, a good videotaped interview may convince the defendant that a guilty plea should be entered (Berliner, 1992). Defense attorneys who witness an emotional but clear indication of abuse may advise the client against a jury trial.

   Used extensively in cases that the author investigated, videotape of the victim was offered to the grand jury as evidence in support of an indictment to superior court. In this instance, no right to confrontation with the accused is expected. Its use is not definitively established, however, as no case testing the constitutionality of videotaped testimony has reached the U.S. Supreme Court.

   Problems do, however, arise in the use of videotaped statements in lieu of testimony in a trial. Although 34 states allow videotaped dispositions to avoid confrontation with the accused as of 1990 (*Maryland v. Craig*), others do not. Congress permitted videotaped or televised testimony by children as the federal standard in 1990 (Sagatun & Edwards, 1995). Efforts to ensure the admissibility of videotaped interviews through legislation have failed to pass the scrutiny of state constitutional objections in both Massachusetts and Texas.

Objectivity on the part of the interviewer is considered crucial for any child interview, videotaped or not (Saywitz, 1994). The vocal inflections and facial expressions of the interviewer can mislead a child to answer inaccurately. Questions must be phrased with the age and developmental stage of the child in mind. It is useless to ask a question that the child cannot understand, so care in phrasing is an important consideration. Open-ended questions are preferred, and closed-ended questions should be avoided. Questions that suggest a yes/no answer limit the child's response and could lead the child to answer inappropriately. Leading the witness by suggestion can taint an otherwise valid disclosure. Experts agree that repeat interviews of young children are potentially harmful and should be avoided. Children can be expected to have varying degrees of memory and varying abilities to communicate their thoughts. A successful interview will depend on the skills of the interviewer, who should have realistic expectations of the child.

Interviewing the Elder Victim. Empowering the elder victim is helpful to both the victim and the officer. The interviewer may accomplish this by giving victims as much control as possible, such as refraining from taking notes before asking permission to do so in the interview and asking where they want the interviewer to sit (Ramsey-Klawsnik, 1993). Communicating respect by referring to the victim by his or her title—Miss, Mrs., Mr. or Dr., for example—can be helpful during the rapport-building portion of the interview. At all times, the dignity of the elder should be maintained. The interviewer should go slowly and use language that is easily understood but not patronizing.

According to the Police Executive Research Forum, the following guidelines are suggested for interviews with elders (Nerenberg, 1993).

- Investigations should be coordinated with adult protective services personnel or the ombudsman when possible, to avoid multiple interviews.
- Joint interviews with public health nurses or others treating medical conditions may assist agencies when appropriate.
- Interviewers should attempt to establish rapport with the person being interviewed.
- Whenever possible, interviewers should use audio and video technology.
- Officers should respect the confidentiality of all parties whenever possible.
- To prevent contamination or collusion, interviewers should avoid disclosure of case information to all parties involved in the alleged offense.
- Interviewers should ask general, nonleading questions.
- Officers should ask all witnesses to identify others who have relevant information and tell how those others may be contacted (Figure 7–8). Interviewers

Figure 7-8 A witness may be able to identify others who will have relevant information. *(Photo courtesy of Mark C. Ide.)*

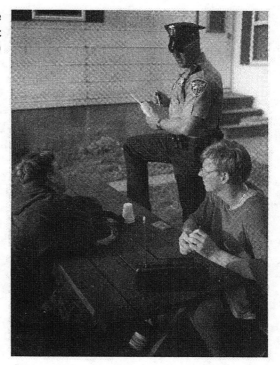

will need to identify the victim's doctor, conservator, attorney, social worker, and any agencies that provide service to the victim.

Goal 3: Provide the Basis for Successful Prosecution

This goal is satisfied when all injuries have been properly documented and evidence has been gathered. In Chapter 8 we explore the legally acceptable methods to satisfy this objective.

CONCLUSIONS

For years, research has been gathered on what police do and how they should be doing it. This difficult task is far from complete. The role of the police officer is more complex because the job is constantly changing to meet new expectations in society. Contemporary problems call for nontraditional responses. Somewhere along the way, the definitions became too clear, too concise, too narrow. This obscured the job of policing!

Are police expected to do it all? In a way. They are expected to provide protection and service to their communities. The job requires techniques in a technical world. Preconceived notions of drama and excitement drown out the reality that domestic violence is the most frequent call for many jurisdictions, although oddly, it has rarely appeared in the profiles of what police do. Often, departments fail to validate this large portion of duty through adequate training or proper incentives.

Since the 1960s, the trend toward proactive policing for crimes of domestic status has followed other examples. The acknowledgment that the forms are varied and the victims are mixed has brought the position of policing one step closer to effective intervention. Arming police with a strategy is paramount if the goals of protection and service to all citizens are to be met. No other area of police work is this muddy. Moving from nonintervention to mediation to arrest, the criminalization of domestic violence has been achieved, and it is up to the policy makers to assure the passage of legislation that will allow legitimate police action.

The foundation for action is the successful interview. Knowing who did what, how, when, where, and why is still necessary to protect the victim and prosecute the abusers. Those questions can be answered with greater accuracy through the use of techniques meant to elicit information. The interview has changed from simply filling out a form to being a skilled art form. In some cases, the use of a professional forensic interviewer will be necessary to overcome expected court challenges.

How should police respond to allegations of domestic violence? They should respond with questions, lots of them, not with preconceived ideas as to who did what based on previous experience or personal bias. Understanding the goals for public safety and the need to elicit truthful information makes clear the actual role for law enforcement: to serve and to protect.

Key Terms

Child credibility

Cognitive interview method

Community policing

Competency

Family crisis model

Forensic interview

Lautenberg Gun Ban

Problem-oriented approach

Rapport

Risk assessment

Questions for Review

1. Name the two most common styles used to describe policing efforts. What are the positive and negative effects of this labeling?

2. Explain the three categories of efforts to prevent domestic violence. What is the policing role within each category?

3. What is the best method to use to conduct a domestic violence interview?

4. What are the three basic phases of the interview process?

5. Why is it important to establish rapport in an interview?

6. To make a risk assessment, what questions should be asked during an interview?

7. Explain the controversy surrounding child statements. Talk about the case that prompted research into the issue.

8. Do you believe that videotape should be used in interviews with children? Why or why not?

9. Discuss some helpful hints to use when interviewing an elder.

ℛEFERENCES

Anon. 1998. "A Shelter for Battered Men." *Advocate*. 764:1–8.

Bard, Morton. 1969. "Family Intervention Police Teams as a Community Mental Health Resource." *Journal of Criminal Law, Criminology and Police Science* 60(2):247–50.

_____. 1970. *Training Police as Specialists in Family Crisis Intervention*. NCJ 000050. Washington, DC: U.S. Department of Justice.

_____. 1973. *Family Crisis Intervention: From Concept to Implementation*. NCJ 148484. Washington, DC: National Institute of Law Enforcement and Criminal Justice.

Berliner, Lucy. 1992. "Should Investigative Interviews of Children Be Videotaped?" *Journal of Interpersonal Violence* 7(2):277–85.

Biggs, Simon, Chris Phillipson, and Paul Kingston. 1995. *Elder Abuse in Perspective*. Bristol, PA: Open University Press.

Buzawa, Eve and T. Austin. 1993. "Determining Police Response to Domestic Violence Victims." *American Behavioral Scientist* 36(5):610–23.

Buzawa, Eve S. and Carl G. Buzawa (eds.). 1996. *Do Arrests and Restraining Orders Work?* Thousand Oaks, CA: Sage Publications.

Carlson, Allan. 1996. "Government Intervention Undermines the Family." Pp. 186–96 in *Family Violence*. San Diego, CA: Greenhaven Press.

Cook, Philip W. 1997. *Abused Men: The Hidden Side of Domestic Violence*. Westport, CT: Praeger Publishers.

Dantzker, Mark L. 1995. *Understanding Today's Police*. Englewood Cliffs, NJ: Prentice Hall.

Davies, Deborah, Judy Cole, Gigi Albertella, Usa McCulloch, Kelly Allen, and Harriet Kekevian. 1996. "Model for Conducting Forensic Interviews with Child Victims of Abuse." *Child Maltreatment* 1(3):189–97.

Dempsey, John S. 1994. *Police: An Introduction to Law Enforcement*. New York: West Publishing Company.

Dickinson, Beth, Sergeant, County of Los Angeles Sheriff's Department. 1985. "Los Angeles County Sheriff's Department Preschool Investigation." February. *www.ieway.com/~csukbr/juslib/mcmartin.html*. 1998.

Frontline. "Other Well-Known Cases Involving Child Sexual Abuse in Day Care Settings." *http://www3.pbs.org/wgbh/pages/frontline/shows/innocence/etc/other.html*. 1998.

Geiselman, Edward R. and Ronald P. Fisher. 1985. *Interviewing Victims and Witnesses of Crime.*
     National Institute of Justice Research in Brief. NCJ 099061. Washington, DC: U.S.
     Department of Justice.

Geiselman, R. E., Gail Bornstein, and Karen Saywitz. 1992. *New Approach to Interviewing
     Children: A Test of Its Effectiveness. National Institute of Justice Research in Brief.* NCJ 135011.
     Washington, DC: U.S. Department of Justice.

Gelles, Richard J. 1996. *The Book of David: How Preserving Families Can Cost Children's Lives.*
     New York: Basic Books.

Goldstein, Seth L. and R. P. Tyler. 1998. "Frustrations of Inquiry." *FBI Law Enforcement Bulletin*
     67(7):1–6.

Helfer, Ray E. and Ruth S. Kempe (eds.). 1988. *The Battered Child,* 4th ed. Chicago: University
     of Chicago Press.

Holmes, William and Trent Headley. 1995. *Cambridge Police Department Operation Safe Home.*
     NIJ grant 94IJCXK001. Boston: Executive Office of Public Safety Programs Division.

Lanning, Kenneth. 1992. *Child Sex Rings: A Behavioral Analysis,* 2nd ed. Arlington, VA: National
     Center for Missing and Exploited Children.

Marx, Sue. 1992. "Checklist for Child Protective Services Investigators: A Prosecutor's
     Perspective." *National Center for Prosecution of Child Abuse* 5:10–11.

Mignon, Sylvia I. and William M. Holmes. 1995. "Police Response to Mandatory Arrest Laws."
     Crime and Delinquency 41(4):430–43.

Nerenberg, Lisa. 1993. *Improving the Police Response to Domestic Elder Abuse.* Washington, DC:
     Police Executive Research Forum.

Pence, Donna and Charles Wilson. 1992. *The Role of Law Enforcement in the Response to Child
     Abuse and Neglect.* Washington, DC: National Center on Child Abuse and Neglect.

Ramsey-Klawsnik, Holly. 1993. "Interviewing Elders for Suspected Sexual Abuse: Guidelines
     and Techniques." *Journal of Elder Abuse and Neglect* 5(1):5–17.

Randall, Teri. 1991. "Duluth Takes Firm Stance against Domestic Violence; Mandates Abuser
     Arrest, Education." *Journal of the American Medical Association* 266(9):1180–84.

Rucinski, Cheryl. 1998. "Transitions: Responding to the Needs of Domestic Violence Victims."
     FBI Law Enforcement Bulletin 67(4):15–18.

Sagatun, Inger J. and Leonard P. Edwards. 1995. *Child Abuse and the Legal System.* Chicago:
     Nelson-Hall Publishers.

Saywitz, Karen. 1994. "Questioning Child Witnesses." *Violence Update* 4(7):3–10.

Shepherd, Jack R. 1988. "Law Enforcement's Role in the Investigation of Family Violence." Pp.
     392–400 in *The Battered Child,* 4th ed., Ray E. Helfer and Ruth S. Kempe (eds.). Chicago:
     University of Chicago Press.

Sherman, Lawrence W. 1997. "Policing for Crime Prevention." In *Preventing Crime: What
     Works, What Doesn't, What's Promising.* Report 104-378. Washington, DC: 104th Congress,
     1st Session, U.S. House of Representatives.

Sherman, Lawrence W., Denise C. Gottfredson, Doris L. MacKenzie, John Eck, Peter Reuter,
     and Shawn D. Bushway. 1998. *Preventing Crime: What Works, What Doesn't, What's
     Promising.* NCJ 171676. Washington, DC: U.S. Department of Justice.

Stark, Evan and Lawrence Sherman. 1994. "Should Police Officers Be Required to Arrest
     Abusive Husbands?" *Health* 8(5):3–4.

Stearns, Richard G. 1998. *The Massachusetts Criminal Law: A District Court Prosecutor's Guide.*
     Dedham, MA: Commonwealth of Massachusetts.

Stern, Paul. 1992. "Videotaping Child Interviews." *Journal of Interpersonal Violence* 7(2):278–88.

Straus, Murray A., Richard J. Gelles, and Suzanne K. Steinmetz. 1980. P. 222 in *Behind Closed Doors: Violence in the American Family*. Garden City, NY: Anchor Press/Doubleday.

Swarns, Rachel L. 1997. "The New York Times: On the Web." October 22. *http://archives.nytimes.com*. July 1998.

Wilson, James Q. 1997. "What to Do about Crime?" Pp. 14–24 in *Criminal Justice 97/98*, 21st ed., John J. Sullivan and Joseph L. Victor (eds.). Guilford, CT: Dushkin/McGraw-Hill.

Wolf, Rosalie S., Michael A. Godkin, and Karl A. Pillemer. 1984. *Elder Abuse and Neglect: Final Report from Three Model Projects*. Worcester, MA: University Center on Aging.

Zahn, M. 1991. "Wolfgang Model: Lessons for Homicide Research in the 1990's." *Journal of Crime and Justice* 14(2):17–30.

Cases

Idaho v. Wright, 116 Idaho 382, 775 P.2d. 1224 (1990).
Kentucky v. Stincer, 482 U.S. 730 (1987).
Maryland v. Craig, 497 U.S. 836 (1990).
People v. Buckey (1984).

Statutes

Delaware Code, Title 11, §§4120, 4121.
Massachusetts General Laws ch. 233, §20.

Other Authorities

Lautenberg Gun Ban, H.R. 3610 (September 1996).

Law Enforcement Response

INTRODUCTION

> The two emotions most readily transmitted from person to person are fear and anger. Both are present in abundance at the scene of a domestic disturbance and they will descend upon you like a demon as soon as you walk through the door. You should know ahead of time that you would feel both of these emotions profoundly. You must be ready to deal with them: "Eat your emotions" and continue to investigate calmly, systematically, and fairly. (Gosselin, 1996)

Obviously missing from discussions on policing domestic violence is the fact that responding officers often feel bad when handling the call. That emotion begins when the peace officer is first dispatched. Fear and anger are present at the scene and are transmitted immediately, heightening the automatic response of the officer. Allegations of severe child abuse may invoke disbelief and often outrage. Many law enforcement officials are parents themselves. It is difficult to see children severely harmed or killed and not be affected. Determining the appropriate response requires the realization that unchecked emotions can direct behavior. Anticipating internal reactions to domestic abuse and the necessity of dealing with them will allow for fair and impartial police action.

Mike's story illustrates the frustration officers frequently experience when they confront a complicated domestic situation. The available options include arresting or summonsing the perpetrator when a clear legal violation occurs. The case can be referred to other services if a formal arrangement has been established with local

---

It was Christmas Eve, and I was filling in for the regular cops as a reserve officer. A woman called the station saying that she wanted her husband out of the house. I responded without a clue about what was going on. She let me in the house and pointed to the living room, saying, "There he is: get him out of here; I can't stand him anymore." He was drunk, really drunk, sitting in a chair watching television, and he didn't even acknowledge that I was there. His nose was bleeding and the rag that he held to it was soaked with blood. "You hit *him*," I told the woman, "don't you know that I should *arrest you?*" "Get him out of here," she kept saying adding, "You won't arrest me—who will take care of our daughter!" Their 12-year-old was hooked up to all kinds of blood and tubes in an upstairs bedroom. I felt sick. What was I supposed to do? Arrest her, call an ambulance for the child, and then what about the husband? He wasn't doing anything wrong, but I didn't think he could take care of himself. Maybe I could put him in protective custody. All this on Christmas Eve! I'll never forget that night, and I still don't know if I did the right thing. No matter who I ask, the answer is always different. Soon after that, I quit the force. I don't need that kind of stuff—it just isn't for me.

---

resources for occasions when a crime has not been committed. Approximately 75 percent of police calls for service do not involve a crime as defined by state law (Hirschel & Hutchison, 1991). An emergency restraining order is an option in cases where the victim requires additional protections. Some states mandate that the officers stay on the scene until they are confident that the victim is safe. Information from the victim along with the analysis of the situation will help the police to make the judgment.

It is not that officers are afraid to respond to intimate disputes, and certainly no two calls are alike. Police routinely respond to life-threatening situations, and it is naive to believe that they do so without emotion. An inordinate fear, however, may be based on the mistaken belief that domestic disputes constitute the most hazardous of calls for assistance. For years, police and the public believed that intimate violence was unusually dangerous. As Eve and Carl Buzawa have suggested, the officer's goal was to extricate himself or herself from the risky and unpleasant situation as soon as possible (Buzawa & Buzawa, 1996). The notion was based on statistics from the FBI showing frequent deaths for officers engaged in disturbance response. When these calls were removed statistically from other altercations, that representation was modified. It is now believed that domestic disputes are no more lethal than other police action (Fagan, 1996). In fact, police are more likely to be shot accidentally by other police officers than to be killed in family quarrels (Sherman, 1986).

Whether or not police face inordinate risk at domestic disputes is still a matter of debate. Given the high numbers of domestic violence calls, a high risk of injury is still evidenced through research (Uchida et al., 1987). The volatility of the situation coupled with easily transmitted emotions has been at the root of training efforts to prepare officers for what they might encounter.

TRAINING

Academies that do offer domestic violence training will frequently provide a four- to eight-hour block of time for instruction. Experts know that without extensive, adequate training police will not implement domestic laws properly (Mignon & Holmes, 1995). Specific programs developed by law enforcement for police officers have netted some interesting results when coupled with additional training.

Portland, Oregon, for example, created a special Domestic Violence Reduction Unit in 1993 that both investigates assaults and educates about the violence (Barbour, 1995). To facilitate communication between the department and the victims, a Hispanic-speaking caseworker was brought on to the team in addition to a Russian-speaking officer. The efforts fit well within the community policing philosophy. Here new recruit officers receive 40 hours of training where they learn about the cycle of violence and practice scripts for supporting and empowering victims. A survey of the officers found that *making an arrest for domestic assaults* rose in importance as a police activity over a two-year period. Arrests, prosecutions, and police perceptions all showed improvement from the initiative.

A specific approach is necessary for the law enforcement community to respond appropriately. An effort to provide that clarity has brought about projects such as the Cambridge Police Department Operation Safe Home (Holmes & Headley, 1995). The authors reported that the improved training brought about significant success in

---

Been There... Done That!

A former student dropped by my office to say hello. He was halfway through the police academy and was proud that he had been selected to tutor other recruits who were having difficulty with the academic portion of the training. Of course, I asked how much time was being dedicated to domestic disputes, since it will ultimately be the most frequent call for the graduates. Four hours, he responded, adding that the instructor tried to cram into that time frame what he had been exposed to during a semester course as my student. The academy class was told that the law requires an arrest for violation of protection orders and that it was preferred that they arrest for all disputes. Failure to make an arrest leaves the officer personally liable. Drill instructors repeatedly shouted, "What do we do at a domestic disturbance?" "We arrest everyone and let the courts sort it out," was the expected reply. They are teaching police recruits to arrest victims, I thought in horror. Why is this still happening?

increasing the identification of domestic violence and in improving collection of evidence needed for prosecution. Determining the level of risk to the victims through a profile of the batterer helped the police officer to select the best manner of response. Liaisons formed with community services offered feasible alternatives. Noting that training itself cannot be assumed beneficial, Holmes and Headley suggest that a training program must be examined and evaluated for its accuracy and relevance to the problem.

A similar project to provide enhanced training on elder abuse was evidenced in the Elderly Protection Project (Kohl et al., 1995). The efforts involved education on the challenges that elders face and the myths surrounding the older population. Elder abuse was identified as a topic about which many departments wanted more information. Future programs need to address this emerging obligation.

Successful policing of intimate violence boils down to the requirement for enhanced personal skills broad enough to meet the contemporary paradigm shift. Police Chief Shanahan sees a need for these changes in law enforcement while urging for service delivery in a professional and competent manner (Shanahan, 1998). Moving toward that goal, training for officers has taken a new turn. Member/citizen interaction training, affectionately referred to as *charm school*, attempts to enlighten those with a John Wayne or Napoleonic syndrome. At least four states have such programs. Developed by the New York State Police, Massachusetts, New Hampshire, and Illinois have programs modeled after the original (Trapasso, 1998). After citizens have complained about an officer's conduct, he or she is scheduled for the 40-hour interpersonal skills training. To keep it a positive experience for the officers, only those identified for the education and the immediate supervisor is notified. Officers are assigned out on paper to other training and simply disappear to a campus setting where they attend in plain clothes. Evaluation has not yet been conducted to measure the relative success of this program.

CRIMINAL JUSTICE AMBIVALENCE

A lack of consensus on how police should respond to domestic violence in the civilian population is mirrored within the criminal justice community. Historically, police intervention has been unpredictable, criminal prosecutions rare, and victims reluctant to report to the police. Victims and their advocates charged police with failure to protect women against domestic abuses. The criminal justice community was charged with failure to respond equally to women alleging violence, researchers documented the struggle, and civil battles began in an attempt to force the system into action. The courts were accused of failing to follow through with prosecuting charges of battering. Stories of failed attempts at justice were made public; women and children were being severely injured and killed.

The police responded vehemently, blaming victims for not following through in signing complaints. Statutes that forbade officers from making an arrest for a misdemeanor not committed in their presence were offered as proof that those legal hands were tied. Legal precedent discouraged and often forbade them from entering a person's home to effect an arrest without a warrant. Further, many officers believed that arrest-ing the perpetrator would cause more harm to the victim than good. As if that were not enough, occupational images of policing involved prosecution, and *that* was not occurring for the majority of domestic cases.

All sides have been openly frustrated and dissatisfied since the feminist move-ment opened the wounds in the 1970s. Close examination reveals that each position holds a kernel of truth. If the criminal justice community remains indecisive in its domestic violence response, a fair argument would suggest that society is also. The truth is, we just don't know yet what works best. The most telling information sug-gests that results are better when domestic violence is recognized as a community problem, not just a police problem. Higher arrest rates have been documented when police are part of a coordinated community response (Stalans & Lurigio, 1995).

THE SYSTEMS APPROACH

Why is vigorous prosecution an issue for police? Officers view themselves as an essential part to a larger group, the criminal justice system (Figure 8–1). They expect to have an impact on the other components. Therefore, even if officers are actively pursuing a preferred arrest policy but see that the district attorney is not prosecuting the offenders they have arrested, they are likely to stop making arrests, believing that the arrest serves no purpose (Hirschel & Hutchison, 1991). Communities interested in the full enforcement of preferred and mandatory provisions cannot ignore the other branches of the criminal system.

The Courts

Prosecutors routinely sign complaints for most crimes but have traditionally required domestic violence victims to sign their own (Stalans & Lurigio, 1995). Programs aimed at simplifying complaint procedures where the prosecutors file on behalf of the domestic victim have led to more prosecutions of batterers in some jurisdictions

Figure 8–1   Branches of the criminal justice system.

(Cahn & Lerman, 1991). Victim witness advocates and community volunteers are now more involved to assist victims in filing the difficult paperwork required for a protection order. It is not uncommon for the request form to consist of five pages. With this assistance it is hoped that the victims of domestic abuse will more consistently follow through with their complaints.

Acknowledging that a prosecutor's failure to act directly affects the officer's future decisions to arrest in cases of abuse, Naomi Cahn and Lisa Lerman note: "Prosecution is the formal expression of social norms. If we want woman abuse to stop, we must prosecute those who abuse women. If we do not prosecute them, we give them tacit permission to continue. Increased intervention could have a significant impact on one of the most serious crime problems in the United States."

Another strategy aimed at increasing successful prosecution is the aggressive stance of proceeding without the victim's participation (Crowe, 1996). Decisions to go forward with a prosecution despite victim preference are based on the premise that victims are not failing to cooperate, just trying to stay alive. This current trend is known as a *no-drop policy*. Courts that force a victim to testify, by subpoena if necessary, have adopted this tough position. Three reasons exist for no-drop policies (Davis & Smith, 1995):

1. It removes responsibility for prosecution from victims, which makes them less likely to be targeted for intimidation attempts by batterers.

2. The state has an obligation to prosecute those who violate the law regardless of victims' wishes; to do otherwise sends the wrong message to batterers (i.e., that it is acceptable to break the law).

3. The state has a compelling interest in prosecuting potentially dangerous domestic violence defendants in the interest of public safety, just as the state has an interest in prosecuting dangerous robbers, rapists, and others who may offend.

The collection of statements and physical evidence by law enforcement will have a large impact on whether the case will result in a successful prosecution. The measure is not without its critics, however. Advocates claim that battered women are being revictimized by a system that will not be satisfied with their decisions to remain in the violent relationship. Jeffrey Edleson reported how a Minnesota judge ordered the police to arrest several women who did not appear after being subpoenaed; and some spent the weekend in jail (Edleson, 1991).

The American Bar Association Commission on Legal Problems of the Elderly recently looked at the trends in elder abuse cases in the courts and made recommendations on how to handle these cases more effectively. The review supported judicial and court staff education on the barriers to court access for the elderly as well as civil and criminal alternatives. The importance of supporting the elder victims in their choice was a main focus of the report (Stiegel, 1996).

Corrections

The most common sanction for convicted batterers is mandatory treatment programs. This alternative to prison is an adequate option for domestic offenders without lengthy abuse histories, since the majority of assaults constitute a misdemeanor. Its acceptance is due to the overall goal in domestic disputes: prevention. The counseling programs that have emerged typically involve group sessions that combine anger control, stress management, and communication skills. Behavior modification and increased awareness are the goals for effective batterers programs.

Convicted child abusers are generally receiving harsher penalties, although treatment is a frequently used option. California enacted mandatory prison sentences for child molesters in 1981, funneling them away from hospitals and into prisons (O'Neill, 1983). Sexual child offenders most recently face chemical castration in California. Effective in January 1997, California became the first state to require chemical castration for repeat molesters. After the second offense, molesters receive weekly injections of the drug Depo-Provera, which dampens sexual desire. Offenders could choose to be surgically castrated instead, under the law.

The Drug-Induced Rape Prevention and Punishment Act of 1996 imposes a prison sentence of up to 20 years for anyone intending to commit sexual assault by distributing illicit drugs to another person without his or her consent. This federal law targets the use of Rohypnol, the date rape drug being used increasingly on college campuses across the country (National Criminal Justice Association, 1996).

Law Enforcement

The systems approach is illustrated through the combination of procedures and technologies to combat domestic violence. The Riverside Police Department uses digital imaging, which allows photographs, fingerprints, mug shots, crime laboratory reports, video segments, witness statements, and even audiotape recording of 911 calls to be stored and electronically accessed (Amato, 1996). Encouraged to be conscientious in gathering evidence, including photographs of the victim and the crime scene, broken furniture, and bloody clothing, the officers know that their efforts will make a difference.

Preferred and Mandatory Arrest Policies.   Regardless of the debates from experts on the best course of action, the mandate to police officers is clear. *Take domestic assaults seriously; treat them criminally.* As most states have adopted preferred and mandated arrest policies, officer discretion is limited. Several different terms are used to express the approach of *preferred arrest*. J. David Hirschel and Ira Hutchison examined the policies, which include *preferred, presumptive,* and *proarrest* as interchangeable terms (Hirschel & Hutchison, 1991). In their study of 20 police departments, officers themselves shied away from using these terms. Supervisors instructed on when they "should" arrest versus "must" arrest for *mandated* policies.

The conditions under which departments apply the policy vary greatly. Look closely at the domestic violence statute in your state and determine how police must respond. In Massachusetts, the preference for arrest is stated in Massachusetts General Laws, ch. 209A, §6. The first paragraph makes the arrest mandatory if an abuse order is violated:

> An officer *shall* arrest any person he witnesses or has probable cause to believe has committed a misdemeanor by violating a temporary or permanent vacate, restraining, or no-contact order, or a judgment issued by any court pursuant to the domestic violence abuse prevention act or during divorce, custody, or support proceedings. This includes failure or refusal to comply with orders for suspension and surrender of firearms, ammunition, licenses for same, FID cards possessed, owned or controlled by the defendant.

The third section makes arrest for domestic violence the preferred response:

> Where no such [abuse prevention order] is in effect, arrest shall be the *preferred* response whenever an officer witnesses or has probable cause to believe that a person has committed (a) a felony; (b) a misdemeanor involving abuse; or (c) an assault and battery.

The statute notes that "the safety of the victim and any involved children shall be paramount in any decision to arrest."

More about It: Full Faith and Credit

Police have a duty to enforce domestic violence restraining orders that were issued from another state under the Violence Against Women Act, passed by Congress as part of Federal Crime Bill of 1994. The act contains the provision for interstate enforcement of protection orders (Title II of VAWA), which is referred to as *full faith and credit*. It establishes that states must recognize and enforce protection orders issued in foreign states or tribal courts. Expressly forbidden is providing full faith and credit in instances where cross or counter petitions have been filed. The provision is otherwise vague, however, and states are left to set up procedures to implement the requirement effectively (Klein, 1995). Any victim with a valid order continues to receive protection until the expiration of that order, regardless of which state she or he has entered and regardless of the issuing state. VAWA does not require that a victim register the foreign protection order in the enforcing state to validate it. Whenever a state fails to provide for full faith and credit, the federal VAWA standards apply. Given this, many states have adopted their own procedures for complying with the VAWA requirement. Check with your state to find the procedures for interstate enforcement. If none exists, the federal statute applies.

HOW DO POLICE GET INVOLVED?

The ways in which the police are notified for domestic violence are as varied as the forms of violence. The three principal methods are citizen complaint, mandated report, and officer initiated. Remember goal number 1 from Chapter 7: *Protect the victim.*

The Citizen Complaint

The majority of calls for service are domestic dispute calls resulting from citizen complaints. These reports of domestic violence are crisis situations where the violence is still likely to be occurring. Most reports will be from telephone calls. The caller may be angry, confused, or injured at the time due to abuse. It may be a child who is frantic because a parent is being beaten up in the next room. It may also be a neighbor or someone else who is fearful of the noises from a fight next door. The dispatcher or desk officer should gather as much information as possible in order to prepare the officers who are responding. If possible, the caller should be kept on the phone until help arrives, in order to update any information on what is occurring.

Part of the reason for the fear that was discussed at the beginning of the chapter was fear of the unknown. Traditionally, officers were dispatched to domestic calls without having enough information to be prepared for what they were responding to. Knowledge is power, and in this case, knowledge of the situation can prevent anxiety and result in a better response. The following are the basic questions asked by the person taking the report and dispatching it to the officers. If the abuse is occurring at the time, any change in the level of violence is important to convey.

- Who is the caller?
- What is caller's telephone number?
- What is the location of the abuse?
- Is anyone hurt?
- Are any weapons involved (guns, knives, clubs, sticks, etc.)?
- Are there guns in the house?
- Who are the parties involved?
- What is happening?
- Is either party drunk or high on drugs?
- Is there a restraining order of protection in effect?
- Are there children in the house?

At the Scene.   Offering aid to the victim and disarming an assailant are the priorities for officers who first arrive (Figure 8–2). The officer must be aware constantly; the violence does not necessarily stop when they arrive. They must look and listen. The level of anger is likely to remain high after the officer intervenes and separates the people involved.

Figure 8–2 Offering aid to the victim and disarming an assailant are the priorities for officers who first arrive at a domestic violence dispute. *(Photo courtesy of Mark C. Ide.)*

How the injured actually get to the hospital is dictated by police department policy. For some jurisdictions, the police and the emergency medical transportation are one and the same. In others, officers are required to transport victims to the nearest hospital in their cruiser. Some departments are forbidden by policy from transporting victims, and they would call for an ambulance. The major reason behind calling for an ambulance is that officers may not be able to render lifesaving care to a victim during transportation.

When it is safe to do so and after the victim has received emergency medical attention if needed, the officer will investigate to determine who is the perpetrator and who is the victim. This is sometimes the most difficult part of the effort to resolve *any* domestic dispute. Spouses and cohabiting adults talk to police the most during a dispute—that usually changes after the anger has subsided.

The next step is to assess the level of risk for injury to the victim. Questions for cohabiting couples and for dating relationships should be specific. Refer to Chapter 11: *Interviewing the Adult.* Many states require officers to request initially that a firearm or weapon be placed temporarily in their custody. Without compliance, the officers may have the right to search for and take custody of a firearm or weapon to alleviate the threat of serious violence that it poses. The weapon might be returned after a check to determine that it is lawfully possessed. Unless the officer is required by law to return the weapon immediately, it is within his or her discretion to make the return at a later date. If the weapons cannot be seized legally, a judge may order the defendant to surrender guns, his or her license to carry, and/or his or her FID card during the pending of an order or criminal prosecution.

There is no exemption for police batterers for retaining a weapon, even if they would ordinarily use the weapon in the course of their employment. Many departments have developed a policy to seize department weapons upon an allegation of abuse or a civil restraining order being issued. Anyone convicted of a domestic violence offense loses the right to carry a gun for any reason, including employment. The New York City Police Department was the first to institute this policy in compliance with the Lautenberg Gun Ban (Anon., 1997). A domestic violence conviction is an automatic disqualifier for the job as a police officer in New York; other states are following the trend.

The final step is to collect the evidence.

The Mandated Report

Police are required to file a report to the state-designated agency when they suspect abuse or neglect of elders and children (Figure 8–3). Additionally, they receive these reports to investigate after an initial substantiation. What does that mean for the police?

Reporting Requirements

1. Officers must be familiar with the conditions that require a mandated report in their jurisdiction. The circumstances under which a report is required vary from state to state. *Severe* abuse or neglect is usually the standard, and a suspicion—not proof—is required. Learning that a child or elder is living in a violent home is one condition that may lead to a report. If it appears that the caretaker(s) are impaired through drugs or alcohol and unable to care for dependents in the home, a reportable condition may exist. Death or severe injury due to abuse or neglect must be reported. Additional conditions that might require a report of elder abuse would be indications of coercion, intimidation, abandonment, and/or financial exploitation.

2. Police need to know where to file the report. Frequently, an initial report will go to the state's child or elder protection agency. Sometimes the district attorney's office will screen the reports for criminal violations.

3. There may be a penalty for a failure to report. The penalty itself is usually not substantial—a fine, for example—and is rarely imposed. More important, it sets up a duty to the officers. Although police cannot be held responsible for protecting a person, the courts have agreed that officers can be statutorily required to protect a class of people, such as elders, children, and domestic violence victims (Lehrman, 1997). Failure to perform an expressed duty

REPORT OF CHILD(REN) ALLEGED TO BE SUFFERING FROM SERIOUS PHYSICAL OR EMOTIONAL INJURY BY ABUSE OR NEGLECT

Massachusetts law requires an individual who is a mandated reporter to immediately report any allegation of serious physical or emotional injury resulting from abuse or neglect to the Department of Social Services by oral communication. This written report must then be completed **within 48 hours** of making the oral report and should be sent to the appropriate Department office.

Please complete all section of this form. If some data is unknown, please signify. If some data is uncertain, place a question mark after the entry.

DATA ON CHILDREN REPORTED

AGE OR

	NAME	CURRENT LOCATION/ADDRESS	SEX	DATE OF BIRTH
1)			Male / Female	
2)			Male / Female	
3)			Male / Female	
4)			Male / Female	

DATA ON MALE GUARDIAN OR PARENT

Name: _____
First   Last   Middle

Address: _____
Street and Number   City/Town State

Telephone Number: _____ Age: _____

DATA ON FEMALE GUARDIAN OR PARENT

Name: _____
First   Last   Middle

Address: _____
Street and Number   City/Town State

Telephone Number: _____ Age: _____

DATA ON REPORTER/REPORT:

_____   **Mandatory Report**   **Voluntary Report**
Date of Report

Reporter's Name: _____ First   Last

Reporter's address: (If the reporter represents an institution, school, or facility please indicate.)

_____   _____
Street   City/Town

_____   _____
State   zip Code   Telephone Number

Has reporter informed caretaker   YES   NO
ABUSE/NEGLECT REPORT - 3

(Revised April, 1983)

Figure 8–3   Sample form for reporting abuse or neglect of children.

COMMONWEALTH OF MASSACHUSETTS - DEPARTMENT OF SOCIAL SERVICES   PAGE 2
REPORT OF CHILD(REN) ALLEGED TO BE SUFFERING FROM SERIOUS
PHYSICAL OR EMOTIONAL INJURY BY ABUSE OR NEGLECT

What is the nature and extent of the injury, abuse, maltreatment or neglect, including prior evidence of same? (Please cite the source of this information if not observed first hand.)

What are the circumstances under which the reporter became aware of the injuries, abuse, maltreatment or neglect?

What action has been taken thus far to treat, shelter or otherwise assist the child to deal with this situation?

Please give other information that you think might be helpful in establishing the cause of the injury and/or the person responsible for it. If known, please provide the name(s) of the alleged perpetrator(s).

Signature of Reporter

Figure 8-3   (cont'd)

would leave the officer open to civil action. Liability is most likely to exist if a child or elder is severely harmed or killed subsequent to police knowledge of conditions ripe for abuse.

Receiving the Report.   As you can see from the sample *report of abuse and neglect*, the information supplied would assist in planning the investigation. Similarities exist between the elder and the child report.

1. The age and gender of the victim is helpful to determine who should conduct the interview.

2. It seems simple, but addresses for parents and guardians are not always the same addresses as those of the children. The report provides a quick and hopefully accurate way to get hold of all interested people who might have information.

3. The original reporter should be contacted to supply further facts. Rarely will a reporter put everything down on paper.

Where the interview takes place is as important as who asks the questions. To facilitate information, the setting must be safe for the victim. That means first that the perpetrator should not be anywhere around. It is unwise to question a child victim at his or her school. Even though it may be a safe place, the child will be affected in some way by the authorities speaking with him or her. Since these investigations allow for time to plan, the place where the statement is taken can be determined in advance.

The Officer-Initiated Investigation

Police can investigate a crime simultaneously with filing a report of abuse or neglect. It is not unusual for a disturbance call to involve a subsequent inquiry into abuse or neglect of a child or elder. Information may come directly to the officer through concerned people in the community or even from public appearances and during community policing efforts.

TO ARREST OR NOT TO ARREST: THAT IS THE QUESTION!

Objectionable behavior does not necessarily constitute criminal conduct. Even when it does, police don't always have the power to arrest. When the power of arrest is available, they may use discretion in exercising that option. Although some accuse police officers of underenforcing the laws against domestic assault, recent research has shown that police have low arrest rates for nondomestic assaults as well (Feder, 1998).

How do police officers make the decision to arrest? Here are three questions that police officers consider when making the decision.

B e e n   T h e r e … D o n e   T h a t !

It is not unusual for police to make public appearances in schools to talk about good touch and bad touch. After one of these guest lectures, a teenager in the group told a friend that her stepfather was abusing her sexually. He had taken a picture of her naked when he raped her, saying that he would show it if she ever told anyone. No one would believe that she had not been willing to have sex with him, he had told her. So she had put a tape recorder under her bed one day to prove what was happening. The friend called me with that information.

I went to the victim's house when I knew her stepfather would be at work. She came to the door, and I quietly asked if she needed help. The fear in her eyes was readily apparent as she nodded. Is there a picture, a tape? Saying nothing, she again nodded, as she looked nervously into the house behind her. "I will be back," I told her.

It did not take long to prepare the affidavit for the search warrant. Armed with the warrant, three officers and I returned to the house. A lengthy search resulted in the photo—it was hidden in the garage inside a box intended for a car air filter. The audio-tape was handed over as well. A social worker waited in a car outside the house until the police were finished; then she took custody of the crying teen. The stepfather came home from work and was promptly arrested for *rape of a child*. Additional charges were brought after an extended interview with the victim.

---

1. Does the action constitute a crime?
2. Does the officer have the power of arrest for that crime?
3. What are the alternatives?

Crimes

The following factors are taken into consideration when making that powerful decision:

- If the violence constitutes a felony, the officer may make a warrantless arrest wherever he or she has the legal right to be present.
- A misdemeanor crime committed in the presence of an officer typically carries the power of arrest (Figure 8–4). Some misdemeanor crimes are specifically written with an authorization for an arrest. Statutes vary widely on arrest procedures for domestic violence.

Questions to consider: Does the violent act fall within the definition of a felony or a misdemeanor? Does the offense constitute a crime that carries with it the power of arrest? Is there a preferred or mandated response that would limit the discretion at

Figure 8-4 Police have the power to arrest for both misdemeanors and felonies committed in their presence. *(Photo courtesy of Mark C. Ide.)*

the scene? In other words, officers need to know what *must* be done and then what *can* be done, in response to the violence encountered in their jurisdiction.

Assaults. The term *domestic assault* is used to describe behavior that ranges from shoving to stabbing, from threatening to punching. Its verbal overuse in this context minimizes the seriousness of the charge. States that have codified their laws classify the assault as simple or as aggravated:

> *Simple assault:* intentionally causing another person to fear immediate bodily harm or death or intentionally inflicting or attempting to inflict bodily harm on the person. It is usually a misdemeanor crime due to minor injury, if any.

Example: You want to go out of the house to visit friends, but your lover grabs your hair and pulls you away from the door, closing it and preventing you from leaving.

> *Aggravated (felonious) assault:* an unlawful attack by one person on another to inflict severe bodily injury. It might also be classified as assault with a dangerous weapon or assault with intent to commit murder.

Example: You fight to get the door open, and your lover pulls a knife and cuts you.

For other states that follow common law, there are numerous charges, each specific to a form of violence that could occur in a domestic relationship.

Assault: any willful attempt or threat to inflict injury when coupled with an apparent present ability to do so, or any intentional display of force that would give the victim reason to fear or expect immediate bodily harm. Under this definition, an assault may be committed without actually touching, striking, or doing bodily harm to the person.

Example: Your spouse shakes his or her fist in anger while threatening to hit you. Next she or he moves in your direction *as if* to hit you, even if no subsequent battery (hitting) occurs. The victim must *believe* that the intent was to cause injury. Past experience is a good predictor.

Assault and battery: any unlawful touching of another without justification or excuse. The battery requires a physical contact of some sort, injury or offensive touching.

Example: You slap or kick a family member, for any reason.

Assault with a dangerous or deadly weapon: an unlawful attempt or offer to do bodily harm without justification or excuse by use of any instrument calculated to do harm or cause death.

Example: You point a gun at someone and threaten to shoot him or her.

Assault with intent to commit rape: a crime of an assault, coupled with an intention to commit the crime of rape. It is the actions that lead up to a rape that does not occur. Lack of consent and force are an issue.

Example: Your date pushes you to the ground and pins your arms while unzipping his fly and ripping off your dress. You fight him off and get away.

Rape.   Sexual intercourse without consent is rape. It can be described as any intrusion into any orifice for sexual gratification. Some states include digital, oral, and anal intrusions (no matter how slight) in this definition. The use of force demonstrates a lack of consent. If there are no physical injuries, the victim must be able to demonstrate that consent was not granted. Recounting the words spoken by the perpetrator or the circumstances under which the rape occurred is one way to show lack of consent. The victim must have in some way articulated the lack of consent. Fear from threats or age (under the age of consent) may satisfy the legal requirement. All states recognize that rape can occur within a marital relationship. Victims of date rape can be adults or adolescents. Forced intercourse in lesbian and homosexual relationships can also reach the legal level of rape.

Example: Your elderly neighbor says she does not like to be alone when her son visits. Over time she confides that he puts his fingers inside her vagina, and that it hurts. You know that she suffers from dementia and lacks the ability to consent.

Stalking.   Any person who willfully, maliciously, and repeatedly follows or harasses another person and makes a credible threat with the intent to place that person in reasonable fear of death or bodily injury commits the offense of stalking.

Example: You receive hang-up calls each night at different intervals designed to prevent sleep. They began soon after your divorce. Getting out of work, you find a flat tire; this happens more than once. During the day, he calls and threatens you if you do not meet with him.

Review copies of the state's penal code to fully understand crimes explicitly intended to address domestic violence offenses. These crimes represent only a portion that may be applied in any given jurisdiction. If the call involves an elder or a child, specific legislation may offer protection in addition to the criminal codes with which the officers are more familiar. The use of protective custody may be helpful when misconduct fails to reach the level of a crime.

Domestic violence is a general term that includes a variety of offenses; think of it as many different crimes that occur within legally recognized relationships. Relationships do not change the duty of the officer to enforce the law and to arrest offenders. All pertinent criminal codes should be considered in determining the appropriate police response and subsequent criminal charges, in addition to offenses specific to domestic violence. Dual arrests are discouraged by most jurisdictions. Police should attempt to identify the primary aggressor, to avoid arresting both parties. Mailing an arrest warrant to domestic violence offenders who leave the scene is a feasible alternative to an arrest (Sherman et al., 1998).

Civil Protection Codes

Violation of a civil restraining order or no-contact order is an additional criminal offense apart from ongoing abuse. Usually, it is a misdemeanor, with the power of arrest given by statute. Since the violation is a separate crime, it should be considered in addition to any other criminal violations, not in lieu of them.

Mutual restraining orders exist when both parties involved in a domestic dispute have applied successfully for an order of protection against the other. The Violence Against Women Act strongly discourages this practice since such restraining orders are not recognized as enforceable outside the jurisdiction in which they were filed. Law enforcement officers should not encourage application for cross complaints. The practice is considered dangerous to the one who has been victimized and serves to minimize the abuse (Zorza, 1996). State statutes may expressly forbid issuance of mutual restraining orders except in rare and extreme instances.

Mental Health Codes

In some instances it may be necessary to remove suspects and to hold them involuntarily for evaluation at a mental health facility. Emergency procedures for overnight commitment are specific to each state, with particular amounts of time allowed before a court hearing. Officers should become familiar with state mental health provisions for involuntary commitments and evaluations.

Use of Available Resources

In addition to any legal requirements that might exist for reporting abuse to another agency, response to domestic violence can be simplified by utilizing local and state resources whenever possible. Networking and developing the sources for extralegal intervention are beneficial to both the victim and the officers. If the crime involves an elderly victim, contact the local elder services or adult protection services for assistance and future follow-up. If an arrest is anticipated in a home where children would be left unattended, contact the local department of social services or child protection agency and request that they take custody. Victim witness programs exist in every state and are helpful in advising domestic violence victims of their rights and of procedures to obtain civil restraining orders. Local crisis centers are valuable in offering emergency shelter for the victim. Referrals of battered women to other agencies have been used as an avoidance tactic. That is not the suggestion here. A coordinated system approach to domestic violence response includes utilizing alternative services in addition to traditional policing.

WHAT ABOUT PROBABLE CAUSE?

Probable cause is a standard of proof that must be satisfied for any search or seizure to occur. An arrest is legally defined as a seizure and therefore falls under the same requirement for probable cause as a search. The requirement is stated in the Fourth Amendment of the U.S. Constitution and in state constitutions: "The Right Of The People To Be Secure In Their Person, Houses, Papers And Effects Against Unreasonable Searches and Seizures Shall not Be Violated...**And** no warrant shall issue except for probable cause."

An officer has the task of determining if probable cause exists to believe that a crime has been committed and that an arrest is warranted. Sources for determining probable cause include

- Collective knowledge doctrine
- Knowledge about the suspect
- Suspect's behavior to police
- Reliable hearsay
- Observations of the police

The U.S. Supreme Court clearly stated the probable cause requirement in *Gerstein v. Pugh* (1975), while referring to past instances of definition: "Probable cause to arrest exists when the facts and circumstances known to the officer are sufficient to warrant a reasonably prudent person in believing that the suspect has committed or is committing a crime" (*Beck v. Ohio*, 1964). The standard is universal; both federal and state laws require meeting this level of proof to justify depriving persons of their liberty under the Fourth and Fourteenth Amendments to the Constitution. Additional states' constitutional provisions echo the sentiment. Exact requirements for the level of information to rise above mere suspicion without reaching the adjudication standard of proof beyond are clarified through both state and federal case law and legislation. "Probable cause to arrest [in Massachusetts] must exist at the moment of arrest. Facts and circumstances, which come to an officer's attention after a person has been taken into custody, may not be used retroactively to justify the arrest. However, an officer need not make the arrest as soon as probable cause arises. Unlike probable cause to search, which is of limited duration, once probable cause to arrest is formed, it will continue to exist for an indefinite period, at least if no intervening exculpatory facts come to light" (Commonwealth of Massachusetts, 1996).

A difficulty in determining probable cause in cases of domestic disputes has led some jurisdictions to conclude that the standard is met by a mere accusation of assault, regardless of any supporting evidence. Thus, when both parties accuse the other of abuse, a dual arrest is the only available option for the police. The dual arrest occurs when both parties are taken into custody. The courts have voiced a preference that police not make dual arrests in disputes, yet they may be appropriate in some circumstances. In addition to the constitutional requirement of probable cause, a police officer must have statutory or common law authorization in order to place someone under arrest (*Michigan v. DeFillippo*, 1976). The lesser standard of *reasonable suspicion* allows police to detain someone briefly in order to investigate suspicious circumstances (*Terry v. Ohio*, 1968).

COLLECTION OF EVIDENCE

Three types of evidence can be gathered: real (or tangible) evidence, documentary evidence, and testimonial evidence (Yeschke, 1997). The first form of evidence, *real* or *tangible* evidence, is physical. Things that you can acquire, such as a fingerprint or a bullet, are examples. The second type of evidence is documentary, something that is recorded, such as financial statements or 911 tapes. By themselves, these items are not evidentiary but may have significance after a crime has been committed. The third type of evidence is *testimonial*; both interviews and interrogations come under this heading. The majority of court-introduced evidence, approximately 80 percent, is testimonial.

The probable cause requirement attaches to searches as well as seizures conducted by government officials. Strict adherence to federal and state constitutional guidelines is imperative to obtain evidence that will withstand the scrutiny of the court. Therefore, it is best to conduct a search with a warrant whenever time permits. The use of searching with a valid warrant is beneficial in domestic cases and should be considered to validate the statements of victims. Its use should not be limited to fatal investigations; tangible evidence speaks louder than words.

Been There... Done That!

The investigation began as domestic but soon turned into allegations of sexual abuse to over a dozen children. The relationship between the perpetrator and some of the victims was incestual and was alleged to include digital rape as well as rape by objects. Due to the nondiscriminatory pattern of boys and girls as victims, I suspected that the man was a pedophile. Children described being given little toys and trinkets that were kept in bedroom drawers. Dolls were frequently used as objects of affection. Putting all the information into an affidavit, I applied successfully for a search warrant. The reward for these efforts was proof beyond a reasonable doubt that the perpetrator was sexually deviant and that children were the objects of his desires. When the evidence was presented at trial, John was committed to a state institution for the sexually dangerous for an indeterminate time, referred to as "a day-to-life" sentence. Should he ever be released, he will serve his sentence of over 40 years. Without the tangible evidence, it would have been the word of the children against his word, a difficult obstacle to overcome.

Search without a warrant is per se unreasonable. Some exceptions to the warrant requirement do exist, however. Places that are not covered by the Fourth Amendment protection that can be searched without a warrant include common areas, entranceways, public places, semipublic places, open fields, and driveways. An open field or driveway that is posted "no trespassing" does not invoke constitutional protection. An officer may commit a trespass and be held separately accountable for that crime but still conduct the search without violating the warrant requirement.

Known as the *state action doctrine*, the Fourth Amendment and relevant state constitutions protect persons only against action by or at the direction of the state or its agents. It is a limitation on the activities of government law enforcement officials only and not on private citizens. Constitutional protections have also been extended to control public school officials in the area of search and seizure, but they do not have to obtain a warrant or meet the standard of probable cause in the same way that police must in order to conduct a search. What that means is that police can accept evidence that has been offered by private citizens or agencies, regardless of how it was obtained, as long as the search was not conducted under the direction, encouragement, or instigation of the police. This includes medical evidence obtained during routine medical procedures not requested by police. A court order to produce medical evidence may be required if the evidence is being withheld.

It is permissible to accept drugs (evidence of date rape) from a college roommate who turned it over to school officials. A videotape or audiotape from a victim may provide evidence of child pornography or rape. Tools or instruments used in the commission of a crime, such as rope or tape discovered, or anything offered by a private citizen can be introduced as evidence. Items that have been discarded in a trash can or outside a window of a moving vehicle carry no expectation of privacy and can be seized without a warrant. It is not legally acceptable to circumvent constitutional protections by asking someone to bring evidence, however, by threat, by promise, or by any inducement whatsoever.

Some of the relevant exceptions to the warrant requirement are presented below, but this is not an exhaustive list.

Exceptions to the Warrant Requirement

The courts specify the conditions under which evidence without a warrant may be collected. Conditions for making an exception are specifically outlined. Attempts to expand their meaning may result in the loss of evidence according to Lt. Gosselin, a 27-year veteran who put together the following description of exclusions for training police recruits (Gosselin, 1996).

Consent Search.   This form of exception is scrutinized more than others and must be used judiciously. Consent must be given freely and voluntarily, not a mere acquiescence to legal authority or intimidation. Although officers may mention the possibility of getting a warrant, they cannot demand, trick, or force cooperation. Consent to enter a home is not equivalent to a search consent, and even if consent is given, it may be revoked at any time. The person providing consent can do so only for areas that are commonly used. People who live together cannot give consent to search

---

Been There... Done That!

Child protection concerns sparked an investigation by the department of social services. The single mother had had five pregnancies that resulted in two miscarriages, a stillborn, a child born with brittle bone disease, and one healthy male child. Severe neglect was the reason for an ongoing department involvement. The social worker thought that an adult incest relationship between the 25-year-old mother and her biological father had caused the multiple birth problems in what they thought to be the fifth generation of incest. Coincidentally, the father and daughter had been separated shortly after her birth and had not met until she was approximately 20 years old. Child protection services obtained DNA profiling on the mother and her father which indicated that both had parented the two living children. When the test results confirmed their suspicions, the department contacted the state police and turned the DNA reports over to me. Since there was no involvement in the department investigation by any police, the court upheld use of the DNA report in a criminal prosecution against both people. In Massachusetts, both parties are held criminally responsible for incest unless there is an indication of force (rape) or lack of consent, including that of age or incompetence.

in areas that are private and used exclusively by the other person. A person who has a locked or private desk, a separate closet, or a library has an expectation of privacy and must be the one to offer consent for those areas. Since domestic violence usually occurs in a place where there is joint ownership or residence, this distinction is quite important.

Exigent Circumstance and Domestic Violence.   Police routinely enter homes for domestic calls and may investigate under this exception to the warrant requirement. This allows for a sweep to be conducted to search for weapons and injured people. It does not authorize a protracted and general search of the entire home.

Search Incident to a Lawful Arrest.   A person who is legally under arrest may be searched (Figure 8–5). The body and areas within the immediate control of the arrested are included. The purpose is to allow an officer to seize weapons, and the search is used for his or her protection. It is not a general search of a house or vehicle where the person is found in order to look for evidence. The scope and intensity of the search are limited.

Plain View Seizure.   Articles in plain view in public places or where the police have a legitimate right to be present, that are readily apparent as contraband or as the fruits or instrumentality of a crime, can be seized. This is not considered a search,

Figure 8–5 The police may search a person who is legally under arrest. *(Photo courtesy of Mark C. Ide.)*

and no warrant is required. To justify the plain-view seizure, the officer cannot move items to find identifying serial numbers to confirm that it is in fact contraband. The key point is that the contraband must be readily apparent, such as drugs, instruments of the crime, or weapons. Plain-view observation can occur where no expectation of privacy exists, such as public bathrooms (not stalls), open fields, public airspace, or a private driveway. Enhanced methods to view suspected contraband such as binoculars are acceptable. Techniques to improve hearing cannot be used where persons have a reasonable expectation of privacy, such as telephone lines in some states.

The plain-view doctrine justifies seizure of items that were not anticipated during the course of a search pursuant to a warrant. A search warrant executed for evidence of domestic violence, for example, may lead to the discovery of illegal drugs. The drugs may be seized without application for a new warrant. In some jurisdictions, the seizure must bear a relationship to the crime under investigation, however, or a new warrant is required.

What Police Look For

A checklist is helpful to remind the investigator of the responsibilities at the scene. The sample provided in Figure 8–6 is used for training purposes (Commonwealth of Massachusetts, 1995b). It can be adapted and changed to fit the needs and specific responsibilities in any jurisdiction.

Evidence of the crime can be seized whenever possible. This includes but is not limited to the following weapons:

1. When the telephone has been used as a dangerous weapon, the responding officers should seize it. Telephones are frequently used as weapons in domestic violence assaults. Sometimes used as blunt instruments, they also provide wire for strangulation attempts.

2. Knives, guns, clubs, or any other article used as a means to inflict harm or threaten the victim should be seized at the time of response.

3. Cords, ropes, or tape that was used to restrict the movements of a victim may be seized.

4. Objects that have been used for penetration of genitalia may be seized. Paper bags, not plastic bags, are the way to store properly items that may contain blood or body secretions.

If the abuse allegations involve physical abuse and injury, evidence must be preserved.

1. Further evidence of the assault, such as bloodstained articles and clothes, should be secured at the scene and placed in paper bags (not plastic!).

2. Photographs of the damage to property can be taken. Such damage may include smashed windows in the house or car, bullet holes, and knife slashes.

DOMESTIC VIOLENCE INVESTIGATION CHECKLIST

Victim Information

Name: _____
Noted date of birth
Noted location upon arrival
Administered first aid, noted if
  medical treatment was sought
Noted time dispatched, arrived,
  and when victim spoke
Recorded excited utterances
Described demeanor
Height and weight noted
Described physical condition
Noted complaints of injuries
Described injuries in detail (size,
  location, color)
Noted relationship to suspect
Detailed description of incident
Recorded history of abuse
Recorded history of court orders
Explained rights
Provided written copy of rights
Recorded temporary address/phone
  (Do NOT include in report!)
Advised of suspect's right to bail

Does this case also involve:

Child abuse   report filed
Elder abuse   report filed
Disabled abuse   report filed

Witness Information

Identified reporting party
Interviewed reporting party
Documented names, DOBs, addresses,
  and phone numbers of all witnesses
Interviewed all witnesses, separately
Listed names and DOBs of children
  present
Recorded names of emergency
  personnel
Identified treating physician
Identified desk officer/dispatcher

Suspect Information

Name: _____
Noted date of birth
Noted location upon arrival
Administered first aid, noted if
  medical treatment was sought
Noted when suspect first spoke
Recorded excited utterances
Described demeanor
Height and weight noted
Described physical condition
Noted complaints of injury
Described injuries in detail (size,
  location, color)
Temporary address noted (if vacate
  order exists)
Noted existence of any restraining
  orders

Following Miranda, when applicable

Asked if she/he wanted to make
  a statement
Noted whether suspect knew of
  and/or understood restraining
  order
Detailed description of incident
Noted history of abuse in any
  relationship

Evidence

Photographed/described crime scene
Took full body picture of suspect
Took full body picture of victim
Photographed victim's injuries
Photographed suspect's injuries
Seized items thrown or broken
Seized firearms for safety
Seized firearms under surrender
  order
Requested medical records
Requested 911 tape

Figure 8–6   Domestic violence investigation checklist.

3. Photographs of the injury to the victim should also be taken (Figure 8–7), but these are normally done at the police department or hospital. Bruising on the victim may not be immediately apparent, so it is important to follow up with the victim in the days following an assault.

4. Photographs of the location can be substituted by a sketch to document where the assault took place and to portray property damage as the result of the assault.

5. If the assault took place in multiple rooms/locations, each location should be documented for damage and any evidence seized.

If the allegation involves sexual misconduct or date rape:

1. Evidence may include bedsheets, underwear from the victim, and any clothing that may be stained by blood or semen.

2. The victim should be taken to the hospital as soon as possible for a full medical examination. A rape kit is commonly used in emergency room protocol to collect evidence of a rape. Signs of force, such as bruising, cuts, and tissue damage, should be properly collected and preserved. It is important to explain to the victim that she or he must not smoke, drink, or eat anything prior to the examination. She should not shower or wash until after the evidence is collected.

Figure 8–7 A victim who is choked may have bruises on the neck that resemble thumbs in the front and fingers toward the back of the neck. *(Photo courtesy of Mark C. Ide.)*

3. An expert in child sexual assault should conduct the examination of a child. The amount of evidence discovered may be improved when a physician with specialty knowledge of child sexual assaults conducts the examination. Medical evidence is found in 10 to 59 percent of child sexual assault cases (Wallace, 1996).

4. The suspect should also be examined for marks, bruises, and other defense wounds inflicted by the victim. A warrant obtained for the collection of evidence and search of the perpetrator's body can yield a tremendous amount of evidence when the crime is recent. The search should include fingernail scrapings, swabbing of the mouth and genitals, and the seizure of clothing for lab analysis for body fluids. Hair combing (both pubic and head) and pulled hair samples should be taken. For convenience, the officer can obtain a rape kit, which is usually used on the victim to collect and preserve evidence.

If the allegation involves elder financial or fiduciary abuse: This investigation poses complex problems for the investigator to overcome. Two model programs, the Los Angeles FAST Program and the Bank Reporting Project, offer guidance for law enforcement in conducting joint investigations with ombudsman and adult protective services (Commonwealth of Massachusetts, 1995a).

1. The victim's bank(s) or other financial institution(s) must be notified about the investigation. Request a temporary administrative hold on all the victim's holdings, including accounts, certificates of deposit, and safe deposit boxes, pending the outcome of the investigation.

2. Establish the victim's mental capacity to handle his or her affairs and obtain a written mental evaluation from the family physician.

3. Determine the extent of the estate through the conservator or other designated person in control of the estate if they are not suspected in the abuse. Alternative sources of information on the estate may be obtained from a relative, bank, and/or through the registry of deeds.

4. Evidence that the elder has been subjected to undue influence in financial matters is the confirmation of coercion, compulsion, or restraint. This confirmation must be documented.

If the allegation involves child neglect: The home should be searched pursuant to a warrant to document the conditions that constitute criminal neglect. Absence of available food, appropriate clothing, and adequate sleeping conditions will be noted. Severe substandard living conditions are best illustrated by photographs.

If death results: Each form of abuse and neglect has found its victims in death. When mistakes or oversights in evidence collection occur, they can be fatal to the case as well. Entry to a home without a warrant can be justified due to exigent circumstances, but the collection of evidence in these crimes is usually painstakingly slow. For that reason, a search warrant should be obtained as directed in *Mincey v. Arizona* (1978).

According to the *New York Times*, her parents killed Elisa in 1996. The other five siblings watched the 6-year-old being sexually assaulted and beaten to death. Forced to drink ammonia and eat her own feces, her white bones gleamed through her brown fingers (Swarns, 1998).

The responding officer first determines that the person is in fact deceased and calls for the medical examiner, who is responsible for the legal determination of the cause of death. The remainder of the home should be checked for other victims. It is not unusual for a domestic killer to commit suicide or to kill other members of the family as well. Once the scene has been combed for victims, it is cordoned off to prevent contamination of the area and to allow for a full investigation of the scene.

The Interrogation of Suspects

A suspect's confession presents the most injurious evidence of a crime. Properly conducted in accordance with legal requirements to ensure voluntariness, an admission provides the best evidence. Supreme Court Justice Byron White wrote: "The defendant's own confession is probably the most probative and damaging evidence that can be admitted against him" (*Bruton v. U.S.*), 1968).

Experts suggest that an interrogation with the perpetrator should always be attempted. Yet debate surrounding *Miranda v. Arizona* (1968) has caused confusion on when the officer must recite warnings. Unless someone has been deprived of his or her freedom in a significant way, *and* he or she is being interrogated, no warnings are legally required (Rutledge, 1994). According to Rutledge, officers should routinely interrogate suspects, despite the reluctance since *Miranda*.

When considering the decision to interrogate, the officer has options in addition to the traditional face-to-face confrontation, which can be considered custodial and/or intimidating. Obtaining statements over the telephone is one possibility. Another method is to interrogate the suspect in a nonthreatening environment such as a home or restaurant. The purpose of *Miranda* is to prevent *compelled* statements or forced confessions through intimidation. Force, intimidation, or threats are not acceptable at any time for the purposes of obtaining a confession.

Some authors suggest that the victim obtain the incriminating statements in a telephone conversation that is recorded (Rawlins & Gassaway, 1993). The victim becomes an agent of the police in this scenario, and caution must be taken to ensure that he or she would not be traumatized by the involvement. This method would not be considered entrapment because the offender has already committed the crime. Before using this technique, investigators should research the laws that pertain to their jurisdiction. Some states prohibit the tape recording of any phone conversations. Others allow one-party consent recording of a conversation. No warnings are required unless the perpetrator has previously been indicted or arraigned on the crimes being investigated. If the victim recorded an incriminating statement without police inducement or involvement, it is evidence that can be received by police.

William Geller suggests videotaping interrogations, noting that an estimated 2,400 police departments in the United States used the technology in 1990 (Geller, 1993). His research into the use of videotaping concluded that it led to improvements in police interrogations. The tapes, which make it easier to show that the statements were voluntary, may be used to discredit a suspect at trial.

CONCLUSIONS

Since domestic violence response can invoke fear and anger, that reaction should be anticipated. Both emotions can be met head on with the power of increased knowledge in handing the situation. Although any form of violence can involve weapons and would pose a danger to the responding officers, these calls are not more dangerous for the police than compared to other calls.

As with any other case, the primary determination for the police remains: Was a crime committed? The officer must determine who committed the crime based on probable cause. Interviewing and interrogation are important tools toward this end. Truthful information gathering is the goal, and officers must take care when interviewing populations that may be influenced by misinformation. An allegation may be substantiated through the collection of evidence obtained. Since legal constraints exist that guide an officer in that task, knowledge of search and seizure law provides power for the skilled investigator to assure that fundamental fairness and decency are always maintained.

B e e n   T h e r e ... D o n e   T h a t !

While I routinely videotaped statements given by child victims and witnesses, my colleague preferred to tape interrogations. He always taped the entire account when a perpetrator volunteered to give a statement. With skill, he would question the assailant and elicit any incriminating statements that were offered. The majority of these amounted to confessions, which were invaluable at time of trial. Once a defense attorney viewed the tape, a plea bargain was offered. The result: Fewer young children were made to testify in a lengthy and potentially traumatic trial.

$\mathcal{K}$EY $\mathcal{T}$ERMS

Assault	Plain-view seizure
Consent search	Preferred arrest
Exigent circumstances	Probable cause
Full faith and credit	Rape
Mandatory arrest	Search incident to a lawful arrest
Neglect	Stalking
No-drop policy	State action doctrine

QUESTIONS $\textit{for}$ $\mathcal{R}$EVIEW

1. What are the preferred and mandatory arrest policies?

2. What questions should be asked during a citizen complaint?

3. What are the requirements for police when reporting abuse?

4. How do police officers make the decision to arrest? What factors influence that decision?

5. What is probable cause? How is probable cause determined?

6. What are the three types of evidence that can be gathered?

7. Explain the exceptions that allow for a warrantless search.

8. Give examples of weapons that police may seize at a domestic crime scene.

9. What evidence do police officers gather to document physical abuse and injury?

10. What evidence do police officers look for to document a claim of sexual misconduct or date rape?

11. What evidence do police officers look for to show elder financial abuse?

12. What is the purpose of *Miranda* warnings?

$\mathcal{R}$EFERENCES

Anon. 1997. "No Gun If Convicted." *Christian Science Monitor* 89(32):16.

Amato, P. 1996. "New Tools to Prosecute Domestic and Child Abuse Offenders." *Law Enforcement Technology* 23(5):40–42.

Barbour, Scott (ed.) 1995. *Rape on Campus*. San Diego, CA: Greenhaven Press.

Buzawa, Eve S.and Carl G. Buzawa (eds.). 1996. *Do Arrests and Restraining Orders Work?* Thousand Oaks, CA: Sage Publications.

Cahn, Naomi R. and Lisa G. Lerman. 1991. "Prosecuting Woman Abuse." Pp. 95–112 in *Woman Battering: Policy Responses*, Michael Steinman (ed.). Cincinnati, OH: Anderson Publishing Company.

Commonwealth of Massachusetts. 1995a. *Investigation of Financial Exploitation: Skill-Building for Protective Services Caseworkers*. Boston: The Commonwealth.

_____. 1995b. *Domestic Violence Investigations*. In-Service Training. Boston: The Commonwealth.

_____. 1996. *Police Training Program*. Middlesex County, MA: Office of the District Attorney.

Crowe, Ann H. 1996. "Stopping Terrorism at Home." Pp. 66–69 in *Criminal Justice 96/97*, 20th ed. John J. Sullivan and Joseph L. Victor (eds.). Guilford, CT: Dushkin Publishing Group.

Davis, Robert C. and Barbara Smith. 1995. "Domestic Violence Reforms: Empty Promises or Fulfilled Expectations?" *Crime and Delinquency* 41(4):541–53.

Edleson, Jeffrey L. 1991. "Coordinated Community Response." Pp. 203–19 in *Woman Battering: Policy Responses*, Michael Steinman (ed.). Cincinnati, OH: Anderson Publishing Company.

Fagan, Jeffrey. 1996. *The Criminalization of Domestic Violence: Promises and Limits*. Washington, DC: National Institute of Justice.

Feder, L. 1998. "Police Handling of Domestic and Nondomestic Assault Calls: Is There a Case for Discrimination?" *Crime and Delinquency* 44(2):335–49.

Geller, William A. 1993. "Videotaping Interrogations and Confessions." NCJ 139962. Washington, DC: U.S. Department of Justice.

Gosselin, Robert C. 1996. "Search and Seizure." Massachusetts State Police Academy Course Content. Unpublished.

Hirschel, J. D. and Ira Hutchison. 1991. "Police-Preferred Arrest Policies." Pp. 49–72 in *Woman Battering: Policy Responses*, Michael Steinman (ed.). Cincinnati, OH: Anderson Publishing Company.

Holmes, William and Trent Headley. 1995. *Cambridge Police Department Operation Safe Home*. NIJ grant 94IJCXK001. Boston: Executive Office of Public Safety Programs Division.

Klein, Catherine F. 1995. "Full Faith and Credit: Interstate Enforcement of Protection Orders under the Violence Against Women Act of 1994." *Family Law Quarterly* 29(2):253–70.

Kohl, Rhiana, Diana Brensilber, and William Holmes. 1995. *Elderly Protection Project*. Washington, DC: U.S. Department of Justice.

Lehrman, Fredrica L. 1997. Pp. 6–25 in *Domestic Violence Practice and Procedure*. Washington, DC: West Group.

Mignon, Sylvia I. and William M. Holmes. 1995. "Police Response to Mandatory Arrest Laws." *Crime and Delinquency* 41(4):430–443.

National Criminal Justice Association. 1996. "New Federal Law Enhances Penalties for Use of Date Rape Assistance Drugs." *NCJA Justice Bulletin* 16(12):1–5.

O'Neill, V. J., Jr. 1983. "Prison for Child Molesters: The Impact of the 1981 MDSCO Repeal and Mandatory Prison Legislation." *Journal of Juvenile Law* 7(1):1–6.

Rawlins, Ray and Dana Gassaway. 1993. "The Telephone: Tool or Tort?" *APSAC Advisor* 6(3):3–6.

Rutledge, Devallis. 1994. *Criminal Interrogation: Law and Tactics*, 3rd ed. Pacerville, CA: Copperhouse Publishing Company.

Shanahan, Michael G. 1998. "Surviving the Policing Paradigm Shift." *www.berettabulletin.com*. October 1998.

Sherman, Lawrence. 1986. "Domestic Violence." National Institute of Justice Crime File Series. NCJ 100736. Washington, DC: U.S. Department of Justice.

Sherman, Lawrence W., Denise C. Gottfedson, Doris L. MacKenzie, John Eck, Peter Reuter, and Shawn D. Bushway. 1998. *Preventing Crime: What Works, What Doesn't, What's Promising*. NCJ 171676. Washington, DC: U.S. Department of Justice.

Stalans, Loretta J. and Arthur J. Lurigio. 1995. "Responding to Domestic Violence Against Women." *Crime and Delinquency* October:387–98.

Stiegel, L. A. 1996. "What Can Courts Do about Elder Abuse?" *Judges' Journal* 35(4):38–43.

Swarns, Rachel L. 1998. "3 Years After a Girl's Murder, 5 Siblings Lack Stable Homes." August 4. *http://archives.nytimes.com*. October 1998.

Trapasso, Philip. 1998. Telephone interview. October.

Uchida, Craig D., L. Brooks, and C. Koper. 1987. "Danger to Police during Domestic Encounters: Assaults on Baltimore County Police, 1984–1986." *Criminal Justice Policy Review* 2:357–71.

Wallace, Harvey. 1996. *Family Violence: Legal, Medical, and Social Perspectives*. Boston: Allyn & Bacon.

Yeschke, Charles L. 1997. *The Art of Investigative Interviewing*. Boston: Butterworth-Heinemann.

Zorza, Joan. 1996. "Women Battering: High Costs and the State of the Law." Pp. 271–77 in *Domestic Violence Law Reader*, Domestic Violence Law (ed.). San Francisco: Austin & Winfield Publishers.

Cases

Beck v. Ohio, 379 U.S. 89 (1964).
Bruton v. U.S., 391 U.S. 123 (1968).
Gerstein v. Pugh, 420 U.S. 103 (1975).
Michigan v. DeFillippo, 443 U.S. 31 (1976).
Mincey v. Arizona, 437 U.S. 385 (1978).
Miranda v. Arizona, 384 U.S. 436 (1968).
Terry v. Ohio, 392 U.S. 1 (1968).

Statutes

Federal Crime Bill (1994)
Full Faith and Credit, VAWA 18 U.S.C.A., 2265 (1994)
Massachusetts General Laws ch. 209A, §6.

Other Authorities

Lautenberg Gun Ban, H.R. 3610 (September 1996).

Part Four

Crime Identification

Generally, the level of brutality in an abuse situation determines the severity of the domestic crime that has been committed. Some crimes stand out and deserve particular attention, due to their unique characteristics. In Part Four we provide an in-depth look at some categories that are usually viewed as *major crime*. This classification may be based on the nature of the offense or the vulnerability of the victim population. Are children particularly vulnerable as abuse victims? Is the problem of child abuse overstated? Do elders need additional legal protections? At what point should police intervene in protecting elders against their wishes? Stalking and homicide are discussed due to the grave nature of these offenses.

In Chapter 9, "Recognizing Child Abuse," we delve into the forms of domestic violence perpetrated against children and the indicators of this abuse category. Emotional and psychological abuses are the most frequently reported types of child maltreatment, which are often indicators of physical and/or sexual abuse crimes. Can the location of abrasions, bruises, lacerations, and welts aid in the difficult determination of child abuse versus child accidents? What is Munchausen by proxy? What are the symptoms of sexual abuse? When should a parent be charged with parental kidnapping? Who are the people mandated by law to report cases of abuse and neglect of children? These are some of the questions answered in Chapter 9.

In Chapter 10, "The Identification of Elder Abuse," we address the unique problems associated with old age. What choices does an elder have when he or she is in ill health and dependent on a family member for care? At what point does gift giving turn into financial exploitation? Who makes this determination? Are adult children responsible for providing care for an infirm parent? Why don't we hear more about the sexual abuse of elders? Who is mandated to report elder abuse and neglect to the authorities?

In Chapter 11, "Associated Major Crimes," we include the crime of stalking and domestic homicide. Stalking has been termed the crime of the 1990s. Although stalking behaviors are not new, they are newly prohibited. Are domestic violence victims more vulnerable to being stalked? How can someone protect himself or herself against becoming a victim of stalking? Have you ever heard of the false victimization syndrome? You may be surprised to learn that the rate of homicide committed by intimates is declining. In Chapter 11 you will also study the prevalence of murder in the family and consider the different forms that it takes. What about the murder scene exception to the requirement for a search warrant in cases of suspected homicide? Does it exist?

chapter

9

Recognizing Child Abuse

INTRODUCTION

> I mentioned to one of our lawmakers that while a parent's death caused by his child is
> called murder and taken very seriously, a child's death caused by his parent usually
> results in lesser charges. He said, half in jest, "They [parents] are adults like me, and
> children don't vote; furthermore, they [children] are not very vocal before my com-
> mittee!" Foreword by C. Henry Kempe (Helfer & Kempe, 1988).

Until the late 1970s and early 1980s, the criminal justice professions rarely intervened
in crimes against children. Allegations of child abuse were investigated only in the
most serious cases or when a death obviously due to abuse had occurred. Even then,
a female matron would probably be assigned to investigate—a strong message to
police officers that child abuse was a "family problem" and not important enough for
real police attention. With limited exceptions, the problem was referred to a social
service agency for family intervention. This attitude reflected a greater social problem: the devaluation of children and the lack of societal protections under the guise of
parental rights. Every state now has legislation to prohibit crimes against children.
The legal transgression depends on the statute language of each state.

In addition to the identification and recognition of child abuse, the impact of
violence is of consequence to the investigator. Insight into the reactions of the victim
may provide an accurate portrayal of the situation that is harmful to the child. The
investigator has a unique opportunity to document the full extent of injury, both
physical and psychological, if those signs and symptoms present themselves. Keeping

---

B a c k   T h e n ...

C. Henry Kempe and colleagues were largely responsible for the shift in public attitude, in the increased awareness, and ultimately in the legal responses to child abuse. They raised consciousness through their first presentation about the battered child syndrome in 1961. Their contributions to our understanding the complexities of child victimization continue through *The Battered Child* (Helfer & Kempe, 1988).

---

in mind that the role of investigators from different agencies may conflict at times, the child protection worker must determine if a child is in need of protection and/or services. The mandate may or may not include family preservation. Law enforcement officers first have the duty to protect, which is emergency intervention only. The job of law enforcement is to determine if a crime has been committed and, if so, by whom.

Civil versus Criminal Action

Should the perpetrator be arrested and prosecuted criminally? The district attorney makes the final decision based on the following factors:

- Age of the child
- Seriousness of the offense
- Reluctance to testify
- Evidence
- Probability of successful prosecution

Recent research indicates that violence toward an intimate partner causes a variety of psychological problems for the children and places them at greater risk for delinquency and adult criminality. Known as indirect abuse, this form might constitute criminal neglect. Those who reside in violent homes are also at greater risk of becoming victims of direct abuse. Ongoing research efforts continue to identify the impact of violence on children in a variety of settings. In this chapter we identify and define the direct forms of child abuse and discuss the indirect effects of witnessing abuse.

Active Maltreatment

An injury or a pattern of injuries that is nonaccidental characterizes direct child abuse. It is damage to a child for which there is no explanation that is reasonable or fitting to the injuries that the child has sustained. The most frequent category of violence that comes to the attention of investigators is the active abuse, sometimes referred to as *maltreatment*. Such abuse may take these forms:

Having been part of the 1980s transition in policing for Massachusetts, I am still frustrated by the lack of understanding and the failure of some police departments to use traditional investigative techniques during the investigations of child abuse. When queried, officers with years of experience will admit to never having executed a search warrant to obtain evidence in child abuse allegations. Although this is not the case in all jurisdictions, rigor and consistency are lacking. Some agencies have created detective divisions to investigate and follow through with the prosecution of crimes against children, but all criminal justice professionals need to be educated to recognize the signs and symptoms of child abuse. I believe the larger problem comes from not understanding the crimes, what might constitute evidence, and how the evidence should be gathered.

What kind of information and evidence might be gathered? Everything and anything that gives credibility to the statement or medical condition of a child! The first step toward the goal of evidence gathering lies in the recognition of abuse, which is the basis of this chapter. Assessing the injury or harm is done through detection (visual and medical diagnosis) along with the medical and family history of the events leading up to the injury.

- Emotional abuse and psychological maltreatment
- Physical injury abuse
- Sexual abuse

Passive Maltreatment

The action or inaction of a legally recognized caretaker who fails to fulfill his or her responsibility to a dependent child identifies the second category of direct violence. These neglectful categories of abuse are becoming more familiar to criminal justice and social service agencies as they struggle to enforce an increasing number of child protection statutes:

- Neglect, which may be physical or emotional
- Educational neglect
- Inadequate care in such areas as food, clothing, and shelter
- Lack of supervision
- Lack of medical care
- Nonsupport of minor child
- Parental kidnapping

A classic case of child abuse is that of Mary Ellen Wilson. In 1874, the 8-year-old child came to the attention of the judicial system due to repeated beatings with a rawhide whip and scissors, as well as severe neglect. Concerned neighbors reported the case to numerous authorities, even the New York City Police Department, which said that there was no proof of a crime! Legend says that the Society for the Prevention of Cruelty to Animals ultimately intervened on Mary Ellen's behalf and persuaded the courts to accept the case because she was a member of the animal kingdom. This account is less than truthful, according to Sallie Watkins, who reports that Mr. Bergh made it clear to the court that he was not acting in an official capacity as president of the Society of Prevention of Cruelty to Animals, but as a humane citizen (Watkins, 1995).

Categories of Secondary Abuse

There are two categories of secondary abuse: witnessing domestic violence and witnessing the homicide of a parent. *Secondary abuse* can be described as the consequence of residing in a violent home. Violence toward an intimate partner causes a variety of psychological problems for the children and places them at greater risk for delinquency and adult criminality. Recent research has suggested that those children subjected to violence through the witnessing of abuse in the home have higher rates of self-reported violence as adolescents (Kelley et al., 1997).

   Those who reside in violent homes are also at greater risk of becoming victims of direct abuse. If a mother is being beaten, the abuse usually predates abuse to the child (Stark & Flitcraft, 1988). Approximately 87 percent of children witness abuse, according to reports by battered mothers. Although we cannot predict which children will become victims of abuse, those that reside in violent homes are at greater risk.

THE VICTIMS OF CHILD ABUSE

The estimated numbers of child abuse victims are staggering. More than 3 million children were the subject of investigation by social protective agencies in 1996, with close to 1 million children whose cases were substantiated or indicated child abuse and neglect in that year (U.S. Department of Health and Human Services, 1998). The study reported that in 1996 there was an approximate 18 percent increase in substantiated abuse since 1990. The most recent estimates of the number of children reported and substantiated as victims of maltreatment and the number of child abuse fatalities nationwide for 1997 have been collected by the National Committee to Prevent Child Abuse (Wang & Daro, 1998). Approximately 3,195,000 children were reported to

TABLE 9–1

Abuse Victims per 1,000 U.S. Children

Year	Average Substantiated Rate of Child Abuse Victims (%)	Estimated Number of Children Confirmed as Victims	Number per 1,000 U.S. Children
1993	34	1,009,000	15
1994	33	1,014,000	15
1995	33	1,032,000	15
1996	32	1,005,000	15
1997	33	1,054,000	15

Source: Data from Wang & Daro (1998).

child protective agencies in 1997. An estimated 1,054,00 children were substantiated as victims of abuse and neglect during that year. The figures represent a slight national increase of reports between 1996 and 1997, with some states reporting a decrease. As shown in Table 9–1, 15 of every 1,000 children in the United States were substantiated victims of child abuse each year since 1993 (but see Figure 9–1). In comparison, the *Third National Incidence Study* estimated that 42 children per 1,000 were harmed or endangered by maltreatment (Sedlak & Broadhurst, 1996). The higher estimate is due to the definition of child abuse in the report, which included the *endangerment standard*: Children who experienced abuse or neglect that put them at risk of harm were included in the set of those who had already been harmed.

Figure 9–1 The majority of children in the United States are happy and well cared for. The statistics on child abuse remind us that 985 children out of every 1,000 are *not* abused or neglected.

A student once said that she could tell if a child was abused by just looking at him or her. Having interviewed over 1000 children who were victims and countless others who were not, I assure you that you cannot tell simply by outward appearances! Disheveled or unkempt appearances are not necessarily signs of abuse. Not all children respond to abuse by becoming surly or openly angry; some children react to abuse by adapting—they learn how to please others and appear overly willing to do so.

When indicators are present, they should serve as the catalyst for investigation, not as confirmation in the determination of abuse. Trained investigators, along with a team of professionals, should be consulted for abuse to be substantiated. The information presented in this book provides guidelines to conduct thorough investigations, and since social and medical research is providing new information constantly, do not expect this book to include every indicator or symptom.

Age

The victims can be found throughout society with no regard to age or gender (Figure 9–2). This does not mean that all children are victimized, but that boys and girls of all ages are represented as victims. A child is defined as a person under the age of 18, except in those states that specify a younger age. The incidence of abuse according to age is difficult to determine with a review of the literature. Young children are reported as the victims most often. Although there is evidence to suggest that physical

---

Susan came into my office with a big smile on her face! A charming 4-year-old, she was sparkling clean—the kind of child whose face shines. Her hair was tied in a ponytail topped with a pink ribbon, which matched her dress. Within moments of meeting, she spun around in circles to show off her frilly outfit! In an apparent effort to please me, she smiled broadly and chatted incessantly.

Yet I already knew that there was a dark side to the life of this little girl. Months earlier, she told her mother that daddy had touched her and that he had hurt her where she pees. Frustrated in her lack of ability to protect the child, her mother fled with her and had been living in hiding ever since. A medical exam had found trauma to the vagina that "might indicate" sexual abuse. During our videotaped interview, Susan told me that daddy had put his pee "down there" and white stuff had come out of it. It hurt her, and she did not want to see daddy again.

Figure 9-2   Percentage of child abuse victims by age. N = 833,115 victims in 45 states. *(Data from U.S. Department of Health and Human Services, 1997.)*

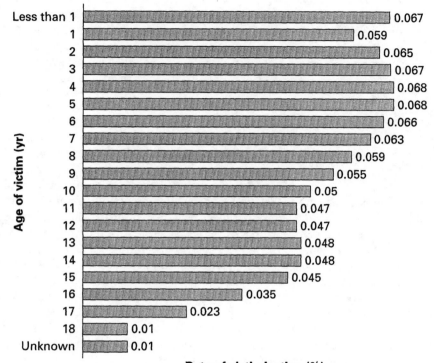

Rate of victimization (%)

maltreatment declines with the age of the child (U.S. Department of Health and Human Services, 1997), the middle years (ages 6 to 11) are now associated with the maximum risk of maltreatment (U.S. Department of Health and Human Services, 1996). Categorizing by age difference has become less important for the investigator, with findings that all age groups are at risk for some form of maltreatment.

Until recently, the frequency of adolescent physical victimization went unnoticed. Approximately 35 percent of abuse reports are for children between the ages of 12 and 17 (American Association for Protecting Children, 1988). Adolescents are thought to be capable of protecting themselves; the numbers indicate that this misconception could cause inappropriate response to allegations of abuse by teenagers.

Gender

Boys and girls are victimized almost equally. In 1996, 52 percent of victims were female, and 48 percent were male (U.S. Department of Health and Human Services,

1997). Boys are at higher risk of *serious* physical injury and for emotional neglect than
are girls (Sedlak & Broadhurst, 1996). Official statistics reflect that girls are sexually
abused three times more often than boys (Sedlak & Broadhurst, 1996). The U.S.
Department of Health and Human Services report that boys were sexual abuse victims in 23 percent of substantiated cases versus girls in 77 percent (U.S. Department
of Health and Human Services, 1998). Keep in mind that the statistics on abuse are
based on cases that are *reported* to social service agencies; the true incidence of sexual
abuse to boys is believed to be equal to the victimization of girls (Hunter, 1990).

Race

According to the U.S. Department of Health and Human Services, more than half of
child abuse victims are Caucasian, approximately 53 percent in 1996. The second
largest group, 27 percent of victims, is African-American. Hispanic children were 11
percent of victims, Native American and Alaska Native children were about 2 percent
of victims, and Asian/Pacific Islander children about 1 percent of victims, according
to the same study. These numbers represent disproportionate numbers of African-
American and Native American victims, almost twice their proportions in the national
child population.

The type of abuse varies between Caucasian and African-American children (U.S.
Department of Health and Human Services, 1998) as well. Caucasian children were
more likely to be the victims of sexual and emotional abuse, but comprised a low
percentage of medical neglect victims. African-American children were represented
disproportionately low in the percentage of victims of sexual abuse and emotional
maltreatment, but accounted for 44 percent of all medical neglect victims.

In contrast, the *Third National Incidence Study* did not find any significant differences in the rates of abuse according to the race of the child. Although this runs

---

B e e n   T h e r e . . .   D o n e   T h a t !

During an investigation of the suspected sexual abuse of a 4-year-old boy, the child drew
a crude picture of an erect penis. His father was thought to have been the perpetrator.
Insufficient evidence of the crime prevented my bringing criminal charges against anyone.
Regardless of my suspicions that the child had been raped, probable cause to make an
arrest did not exist in this case. Here is just one example of sexual abuse to a male child
that would not be included in the statistics.

Whenever I made an arrest for sexual abuse crimes, an attempt was made to determine
whether the men had themselves been victimized. Many told me "off the record" about
their own childhood victimization. Almost all the male perpetrators who had been sexually
abused as children knew that their offenders had never been prosecuted.

counter to the representation of minorities in the child protection agencies, the authors suggest that this may be due to differential attention during the process (U.S. Department of Health and Human Services, 1996).

THE MAJOR FORMS OF ABUSE

It is not unusual for a victim to present more than one form of abuse at the same time. A child who is battered will frequently have been subjected to emotional or psychological maltreatment and/or neglect. A legitimate criticism about the frequency of child abuse is that some states report more than one type of maltreatment as separate cases of abuse, which makes it difficult to determine exactly how many children are abused. These criticisms have brought attention to state reporting methods and point to the need for clear and standardized procedures.

Statisticians echo this concern and are making diligent efforts to address this issue. Notice in Figure 9–3 that the numbers add up to 111.2 percent. That is because substantiation of victims with multiple maltreatment has occurred; this table is not meant to tell you how many victims of abuse exist, but the frequency of the types of maltreatment.

Emotional Abuse and Psychological Maltreatment

Emotional abuse involves a pattern of behavior that impairs a child's emotional development and sense of well-being. Approximately 5 percent of substantiated child abuse cases involve emotional abuse or psychological maltreatment (U.S. Department of Health and Human Services, 1997). In the mildest form, this occurs when a caretaker belittles or ridicules a child frequently. It also includes the absence of supporting

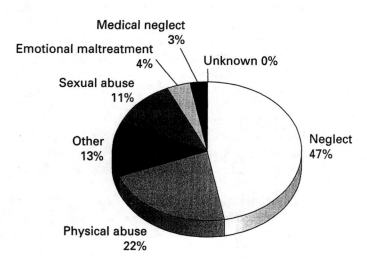

Figure 9–3 Percentage of child abuse victims by maltreatment. *(Data from Wang & Daro 1998.)*

language such as praise or expressions of love and concern. Most often, emotional abuse is considered reprehensible behavior that may indicate the need for social service or therapeutic intervention, but is not criminal. However, emotional maltreatment often accompanies other forms of abuse to children and should serve as a "red flag" to investigators that other types may be occurring. A full investigation of abuse should document emotional and psychological maltreatment in addition to other forms to show the atmosphere of abuse under which the child resides, even if it is not criminal conduct. In its most extreme form, emotional abuse is considered criminal activity. When a caretaker uses extremely restrictive methods to bind a child or places a child in close confinement such as a closet or trunk for an extended period of time, the victim suffers emotional abuse.

Indicators of Physical Abuse

Criminal prosecution of physical abuse is more common than the prosecution of emotional maltreatment, but it is less frequent than prosecution for sexual abuse (Smith, 1995). The recognition of abuse and collection of substantiating evidence becomes extremely important in these cases. The line between accident and intentional harm can be blurry, making the determination difficult. The multiagency or interdisciplinary team approach is helpful in gathering information from various sources to portray an accurate picture of the abuse.

Regardless of the nature or role of the initial investigating agency, any reports and other documentation generated may become the focus of the court if prosecution proceeds. Whenever possible, obtain a written report from a medical professional on his or her opinion of the cause of injury. Medical records of the victim may be summoned if necessary. Gathering information on the nature, type, and location of injury is the first step toward a determination of physical abuse. This history should be collected *before* the victim is interviewed, then compared with the explanations. An allegation of abuse is not confirmation that a child has been victimized. Approximately two-thirds of the cases reported to child protective agencies were not substantiated after an investigation (Wang & Daro, 1998).

Since bruises and cuts are often legitimate accidental injuries (Figure 9–4), the age and mobility of the child is considered along with the explanation given for the injury. The greatest asset that an investigator can possess is the ability to remain objective and nonjudgmental when a child has suspicious injuries. Children can become injured during play; bruises, burns, and even broken bones do occur that are not due to parental abuse. Gather information on the location and type of injury, and speak with the caretaker about the incidents that preceded the injury.

Location of Abrasions, Bruises, Lacerations, and Welts.   Infants who are not mobile are not capable of inflicting severe injury to their bodies. In the absence of a medical condition such as *brittle bone disease*, such an explanation is not

Been There... Done That!

The interdisciplinary or multiagency team is an example of recent attempts to provide coordination among child protection workers, the police, the medical community, and the prosecutor's office. It is helpful to include a forensic mental health specialist or child psychologist on the team if possible. They share information and discuss options for the child. In 1984, I was a member of one of the first interdisciplinary teams to investigate child abuse in Massachusetts at the Northwestern District Attorney's office under Michael Ryan. It worked like this: Once a week, the team would meet for one to two hours. The department of social services investigator would bring the week's list of child abuse allegations of serious physical or sexual abuse. The team, including a doctor, prosecutor, mental health worker, victim witness assistant, and me as the police representative, would discuss the cases.

We determined who would conduct the interview of the child in order to minimize the number of interviews. The interviewer could be any team member or a forensic interviewer. Then we discussed the cases already in the process of investigation.

In cases that the prosecutor thought were likely to go to trial, I would conduct the interview because I also videotaped the first interview with the victims. The videotape would be shared with the necessary agencies, or they could watch through a two-way mirror as the interview was being conducted. The police would always interrogate the perpetrator, with a full report made to the social service agency to complete their mandate to talk with the abuser.

When present (it was difficult to have a doctor or representative present at all meetings), the physician or representative would advise on the necessity of a physical exam. He or she would explain the findings if an exam had already been done. The victim witness advocates and mental health professional would express their concerns about any mental health problems and address the victim's perceived ability to withstand the rigors of a criminal trial. We discussed the reliability of the victim and the consistency of any reports regarding the abuse. This coordinated response resulted in many child abuse cases never coming to trial, for any number of reasons that the team might bring up, including the needs of the victim. Successful prosecution of these difficult cases increased with the team approach.

Since my own experiences, multidisciplinary teams have sprung up across the nation. Experts suggest the team approach as the best method of investigation for child abuse cases (Sgroi, 1984; Smith, 1995). I agree.

plausible. Infants who are thrown or dropped, hit or slapped, burned, or poisoned may have visible signs of injury. Any location of injury on an infant is cause for concern. Note the bruise on the infant in Figure 9–5; the outline of fingers is readily identifiable on the cheek.

Figure 9–4   Normal bruising encountered on the legs of an active child. *(Photo courtesy of the American Academy of Pediatrics.)*

Been There... Done That!

Interviewing parents or the caretaker of a child should always be done with respect. The feelings or personal opinion of the investigator should never enter into the conversation, no matter how severe the injuries may be. There is a distinct difference between an interview and an interrogation of the suspect. The interview is a gathering of information and should not be confrontational. Keep it nonjudgmental and thorough to assure compliance of the interviewee; there is always time later for an interrogation if a suspect is identified.

Once an accusation is made, or the parents feel they are being accused, they will hesitate to answer the many questions that you have. The majority of parents whose children have injuries did not intend to harm the child. Some may believe that they have the right to punish in any form they choose, or have gone too far in the form of punishment they gave. It is the role of the court to make these parents accountable, not that of the investigator.

Additionally, leave the door of communication open, taking care not to accuse someone falsely of abuse. The consequences of false allegations by authorities cannot be underestimated: Humiliation, shame, loss of job, and in some cases loss of the custody of their children can result.

Figure 9–5   This child was slapped with a human hand. *(Photo courtesy of the American Academy of Pediatrics.)*

More about It: Osteogenesis Imperfecta

The technical term for brittle bone disease is *osteogenesis imperfecta* (OI). Bones that break easily characterize the condition. There are four forms of OI, with bone fragility ranging from mild to very severe, depending on the type. A minor accident may result in a fracture; some fractures may occur while an infant with the condition is being diapered, lifted, or dressed.

Child abuse is also characterized by broken bones. Consult a physician in cases of multiple fractures in multiple stages of healing, rib or spiral fractures, and when there is no adequate explanation for the trauma. In most cases, radiographic, clinical, and historical features are present and obvious, allowing easy detection (Ablin, 1998). A skin biopsy for collagen analysis in difficult cases may help to identify mild forms of OI. Since child abuse and OI have been reported together, the presence of OI does not exclude the possibility of child abuse.

Infants are not capable of "falling" down, but once they begin to walk, they begin to fall. Young children who are active are more capable of hurting themselves physically.

When an injury is caused through discipline or for the purpose of inflicting injury, it is an example of nonaccidental injury (compare Figures 9–6 and 9–7). If a child is punched, kicked, thrown, or shaken and sustains injury, no matter how slight, the abusers could be held legally responsible regardless of a preexisting medical condition.

Age Dating of Bruises.   Multiple bruises, abrasions, or other wounds in varying stages of healing may indicate repetitive physical assault, particularly if they are in the same location on the child. Documenting the color of the bruises will assist in determining if repetitive abuse has occurred. It may also be helpful to see if the age of the bruise matches the explanation for the presenting injury, since a timeline of the injury is possible. The age of a bruise is generally determined by its color, although the location can change the color somewhat.

- Bright red bruises are indicative of an injury 0 to 2 days old.
- Bluish or purple bruises are 2 to 5 days old.
- Green indicates a bruise 5 to 7 days old.
- Yellow bruises are 7 to 10 days old.
- Brown bruises are 10 to 14 days old.
- No evidence of bruising occurs after 2 to 4 weeks.

Patterns of Bruising Abrasions, Bruises, Lacerations, and Welts. Common household items are frequently used as weapons against children in abusive situations. Examples include hairbrushes, flyswatters, hangers, belts, and baseball bats. The most common dangerous weapon remains the hand. Look for the patterns on the locations that have been identified as suspicious. Even if the child is unable to articulate, bruise patterns on the child may help to identify and retrieve the weapon as evidence.

Small oval patterns or imprints suggest an inflicted injury due to being grabbed, pinched, squeezed, or slapped. Figure 9–8 shows a grab mark on the upper arm: Notice the two bruises caused by fingers; there may be a thumb mark on the other side of the arm of the child. These oval marks, which are characteristic of fingertips, may be found on the trunk of a child who has been shaken, and around the throat if strangulation was attempted.

Figure 9–6 Accidental injury locations, front and back. Bruises on the walking child are usually accidental if they appear on the forehead, elbows, and stomach, and the outside of the thighs, knees, and ankles.

Figure 9–7 Nonaccidental injury locations, front and back. Bruises or fractures to a child that are suspicious for an intentional injury are located on the ears and cheeks, neck, shoulders and upper arms, genitals, and inner thighs. Bruising on locations other than bony prominence is questionable. Defense posturing can cause injuries to the outside of the lower arm. Suspicious bruising locations include the buttocks, lower back, ear lobes, mouth, and neck.

B e e n   T h e r e …   D o n e   T h a t !

Child protective services, known as the Department of Social Services in Massachusetts, called to notify me of a young child at the local hospital who was suspected to have been shaken. The child was presumed to have serious brain damage and was not expected to live through the night. The child's infant brother, who had brittle bone disease, had died on the previous day. The initial determination was that the infant had died of complications due to the osteogenesis imperfecta.

An interview with the mother provided information that she and her boyfriend shared a one-bedroom apartment with the two children. In the middle of the night, the crying of the sick child, who in turn woke the other child, awaked the boyfriend. The desperate mother had carried both children into the kitchen to appease her boyfriend. She said that she stumbled over a toy in the doorway and had dropped the toddler. A search warrant executed at the apartment found there were no toys in the apartment. A dent on the side of the stove was noted in the doorway where the mother claimed to have stumbled. Her story of how the child "rolled" to the opposite side of the room was indicative of his having been thrown against the stove before coming to rest a few feet away in the opposite direction. In addition to the brain damage, he presented with retinal hemorrhage, suggestive of *shaken baby syndrome*. This child became ill the next day, throwing up, and he had stopped breathing before he was rushed to the hospital. Although the toddler lived, his doctor predicted that the brain damage would prevent him from developing past his age of 2.

The infant was presumed to have died immediately from the incident. It was never clear whether he was also thrown or had been mishandled, causing his brittle bones to break.

Figure 9–8 Grab mark. *(Photo courtesy of American Academy of Pediatrics.)*

Another indication of attempted strangulation is a wrapping mark around the throat indicating that a rope, cord, or wire might have been used. Tethering or tying up of the child may also cause a bruise around the mouth, neck, wrists, or ankles. Wraparound or tethering or binding injuries on the neck, ankle, or wrist suggest that a child is being tied with a rope or cord.

As stated earlier, punishment gone too far is at the root of most abuse. Refer to Figure 9–9 for a clear example of punishment that is considered abusive. Not all physical abuse cases are this extreme. When minor injury is present, the investigation becomes difficult. The final resolution for the child should not be the result of a gut reaction, however. Consider the physical evidence as an outside indication of abuse; look to see if behavioral symptoms and signs are present. Look for other forms of abuse, such as emotional or psychological abuse, sexual abuse, or neglect. If you do not find signs of these, the case may have to be closed.

Figure 9–9 This child was beaten on the buttocks with a plastic pipe. Notice the outline of the pipe that was used. *(Photo courtesy of American Academy of Pediatrics.)*

Objects used to hit a child may leave a distinguishable pattern of bruise identifiable, for example, as that of a hairbrush, cord, or coat hanger. The doubled-over cord or coat hanger will leave a loop mark, as shown in Figure 9–10.

A human bite also leaves a distinguishable pattern of injury that can be distinguished from animal bites by the configuration of the teeth (Figure 9–11). Tearing or shearing injuries are more likely to be caused by an animal (Jenny & Day, 1994).

Munchausen by Proxy.   Within the mental health field, a new and rapidly changing field of study has emerged, *Munchausen by proxy*. The recognition of this disorder is recent, and prevalence rates have not yet been determined. It is characterized by repeated unnecessary medical tests and procedures, which are demanded by a caretaker and cause physical injury to the child. An individual diagnosed with *Munchausen by proxy syndrome* intentionally plans and conceals their behaviors, which may include suffocating a child or demanding painful medical tests and procedures for the child. To assure hospital admission for the child, case studies indicate that the parent has used a range of intentional behaviors, including an injection of urine or fecal matter and the administering of large amounts of laxative. The medical procedures or inflicted medications may kill the child. An estimated 9 to 31 percent of Munchausen by proxy victims die as a result of the abuse (Parnell & Day, 1997).

Figure 9–10   Looped cord mark. *(Photo courtesy of American Academy of Pediatrics.)*

Figure 9–11   Human bite mark. *(Photo courtesy of American Academy of Pediatrics.)*

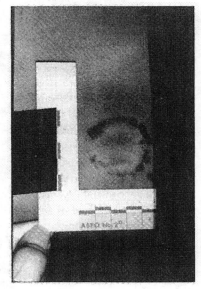

The vast majority of Munchausen by proxy perpetrators are women, approximately 98 percent, according to Teresa Parnell. She reports that the victims are equally divided among male and female children. It is a difficult diagnosis to make because the perpetrators believe or have convinced themselves that the child is sick, even though they have caused the ill effects by their own behavior. There is an absence of motivational incentives for the behavior, and it cannot be explained by any other mental disorder (Parnell & Day, 1997).

Injuries to the Head.   Infants rarely suffer head injuries that are accidental. A child riding a bicycle, roller skating, dirt biking, or four-wheeling might suffer accidental head injuries. Car accidents may also be responsible for the harm to a child. Examples of intentional injury include:

- Hemorrhaging beneath the scalp or when hair is missing due to being pulled
- Retinal hemorrhage, the hallmark of *shaken baby syndrome* and only rarely associated with some other kind of injury
- Injury from multiple slapping or hitting on the head, causing neck injury, with the child unable to turn his or her head
- Whiplash (without an auto accident history)
- Any bruising to the ear, a cause for suspicion that the child has been hit on the side of the head
- A "cauliflower ear," similar to a boxing injury, is caused when the ear is hit numerous times.
- A black or swollen eye, which can be accidental or the result of abuse (the history of the accident is important)

More about It: Munchausen Syndrome by Proxy

The real Baron Hieronymous Karl Fredrich von Munchausen, a German baron, lived from 1720 to 1797. His tall tales about his feats in the Russo-Turkish wars were published after his death. Remembering the outlandish baron, Richard Asher took his name to describe patients who told dramatic and plausible but untruthful stories about their medical symptoms, which resulted in an astounding number of hospital admissions (Parnell & Day, 1997). The term *Munchausen syndrome* was coined in 1951. Today, *Munchausen syndrome* is a recognized psychiatric disorder. The American Psychiatric Association's *Diagnostic and Statistical Manual of Disorders* (DSM III-R) describes it as the "intentional production of physical symptoms."

Munchausen syndrome by proxy is used to describe the situation where a person with Munchausen syndrome causes the injuries or fakes the illness of another, usually a child. The motivation for the behavior is to assume the sick role by proxy.

Shaken Baby Syndrome.   *Shaken baby syndrome* (SBS) is the medical term used to describe the violent shaking of a child and the injuries that can occur. Children from birth to age 2 are at the highest risk of suffering harm from shaking because their neck muscles are underdeveloped and their brain tissue is fragile. Repeated vigorous shaking causes the brain to slam against the skull from side to side. It can cause brain damage, blindness, paralysis, seizures, and death. Most of its victims present with retinal hemorrhages that look like broken blood vessels and small pooling of blood on the white of the eye. Violent shaking of infants accounts for the most common abusive brain injury (Jenny & Day, 1994).

Few states keep statistics on SBS, so it is impossible to determine how widespread the problem really is. In New Hampshire, 100 injuries due to shaking were estimated for 1997, according to the New Hampshire Coalition to Prevent Shaken Baby Syndrome. There were two deaths in New Hampshire that year because of shaking.

Burns.   Punishment in the form of burns may involve forcing a child under hot water, inflicting cigarette or lighter burns, or pushing/holding a child on a heating or electrical unit. In extremely rare cases, children have been placed in ovens and in a microwave, which caused death. When a child has a burn that is described as accidental, the injury is probably located on the front of the child's body. This can happen if a child pulled over a pot on the stove or a container of hot liquid. A young child might also touch or step on a heating unit, injuring the bottom of a foot or hand.

Nonaccidental cigarette burns may also be self-inflicted. Having all the characteristics of abusive burns, the marks tend to be found in areas that are easy to reach, such as the forearm or leg. This is a form of self-mutilation, a practice engaged in by troubled teenagers (Helfer & Kempe, 1988). Purposeful cigarette burns are often located on the child's body to avoid detection, such as the bottom of the feet, the pelvic and genital area, or the inside of the thigh. A deep circular burn of approximately 1/4 inch is caused by a cigarette or a match being held against the skin.

Immersion in hot water causes symmetrical patterns that are distinct from accidental burns and are the most common burns caused by child abuse (Jenny & Day, 1994). A person who steps into a hot bath or bumps into a pot of boiling liquid that spills on them will move away and jump in pain—the burns caused by this are not even across the body; splash marks result. Immersion, on the other hand, is when a child is held or forced into the hot water. What results is a distinct shape or series of burns:

- An *oval* burn usually includes buttocks and genitals; it is caused when a child is submerged and held in hot water. The burn may not be totally symmetrical; some areas of the body can be protected from the burn, due to the position of the arms and legs of the child.

- A *glove* or *stocking* burn results when a hand or foot is held in hot water. An example of a stocking burn is seen in Figure 9–12. Notice the splash marks on the less severely burned leg, which indicates that the child managed to free that leg partially while being held.

- A *donut-shaped* burn surrounding the buttocks indicates being forced to sit on a hot object, which could be an electric heater, stove, or other electrical unit.

Forms of Sexual Abuse

In the area of child abuse, no other category is as universally condemned as sexual victimization. Approximately 1.8 million children have been victims of a serious sexual assault, comprising 11 percent of substantiated reports of child abuse in 1995 (Kelley et al., 1997). Still, it is commonly accepted that sexual crimes are underreported, and self-report studies typically suggest higher levels. In a study on histories of child sexual abuse among African-American college students, the results indicated that 25 percent of female respondents and 12 percent of male respondents had been sexually abused before age 17 (Priest, 1992).

The majority of substantiated cases of sexual abuse to a child involve a female victim with an average age of 7 to 8 years old (Hammerschlag, 1996). When family members perpetrate the abuse, it usually involves multiple episodes from one week to years. Over 50 percent of male victims experienced anal penetration (Hammerschlag, 1996). A sexual assault on a child is any forced, exploitive, or coercive sexual contact or experience with a child. Statutes typically address the issue of "force," and they vary widely. Due to the usual age difference in sexual victimization and the lack of sexual maturity in a young person, force can be as minimal as instructing a child in a sexual activity. The three elements of sexual abuse are these:

1. *A significantly older person.* Five years or more is a significant difference. The power differential is also a good indicator to consider. The child perceives a person in a authority position, such as a babysitter, teacher, parent, police officer, or priest, as someone the child must obey. Relationships involving

Figure   9–12   Immersion burn. *(Photo courtesy of American Academy of Pediatrics.)*

power and control are always considered abusive. Children can be sexual offenders in addition to having being victimized. The younger the child perpetrator, the more likely that he or she is also a victim.

The most difficult situations in which to determine abuse are the teenage category of 13- and 19-year-olds. A 19-year-old is a legal adult and can be held responsible for statutory rape even in a consensual sexual relationship. In Massachusetts, for example, a child under the age of 16 is legally incapable of giving consent to a sexual relationship. Therefore, the 19-year-old could be criminally charged and tried with statutory rape of a child if he or she has sex with someone under age 16.

2. *A person who engages in sexual activity.* This is any activity committed for the sexual gratification of the offender. We tend to think of more common forms of sexual activity with respect to children. In reality, sexual activity can also include bondage, urination (referred to as "golden showers") or defecation on a child, in addition to fondling and/or intercourse. Cross-dressing the child or posing a child in underwear can be sexually appealing to the pedophile and should not be overlooked as sexual activity.

3. *Activity involving someone who is legally a child.* Achieving age 18 most often defines an adult. Some states may specify a younger or older age; some states specify different ages as legally consenting participants in particular crimes. For example, a child in Massachusetts cannot consent to intercourse until age 16, yet can be indecently touched with consent over the age of 14. The federal standard for child pornography considers a minor to be someone who has not yet achieved the age of 18. Obviously, age becomes less of an issue for clinical intervention, but the law of each state supersedes in cases involving legal intervention.

Most often, there are no physical signs of the sexual misuse of children. Types of sexual assault include:

- *Molestation:* involves indecent touching of the child or forcing the child to touch the perpetrator on the genitals or breasts.
- *Rape:* the insertion of any object into any orifice for sexual gratification. Penile penetration usually comes to mind, but rape also includes digital penetration into the child's vagina or anus (use of fingers), or oral penetration of breasts, penis, or vagina (use of the mouth). In fact, any object can be used to effect a rape; common weapons include bottles, sticks, and curling irons. Any object used to penetrate a child is a weapon of rape. Rarely, there may be a visible indication that force was used in the attempt of a rape. Notice the bruise around the neck of the rape victim in Figure 9–13.
- *Voyeurism:* includes looking at the victim in various stages of undress. The victims may or may not be aware that the perpetrator is watching them.

Figure 9–13 Bruise due to strangulation attempt. *(Photo courtesy of American Academy of Pediatrics.)*

- *Exhibitionism:* when a person exhibits his or her genitalia to a child.
- *Pornography:* for the crime to be pornography, the victim does not have to be aware that the perpetrator is filming or videotaping.
- *Forced prostitution:* a child is always considered to be forced when she or he is engaging in prostitution at the instruction of an adult.

Incest.   When a blood relative perpetrates sexual abuse, it is known as incest. If the sexual relationship is between a parent and child, the power position of the parent identifies the perpetrator. Parental/child incest is the type that is most commonly reported, but sibling incest may be the most frequent form (Sgroi, 1984). Including stepparents or foster parents is common in nonlegal definitions of incest, particularly in clinical settings. When sexual interactions take place between children who have the same parents, they are incestual. The relationship may be consensual in the absence of threats or harm in order to gain compliance.

Symptoms of Sexual Abuse

Sexually Transmitted Diseases in Children. Gonorrhea, syphilis, AIDS, herpes, venereal warts, and pubic lice are examples of sexually transmitted diseases (STDs). The presence of an STD in a child over the age of one month is suggestive of sexual abuse, but exceptions do exist (Hammerschlag, 1996).

Physical Indicators,

1. Enlarged vaginal or anal opening
2. Bleeding or discharge from the vagina, penis, or anus
3. Scratching or rubbing the genitals

4. Walking with the buttocks and legs apart (as if the child has to have a bowel movement)

5. Current physical injury accompanied by signs of multiple prior injuries

Behavioral Indicators

1. Complaining that his or her genitals hurt or were touched
2. Acting out sexually with other children
3. Inappropriate sexual knowledge for his or her home environment and age
4. Child fearful or unwilling to explain the cause of any injury
5. Regression

Caretaker Indicators

1. Delay or failure to seek medical treatment for a child
2. History not consistent with the child's developmental level or ability to harm himself or herself
3. Historical details change or are different from the caretakers' original version

Sexual Abuse in Social Settings.   The high level of media coverage of sexual abuse in day-care settings leads us to believe that the incidence is quite high. Research indicates that in fact it is rare, representing less than 1 percent of substantiated abuse (Wang & Daro, 1998). Additionally, there does not appear to be a high risk of sexual abuse for children sent to a day-care setting (Finkelhor & Williams, 1988). When abuse does occur in such social settings as a day-care center, Boy Scout troop, or Little League team, the settings are usually referred to as *child sex rings*. Ann Burgess suggests three types of child sex rings: solo, transition, and syndicated (Burgess, 1984). Multiple victims are characteristics of these sex rings. Special Agent Lanning identified two types of child sex rings that involve multiple victims and multiple offenders. A structure such as day care or social organizations is necessary for this type of abuse to flourish (Lanning, 1992). Fear and bizarre or ritualistic activities are controlling factors for what Lanning calls the *multidimensional child sex ring*. Seduction is the primary control for victims in the *historical sex ring*.

Neglect

Child neglect is the form of violence that is most commonly found in cases of abuse. Of the reports substantiated in 1995, NCPA estimated that 54 percent involved neglect (Wang & Daro, 1998). According to the Department of Health and Human Services, neglect was involved in 52 percent of substantiated cases in 1995 and 57.7

One of the most recent child sexual abuse cases that attracted national attention was the sex ring in Wenatchee, Washington, known as "The Circle." It began in 1994 when a 9-year-old girl was placed in foster care with Bob Perez and his wife. Bob, the city's chief sex-crimes investigator, was investigating a series of unrelated sexual abuse cases at the time. The foster girl came from a poor home; her father was illiterate and her mother had an IQ of 58. She had testified in a trial resulting in the conviction of a friend of the family previous to living with the Perez family.

During the fall of 1995, she told Perez that her biological parents had molested her and her siblings. The story was confirmed, and the mother confessed; she and her husband pled guilty and were sent to prison. Soon after, the girl made further accusations about other members of the community. Included were stories of a sex ring at the local church, where adults would take children six at a time to a room, having sex with them. Incredible stories of the circle grew from two dozen adults to 100 members who were accused of thousands of counts of abuse. The case against the Robinsons (the pastor and his family) was based on the testimony of the foster child, a 13-year-old friend of hers, and a 35-year-old member of the church. The woman told prosecutors that she had participated in the sex ring activities, but later told a television station that Perez and his investigative team pressured her into the confession. The Robinsons were acquitted on all 14 counts of abuse on December 11, 1995. They had been in jail for nine months at the time of their release. Journalists covering the cases noted that all the defendants who could afford a private attorney were acquitted or had charges dismissed; most of those who had public defenders received prison sentences. All the adults accused of being part of the circle were poor; many are illiterate, and some have been tested below average intelligence.

In June 1996, the foster child called a local TV station and in a 1 1/2-hour videotaped statement officially recanted her earlier stories of abuse, saying that Perez had pressured her. Some defendants filed appeals based on her recantation. Many of those acquitted or with charges dismissed filed civil suits for wrongful prosecution against Perez and other investigative officials.

Source: PBS Online (1998).

What could be done to prevent this kind of outcome? What safeguards should professionals put into place when investigating cases of suspected sex ring abuse?

---

percent in 1996 (U.S. Department of Health and Human Services, 1997). Neglect is often present when other forms of abuse are reported. In some states, that would constitute a separate report; in others, it would not be substantiated if it were the "minor" form that the child presents. The accuracy of our statistics is questionable, due to obscure definitions and differential reporting methods. Still, the problem of assuring adequate care for children is a huge one that requires education. When neglect is noted, it should be documented in a comprehensive report of the child's situation.

Neglect is difficult to define because there is no consensus. Inadequate parenting can include a number of different acts or omissions that might be considered neglectful. The concept of neglect is predicated on a parental duty to provide the basic needs for one's children. These needs include food and adequate shelter. A parent is expected to seek medical attention and provide educational opportunities for the child. Providing supervision and nurturing is also expected. The failure to provide these necessities within socially acceptable standards may be considered neglectful.

Along with the idea of parental duty, the concept of children's rights has been established. Children have been afforded legal protections to assure that the parent is providing the necessities of life and promoting well-being. As early as 1838, the U.S. Supreme Court ruled in *Ex Parte Crouse* that the right of the parent is not inalienable. The extent to which children must be protected and the expanse of child rights has always been controversial in social and legal forums.

Educational Neglect.   At the most basic level, the education of a child includes providing behavioral limits that are age appropriate. All states have mandatory formal educational requirements that a child must attend school until age 16. Educational neglect includes failure to enroll a child of mandatory school age in school, the allowing of chronic truancy, and the failure to attend to a special educational need.

Inadequate Care Such as Food, Clothing, and Shelter.   Children are unable to seek out nutrition that is necessary for body growth and development. A healthy baby should double his or her birth weight by four to six months and triple it by about one year (Rosenberg, 1996). Food should be of the quality and amount that is appropriate for the age of the child. *Failure to thrive* is a term that has been used since early in the twentieth century to describe the condition of children who, due to lack of adequate nutrition, did not gain weight expected for normal growth (Helfer & Kempe, 1988). Inadequate nutrition or a disease may cause it. *Acute starvation* is the result of lack of nutrition on a short-term basis. If a child has been *dehydrated* (by a failure to provide fluids), the child may present with severe vomiting or diarrhea. If failure to thrive, dehydration, or starvation is suspected, the child requires immediate medical attention, as illness or death can result.

Clothing should be sufficient to protect the child from the elements, minimally clean, and in decent repair. Infants must have diapers that are cleaned and changed frequently to avoid severe diaper rashes. Shelter must provide protection from extreme weather and allow a safe place for sleep.

Lack of Supervision.   Supervision is necessary to prevent harm or to intervene when harm is occurring. Leaving a young child unattended or locking the child in a room are examples of failure to provide supervision if the age and maturity of the child is insufficient to respond to problems that might occur. Young children have been known to play with matches and lighters while locked in a room, which has led

---

More about It: Maltreatment

Keep in mind that as individuals, we have our own perspective on how children should be raised, based on our upbringing and family history. Be careful not to impose your standards on another family! Additionally, families living in poverty will appear different due to a lack of resources and should not be accused of abuse simply because they don't live the way you do! Abuse is a *maltreatment*, not a result of the living standards or values of other families.

---

to a fire and ultimate deaths. Parents must assure that when children are left alone—such as latchkey kids—that they are reasonably able to care for themselves in case harm arises.

Failure to Seek Medical Care.   The parent has the duty to seek medical care for a child when necessary. Withholding of medically necessary treatment has been defined by the Child Abuse Prevention and Treatment Act of 1996 as the failure to respond to an infant's life-threatening conditions by denial of treatment that would probably be effective in ameliorating all life-threatening conditions. A religious exemption from medical neglect is permitted in some states if the withholding of medical care is based on religious grounds. Each state determines if it will recognize this federal standard expressed by the U.S. Department of Health and Human Services. Under the same standard, however, states cannot have an exemption from finding a child to be neglected (Swan, 1994).

Been There...Done That!

Although I was not a narcotics investigator, there were times when that unit would ask for assistance in executing warrants. I remember such a case where we "hit" an apartment with a search warrant for drugs. As I came through the door, I couldn't help but notice a child of about 6 years old sitting at the breakfast table. He would put his fingers into the bowl and pull out a cockroach, then take a spoonful of cereal. He repeated this until he had finished eating, literally "flicking" the cockroaches across the room each time. As I searched his bedroom, the contents of each dresser drawer would appear to "move" in unison when opened to the light. When I lifted his mattress to look at that space between the mattress and box spring, thousands of cockroaches scurried to the same beat. *Was this child neglect?* I spoke with a social worker who reminded me that the apartment was one of approximately 150 in the block and that cockroaches are a hazard of the poverty in that neighborhood.

Nonsupport.   The court determines child support when a family divorces or separates. It is like an allowance for the child that is administered by the parent who has legal physical custody. It allows the custodial parent to provide adequate care for the child who lives with him or her at a level roughly equivalent to the family's status had the separation not occurred. Both biological parents have the responsibility to care for their offspring; this method attempts to share the financial assets of the parents for the benefit of the child. Failure to provide for a child financially directly affects the quality of life for the child and may cause illness or neglect. Recent campaigns to decrease nonsupport have attained a high level of media coverage. Most people are familiar with the terms *deadbeat dad* and *deadbeat mom*. These refer to parents who attempt to avoid their financial responsibility through nonsupport of a minor child.

Parental Kidnapping

The second most common missing child case is *parental kidnapping* (Patterson, 1987). The term is used when a parent abducts a child in violation of custody or visitation rights, or prior to the filing of a custody decree. Approximately 354,100 family abductions took place in 1988 (Laney, 1995). Abductors may flee to avoid further abuse to themselves or children, or the abuser may abduct in an attempt to intimidate a battered parent who is attempting to leave the relationship.

   Due to the seriousness of the problem and the consequences for the child, all 50 states and the District of Columbia have enacted criminal parental kidnapping statutes. Still, the investigation of parental kidnapping is complex, since allegations of neglect or abuse by both parents frequently surface, often during the time between separation and divorce (Klain, 1995). When confronted with an allegation of child kidnapping by a parent who names the other, a check begins with a determination as to who has physical legal custody. The reporter should be able to supply documentation from a family court or from a divorce proceeding on the custody and specifics for child visitation if the parents have appeared before the court. A frequent resolution in the absence of child abuse allegation is the awarding of shared legal custody to the parents upon separation and divorce. When an allegation of parental kidnapping is made, a thorough investigation must include separate allegations and legal custody (Patterson, 1987).

MANDATED REPORTING

The primary objective for agencies that investigate child abuse is to determine whether the child is in need of care and protection. The investigator must next assess the level of risk to the child in his or her present living arrangements. All 50 states and the District of Columbia have legislation that mandates reporting of child abuse and neglect. Protection options include the removal of the suspected offender from the home if he or she lives with the child. A parent or legal guardian of the victim should be encouraged to file for a no-contact restraining order to protect the child during the investigation from further violence and threats, whether or not the suspect resides with the child.

To prevent the child from feeling punished for having divulged abuse, removal of the child from his or her home to a safe living environment is an option that should be exercised only if a nonoffending parent or guardian is unwilling or unable to protect the child from the suspect. Additional social services are provided according to the resources of the area in which the abuse is alleged to have occurred. An investigation to determine if a crime has been committed is conducted by law enforcement officials and may be done jointly with a social service agency or independent. Although the initial concern of any investigation involving a child is the safety of the child, law enforcement and social services have different mandates for investigative procedures.

Who Must Report?

Any person who has a duty to care or protect a child may be considered a mandated reporter, governed by the requirements of each particular state. Typical mandated reporters include physicians, childcare givers, police officers, and teachers. It is difficult to determine the exact number of children who are reported and substantiated for child abuse because of the wide variation among states' data collection procedures. Compliance for reporting of child abuse is also difficult to determine, and we can only speculate on the cases that are not investigated due to a lack of reporting.

CONCLUSIONS

The recognition of child abuse and neglect is an important step in the determination of domestic violence involving children. Victims may have experienced numerous kinds of injury and harm that can sometimes be confused with nonabusive injury. Forms of direct abuse include active and physical maltreatment; the general categories include physical, sexual, and emotional maltreatment. Secondary abuse is the consequence of witnessing violence in the home.

No profile can be drawn to describe the victims of abuse. All ages, gender, and races are represented. Although confusion may exist on the exact numbers of those maltreated, certainly we can conclude that it is high—unacceptably high for our society. Medical history and injury inspections are part of the process in determining abuse. Age dating of bruises and pattern identification are tools to assess the condition of the child and provide the necessary protection options. Multidisciplinary teams are helpful to provide insights to the injury and harm and for decisions on intervention. Ultimately, it is the responsibility of the parents or legal guardians to provide for the care and protection of their children physically, mentally, and financially. Intervention must take place only when the needs of the child are not being met to a minimum standard of care or when abusive conditions exist.

$\mathcal{K}$ EY $\mathcal{T}$ ERMS

Active physical maltreatment
Battered child syndrome
Brittle bone disease
Child sex rings
Direct abuse
Failure to thrive
Historical sex rings
Immersion burn
Incest

Mandated reporting
Multidimensional child sex ring
Multiagency team
Munchausen syndrome
Osteogenesis imperfecta
Parental kidnapping
Passive child maltreatment
Shaken baby syndrome

$\mathcal{Q}$ UESTIONS $\mathcal{f}$ OR $\mathcal{R}$ EVIEW

1. What made the public shift attitudes toward child abuse?

2. Describe direct abuse. What is the difference between active and passive maltreatment?

3. What is secondary abuse?

4. What are the major forms of child abuse?

5. What is brittle bone disease?

6. How can one determine the age of a bruise?

7. What is Munchausen by proxy?

8. What are the elements of sexual abuse?

9. List and define the types of sexual abuse.

10. Who is obligated by law to report abuse?

$\mathcal{R}$ EFERENCES

Ablin, Deborah S. 1998. "Osteogenesis Imperfecta: A Review." *Canadian Association Radiological Journal* 49:110–123.

American Association for Protecting Children. 1988. *Highlights of Official Child Neglect and Abuse Reporting, 1986.* Denver, CO: American Humane Association.

Burgess, Ann W. 1984. *Child Pornography and Sex Rings.* Lexington, MA: Lexington Books.

Finkelhor, David and L. Williams. 1988. *Nursery Crimes: Sexual Abuse in Day Care.* Newbury Park, CA: Sage Publications.

Hammerschlag, Margaret R. 1996. *Sexually Transmitted Diseases and Child Sexual Abuse.* NCJ 160940. Washington, DC: U.S. Department of Justice.

Helfer, Ray E. and Ruth S. Kempe (ed.). 1988. *The Battered Child*, 4th ed. Chicago: University of Chicago Press.

Hunter, Mic. 1990. *Abused Boys: The Neglected Victims of Sexual Abuse*. Lexington, MA: Lexington Books.

Jenny, Carole and Thomas Day. 1994. *The Visual Diagnosis of Child Physical Abuse*. Denver, CO: American Academy of Pediatrics.

Kelley, Barbara T., Terence P. Thornberry, and Carolyn A. Smith. 1997. "Juvenile Justice Bulletin." In *In the Wake of Childhood Maltreatment*. Washington, DC: U.S. Department of Justice.

Klain, Eva J. 1995. *Parental Kidnapping, Domestic Violence and Child Abuse: Changing Legal Responses to Related Violence*. Alexandria, VA: American Prosecutors Research Institute.

Laney, Ronald. 1995. *Parental Kidnapping*. FS-9534. Washington, DC: Office of Juvenile Justice and Delinquency Prevention.

Lanning, Kenneth. 1992. *Child Sex Rings: A Behavioral Analysis*, 2nd ed. Arlington, VA: National Center for Missing and Exploited Children.

U.S. Department of Health and Human Services. 1996. *Study of the National Incidence and Prevalence of Child Abuse and Neglect*. FS-13. Washington, DC: DHHS.

Parnell, Teresa F. and Deborah O. Day (eds.). 1997. *Munchausen by Proxy Syndrome: Misunderstood Child Abuse*. Thousand Oaks, CA: Sage Publications.

Patterson, John C. 1987. *Investigator's Guide to Missing Child Cases*, 2nd ed. Washington, DC: U.S. Department of Justice.

PBS Online. 1998. "Innocence Lost: The Plea." *http://www3.pbs.org/wgbh/pages/frontline/shows/innocence/etc/chronology.html*.

Priest, R. 1992. "Child Sexual Abuse Histories among African-American College Students: A Preliminary Study." *American Journal of Orthopsychiatry* 62(3):475–76.

Rosenberg, Donna. 1996. *Child Neglect and Munchausen Syndrome by Proxy*. NCJ 162841. Washington, DC: U.S. Department of Justice.

Sedlak, Andrea and Diane Broadhurst. 1996. *Executive Summary of the Third National Incidence Study of Child Abuse and Neglect*. Washington, DC: U.S. Department of Health and Human Services, Administration for Children and Families; and the National Center on Child Abuse and Neglect.

Sgroi, Suzanne M. 1984. *Handbook of Clinical Intervention in Child Sexual Abuse*. Lexington, MA: Lexington Books.

Smith, Barbara. 1995. *Prosecuting Child Physical Cases: Lessons Learned from the San Diego Experience*. NCJ 152978. Washington, DC: U.S. Department of Justice.

Stark, Evan and A. Flitcraft. 1988. "Women and Children at Risk: A Feminist Perspective on Child Abuse." *International Journal of Health Services* 18(1):97–118.

Swan, R. 1994. "Discrimination de Jure: Religious Exemptions for Medical Neglect." *APSAC Advisor* 7(4):35–37.

U.S. Department of Health and Human Services. 1997. *Child Maltreatment 1995: Reports from the States to the National Child Abuse and Neglect Data System*. 2–7. Washington, DC: National Center on Child Abuse and Neglect .

_____. 1998. *Child Maltreatment 1996: Reports from the States to the National Child Abuse and Neglect Data System*. Washington, DC: DHHS.

Wang, Ching-Tung and Deborah Daro. 1998. *Current Trends in Child Abuse Reporting and Fatalities: The Results of the 1997 Annual Fifty State Survey.* Working Paper 808. Chicago: National Committee to Prevent Child Abuse.

Watkins, Sallie A. 1995. "The Mary Ellen Myth: Correcting Child Welfare History." Pp. 46–53 in *Family Violence: Readings in the Social Sciences and Professions,* James Makepeace (ed.). New York: McGraw-Hill.

Case

Ex Parte Crouse, 4 Wharton 9, PA 11 (1838).

The Identification
of Elder Abuse

INTRODUCTION

> I'm growing fonder of my staff; I'm growing dimmer in the eyes;
> I'm growing fainter in my laugh; I'm growing careless of my dress;
> I'm growing frugal of my gold; I'm growing wise; I'm growing—yes—
> I'm growing old. (J. G. Saxe; *I'm Growing Old*)

People age 65 or older are the least likely to become victims of violent crime in the United States (U. S. Department of Justice, 1994). Retirement can be a peaceful age, a time to sit back and reminisce on the accomplishments of a more active period. Increased leisure time becomes available for activities that were not possible in younger years. Elders as a group are doing well in a number of ways. While the number of children living in poverty has risen, elders on the whole are more financially secure than ever before. In 1959 one-third of elderly were poor; today, the poverty rate for elders is less than the national average (DiLeonardi, 1995).

For some, however, growing old can become a time of increased fear and victimization (Figure 10–1). The most probable source of violence is adult children, spouses or partners, friends, and other caregivers (Executive Office of Elder Affairs, 1998). Yet this area of domestic abuse is unlike any other; a "Just the facts, ma'am" approach will not work. Policing elder violence for the upcoming generation will involve intellect and patience on the part of the officer. Strength and aloofness must be replaced with confidence and compassion when responding to

Figure 10-1 Elders are the least likely to be victimized by violent crime but have the highest rate of fear of victimization. *(Photo courtesy of the Administration on Aging.)*

this population. Some consider this a departure from traditional police work; it is. Now the job of law enforcement means incorporation of appropriate responses to reports from older Americans so that it becomes the tradition of good police work in the future.

Compared to the other forms of domestic violence, elder abuse response is in its infancy. Some credit the report entitled *Battered Parents* and its author with bringing the idea of elder abuse to contemporary study. Much later, the work of researchers Finkelhor and Pillemer first looked at its prevalence and characteristics (Finkelhor & Pillemer, 1988).

The criminal justice community has been slow in responding to the needs of the elderly. Prosecutions of elder abuse have been rare. Community policing for the elderly is the most recent attempt to remedy this problem and to combat the excessive fear that plagues many elderly citizens. The American Association of Retired Persons (AARP), the International Association of Chiefs of Police (IACP), and the National Sheriffs' Association (NSA) signed an agreement in 1988 to work together to reduce crime against the elderly and to improve law enforcement services to older citizens (National Committee for the Prevention of Elder Abuse, 1995b). Referred to as *triad*, community-based programs that involve law enforcement, concerned citizens, and advisory boards are being formed across the United States to improve education and police response to this population of citizens.

Back Then ...

Early references to elder abuse in Britain coined such phrases as *granny battering, granny bashing,* and *granny abuse* according to the authors of *Elder Abuse in Perspective* (Biggs et al., 1995). These terms conjure up images of the little old white-haired lady, someone frail and considered incompetent. Now the stereotypical elder is anything but typical, and current research cautions against identifying elders as one age group of 65 and beyond (Doerner & Lab, 1998). Approximately 34 million elders span four decades as senior citizens (Administration on Aging, 1998). Their health and functional abilities have greatly improved with innovations in medical technology. Increased income, educational attainment, and access to support services for some elders accompany improved standards of care.

Early retirement programs have brought people aged 50 to 55 into the category of senior citizens. Qualifying membership into the American Association of Retired Persons (AARP) is age 50. The spouse of an AARP member is admitted at any age. Since the category of senior citizen has expanded along with the life expectancy, social investigation may necessitate more specifically defined categories of elders. Although states have the flexibility to define elders in law, they do not differentiate between categories such as *early old age* or *advanced old age*. The ability or lack of ability to protect oneself is of little consequence when applying legal protections to the elderly. It does, however, make prosecutions more difficult. Social intervention can and often does differentiate between those who are able and those who require additional consideration. The term *granny bashing* is no longer applicable to describe elder victimization, if it ever was.

Civil versus Criminal Action

Should the perpetrator be charged criminally? The determination on civil versus criminal action for elder abuse is extremely complex. Prosecution is rarely presumed, as with other adult domestic crimes. Neither is the decision made with purely protective concerns, as with child domestic cases. The elder victim is assumed to have an interest in protecting family relationships due to some dependence on the perpetrator. Often, the relationship is of value to an increasingly isolated elder, and threats of abandonment or commitment to an institution make the elder reluctant to follow through with criminal court proceedings. Institutional settings often prefer to handle their own "problems" and historically do not pursue criminal avenues for redress. An institutionalized resident is already limited in ability and may be severely disabled, further complicating determinations in an abusive situation.

Examples of civil actions include assault and battery for physical abuse; false imprisonment when excessive restraints have been used, negligence for mismanagement of funds; and/or restraining orders against perpetrators of abuse. Although this approach could serve to free assets or provide compensation to the victim, he or she must be competent and able to pay the costs of litigation.

More about It: TRIAD

Since its inception in 1988, 32 states have formally committed to work together to increase use of the triad approach, according to the National Sheriffs' Association. In several other states, the office of the attorney general is involved in promoting triad. The national model now includes state and local efforts that survey the needs and concerns of older citizens, expand crime prevention programming, and provide reassurance programs to local seniors. It is called triad because it consists of a partnership with seniors, law enforcement, and the community to provide much needed services. Increasing public awareness and decreasing victimization against older people are the guiding principles. A senior advisory counsel called SALT is established for each chapter to integrate the triad activities and tailor them to fit a community's particular needs.

Providing law enforcement services for elders means accepting that this group of citizens is not incompetent. Understanding the unique character and needs of the people in every age category allows dignity and life choices. These are adults with constitutional protections. Sometimes an elder will make decisions in a manner that is perceived as inappropriate. Could it be that their concerns and considerations are simply different? When age or illness overcomes an elder's ability, interventions become more complex and crucial. Although technically not "domestic," institutional abuse is included because of the caretaker status that nursing homes take on in behalf of the elder.

Criminal actions include assault and battery for physical abuse, burglary or extortion for financial abuse, as well as specific elderly crimes with enhanced penalties. Some states have a caretaker statute that makes it a specific crime to omit care to a dependent or vulnerable person. The advantage to criminal prosecution is the possibility of court-mandated counseling or removal from the victim's presence. Prosecution may serve as a deterrent to future abuse. However, the elder may refuse to press charges due to a fear of retaliation, or may change his or her mind and drop all charges. It is not uncommon for an older adult to be ashamed or embarrassed to admit that his or her family member is abusive.

Prosecution attorneys make the final decision on criminal complaints and must consider the status of each person as well as the severity of the abuse. In some cases adult protection services seek custody of the elder who is unable physically or mentally to make determinations for his or her best interests. Although criminal statutes do not differentiate by age category and ability to self-protect, the choice between civil intervention and criminal prosecution may involve that differentiation.

Categories of Abuse

There are two general categories of elder abuse. The use of these terms may be a bit confusing; remember that they all refer to family or domestic violence. We specify the

---

B a c k   T h e n …

The apparent lack of criminal justice response to this category of maltreatment is evidenced in this historical example of elder abuse. Referring to the preference for health care facilities to deal internally with problems, one author cites *Long v. Brookside Manor*, 1994 (McDaniel, 1997):

> This negligent hiring action suit was brought against a nursing home, based on the assault of a resident by a nursing home employee. Facts indicate that an employee, upon observing that the nursing home resident had accidentally soiled herself, became enraged and grabbed the elder by the hair, jerking her out of the chair and then began beating her about the head, kicking her and punching her. Judgment for plaintiff was reversed and claims dismissed because the court of appeals found that the plaintiff had failed to show that the nursing home's failure to do a background check on the employee was the proximate cause of her injuries.

Based on the information above, should this case have proceeded with criminal charges of assault and battery? Should the law be applied equally to residents in institutional facilities? What do you think?

place of elder maltreatment because this population can reside both at home and in institutional settings. The relationship of the perpetrator to the victim along with the loose definition of residence will allow elder abuse to come under the umbrella of domestic violence, regardless of the setting. The location of the victimization is important to distinguish in order to understand the differences in abuse and likeliness of perpetrator. Bear in mind that these categories are terms used to specify the setting in which the maltreatment occurs.

Domestic elder abuse refers to the victim who lives in his or her own home or in the home of a caregiver. Abuse of an elder who lives in a nursing home, foster home, or group home is termed *institutional*. The forms of abuse remain the same regardless of the environment. For example, physical abuse may occur in a domestic abuse situation or institutional setting. The category of abuse does influence the appropriateness of the responding agency. Ombudsman, health care services, or adult protective services would probably respond to allegations of institutional abuse and neglect, since the majority of complaints would not be criminal. Police would be more involved in the investigation of physical or sexual violence in domestic settings (alone or in conjunction with social service organizations) but may also become involved in severe institutional abuses. It is necessary that all agencies that are charged with response contact each other and work together to resolve conflicts and protect the elder victims.

In any category of abuse, the maltreatment may be either active or passive. This refers to the difference between intentional abuse of the elderly and benign neglect,

---

More about It: Elder at Risk Program

The elder-at-risk program is a short-term, program-focused, goal-oriented crisis intervention. Offered to self-neglecting and/or self-abusing elders aged 60 years and older, it is strictly voluntary. Usually, its clients have demonstrated reluctance to accept interventions by more traditional efforts. The programs provide nontraditional services for those elders seriously in need.

---

which could be unintentional. Intervention may be necessary for the protection of the elder in either case, and a determination would have to be made as to whether the action or inaction of the caregiver was criminal behavior. Social services are provided to elders on a consent basis. If elders refuse services, they may be enrolled in an *elder-at-risk* program and offered whatever services are appropriate. Law enforcement has a responsibility to uphold the law.

Active Abuse and Neglect

The forms of active abuse and neglect should sound familiar to you by now, because they exist in other categories of domestic violence. Financial exploitation and misuse of restraints are examples of specific offenses in this category (Figure 10–2). Self-neglect, a noncriminal activity, might result in civil intervention on the victim's behalf.

Figure 10–2   Financial exploitation and misuse of restraints are examples of specific offenses committed against the elderly. *(Photo courtesy of the Administration on Aging.)*

- Financial exploitation
- Misuse of restraints
- Neglect and abandonment
- Physical abuse

- Psychological abuse and emotional abuse
- Self-neglect
- Sexual abuse

Passive Maltreatment

Caring for an infirm or impaired person that results in unintentional injury or neglect is a passive category, necessitating social intervention.

THE VICTIMS OF ELDER ABUSE

Authors found a victimization rate of 32 elders per 1,000 in the first major study of elder maltreatment (Finkelhor & Pillemer, 1988). Suggesting that a unique classification of elder abuse be recognized, they encouraged professionals to define this category and begin work on profiling the victims involved. Over 1 million older Americans were estimated to have been victimized in 1988 alone.

In part due to the demographics of aging in the United States, increased attention has been focused on elder issues. In 1900, the over-65 age group accounted for just 4 percent of the population. Between 1989 and 2030, the 65-year-old and over population is expected to more than double (Figure 10–3); the 85-year-old and over group is expected to triple. An increased demand for domestic violence protective services has already been noted for this second age group. A survey of state social service departments by NCEA noted a 50 percent increase in elder abuse between 1980 and 1990 (National Aging Resource Center on Elder Abuse, 1992). In one recent study, a steady increase in reported elder abuse cases was noted each year between 1990 and 1994 (Kohl et al., 1995). Indications are that resources will continue to be in demand as the elder population explodes.

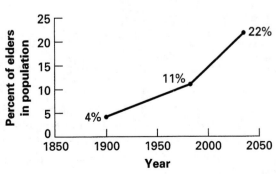

Figure 10–3 Percentage of elders in the population. By 1980, the elderly population had increased to 11 percent and is expected to make up 22 percent of the population by 2030. *(Data from Nerenberg, 1993.)*

In 1996 it was estimated that there were between 820,000 and 1,860,000 abused elders in the country (Tatara, 1996). In 1986 there were 117,000 state-reported cases of elder abuse according to the NCEA. Twenty years later the figure had increased by 150 percent, to 293,000 cases (see Figure 10–4). In 1997, they estimated that 2.1 million older persons were abused, neglected, or exploited (Administration on Aging, 1998).

Both social service agencies and the criminal justice community are affected by these changes. All states and the District of Columbia have passed legislation to protect this population because of the impairments associated with old age. Every state has also passed legislation that mandates police to intervene in domestic violence. Police already respond to domestic elder abuse because law requires it.

Age

A baby born in 1900 was expected to live an average of 47.3 years. In the United States, this figure rose to an average of 75 years in 1987! Males average 72 years of life, and the average woman lives to 79 years old (Administration on Aging, 1998). This trend in life expectancy changes the face of Americans from visions of the young to the wrinkles of the old. If there were such a thing as a "typical" victim, he or she would be between 75 and 80 years old. According to 1994 data (excluding self-neglecters), the median age of victims was 76.4 (National Center on Elder Abuse, 1994). This figure rose only slightly, to 77.9 years, in 1996 (National Center on Elder Abuse, 1996).

Illness and disability associated with old age complicate the investigations of elderly maltreatment. Excluding those who do not live in institutions, approximately 12 million elderly are limited by chronic conditions (Administration on Aging, 1997b). Of these, 3 million are unable to perform by themselves activities such as bathing, shopping, dressing, or eating.

Figure   10–4 In addition to the population growth is an increased incidence of elder abuse reporting. *(Data from the Administration on Aging, 1998.)*

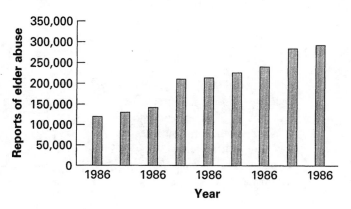

Gender

Women outlive men, and the elderly women outnumber elderly men at a rate of three to two. In addition to having a longer life expectancy, women tend to marry older men. This accounts for the fact that 40 percent of the elderly women in America are widows, whereas only 16 percent of elderly men outlive their wives (Nerenberg, 1993). There are more women in the elder population, which may give the impression that they primarily are victimized (Figure 10–5). The future will shed light on this issue as the gender gap becomes narrower. Between 1990 and 1996, the reports involving female victims dropped from 68.3 percent to 67.3 percent (National Center on Elder Abuse, 1998).

During their elder years, men and women are as like to become victims of physical abuse according to a prominent study (Pillemer & Finkelhor, 1988). In general, female elder victims are represented more frequently than men and are at greater risk for physical injury due to abuse. Age or gender of the perpetrator, however, does not excuse abusive behavior defined as criminal, nor does it exclude law enforcement action.

In addition to the general criminal codes that address domestic violence, legislation provides protections that are specific to the elderly. Some of these laws are criminal, and some are civil. Financial exploitation in a domestic setting is criminal, for example. Self-neglect is usually a civil matter. National standards for protection have been established through the Older Americans Act. Each state interprets the mandates and makes the laws for its jurisdiction. It is important to research the civil as well as criminal statutes to know the exact duties and responsibilities.

Elders have the highest rate of suicide of any age category. If a person is considered a risk to himself or herself or others, regardless of age, either law enforcement or social service agencies may seek assistance from the civil or family court. Even abuse that is not defined by state law as elder crimes may be addressed by using other provisions of the mental health, social service, or penal code (Nerenberg, 1993).

Only women have been identified as victims of sexual assault. We know that younger male victims have been slow in coming forward with complaints of sexual assault, and therefore cannot assume that elder males are not also at risk of sexual abuse. In the Ramsey-Klawsnik study, all the victims were limited in their ability to

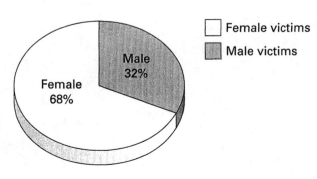

Figure 10–5   Elder abuse victims. In general, female elder victims are represented more frequently than men and are at greater risk for physical injury due to abuse. *(Data from the Administration on Aging, 1998.)*

No one tells the rookie officer what to expect during routine patrol. You have to experience it yourself. Let me tell you of my first experience with Gertrude.

One night while on highway patrol, I noticed a car swerving from lane to lane. Pulling the vehicle over, I expected to find a drunk driver. To my surprise, a petite gray-haired lady opened the door and stepped out as I approached. She took a swing at me, knocking my hat into the travel lane, where the oncoming truck driver delighted in running it over. Admittedly, it took me a moment to reconcile that some little old lady had just hit me, for no reason! I hadn't even said anything yet!

She took off, running up an embankment to the right of the highway. On hands and knees I reached her, holding her first by the ankle so she couldn't go any further. While I was trying to talk to her, she bit me, punched me, and kicked me. I remember yelling, "What is the matter with you? You should be home knitting!" It is really difficult to put someone under arrest when you are afraid of hurting him or her. Ask any police officer; it is a dangerous situation. You are the one most likely to get hurt in the process.

The next day in court, my fellow officers kidded me on my "big" arrest of that poor little old lady for assault and battery on a police officer. I felt so humiliated until the judge yelled at my victim: He was tired of her picking fights with the cops, he said. Then and only then, my fellow officers told me that Gertrude had been beating up her husband for over 50 years. Since he had died, she resorted to fighting with any police officer she could get to approach her.

---

protect themselves (Ramsey-Klawsnik, 1991). The majority of elders were aged 70 to 80 years old. In 61 percent of the reports, the victim had been raped at least once; vaginal rape was the most common form. Surprisingly, a third party witnessed the sexual victimization of these women in approximately one-third of the cases. In institutional settings, the typical victim of abuse is thought to be a female and in poor health (Pillemer, 1988).

Race

By the year 2020 the elderly minority populations will have increased substantially, from 14 percent in 1985 to approximately 21 percent. Minority populations are believed to be increasing at a faster rate than the white population. Because cultural and ethnic factors are thought to influence whether or not families turn to law enforcement or social service agencies for help, it is difficult to assess the risk of elder abuse in this rising portion of our population (Nerenberg, 1993). In 1996, most victims were white, 66.4 percent of total reports; African-American victims made up 18.7 percent of cases; Hispanic elder abuse accounted for 10 percent of victims; and Native

Americans and Asian Americans/Pacific Islanders were each less than 1 percent of total reports (National Center on Elder Abuse, 1996).

Cultural Differences

Cultural differences among minority elderly may have an impact on the reporting of abuse. Since the minority population is expected to comprise 33 percent of the over-65 population by the year 2050, these differences are important (Nerenberg, 1993). If a translator is necessary to conduct interviews with the victim, care must be taken to assure that exact words are translated, not paraphrasing of the statements. Brief profiles offer the following to consider when responding to reports of elder abuse:

1. Older African-Americans form the largest group of minority elderly in the United States (Figure 10–6). Often residing in central city areas, the average have lower income and health status than elderly Caucasians (Nerenberg, 1993). This population is more likely to have dependent children or grandchildren living with them. According to a recent study, African-Americans are four times more likely to be affected by Alzheimer's disease (Mayeux, 1998). These characteristics may increase the vulnerability to abuse.

2. Hispanics/Latin Americans represent the fastest-growing segment of the elder population. They are twice as likely to live in poverty and may have a limited command of the English language (Nerenberg, 1993). Their lack of resources teamed with insufficient communication skills makes intervention difficult.

Figure 10–6   African-Americans comprise the largest group of minority elderly in the United States. *(Photo courtesy of the Administration on Aging.)*

Their risk for Alzheimer's is now thought to be twice as likely as for whites (Mayeux, 1998). Bilingual investigators are important resources for these cases.

3. Older Asian Americans represent still another set of challenges. Their suicide rate is three times higher than the national average for seniors (Nerenberg, 1993). Language barriers inhibit intervention.

4. Native Americans reside in each of the 50 states and the District of Columbia, according to the 1990 census (Administration on Aging, 1997a). They are twice as likely to be rural dwellers. Although they make up less than 1 percent of the total population, the number of elder Native Americans increased 35 percent more than the total non-Indian older population in the United States.

CATEGORIES OF ELDER ABUSE

The environment under which elder abuse occurs provides some insight into the condition of elders as well as their ability to protect themselves. Knowledge of that environment is extremely important to assure that everything that can be done for the elder is put into motion. In each setting, the rights of the victim must be fully protected. Adult protective services are available in every state and the District of Columbia to assist in the protection of elder abuse victims, alone or in conjunction with law enforcement.

Domestic Abuse

Law enforcement is encouraged to use a multidisciplinary approach to elder abuse and neglect investigation. Overlapping responsibilities of multiple state agencies, including long-term ombudsmen, adult protective services, department of social services, and law enforcement, make this category of abuse particularly amenable to agency cooperation. As mentioned earlier, the call for services from all agencies is expected to increase dramatically in future years. A 1992 survey by the Police Executive Research Forum (PERF) identified elder abuse training as the most necessary, according to 81 percent of police chiefs (Nerenberg, 1993).

Due to the dependence that an elder may have on an abusive caretaker, PERF recommends a modified police response to this category of domestic violence. Arrest and removal of the perpetrator may sometimes cause more harm than good. Research suggests that mandatory arrest may sometimes lead to further violence. The situation must be evaluated, and flexibility must be part of the standard operating procedure. Knowing the resources in your area beforehand will make assisting the domestic violence victim much more efficient. Is there emergency care that can be arranged in the event that the abuser/caretaker must be removed from the home? Where is the emergency care provider, and has a protocol been set up with that agency for quick response?

Been There... Done That!

Phyllis, a woman of around 70 years old, opened the door when I knocked. My visit was the result of her call to the office of the district attorney; Phyllis had voted for the DA and hoped that he would send someone to stop her son from stealing her money.

Phyllis lived alone, widowed for many years. She had only one child and no one else to turn to for help. What could she do? she asked. She loved her son, but she didn't have much money and was afraid that he was going to take it all. Her son was taking money out of her purse after she had cashed her social security check. He had a drug problem, she confided, and she was afraid to confront him about the missing money.

She did not know exactly how much money had been taken, or when the stealing had begun. She had never seen her son go into the purse; it must have happened while she slept. No, Phyllis did not want to press criminal charges against her son. Phyllis wanted me to make her son stop taking her money—that's all. Hardly the job for a supercop, I thought. This was not really what I expected to be doing in the major crime bureau! It was easy, though; a little time spent with Phyllis to assess the problem made the choices clear.

First, I spoke to Phyllis about a security alarm for her house—it might make her feel more comfortable knowing that she had the ability to decide who would enter her home while she slept. We discussed having her checks sent by direct deposit to her bank so that she would not have large amounts of cash in the home. Finally, I told her about adult protective services, the social service agency that could help her to make those things happen. They could check up on her and provide a place to call if she had further problems. A small thing, right? Phyllis sent a letter of thanks to the district attorney, which didn't hurt me a bit. It has occurred to me that I had the opportunity to make a difference, a small one to be sure, but it might have made her life a little better. All it cost was my time, and I was already being paid for that! Although the lack of evidence made prosecution impossible, we found an acceptable alternative.

Institutional Abuse

Elders enter nursing and adult foster homes when they become limited in the ability to care for themselves in some way. An elder may have become ill or injured and need this form of temporary assistance until she or he is able to care for himself or herself. It is false to assume that going into a nursing home is permanent. Approximately 30 percent of elders return to their own homes or to assisted living situations after a recuperative stay in a nursing home.

It is also false to assume that all residents of nursing home are demented. Symptoms of maltreatment can be confused with conditions that are nonabusive. When an elder's abilities appear to deteriorate quickly in the institutional setting, it should be standard procedure to seek a medical cause. A simple cold would not seriously affect a 25-year-old, yet to a 90-year-old who weighs only 85 pounds, a cold could involve a number of unexpected side effects, such as increased confusion, restlessness, or rapid weight loss. A medical checkup should be a standard part of the investigation into elder abuse since it may help to confirm or negate abuse allegations.

Aggression, agitation, and depression may be symptoms of a form of dementia such as Alzheimer's disease. These symptoms may be mistaken for abuse if organic causes have not been ruled out. At the same time, dementia is a factor that also puts the resident at higher risk for abuse. Present in 50 percent to 75 percent of patients who reside in nursing and foster homes, dementia is the leading risk factor for maltreatment (Weinberg & Wei, 1995). So although illness or disease may explain away the behavioral indicators of abuse, it does not mean that abuse is not occurring. Diminished capacity does not mean that abuse cannot occur: It can and does. However, only 4 percent of elders resided in nursing or foster homes in 1997; therefore, the risk of abuse in institutional settings is considered relatively small (Doerner & Lab, 1998).

Both state and federal statutes regulate and monitor nursing homes in the United States. The responsibility for protection, however, rests principally with the states. Obtaining a clear picture of maltreatment to the elderly is difficult in part due to the diverse agencies and definitions that are involved. In some states, as many as seven different agencies may investigate complaints of institutional abuse. Primarily, the state long-term care ombudsman's office and adult protective service agencies handle these allegations; however, law enforcement or state health department officials might be charged with the task. In light of President Clinton's announcement in July 1998 of a new initiative to improve the quality of nursing homes, the future involvement of law enforcement is likely to increase. Included in this announcement

---

More about It: Dementia

The term *dementia* comes from Latin for "madness" or "senseless." We use the word to describe the deterioration of intellectual faculties, such as memory, concentration, and judgment. Many conditions can cause dementia. It may be related to depression, drug interaction, thyroid imbalances, and other problems. Emotional disturbance and personality changes are indicative of this brain disorder or disease. Some diseases that can cause dementia include Parkinson's, Creutzfeldt–Jakob, Huntington's, and multi-infarct or vascular disease, caused by multiple strokes (Alzheimer's Association, 1998).

Alois Alzheimer (1864–1915), a German neurologist, first diagnosed Alzheimer's disease in 1906. This is the most common form of dementia. Nearly half of women over the age of 85 suffer from this disease, which involves memory loss and decline in cognitive abilities. The Alzheimer's Association reports that 4 million Americans have Alzheimer's disease now and that experts expect that 14 million will be affected by the middle of the next century if a cure is not found.

is "the need to prosecute egregious violations of care practices through civil and criminal investigation and prosecution..." (National Senior Citizens Law Center, 1998).

Compounding the problems associated with obtaining reliable statistics, states report instances of institutional abuse differently. Although the majority of states do provide statistics for institutional abuse separately from those for domestic abuse, some do not collect data on this category at all (Tatara, 1990). Although we don't know the exact prevalence of maltreatment in this setting, reports received by authorities have been increasing steadily in the past few years.

What we do know is that nursing home residents can be vulnerable due to low staff ratios, poor working conditions and wages, and inadequate supervision, to name a few of the problems. In any case of suspected abuse, it is critical that documentation begin at the onset of an investigation. Once the facility records abuse, it may become admissible in a criminal court and therefore should be stored properly and with limited access allowed to the professional staff of the facility.

Current controversies surrounding institutional abuse and neglect involve the character of nursing and foster home care. In a society that is ambivalent about institutional residential settings, there is little consensus on the nursing or adult foster home. Some authors suggest that the institution itself is oppressive, due to the invasion of personal privacy and forced dependency, a setting that by its very nature abuses residents (Biggs et al., 1995). Others argue this perspective while citing the need for increased awareness that institutional abuse is a category of family violence, deserving attention and concern. This view can be summarized with this statement: "The first step towards resolving mistreatment is to uncover it" (Biggs et al., 1995). Investigations require knowledge of state and federal regulations concerning nursing and foster homes. Most often, an ombudsman investigates in these settings initially. Joint interviews with adult protective services and law enforcement personnel can be valuable, since determinations must be made on the victim's mental status.

THE MAJOR FORMS OF ABUSE

In part, the problems of elder abuse are confusing because of the lack of definitional consensus within the professions that investigate, research, and document cases concerning elders. Hudson (1991) does not include self-neglect as a category of abuse. Additionally, his classification considers sexual abuse as a subgroup of physical abuse (Hudson, 1991). Another author includes "violation of individual or constitutional rights" as an abusive category (Boudreau, 1993). Vague categories that are difficult to understand assure the continuing controversy on the meaning of elder abuse. For the purposes of this book, seven forms of abuse, in two categories, domestic and institutional, have been identified.

Just as with other victims of abuse, it is not unusual for an elder to have more than one injury or different forms of abuse and/or neglect. Physical abuse may be the tool to accomplish financial exploitation, and vice versa. Determining the cause of

---

More about It: Ombudsman

Federal legislation has provided the standards for elder care through the Older Americans Act of 1965. An amendment in 1987 provided for the creation of a long-term care ombudsman's office to act as the agency for nursing home certification and licensure. The amendments of 1987 and 1992 included services to prevent abuse of older people. Bringing together the long-term care ombudsman program with programs for the prevention of abuse, neglect, and exploitation and state elder rights and legal assistance development programs, the act calls for a coordination and linkage within each state. It establishes a requirement that each state agency on aging provide a person who...will investigate and resolve complaints made by or on behalf of older persons who are residents of long-term care facilities. This person, the ombudsman, is responsible for investigating complaints and providing or arranging appropriate resolutions for complaints. He or she might become a reporter of abuse that is discovered and provide information to criminal justice or health department agencies. An ombudsman may be a paid staff member or a trained volunteer. In addition to being an impartial fact-finder, the ombudsman is an advocate for improving the quality of life for nursing home residents.

---

injury begins with ruling out the obvious and looking toward possible explanations that are nonabusive. If an elder is mentally incompetent, his or her patterns of behavior should be observed to assure that the person is not self-neglecting.

When abusive conditions seem likely, the ability of some elders to protect themselves against abuse must be assessed. Elders are often dependent on others for their care, which is a factor contributing to their vulnerability. What is the source of the maltreatment? Is the elder able to take adequate steps in preventing further abuses? Cognitive, physical, and sensory impairments may make elders susceptible to many forms of abuse, including financial exploitation (Wilber & Reynolds, 1996).

Financial Exploitation

Financial exploitation is also known as *fiduciary abuse, financial abuse, economic abuse,* and *financial mistreatment.* It covers a broad range of conduct that is difficult to define and to prove. The determination is often subjective, and rarely is it possible to prove criminal knowledge of incompetence and intent (Commonwealth of Massachusetts, 1995). Although prosecution of the perpetrator has been rare (Wilber & Reynolds, 1996), it is possible in some cases. A civil lawsuit, for the purpose of recovering misappropriated property, is also an option for the victim. As the phenomenon of exploitation becomes better understood, its indicators will increasingly be recognized and successful intervention more commonplace. This form of violence to the elderly could be called the *invisible tragedy*; without the external signs of abuse, it has often been unrecognized and its effects minimized.

More about It: Adult Protective Services

Most states have an adult protective services program. The purpose is to provide services and receive reports of adults who are abused, neglect, exploited, or otherwise mistreated by their families or caretakers (American Association of Retired Persons, 1987). Social services are offered to consenting older adults and personnel may intervene following court authority on behalf of incompetent persons without consent. There is no national consistency, however. APS may be part of a social services department or contracted to a private, nonprofit agency; eligibility may be based on age (50, 60, or 65), incapacity, or vulnerability. It is believed that APS originated in 1958 (Mixson, 1996). At that time, the National Council on Aging created an ad hoc committee to investigate the need for national protective services for the elderly. Implementation of elder protective services nationwide was slow since federal funds were not appropriated until 1991.

Since people over the age of 50 control 70 percent of the nation's wealth (Nerenberg, 1996), the motivation for this form of abuse is clear. The impact of financial exploitation is not as obvious. Losing financial resources can be especially worrisome to a person who is of an age when he or she cannot replenish them. Anguish about the lack of adequate resources and confusion over financial arrangements can be devastating. Loss of property rights to one's home may mean institutional commitment or dependence when the elder would have otherwise been able to care for himself or herself. Approximately 12 percent of cases investigated by protective services involve financial exploitation (Fox et al., 1995).

The National Center on Elder Abuse warns that the following may be indicators of financial abuse (Nerenberg, 1996). By no means is this an exhaustive list.

- Uncharacteristic bank activity is noted for an elder.
- Suspicious activity appears on the person's credit card accounts.

Since the banking industry has a stake in protecting its clients, educational efforts should be aimed at bank personnel in addition to protective service agencies and law enforcement. This model, which includes the banking business in efforts to combat financial exploitation, is outlined in *The Bank Reporting Project* (Fox et al., 1995). The design includes a sample protocol for reporting and responding to financial exploitation by bank personnel in addition to consumer education. A similar program with the Milwaukee Police Department and area banks reduced confidence crime against elders in that city by 80 percent, according to the Fox report.

- Bank activity is noted that is inconsistent with the abilities of an elder.
- There are changes in property titles, will, or other documents of the elder.

Tellers are trained to be observant of client behaviors, such as the behavior of elders when withdrawing large cash amounts or those accompanied by others who appear domineering. Elders who appear confused or coerced into banking activity would prompt the senior bank officers or security to speak privately with the client about the transaction.

- An elder does not understand recently completed financial transactions or seems unaware of the transactions.
- An older person is uncared for.
- An elder seems to be isolated by others.
- An elder has untreated medical or mental health problems.
- A power of attorney is executed by a confused older person.
- Forged and/or suspicious signatures appear on an elder's documents.

Police officers from Los Angeles found themselves inundated with investigations involving complex misappropriation of property through powers of attorney, quitclaim deeds, wills, and living trusts (Nerenberg, 1995). Police departments traditionally had not become involved with cases involving legal documents that had assigned authority because they believed them to bring the case into the civil rather than the criminal arena. This was referred to as *civil mirage*. Since 1987, the Los Angeles Police Department responded with a formal unit called the *Fiduciary Abuse Specialist Team* (FAST), which works together with local protective service workers in investigations of elder exploitation. The FAST team approach combined criminal investigation techniques and cooperation with local banks and businesses.

Misuse of Restraints

Although misuse of restraint is usually associated with institutional settings, it may also be identified in an abusive home. It involves the chemical or physical control of an elder beyond physician's order or outside accepted medical practice. The U.S. Department of Health Services concluded in a 1990 report that 24 percent of nursing homes improperly administered drugs against the written orders from attending physicians.

Restraints (cloth bindings on chairs or beds) may be used in nursing homes only under two conditions:

1. When a person is confused and unable to comprehend or remember that by moving about, he or she may harm himself or herself or someone else.
2. When a person is unable to maintain his or her position because of a severe physical handicap such as paralysis.

Restraints are used only for a resident's safety; they are never to be used without a physician's order and even then only for the span of time absolutely necessary. A restraint used for the convenience of the caretaker is never acceptable. Used in anger or for punishment, a restraint constitutes abuse. Caretakers at home may not be familiar with state laws on abuse and need to be educated about its limited acceptable use. Educating the caretaker on alternative methods may be helpful. If the restraints are used as a punishment or for the purpose of inflicting pain, particularly if the practice is an ongoing or repetitive action, prosecution may be a feasible option.

Neglect and Abandonment

The frequency of neglectful behavior, and its duration, intensity, severity, and consequences, all are taken into account when making a determination as to elder abuse and neglect (Wolf, 1996). It is not a simple decision that can be made haphazardly. Controversy exists between the child abuse model and spousal abuse model, both of which have been applied to address the needs of the elder victim. The child abuse model uses language similar to child abuse protective statutes and takes a stronger view of victims as unable to protect themselves. Conversely, the spousal model assumes the elder to be victimized, yet legally independent adults. Some researchers claim that the family violence paradigm is not suitable for these cases because cases of neglect are forms of inadequate care, not violence. Concerned about the civil rights of elders, professionals disagree on this area of government interference (Biggs et al., 1995). Since many adult protective services have modeled legislation after child abuse statutes, this raises questions on freedom of choice. Some suggest that the government-defined level of care denies elders basic constitutional rights.

Abandonment.   If a special relationship exists between a caretaker and the elder, the caretaker can be held legally responsible for a failure to act on that duty of care in some states. California is one state among six that has adopted criminal abandonment legislation, making it a felony to cause or permit a dependent elder to suffer harm. In 1995, the California Supreme Court put that law to test. They tried family members for "abandonment" after the death of 67-year-old Robert Heitzman, Sr. His "body was found in his bedroom on a mattress covered with feces and rotted through with urine" (National Committee for the Prevention of Elder Abuse, 1995a). Two sons who lived with the elder were found guilty of 368(a) of the California Penal Code. Upon appeal, the California Supreme Court held that the statute was not unconstitutional or vague—yet a duty to care for an elder, through a special relationship, must be present for legal liability to attach. A daughter who did not live full-time with her father was found not guilty.

Active Neglect.   A deliberate attempt by a caregiver to inflict injury or emotional stress on an older person characterizes active neglect. This is an intentional condition that is inflicted on the elder by an act or an omission: for example, failure to provided needed medication for the elder because of the high cost of the prescription.

Passive Neglect.   The passive form of neglect occurs when a caregiver is unable to provide the necessary care for an elder. Passive neglect may be caused by caretakers who are too young or inexperienced to take care of an older person who has special needs. Sometimes the person responsible for elder care is handicapped by mental or physical disability and is unable to handle the difficult chores of caring for an elder. Passive neglect is defined by AARP as the unintentional failure to fulfill a caretaking obligation. There is no willful desire to inflict physical or emotional distress on the older person.

Symptoms for both types of neglect include the following:

1. *Withdrawal or denial of health services.* Overmedication may be purposeful to keep an elder "quiet" or might be due to ignorance and carelessness on the part of the caretaker. Either way, it can be extremely dangerous to the person, and intervention is necessary. This could be a life-threatening situation for the elder. Deliberate overmedication is a form of an improper use of restraint. In some instances, a lack or perceived lack of financial resources could cause the withdrawal or denial of health services. Medical attention for the elder should be sought to determine the condition and provide necessary medications. Untreated injuries and illnesses may alert the responder to neglect or abuse. Although it is not life-threatening to be denied eyeglasses, dentures, or hearing aids, this would constitute a lower standard of life for the senior and is neglectful.

2. *Denial of adequate food.* The elder may become malnourished or dehydrated as a result. If the elder is living alone, the investigator should look into the refrigerator and cupboards to confirm suspicions that food is not being supplied or made available to the elder.

3. *Lack of proper hygiene.* If the older person smells of old urine or is caked with feces, he or she is not being cleaned properly. Other signs of neglect include matted, unclean, or uncut hair, bodily crevices caked with dirt, or overgrown finger/toe nails. The presence of a serious rash, bedsores, urine burns, or impetigo is also suggestive of neglect.

The neglected elder's environment may also provide clues that abuse is occurring (Ramsey-Klawsnik, 1997). Evidence demonstrating neglect include:

- An excessively cluttered or dirty home
- Lack of heat, running water, electricity, or air conditioning in extremely hot climates
- Infestation by cockroaches or rodents

Self-Neglect and Abuse

When an older person threatens his or her own health or safety, it is called *self-neglect* or *self-abuse*, depending on the actions of the elder. Self-neglect is the most common form of elder mistreatment and must be differentiated from maltreatment caused by another person. Nationally, about 51 percent of elder abuse cases involve self-neglect (Biggs et al., 1995). Self-neglect and self-abuse are included as a separate form of violence because it is extremely rare that they would be considered a criminal offense. This type of abuse may accompany other forms for which there are criminal consequences. The differences are important, and an investigation of neglect must include the consideration that abuse may be in part or wholly self-inflicted.

The National Association of Adult Protective Services Administrators (NAAPSA) formed a committee to study and report on the characteristics of adults identified as self-neglectful in addition to providing a definition for this form of abuse (Virginia Department of Social Services, 1991). As a result, NAAPSA adopted the following definition:

> *Self-neglect:* the result of an adult's inability, due to physical and/or mental impairments or diminished capacity, to perform essential self-care tasks, including providing essential food, clothing, shelter, and medical care; obtaining goods and services necessary to maintain physical health, mental health, emotional well-being, and general safety; and/or managing financial affairs.

The report stated that 79 percent of APS clients are self-neglecters, some of whom may also be victims of another. Generally noninstitutionalized, they frequently have a mental and/or physical impairment. Service needs for this population can be substantial. Recognition of this form of abuse by law enforcement is crucial to make the appropriate referrals to social service agencies that can provide appropriate intervention.

M o r e   a b o u t   I t :   A t t e m p t e d   S u i c i d e

There is at least one situation where self-neglect or abuse may be a criminal offense: Some states outlaw suicide. The law of Massachusetts, for example, allows for a person to be brought before the court on a complaint of "attempted suicide." This is common law crime, but rarely is it enforced.

An officer in western Massachusetts has used it, however. The case involved a man who after repeated unsuccessful suicide attempts refused medical assistance or evaluation. Brought before the court on criminal attempted suicide, he was ordered to have a psychiatric evaluation and a temporary commitment to a local hospital. This method was used to obtain emergency help for the victim.

This issue raises some important considerations for criminal justice on the acceptable extent of government interference. The suicide rate for the elderly is higher than for any other age group. Is it the role of law enforcement to prevent or intervene in such attempts? Jack Kevorkian has brought the issue to the forefront in the United States through his multiple assisted suicides for terminally ill patients.

Self-abuse is not a criminal violation, and necessary emergency intervention should come from a social service or adult protective service agency.

Physical Abuse

The symptoms of elder physical abuse are similar to the other categories of domestic violence. Human bite marks, bruises, bleeding, and burns are all indicative of maltreatment. Gag marks, or the indication that the elder has been tied or taped, should make investigators highly suspicious of elder abuse. Slapping an elder is an example of physical abuse. Injuries that are not consistent with the explanation given for their cause are a "red flag" that should cause an investigator to look deeper into the situation. Does the elder have a history of similar injuries or hospitalizations? Do people in the household give varying accounts of how the elder was injured?

However, injuries due to falls or accidents may not be caused by abusive conditions. Observing the behavior of the elder may help to clarify the situation if abuse is suspected. Presence of fear, agitation, contradictory statements, or refusal to talk openly should alert officers of a potential abuse situation. It is not confirmation of abuse, but should focus further investigation.

Psychological and Emotional Abuse

Psychological and emotional abuse is the willful infliction of mental or emotional anguish by threat, humiliation, intimidation, or other abusive conduct. Psychological and emotional abuses are the most difficult forms to identify. Isolation, name-calling, or being treated like a child by a caretaker are recognizable conditions. Usually, there is a lack of evidence to support these claims. If an elder is suffering from another type of abuse, it is not unusual for psychological and/or emotional abuse to be present also. Documenting signs of psychological and/or emotional abuse in conjunction with other more visible forms of abuse will provide an accurate statement of the general living conditions that are indicators of abuse as well as strengthening the case against the suspect.

Additionally, investigation may find the elder to be in need of services. A referral to the local elder protection agency is warranted when the complainant seems confused or unable to distinguish between reality and fantasy. It is appropriate to contact a caregiver or protection agency to let them know when a person is displaying inappropriate behaviors.

Sexual Abuse Indicators

Research on sexual abuse to the elderly is rare (Ramsey-Klawsnik, 1993). We know that it is happening because the professionals in the field are identifying cases. Sexual maltreatment may be "covert" or "overt," as described in one major study from Massachusetts (Ramsey-Klawsnik, 1991). The author describes covert sexual abuse as a sexualized relationship. It involves sexual interest, jokes, comments, and harassment

---

Been There... Done That!

A report came into the barracks of theft from an elder. When responding to the call, I found the man extremely agitated as he described his wallet being stolen. His fear of being victimized was real, but the account of how it happened didn't sound plausible. After careful consider of his narration and interviewing of the suspect, I doubted that the wallet had been taken. We slowly retraced his steps throughout the day. Actually walking the property where he had been, I found the wallet lying on the ground in the barn. He was embarrassed to find that it had been dropped, not stolen.

Complaints from seniors should never simply be dismissed. If possible, they should be resolved. The elders' fear of victimization is high even though the actual incidence may be low. Failure to be sensitive to elderly fears will leave the person in emotional turmoil, if not psychological pain. Although frivolous complaints may occur from time to time, we have no way of determining if the abuse is occurring without an investigation. A case solved is a case solved, regardless of the complaint!

---

of the victim or discussion of sexual activity in front of the victim. Overt sexual abuse is any type of unwanted or forced sexual conduct with an elder. Overt sexual abuse can be any form of sexual activity, including but not limited to kissing and fondling, oral–genital contact, penetration of the vagina or anus, voyeurism, and exhibitionism.

Sexual assault victims share the same or similar symptoms regardless of their age or gender. The following signs are suspicious for sexual abuse, although their presence doesn't verify that abuse to the elder is occurring and may be indicative of other problems.

Sexually Transmitted Diseases. Presence of a sexually transmitted disease if the elder is not engaged in consensual sexual activity and does not have a prior record of STD is cause for concern when present with other indicators, such as fear, apprehension, or neglect. Some STDs are related to poor hygiene and would not indicate abuse, so caution is recommended. Examples of STDs that could be caused by poor hygiene *or* sexual abuse include *Trichomonas* vaginalis (vaginitis) and bacterial vaginosis (Hammerschlag, 1996). Herpes and herpes simplex may be self-infected in the genital area if the person was infected with mouth sores previously. Severe and untreated infections may be indicative of neglect rather than abuse.

Physical Indicators

1. Injury such as bruising, bleeding, or pain to the genitals, rectum, mouth, and breasts should be investigated thoroughly. Urinary incontinence would

complicate the diagnosis for abuse if the elder is not cleaned and cared for properly. Redness of the genital area could be caused by poor hygiene.

2. When bruising or pain is evidenced with injury to the face, neck, cheek, abdomen, thighs, or buttocks, the patterns of bruising might be suggestive of grab marks or the use of restraints.

3. Evidence of torn, stained, or bloody underwear is highly indicative that sexual abuse is occurring.

Behavioral Indicators

1. Intense fear, anxiety, or mistrust of one person, along with other indicators of sexual maltreatment, is a sign of sexual abuse.

2. The victim of sexual abuse may offer a "coded" disclosure to someone that she or he trusts. Ramsey-Klawsnik suggests that the elder may give hints about the sexual abuse, described as "testing of the waters" (Ramsey-Klawsnik, 1993). This may include statements about a dislike for a particular caregiver or a reluctance to be bathed by that person.

3. Depression without other explanation or cause may indicate sexual abuse.

4. Self-destructive or suicide attempts without a history of mental illness or underlying medical causes may indicate sexual abuse.

DUTIES AND RESPONSIBILITIES

Since elder abuse and neglect is a new area of intervention for the criminal justice community, it is important to consider the duties and responsibilities that are in place to direct law enforcement. Police officer liability is a factor that must be taken into account. If your state has a mandated or preferred arrest policy for domestic abuse that does not specifically exclude elders, it must be enforced. If the state has a more liberal policy involving discretionary action, police can consider the entire situation before taking any action. Depending on the severity of the abuse and the likelihood of repeated assaults, an arrest, further investigation, or referrals are all options to consider.

In neglectful situations, it may be more difficult to determine an appropriate course of action. Any investigation is first concerned with the safety of the victim (Figure 10–7). Can the person protect himself or herself against further abuse or neglect? Referrals, arrest, or continued investigation are all options. The first guiding principle should be the determination of probable cause. If probable cause to believe a crime has been committed does exist, officers must consider already existing domestic violence law in their state. Does your jurisdiction mandate arrest in an abuse situation?

Figure 10–7   The first concern of any abuse investigation is the safety of the victim. *(Photo courtesy of the Administration on Aging.)*

MANDATED REPORTING

Forty-two states and the District of Columbia have mandatory reporting laws under which physicians, nurses, social workers, and others designated by the state are legally required to report suspected elder abuse (American Association of Retired Persons Foundation, 1998). The remaining states have voluntary reporting laws. A mandated reporter is required to report when he or she saw abuse or when there is a reasonable belief that it is occurring. It is difficult to identify abuse in some instances, since many elderly are reluctant to tell and since many physical and mental difficulties that older adults suffer from have results that can easily be mistaken for some forms of abuse. Since it is so hard to determine if elder abuse is actually occurring, the trend in most states is to grant immunity from legal sanctions for reporting abuse when in fact it is not occurring, if that report was based on a good faith belief that it was.

States that have mandated reporters seem to create a duty to report for almost all professionals with whom the elderly come into contact. Following is a list that identifies the percentage of state laws that include the professionals cited as mandated reporters (Tatara, 1995): social workers, 75 percent; physicians, 70 percent; nurses, 69 percent; police, 52 percent; and dentists, 50 percent. If a mandated reporter believes that abuse is possible but fails to report it, legal repercussions could be taken against the reporter. For failing to report abuse, for example, a reporter can be found to have committed a misdemeanor (Stiegel, 1995). Most states do not, however, take such aggressive action against this omission. In fact, only one prosecution occurred in the United States between 1994 and 1997 under these mandated reporting laws (Moskowitz, 1998).

CONCLUSIONS

As a society, we are faced with many challenges in the upcoming years. Our elder population is exploding, and the call for services is increasing as well. In an area where law enforcement has been involved only sporadically, the need for continued self-education and involvement is imperative. Community triad programs demonstrate the commitment of this generation of law enforcement personnel toward protecting the next. Fiduciary investigation units such as LAPD's FAST provide an example of one police department's response to the unique problems that elders face. Most officers can expect to be faced with these elder issues throughout their careers and should remember that they, too, will one day be elderly.

Physical and sexual abuse of the elderly shares many identifying physical characteristics with other forms of family violence. The signs and symptoms are nearly the same; injury is still the obvious indicator. The possible extent of injury for the elderly can be higher than for other populations, however, due to infirmity and old age. The emotional and psychological harm of abuse, which is impossible to measure, may be taken to the grave.

Change in abilities and dependencies make elders susceptible to abuse in ways that don't apply to other age groups. Due to the vulnerability of elders, legislation has been enacted that will guide enforcement action for the future. Financial exploitation, the invisible abuse, should be a growing area of specialization for law enforcement in the future. Compassion and empathy will go a long way toward preserving the dignity of seniors in the United States.

KEY TERMS

Abandonment

Active maltreatment

Adult protective services

Alzheimer's disease

Dementia

Domestic abuse

Fiduciary abuse specialist team

Financial exploitation

Institutional abuse

Misuse of restraints

Ombudsman

Passive maltreatment

SALT

Self-neglect

Triad

QUESTIONS FOR REVIEW

1. Name criminal actions against the elderly.

2. What are the two types of elder domestic abuse, and what agencies handle each?

3. Name the forms of active elder abuse.

4. Define *passive maltreatment*.

5. Describe the demographics of the "typical" elderly victim of abuse.

6. What is dementia, and how is it related to abuse?

7. What is an ombudsman?

8. What is financial exploitation?

9. Explain the category of self-neglect and abuse. What is the seriousness of this type of abuse?

10. Name some of the symptoms that indicate physical abuse of an elder.

$\mathcal{R}$EFERENCES

Administration on Aging. 1997a. *Native American Elder Population, 1990*. Washington, DC: U.S. Administration on Aging.

_____. 1997b. *Older and Younger People with Disabilities: Improving Chronic Care Throughout the Life Span*. AOA Fact Sheet. Washington, DC: U.S. Department of Health and Human Services.

_____. 1998. *Older Women: A Diverse and Growing Population*. AOA Fact Sheet. Washington, DC: U.S. Department of Health and Human Services.

Alzheimer's Association. 1998. "Alzheimer's disease: A Major Health Issue for Women." *www.alz.org/news/right.htm*. August 1988.

American Association of Retired Persons. 1987. *Decision-Making, Incapacity, and the Elderly*. Washington, DC: Legal Counsel for the Elderly.

American Association of Retired Persons Foundation. 1998. *Elder Abuse: Training Module*. Washington, DC: National Legal Assistance and Elder Rights Project.

Biggs, Simon, Chris Phillipson, and Paul Kingston. 1995. *Elder Abuse in Perspective*. Bristol, PA: Open University Press.

Boudreau, F. A. 1993. "Elder Abuse." Pp. 142–58 in *Family Violence: Prevention and Treatment*, R. L. Hampton, T. P. Gullotta, G. R. Adams, E. H. Potter, and R. P. Weissberg (eds.). Newbury Park, CA: Sage Publications.

Commonwealth of Massachusetts. 1995. *Investigation of Financial Exploitation: Skill-Building for Protective Services Caseworkers*. Boston: The Commonwealth.

DiLeonardi, Joan W. 1995. "Families in Poverty and Chronic Neglect of Children." Pp. 145–51 in *Family Violence: Readings in the Social Sciences and Professions*, James Makepeace (ed.). New York: McGraw-Hill.

Doerner, William and Steven Lab. 1998. *Victimology*, 2nd ed. Cincinnati, OH: Anderson Publishing Company.

Executive Office of Elder Affairs. 1998. *Elder Protective Services 1997 Program Report*. Boston: Commonwealth of Massachusetts.

Finkelhor, David and Karl Pillemer. 1988. "Elder Abuse: Its Relationship to Other Forms of Domestic Violence." Pp. 244–54 in *Family Abuse and Its Consequences: New Directions in Research*, Gerald Hotaling, David Finkelhor, John Kirkpatrick, and Murray Straus (eds.). Newbury Park, CA: Sage Publications.

Fox, Craig R., Gillian Price, John S. Scheft, and Bonita Irving. 1995. *The Bank Reporting Project: An Edge against Elder Financial Exploitation.* Boston: Commonwealth of Massachusetts, Executive Office of Elder Affairs.

Hammerschlag, Margaret R. 1996. *Sexually Transmitted Diseases and Child Sexual Abuse.* NCJ 160940. Washington, DC: U.S. Department of Justice.

Hudson, M. F. 1991. "Elder Mistreatment: A Taxonomy with Definitions by Delphi." *Elder Abuse and Neglect* 3(2):1–20.

Kohl, Rhiana, Diana Brensilber, and William Holmes. 1995. *Elderly Protection Project.* Washington, DC: U.S. Department of Justice.

Mayeux, Richard. 1998. "The APOE-E4 Allele and the Risk of Alzheimer Disease among African Americans, Whites and Hispanics." *Journal of the American Medical Association.* 280(19) November pp. 1661–63.

McDaniel, Christine L. 1997. "Elder Abuse in the Institutional Setting." May. *www.ink.org/public/keln/bibs/medaniel2.html.* August 1998.

Mixson, Paula M. 1996. "How Adult Protective Services Evolved, and Obstacles to Ethical Casework." *Aging* 367:14–17.

Moskowitz, Seymour. 1998. "Private Enforcement of Criminal Mandatory Reporting Laws." *Journal of Elder Abuse and Neglect* 9(3):1–22.

National Aging Resource Center on Elder Abuse. 1992. *Elder Abuse: Questions and Answers.* Washington, DC: NARCEA.

National Center on Elder Abuse. 1994. *Findings from a National Study of Domestic Elder Abuse Reports.* Washington, DC: NCEA.

_____. 1996. *Highlights of a National Study of Domestic Elder Abuse Reports.* Washington, DC: NCEA.

_____. 1998. "Elder Abuse in Domestic Settings: Elder Abuse Information Series 2." *wwww.gwjapan.com/NCEA/Statistics/p2.html.* August 1998.

National Senior Citizens Law Center. 1998. "Betrayal: the Quality of Care in California Nursing Homes." July 27. *www.nsclc.org/testate.html.* August 17, 1998.

National Committee for the Prevention of Elder Abuse. 1995a. "California Supreme Court Rules on Family and Neglect." *Nexus* 1(2):6.

_____. 1995b. "Triad: Community Policing for the Elderly." *Nexus* 1(2):3.

Nerenberg, Lisa. 1993. *Improving the Police Response to Domestic Elder Abuse.* Washington, DC: Police Executive Research Forum.

_____. 1995. "LAPD's Fiduciary Swat Team: An Interview with Detectives Dave Harned and Chayo Reyes." *Nexus* 1(2):4–5.

_____. 1996. *Financial Abuse of the Elderly.* San Francisco: San Francisco Consortium for Elder Abuse Prevention.

Pillemer, Karl A. 1988. "Maltreatment of Patients in Nursing Homes: Overview and Research Agenda." *Health and Social Behavior* 29:227–33.

Pillemer, Karl and David Finkelhor. 1988. "The Prevalence of Elder Abuse: A Random Sample Survey." *Gerontologist* 28(1):51.

Ramsey-Klawsnik, Holly. 1991. "Elder Sexual Abuse: Preliminary Findings." *Journal of Elder Abuse and Neglect* 3(3):73–89.

_____. 1993. "Interviewing Elders for Suspected Sexual Abuse: Guidelines and Techniques." *Journal of Elder Abuse and Neglect* 5(1):5–17.

_____. 1997. "Sessions I and II; III and IV, Workshop Handouts." Canton, MA: Massachusetts Executive Office of Elder Affairs.

Steinmetz, Suzanne K. 1978. "Battered Parents." *Society*:July/August 54–55.

Stiegel, Lori. 1995. *Recommended Guidelines for State Courts Handling Cases Involving Elder Abuse.* Washington, DC: American Bar Association.

Tatara, Toshio. 1990. *Elder Abuse in the United States: An Issue Paper.* Washington, DC: National Aging Resource Center on Elder Abuse.

_____. 1995. *An Analysis of State Laws Addressing Elder Abuse, Neglect, and Exploitation.* Washington, DC: National Center on Elder Abuse.

_____. 1996. *Elder Abuse in Domestic Settings.* Washington, DC: National Center on Elder Abuse.

Tennessee Department of Social Services. 1991. *A National Study of Self-Neglecting Adult Protective Clients.* NAAPSA #1. Nashville, TN: National Association of Adult Protective Services Administrators.

U. S. Department of Justice. 1994. *National Crime Victimization Survey: Elderly Crime Victims.* NCJ 147186. Washington, DC: DOJ.

Weinberg, Andrew D. and Jeanne Y. Wei. 1995. *The Early Recognition of Elder Abuse.* Bayside, NY: American Medical Publishing Company.

Wilber, Kathleen H. and Sandra L. Reynolds. 1996. "Introducing a Framework for Defining Financial Abuse of the Elderly." *Journal of Elder Abuse and Neglect 8(2):61–80.*

Wolf, Rosalie S. 1996. "Understanding Elder Abuse and Neglect." *Aging 367:4–17.*

Cases

Long v. Brookside Manor, 885 S.W. 2d 70 (1994).

Associated Major Crimes

INTRODUCTION

> "Being the victim of a stalker is a hideous and insidious situation," says actress Theresa Saldana. "It never goes away. When someone is after you, it's like the proverbial bogeyman, only it's real life." (Moret, 1997).

Celebrity accounts on the terror of being stalked heightened public awareness during the 1980s. Actresses Theresa Saldana, Jodie Foster, and Madonna are among those victimized. John Lennon was killed, and David Letterman is still pursued by stalkers. Those who stalk go to great lengths to get noticed by their victims. They may do bizarre things to gain attention. Her assailant, who had obtained her address through a private detective, stabbed Theresa Saldana; John Hinkley shot President Reagan to impress Jodie Foster; a woman who claims to be the wife of David Letterman repeatedly breaks into his house and steals his car. When her stalker killed Rebecca Shaefer in 1989, California responded as the first state to pass antistalking laws.

Stalking itself is not new. We have referred to it as harassment, annoyance, and know it as domestic violence. The pioneering legislative action in California coined the term *stalking* and defined a set of behaviors that constitute the deviant conduct that is now prohibited by law. Unprecedented interest in all aspects of stalking has followed. Since that time, antistalking legislation has been passed in every state and in Washington, D.C.

Research on the identifying features and motivation of perpetrators and the relationships to their victims has resulted. The first national study to determine its prevalence was undertaken in the National Violence Against Women (NVAW) Survey

(Tjaden & Thoennes, 1998). Using a definition of stalking that requires the victim to feel a high level of fear, the NVAW survey found it was more prevalent than previously thought. Eight percent of women and 2 percent of men surveyed said they had been stalked at some time in their life. Estimating that approximately 1 million women and 371,000 men are stalked annually in the United States, the report concluded that stalking should be considered a serious criminal justice and public health concern.

Stalking may have entered the public consciousness through highly publicized cases, but it affects many people every day. It is a gender-neutral crime that is perpetrated by both men and women; it crosses all racial, social, religious, ethnic, and economic lines. Like all crimes, it can be perpetrated by strangers or by offenders known to the victim. When the victim and offender are related by marriage, intimacy, or family ties that are legally recognized as "domestic relationships," the crime is also one of domestic violence.

Until recently, there was little scientific data on the prevalence of stalking. The relationship between homicide and domestic violence was assumed but not documented. On the other hand, statistics on homicides in the United States have been collected from police reports for years. There is no mistake that men, women, and children are being killed by those related to them. In this chapter we deal with stalking and homicide, the relationship between stalking and homicide, and their association to domestic violence.

STALKING

Once thought to be a crime committed against celebrities and politicians, stalking has become the crime of the 1990s. In addition to the fear generated by stalking behaviors, it is estimated that stalkers are violent toward their victims between 25 and 35 percent of the time. The group most likely to be violent are those that have had an intimate relationship with the victim (National Institute of Justice, 1998).

What Is Stalking?

Stalking is a distinctive form of criminal activity because it is a pattern of behavior that is intended to cause harm or to instill fear in a person. Following or harassing someone typically characterizes the offense. It is different from the majority of crimes because it consists of a series of actions rather than a single act. When the events are considered individually, they may not constitute illegal behavior. For example, sending flowers, or love notes, and telephoning someone are perfectly legal activities. When the repetitive actions of the perpetrator install significant fear of bodily harm or cause injury to the person, it then constitutes the pattern of behavior that is legally prohibited. Intent is therefore an important element of stalking, but it is not the stalker's motives or the context in which the stalking occurs that should be considered when the crime is charged. Attempts to force the victim to comply with the desires of

---

A   B o y f r i e n d   T u r n s   M u r d e r e r

Kristin Lardner, 21, dated Michael Cartier for about two months before breaking up with him on April 16, 1992. Angered over her decision to end their relationship, Cartier followed her down the street, beat her, and left her lying on a curb. In the following weeks, he continued to contact and follow her. She notified the police and obtained a temporary restraining order. She also learned that he had committed inhumane acts, such as killing cats, and had a criminal record–he had beaten ex-girlfriends and had been caught injecting his own blood into a restaurant ketchup bottle. At the time he was stalking Lardner, Cartier was on probation for having attacked a previous girlfriend with scissors.

The judge who granted the temporary restraining order on May 11, however, was unaware of Cartier's criminal history and the fact that he was on probation. The judge scheduled a hearing for a permanent injunction to be held the following week. On May 19, when Lardner returned to court to obtain a permanent injunction, a different judge, who was also unaware of the man's record, treated the case routinely. He issued an order prohibiting Cartier from any contact with Lardner and requiring that he stay 200 yards away from her. Approximately two weeks later, just six weeks after he had first beaten her, Cartier shot and killed Kristin Lardner in broad daylight outside a Boston sandwich shop. Cartier later killed himself in his home. (Lardner, 1997)

---

the offender by the use of threats or intimidation can turn the scenario into a nightmare. If the conduct of the person is seriously threatening, it should be charged as stalking, regardless of the defendant's motivations or relationship to the victim.

Since stalking is a newly created and defined criminal offense, it can be confusing. Broadly written statutes in some states have caused difficulty for criminal justice implementation and resulted in constitutional challenges. At least 20 states have faced or will face constitutional objections based on the lack of clarity, broadness of the statutes, and on First Amendment grounds (National Conference on State Legislatures, 1997). Typically, statutes define stalking as willful, malicious, and repeated following and harassment of another person. Some states further require that the perpetrator make a threat of violence that is credible. New York's laws use the term *menacing* (Chapter 353) and *aggravated harassment* (NY Public Law Code, §240.30), yet both provisions refer to stalking behaviors.

It is not unusual for constitutional challenges and revision through case law to clarify some of the problems with newly established laws, and "stalking" is no exception. It may take years for the bugs to be worked out of the state statutes and for clarification to occur. There is a federal offense of stalking in addition to the individual state versions. These versions may vary widely. The following was used in the NVAW survey and offers a general definition of stalking that is not specific to a particular state law (Tjaden & Thoennes, 1998):

Stalking: course of conduct directed at a specific person that involves *repeated* visual or physical proximity; nonconsensual communication; verbal, written, or implied threats; or a combination thereof that would cause fear in a reasonable person (with *repeated* meaning on two or more occasions).

For NVAW, only those victims who reported being very frightened or those who feared bodily harm were counted as stalking victims. The survey used the following questions to screen for stalking victimization: Not including bill collectors, telephone solicitors, or other salespeople, has anyone, male or female, ever...

- Followed or spied on you?
- Sent you unsolicited letters or written correspondence?
- Made unsolicited phone calls to you?
- Stood outside your home, school, or workplace?
- Showed up at places you were, even though he or she had no business being there?
- Left unwanted items for you to find?
- Tried to communicate in other ways against your will?
- Vandalized your property or destroyed something you loved?

Stalking Behaviors

The motivations of a stalker are varied. Offenders routinely attempt to intimidate and control their victims. Some attempt to scare the victim. Others may have a fanaticized love interest in their target. A significant factor is the desire by the stalker to keep the victim within a personal relationship, since more than half of the stalkers begin before the intimate relationship has actually ended. Approximately half of the women who are stalked report the offender to be a current or former marital or cohabiting partner (Tjaden, 1997).

Common elements in the crime of stalking include *following, harassing,* and *threatening* the victims. The actions are not only multiple events that taken together indicate a single pattern of conduct, but they must also *cause fear* and be *intentional* or *willful* in order to satisfy legal definitions of stalking.

Following.   The most common stalking behavior is *following.* Stalkers follow and spy on approximately 75 percent of victims (Tjaden, 1997). They may stand outside a person's home. Still, the crime is more complex than simply following or spying on someone. It is done for a specific purpose, although each stalker is different and the range of behaviors is equally unpredictable. Achieving a victim reaction is routinely the objective of the stalker. The stalker's motivations will determine what reaction is the desired one.

Often, the offender will alert the victim to ensure that he or she is aware of the presence or intent of the perpetrator. The purpose here is to control and to intimidate the victim. For example, a note or telephone message may be sent indicating places that the victim frequents, stores that he or she shop at, and where he or she works or resides. The actions of the stalkers therefore assure that they get the attention of the victims and make them aware that they are being followed or spied upon. A stalker may or may not initiate conversation if seen by the victim. It is meant to cause fear on the part of the victim and bolster the self-esteem of the assailant.

Harassing.   It is difficult to list all forms of harassment that are possible. Harassing is generally recognized as a knowing and willful pattern of conduct or series of acts over a period of time directed at a specific person, which seriously alarms or annoys the person. A reasonable person would be expected to suffer substantial emotional distress as a result of harassment.

A co-worker who consistently stands uncomfortably too close to the victim in conjunction with other acts may rise to the level of harassment. A stalker who breaks into (by key or force) the victim's home and leaves evidence that someone was in the house is also guilty of a form of harassment. Common examples, such as unwanted phone calls, unwanted letters, or items left for the victim and vandalized property, are noted in Figure 11–1.

Females report harassing phone calls more frequently than do male victims. The calls may be excessive, repetitive, and at odd hours of the day or night. They may be hang-up calls or heavy breathing. Depending on the pattern and type of the calling, a

Figure 11–1   Five common stalking behaviors. *(Data from the National Institute of Justice, 1998.)*

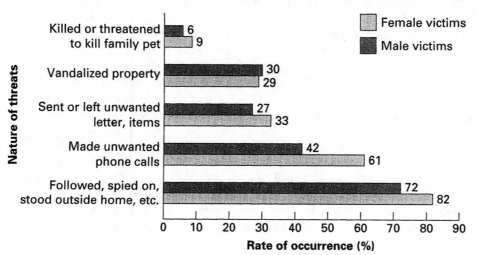

purpose may be determined in some instances. For example, calls may come frequently in the middle of the night to deprive the victim of sleep.

A stalker frequently attempts to contact the victim by sending or leaving unwanted items or letters. Numerous attempts at communicating with the victim routinely contain veiled threats. It is imperative that the item is looked at closely not only for its physical properties but also for its intended meaning. Flowers or a gift may be sent on an anniversary or date of significance to reaffirm the existence of a relationship that in reality no longer exists.

Threats. The legal requirement of a credible threat against the victim can be the most difficult element to establish. Not all statutes require this ingredient, however, so it is important to know the law in your state. The threat does not need to be written or verbal to instill fear; delivering a dead animal to the doorstep or pointing a finger toward someone as if it were a gun are examples. Some states require additional conduct after a threat has been made; others specify that the threat must be one causing fear of serious harm. For example, Massachusetts law requires "a threat with the intent to place that person in imminent fear of death or serious bodily injury" (Massachusetts General Laws ch. 265, §43).

This requirement might seem like an impossible obstacle to overcome since less than half of victims (male and female) are overtly threatened by their stalkers (National Institute of Justice, 1998). However, prior acts of violence against a person by the stalker may properly be admitted to prove that the threats were intended to instill fear of death or serious injury (*Commonwealth v. Martinez*). A person who had been victimized previously due to a partner relationship who then receives a veiled threat may properly react with the level of fear required to satisfy the elements of the crime, even though the "threat" at hand was not itself serious.

The Massachusetts example illustrates the importance of considering the crime of stalking from the entirety of the situation rather than as separate deviant acts. Thinly veiled threats are much more common and may rise to the level of credible threat in the face of a past or current abusive relationship. It ultimately falls on the court to determine if the action will satisfy the requirement of fear.

Threats come in unusual packages that may have meaning to the stalker and to the victim alone. Asking the victim *why* she or he feels threatened can enlighten others. Ripped, torn, or mutilated objects that are sent signify anger and are meant to scare the victim. They may include dolls, photographs, or broken statues, to name a few. Sending black roses or a game called "Hangman" can be threatening if the victim is afraid of the stalker or believes that the gift signifies a step closer to fulfilling an earlier threat to hurt him or her. Killing or threatening to kill a family pet indicates an extremely dangerous situation for the victim. In approximately 10 percent of cases the stalkers threatened to kill or did kill the pet(s) (Tjaden, 1997). Should this occur, safety precautions should be taken and the victim should be considered to be in imminent personal danger.

Characteristics of Stalking Perpetrators

Although stalking is described as a gender-neutral crime, the majority of perpetrators (87 percent) are male (Tjaden, 1997). There is no single profile of a stalker; they are categorized by their relationship to the victim and within broad categories due to their behaviors. A progression that is similar to other domestic violence crimes is also apparent in stalking. If the stalker is spurned, he or she may escalate the behavior to intimidation. In rare instances, the contacts become a persistent pattern of behavior that turns threatening and violent. The majority of stalking does not involve offenders who are mentally ill, although the behavior is not normal or appropriate.

The relationship between the victim and the offender characterizes the first stalker category:

1. *Intimate or former intimate.* The stalker and victim may be married, divorced, or separated. They may be current or former cohabitants, serious or casual sexual partners, or former sexual partners. A history of domestic violence may exist.
2. *Acquaintance.* The stalker knows the victim casually. They may be co-workers or neighbors, or they may have dated once or twice.
3. *Stranger.* Cases involving celebrities and other public figures generally fall into this category where the victim and stalker do not know each other at all.

Forensic psychologists refer to stalkers using this second method of characterizing stalkers; it is based on psychological and behavior profiling.

Relationship or Simple Obsessional Stalkers.   This is the most common type of stalker; it is also the best known. The perpetrator and victim typically have a previous relationship that could be marriage, friendship, or that of co-workers. Most stalkers in cases of domestic violence and dating relationships are simple obsession stalkers. The use of "simple" as a descriptor refers to the fact that this is a common type of stalker, not that the issue is simple or that the victim is not at risk.

People in this category are more frequently those who batter. It should not be a surprise that their characteristics resemble those of the domestic violence offender; they are, in general:

- Emotionally immature
- Socially incompetent
- Unable to maintain relationships

- Overly jealous
- Insecure
- Low in self-esteem

Love Obsessional Stalkers.   People in this group develop a love obsession or fixation, generally targeting celebrities and politicians. There is no personal relationship between the victim and offender; therefore, the target might also be a casual acquaintance. These stalkers tend to be persistent in their pursuit of their victims. They fantasize about the victim being their love partner and may go to drastic means to get attention. The bizarre attempts may be lethal to the victim since the stalker does not care if the attention is negative or positive.

Whereas the common stalker is believed to suffer from a personality disorder, these offenders may have a mental disorder, such as schizophrenia or paranoia (Schaum & Parrish, 1995). Unlike the person suffering from erotomania, the love obsessional stalker does not believe that the target loves them. They may believe that they are destined to be with their target and only need to try harder to convince their victim.

Erotomania.   This term is usually associated with a stalker who has severe mental problems, including delusions. The perpetrator may actually believe that the victim knows and loves him or her. These stalkers expect the target to play the role the stalker has determined, and when threats or intimidation does not work, they may resort to violence. This stalker may continue to pursue the victim for long periods of time, up to eight or ten years.

Stalking Victims

Anyone, male or female, can become the victim of a stalker. The person targeted for this crime has not done anything to provoke the behavior of the offender. Examining victim characteristics is part of the attempt to understand the stalker and of the phenomena that occur. According to NVAW, four of five victims of stalking are female. Men were stalked in approximately 22 percent of the total cases surveyed. Young adults are the primary targets of stalkers; over half are between the ages of 18 and 29. Many victims know their stalker (Figure 11–2). Approximately 59 percent of female victims compared with 30 percent of male victims were stalked by some type of intimate partner.

Investigative Strategies

Half of all victims reported their stalking to the police, according to the NVAW survey. Some suggested that the police did not take them seriously; approximately half were satisfied with the response. Here are a few key points to consider in an investigation into the complaint of stalking.

Assessing the Victim's Credibility.   Assessing the victim's credibility is accomplished by observing the conduct of the victim during the investigation. This is important since there are instances of perpetrators who report themselves as being the victim. How articulate is the victim? What are the motivations for reporting this stalking crime? What did he or she do to reach out for assistance, and was it at an appropriate time? What is the mental health and criminal background of the reporter? Determine

Figure 11-2   Most stalking victims are targeted by someone they know. *(Data from the National Institute of Justice, 1998).*

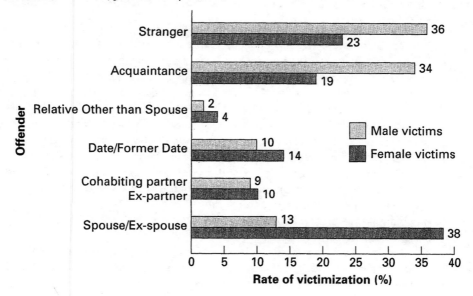

if the statements are consistent with the injuries or documentation provided. Has this victim reported being a victim of other domestic violence crimes?

False Victimization Syndrome. Professionals have long recognized that a small percentage of violent crimes reported appear to be false allegations. Those who suffer from Munchausen and Munchausen by proxy (see Chapter 9) provide examples of recognized disorders of individuals who make false claims. False victimization syndrome is believed to be involved in an estimated 2 percent of stalking complaints that are encountered by law enforcement (Mohandie et al., 1998). Although this appears to be an insignificant number, even one case that involves a false complaint causes many problems for police officers who want to protect the victim from this horrible crime. As the case example illustrates, it is imperative that suspected false complaints be thoroughly investigated and all attempts to find the perpetrator exhausted before concluding that it is a fantasy crime. Gently confronting the victim may be necessary at some point. Mohandie and colleagues further suggest that mental health intervention should be considered for the benefit of the person and a determination made whether charges of perjury or filing a false police report will be pursued in the future (Mohandie et al., 1998).

Assessing the Offender's Conduct.   Does the offender have a mental health or criminal background? What is the employment record of the offender? Has this offender committed prior domestic violence, or are there outstanding restraining orders against him or her? The answer to these questions helps the investigator to

For three years, the police responded to fearful complaints of a woman who was being stalked. Since stalking victims frequently endure for years, this was not unusual. She produced letters that had been written to her from the unknown assailant, mailed from various locations. Often, they included graphic descriptions of his sexual prowess. He described her in detail in the accounts of bizarre sex play and professed love. She received flowers at her place of business and delivered to her home. There were countless hang-up calls to her house. She came to the police station twice with bruises and cuts to her arms and face that were the result of confrontations with the assailant. A beautiful 25-year-old woman, she was a perfect target for this sick predator, thought the officers!

But for the police officers involved, it was a frustrating experience. They were unable to identify the perpetrator, and from the onset, they were concerned for her safety. Responding quickly to her home each time, they even put a tap on her telephone line and put surveillance on her house. Their efforts were to no avail. The only contact occurred when there were no witnesses.

As time went, by the officers began to suspect that she was fabricating the "evidence" of the crime. They noticed that she would request specific officers that she liked. Always she was freshly made-up and particularly well dressed when they arrived. Her demeanor would often change from extremely fearful to gleeful. Still, they were hesitant to ignore her complaints, especially since there had been physical assaults.

Asked to consult and offer advice to the other officers, I reviewed the evidence. The tone of the letters suggested to me that they had been written by a female rather than a male. The acts that were graphically described contained too much detail. They were literally impossible from a physical standpoint. Rather than intimidating, they were erotic stories that were meant to be so. Pictures of her injuries appeared suspicious also. The facial injuries were minor, with superficial cuts on her cheeks, but not across her nose. The bruising from being hit looked more like blush than what one might expect from an attack from assailant. The facts did not match the evidence.

The "victim" was not pleased when she was told that the local officers would no longer respond to her calls and that a female police officer had been assigned to help her. When I met with her, my gut reaction was exactly what the other officers felt—that she was making up the whole thing. Eventually, I confronted her and she confessed that there was no stalker. She smiled broadly when I told her she had great imagination and complimented her writing ability!

determine if the victim's perception of a threat is accurate. Some victims may tend to underestimate the potential harm in a stalking situation.

Since perpetrators of violence often have a traceable history of problems, conflicts, disputes, and failures, their background and coping ability is helpful information to know (Fein et al., 1995). Recognizing that there is a difference between making a threat known as "venting anger" and actually "posing" a threat, law enforcement should evaluate the possibility of violent action through the suspect's past history. The task of the investigator is to gather information about the subject's thinking and to encourage change in the subject's behavior (Fein et al., 1995). Interviewing the subject may be beneficial to permit the subject's story to be related to a third party. It allows an opportunity to communicate that the subject's behavior is unwelcome, unacceptable, and must cease.

Gathering Physical Evidence.   Investigating a complaint of stalking requires full and often lengthy documentation of the actions that present an accurate portrayal of the stalking. Victims need to be aware of the need to save any form of harassment, such as photos of vandalism, injuries, answering machine messages, or notes; these are the kind of evidence necessary to form probable cause that the crime of stalking has been committed. Keeping a journal or diary is one method of gathering additional important information.

Obtain a search warrant or summons for the telephone records of the offender if the communications are by telephone. Encourage the victim to install "caller ID" to track the calls. If e-mail is the medium, trace the address to the suspect and consider intercepting all e-mail messages designated for the victim.

Documenting Previous Law Enforcement Response.   Obtain actual reports on prior incidents of violence. Read the statements and determine whether they reflect the present situation accurately.

Interviewing Third Parties.   Talk to family members of the victim, neighbors, and co-workers to assess the level of danger that may exist. Determine the reasons the victim has come forward at that particular time. What has happened to explain the escalation or change in the behavior of the stalker? Should the police consider this an ongoing stalking that places the victim at risk to probable danger, or is the victim in imminent danger? What can be done to protect this person?

Considering Circumstantial Evidence.   Anything can be considered circumstantial evidence. Does the stalker have access to the types of messages that have been sent to the victim? For example, if the notes are sent through e-mail, does the stalker have access to a computer? Where? Do not overlook any correspondence, pattern of behavior, or gift that may have significance to the victim or the offender.

Assisting the Victim in Obtaining a Restraining or No-Contact Order.   Although the investigation is ongoing, direct the victim to obtain a restraining or no-contact order if possible. Be aware that this may give the victim a false sense of security, however. One-fourth of the women in the NVAW obtained a restraining order and the assailant later violated the vast majority of these. Victims who believe that the stalker will persist, regardless of a court order, must be taken seriously. A restraining or no-contact order does not replace day-to-day efforts to reduce vulnerability. The victim cannot let his or her guard down thinking that the piece of paper is itself full protection.

Since all states have arrest provisions for violation of restraining or stay-away orders, it does permit a faster police response if one is in effect. For the stalker who is rational and can control his or her behavior to avoid legal consequences, this is the best way to make the person accountable. Restraining orders are ineffective, however, if the stalker has little regard for the consequences of the stalking behavior and is obsessed with harming or harassing the victim.

Police officers should attempt to assess the level of threat that the perpetrator poses to the victim. Additionally, officers should suggest that the victim take additional safety precautions and make contact with a local victim assistance unit. These include, but are not limited to, those suggested in the next section.

Safety Precautions for Stalking Victims

Doreen Orion, author of *I Know You Really Love Me*, suggests that stalking victims must acknowledge their being a target of this crime and take extra safety precautions (Orion, 1998). She suggests the following commonsense approaches for persons who suspect that they may be targeted by a stalker.

- To reduce the feeling of vulnerability, the author suggests getting a dog. The Los Angeles Police Department's Threat Management Unit suggests that this is one of the most effective (and least expensive) alarm systems. Installing a house alarm is an alternative.

- Never give out your telephone number or home address. Get a mail box address other than with the U.S. Post Office. List the mailbox as "apartment 111" rather than "box 111." Have personal checks and business cards changed to reflect this new "address."

- If a stalker gets your telephone number, keep an answering machine on it at all times. In addition, get a new and unlisted number to give out to your friends. The stalker will believe he is still getting through to you. Get a cell phone and keep it with you at all times, even inside your home, in case a stalker cuts your telephone lines.

- Document everything. Keep all machine tapes, letters, gifts, or other correspondence. Keep a log of suspicious occurrences.

- File for confidential voter status and get a new driver's license with the mailbox "address."

- Always park your car in a well-lit area and lock your doors. While driving, keep the doors locked. Alarm your car if possible.

- If you think you are being followed while in your car, make four left- or right-hand turns in succession. If the car continues to follow you, drive to the nearest police station, never home or to a friend's house.
- Never be afraid to sound your car horn to attract attention if you are in danger.

It is important that the stalking victim attempt to assess the probability of impending danger. When emotions run high, it may be helpful to allow common sense to replace fear. Contrary to popular belief, the majority of stalking incidents begin before an intimate relationship has actually ended (National Institute of Justice, 1998). Be aware of the possibility that the violent domestic relationship may also include stalking.

Threat Assessment

The role of criminal justice has traditionally been one of response, not of prevention. This trend is changing, however, and is most notable with respect to violent crimes. Proactive policing includes advanced knowledge about the population that is most likely to commit crimes of violence. Threat assessment is a current project for stalking of public figures and has applicability to stalkers in general. Recently, the Secret Service provided findings about the histories and personal characteristics of attackers and near-lethal approachers that include the following (Fein & Vossekuil, 1998):

- Almost half had attended college or graduate school.
- They often had histories of mobility and transience.
- About two-thirds were described as socially isolated.
- Few had histories of arrests for violent crimes or for crimes that involved weapons.
- Many had histories of harassing other people.
- Most had histories of explosive, angry behavior, but only half had histories of physically violent behavior.
- Many had histories of serious depression or despair.
- Many were known to have attempted suicide or to have considered suicide at some point before their attack or near-lethal approach.

This information suggests that stalkers are generally intelligent, have violent or deviant pasts, and suffer from emotional and behavior disorders. Revenge and the need for vindication may motivate them.

DOMESTIC HOMICIDE

The loss of a family member and loved one is difficult when the causes are natural. When a person is killed, it is a tragedy not only for the victim, but for those that are left behind to mourn. Over 6 million adult Americans lost an immediate family member, other relative, or close friend to criminal homicide in one year alone (Amick-McMullen et al., 1991). The nature of intimate relationships provides both the intensity and the opportunity for hostile aggression and even murder. Research confirms that men, women, and children are at risk to domestic homicide.

Homicide is defined as the killing of a human being by the act, procurement, or omission of another human being (Black, 1990). The term *homicide* is neutral and a necessary component to what most people think of as murder. Intentionally causing death to another may be homicide, but not necessarily murder. Three general categories are recognized to describe the forms of homicide: justifiable, excusable, and felonious.

Justifiable Homicide

Justifiable homicide is the intentional taking of another's life that is lawful, such as police officers responding to the commission of a felony with deadly force that could not be avoided. Carrying out the death sentence of an inmate and killing during combat are other examples of homicides where death is intentional but not criminal. These are killings completed as part of a person's duty. The justifiable homicide is viewed by society as appropriate behavior, even though death resulted.

Excusable Homicide

Excusable homicide occurs when a person kills in self-defense or in the defense of family members. Excusable homicide is often treated as another form of justifiable homicide; they both pardon the defendant from criminal liability. A person who commits homicide that is excusable must be released from responsibility for the death through the determination of a court, after investigation by the state's prosecutor, and in rare cases through clemency. The homicide that is excusable is perceived by society to be wrong, but is tolerated because of the actor's state of mind (Balos & Fellows, 1994).

Psychiatrists and psychologists frequently testify in both criminal and civil courts on the mental health of persons accused of major crimes, including murder. It is not uncommon for evidence that relates to the person's state of mind to be presented in an attempt to show a diminished responsibility for the offender who committed a crime. The best known defense is insanity. As the behavioral sciences advance, other mental health disorders, such as multiple personality disorder, postpartum psychosis, and diminished capacity, have been recognized. One highly publicized and controversial defense specific to domestic violence is the battered women's syndrome.

The Battered Women's Syndrome. An example of excusable homicide is the defense referred to as the *battered women's syndrome*. Proponents suggest that the continuum of violence in battering relationships excuses the woman who kills her intimate assailant. Some argue that battered women who kill their oppressors should be considered legally justified, not merely excused of the act. Opponents are divided about whether battered women's syndrome is a valid defense or a claim by someone trying to escape a murder conviction. As in any defense that is raised on behalf of the defendant, some may be legitimate applications of the concept and others are not. There is always the possibility that any defense will be used illegitimately.

The battered women's syndrome is based on the theory of learned helplessness and the cycle of abuse discussed earlier in this book. According to these theories, the battered victim begins to believe that she or he cannot influence or escape the abuser's violence. One rare reaction when faced with the "reality" is to resort to the only perceived option, that is, to kill the abuser. It is considered self-defense even though the victim may not have been in imminent danger of death or great bodily harm at the exact time that the killing occurred.

The primary source of evidence comes from expert testimony on the battered spouse syndrome. Early attempts to introduce the syndrome through psychiatrists had met with several objections, including lack of its acceptance as scientific knowledge. Although jurisdictions do not handle expert testimony on battered spouses in a uniform way, increased judicial recognition has been noted (Moenssens et al., 1995). Some courts still require a showing of abuse; others have interpreted the syndrome as a gender-neutral defense. In Massachusetts, for example, evidence of battering is referred to as the *battered person syndrome* (Massachusetts General Laws ch. 233, §23F).

Clemency.   As the defense of battered spouse syndrome became increasingly admissible, a clemency movement began. Requests to state governors for the release of those women who had been convicted of murdering or assaulting an intimate began in the early 1990s. Ohio Governor Celeste and Governor William Donald Schaefer of Maryland granted clemency to 34 women who were incarcerated for killing or assaulting abusive husbands or boyfriends (Balos & Fellows, 1994). Other states' governors have since followed the lead. Most of those released had been denied the opportunity to offer evidence on battered syndrome. Media attention to the clemency action fuels the controversy for this justification, which is likely to continue into the next millennium.

Felonious Homicide

The wrongful killing of a human being is criminal behavior; generally it is referred to as *felonious homicide*. Murder, manslaughter, or negligent homicides are categories of death with varying degrees of culpability. The term *murder* refers to the killing of any human being by another with malice aforethought. Most states provide different degrees of culpability that are designated by the criminal statute itself or through a trial in a court of law, often referred to as nonneglect homicide. Murder is considered the most serious crime in our society. The penalties reflect this belief: Murder can be punished by life imprisonment or by death. There is no statute of limitations on murder; a person can be tried in a court of law at any time that sufficient proof exists to do so, regardless of how many years have elapsed since the offense (Figure 11–3).

Murder in the Family

Intense emotion, ability, and opportunity are the key ingredients common to murders committed by family members. Familiarity develops when people live together or have a close personal relationship. Often mistaken for intimacy, familiarity occurs whether the relationship is good or bad. Intimate domestic partners frequently share information about themselves during the courtship process, fulfilling the need to love and be loved; they also leave themselves vulnerable to the abusive personality. The beginning of a sexual relationship can be characterized by its intense emotions, completing the first element of intimate homicide. Individuals with poor self-concept and lacking self-control are unable to channel intense emotions, which can turn quickly from love to hate when the relationship ends or fails to be satisfying.

A second ingredient to intimate homicide is that the abuser must have the ability to carry out lethal violence. Since males commit approximately 90 percent of all murders in the United States (Burnley et al., 1998), it is not surprising that they also commit the majority of intimate murders. Generally, men have the physical attributes to overcome their female partners if they choose to. Coupled with the psychological and social explanations for battering, there appears to be a greater willingness to engage in violent encounters in order to maintain power and control in intimate relationships. According to the FBI *Uniform Crime Reports*, 30 percent of female murder victims were slain by husbands or boyfriends in 1996.

Figure 11–3 There is no statute of limitations on murder. A person can be tried at any time after the crime when sufficient proof exists to do so. *(Photo courtesy of Mark C. Ide.)*

In the News: Police Officer Kills His Wife

On December 22, 1998, Pamela Selby, 35, was shot twice in the head while sleeping at home. On the wall was a message written in lipstick that read, "I told you I'd get you in my letter." A typewritten note was found in the home; it stated, "I'm going to kill your wife because you arrested me." Pamela and her husband, Philadelphia Police Officer Carl Selby, had a history of domestic violence. Mrs. Selby was about to leave her husband.

Several neighbors, who were interviewed by police, stated that Carl was a pleasant and quiet man. Forensic testing revealed that Officer Selby wrote the handwritten notes from the crime scene and that letters sent through the mail also originated from him. He was arrested for the murder of his wife (Sarlat, 1999). On April 30, 1999, he was found guilty of first-degree murder and sentenced to life in prison.

The good news is that the homicide rate of intimates has declined over the past two decades (Fox & Zawitz, 1999). The most pronounced decline has been in the number of men killed by intimate partners (Figure 11–4). The number of women killed by intimates has also declined in recent years. When intimate homicide was broken down by gender and race, the biggest difference was noted among blacks. Over the past two decades, the rate of homicide among black female victims fell by 46 percent and among black males by 77 percent.

The availability of guns has been the most frequently noted factor contributing to all forms of homicide. Despite a recent decline, firearms were the weapons used in

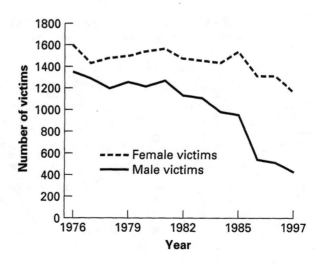

Figure 11–4 Intimate homicides by gender of victims, 1976–1997. The rate of homicide committed by intimates is declining. *(Data from Fox and Zawitz, 1999.)*

65 percent of all intimate murders in 1996 (Greenfeld et al., 1998). More wives (95 percent) than husbands (69 percent) used a gun or knife to inflict death (Langan & Dawson, 1995). The opportunity for lethal violence is seized with the means to carry out the threat immediately with deadly force. These wives use a weapon as an equalizer when faced with an assailant who is larger and stronger.

Spouse Murder Defendants.   Husbands and wives kill each other in a proportion that is closer to those of other intimate relationships. According to Langan and Dawson, spousal homicides are committed by husbands in 51 percent of the cases; wives are the offenders who kill their husbands in 41 percent of these cases. The offenders are older than any other group of killers, an average of 39 years old, and they represent 6.5 percent of the total number of homicides in the United States (Dawson & Langan, 1994).

As noted earlier, the recent trend in rates of intimate murders has been declining. The number of spouse murders, the largest portion of intimate murder, is now half of what it was 20 years ago (Greenfeld et al., 1998). This welcome development has been studied, and explanations are being offered to account for this downward trend. One explanation being offered is that people are not getting married as frequently. In one study, the decline in the number of people getting married was closely related to the decline in rates of intimate homicide (Rosenfeld, 1997).

Wife defendants are not being convicted as frequently as males, and they are receiving substantially fewer prison terms than for husbands who kill. A possible explanation is the high rate of victim provocation noted in these cases that may justify the battered women's syndrome defense. A small percentage of spouse murders are not prosecuted: examples are provided below.

Risk Factors in Spousal Homicide.   Several studies have looked at the risk factors and death rituals associated with spousal homicide in an effort to understand why it happens. The National Victim Assistance Academy outlined some major considerations (Burnley et al., 1996):

- Prior history of violence
- Frequency and severity of violence over time
- Addiction to illegal drugs, especially crack, PCP, and methamphetamine
- The practice of threatening death rituals
- Homicidal and/or suicidal ideation
- Access to weapons, especially firearms
- Announcement of the intimate partner that she or he is leaving the relationship

In one study, an increased risk of homicide in domestic homosexual relationships was noted when there was a large disparity between the couple's ages or when the offender had an arrest history for a violent offense (Block & Christakos, 1996).

More about It: Spouse Murder Defendants Not Prosecuted

Approximately 13 percent of spouse murder defendants are not prosecuted. Here are some case examples from notes taken on prosecutors' records.

- *Dallas case 79.* The wife (victim) is 89 and has been married 65 years. A recent stroke leaves her in terrible pain. She pleads with the doctor to kill her. The doctor refuses. The 87-year-old husband goes to the hospital and shoots her.

- *New Orleans case 54.* For years, the 43-year-old husband (victim), a dry cleaning operator, has beaten his 35-year-old wife. At the time of the murder, the two are fighting, and the husband stabs her in the back. She grabs the knife and stabs him, causing him to bleed to death. She claims self-defense, and the victim's family voices no objection.

- *Los Angeles case 21.* During an argument, the 50-year-old housewife (victim) pulls out a gun and threatens to kill her 39-year-old unemployed husband. The two struggle. He flees the house and gets in his car. She moves in front of the car, raises the gun and takes aim. He runs over her. He is arrested a day later.

Source: Langan & Dawson (1995).

The term *death ritual* refers to the pattern of abuse that may lead to homicide. It begins when the abuser talks about weapons, then displays weapons, then brandishes weapons. This occurs while he or she is making threats to the victim. The offender may actually take the partner to a secluded area and threaten to kill him or her there if the partner ever tries to leave. The more these rituals are acted out, the more likely it is that the abuser will carry out his or her threats.

Familicide.   An extremely rare form of domestic lethal violence, *familicide* is defined as a multiple-victim homicide incident in which the killer's spouse or ex-spouse and one or more children are slain. The extent of this form is unknown in the United States because the Uniform Crime Reporting System is too limited in its data collection to allow analysis of this event.

Researchers Wilson and Daly used information from Canada, England, and Wales to examine the phenomenon (Wilson & Daly, 1996). They found that the majority (93 to 96 percent) of familicide incidents were perpetrated by men. The child victims are almost equally divided between sons and daughters. The recording of pertinent data in Chicago between 1965 and 1989 allowed analysis for familicide in that city. Of the 15 familicides during the 25-year period, one was committed by a female.

Additionally, Wilson and Daly report that suicide is particularly prevalent in familicide cases. Interviews showed that perpetrators (some who had failed at their suicide attempt) were often despondent at the time of killing their family. Experiencing a recent devastating experience of personal and financial failure, and dwelling on the probable shame to the wife and children, are justifications for taking all their lives. Sorrow rather than anger appears to be the motivating factor for these killings.

Parricide.   Parricide is the killing of one's parent. When a mother is killed by one of her children, the term *matricide* is used to describe the specific form of criminal homicide. *Patricide* is the act of killing one's father. In the majority of cases where a mother or father is killed by his or her offspring, the perpetrator is an adult. Adult parricide offenders are different from juvenile offenders. They generally have a history of severe mental illness with little or no history of parental abuse. According to Weisman and Sharma, mothers are the targets more often than fathers with both sons and daughters. Sons almost exclusively commit double parricides, in which both parents are killed (Weisman & Sharma, 1997).

Compared to the other categories of lethal violence, this is relatively rare. Approximately 300 victims a year, and less than 2 percent of the total murder victims, are killed by their offspring (Dawson & Langan, 1994). In *Why Kids Kill Parents*, author Kathleen Heide examined the existing literature on juvenile murderers and concluded that the victim's death was perceived as a relief by the offender (Heide, 1992). This was evidenced by the apparent lack of remorse initially observed in the offender. Severe family violence was characterized in all homes where the juvenile ultimately took the life of parent(s). Parental brutality against the youth included numerous forms of domestic violence and the witnessing of spouse abuse. Alcoholism and heavy drinking by the father were cited frequently. Heide noted that the easy availability to a gun was a critical factor in the majority of parricide cases.

Infanticide.   The term *infanticide* refers to the murder or killing of an infant soon after its birth (Black, 1990). Reports on infanticide often include murdered children over the age of 5, an incorrect use of the term. Children killed under the age of 5 are included as infanticide victims in the figures reported by the Bureau of Justice Statistics. Parents and stepparents have consistently been the most frequent killers of infants since 1976 (Figure 11–5). Most of the children killed are male, and most of the offenders are male. The numbers of children killed under 5 have risen, roughly in proportion to the number of young children in the population.

The felonious destruction of the fetus is called *feticide* or criminal abortion. An estimated 17 percent of adult women are battered during pregnancy; teenagers battered during pregnancy may be as high as 21 percent (Burnley et al., 1996). A pregnant woman who aborts due to injury caused by her batterer that results in the death of the fetus would be included as feticide. There is no accurate numbers of these deaths.

Case Example

The body of an adult woman was placed under a bridge abutment along a major highway. She was in her nightgown, and her hands were tied in front of her. Less than a mile away the victim's vehicle was found, out of gas. The victim was soon identified as a person reported missing from a neighboring state. She had lived with her teenage daughter in an upscale neighborhood. Signs of struggle in her bedroom indicated that she had been killed in her own home. It was an odd case; investigators sat around wondering why the body had been moved. It did not seem to make sense to the seasoned detectives. One finally remarked that the only reason to have moved the body was to move suspicion away from the house. It pointed to the daughter as the most likely perpetrator; she was the only one who would gain by the distance.

Ultimately, the daughter was charged with the crime. She had been fighting with her mother over a boyfriend of whom the mother did not approve. That disapproval cost the mother her life; it was a joint killing committed by the teenage daughter and the controversial boyfriend.

A large percentage of infant deaths have been attributed to natural cases, most notably *sudden infant death syndrome* (SIDS). Advanced investigation into some SIDS-related deaths have revealed criminal homicide in recent years. Mistaken identification of infanticide may be attributable to the lack of evidence generally and criminal intent specifically. Concern for the mother's loss of a child may sometimes prevent further inquiry into the death. Recent controversy surrounding SIDS death has brought an increased awareness to criminal investigation.

Many people believe that in SIDS-related deaths the infants suffocated themselves because they were found with their faces pressed into the mattress. Studies have repeatedly disproved this theory. When death is caused by suffocation, it cannot immediately be attributed to SIDS; further investigation is warranted. Petechial hemorrhages, broken blood vessels on the eyes and surrounding area, will be apparent in most cases of suffocation. Investigators should be aware that SIDS is actually quite rare, and multiple SIDS deaths in the same family or day-care facility are immediately suspicious.

Filicide. *Filicide* is the killing of children by parents; it is a nonlegal term that in some studies may include victims of infanticide. Although all murder is tragic, a parent's killing of a child is a form of abuse that is difficult to understand. Children are unable to protect themselves against abuse and have no alternatives when confronted with lethal violence. Over half of children murdered by a parent (55 percent) were killed by their mother (Dawson & Langan, 1994).

Figure II-5   Circle of death: homicides of children under the age of 5 by relationship with the offender. *(Data from NCJ 173956, 1999.)*

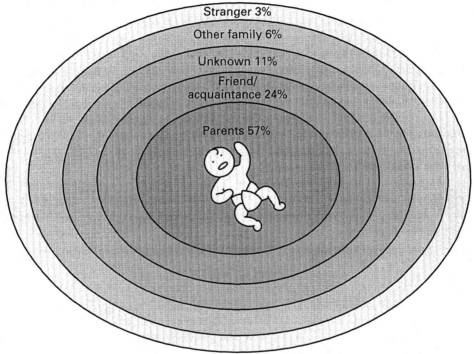

Stranger 3%

Other family 6%

Unknown 11%

Friend/
acquaintance 24%

Parents 57%

Officially, 1,271 children were killed as a result of child abuse or neglect in 1994 (Wiese & Daro, 1995). The official estimate includes only those cases that have come to the attention of authorities and were substantiated as abuse. Law enforcement officers know that abuse is not always a clear determination and that the statistics do not include those investigations where proof was lacking, or when an allegation was plea-bargained to a lesser charge.

From the 29 states that provided fatality data for 1997, a trend was determined that indicated an 8 percent decrease in child fatalities. The actual number is expected to increase as information is received from the remaining states (Wang & Daro, 1998). The vast majority of the child abuse deaths in 1997 (41 percent) were from families who had prior or current contact with child protective services. Between 1995 and 1997, 44 percent died from neglect, 51 percent died from abuse, and 5 percent died as a result of multiple forms of maltreatment.

There is no one explanation that can be offered as to why parents or caretakers abuse and sometimes kill their children. Richard Gelles suggests that distinct types of

---

More about It: Sudden Infant Death Syndrome

Sudden infant death syndrome (SIDS) is the unexplained death of an apparently healthy infant under 1 year of age. It is sometimes called crib death because most of these children die in their sleep. We don't know exactly what causes these children to die, but the U.S. Department of Health and Human Services has predicted a possible 50 percent decrease in the incidence of death through precautionary measures. Known as the "Back to Sleep" campaign, the American Academy of Pediatrics in 1992 recommended that babies be placed on their backs or sides to sleep, which significantly reduces the risk of SIDS. This effort was credited with a 30 percent actual reduction in SIDS deaths between 1992 and 1995 (U.S. Department of Health and Human Services, 1996).

---

abusers exist, with an overlap (Gelles, 1996). Most parents, he suggests, punish children within guidelines so that injury does not occur with physical punishment. The other type purposefully causes mild to severe injury. The overlap occurs when the first type goes beyond the boundaries due to anger or bad aim, and when the second type fails to cause severe injury due to intervention or lack of anger.

Deaths of children due to Munchausen by proxy are slowly becoming evident as we learn more of this disease. It is difficult to predict accurately the number of deaths due to this condition (Parnell & Day, 1997). Researchers estimate the mortality rate for victims to be somewhere in the range 9 to 31 percent of cases where Munchausen by proxy has been diagnosed. When the child dies, it may be an unintentional consequence of the perpetrator's intentional actions to feign illness for medical attention.

Fratricide.   The killing of a brother or sister is called *fratricide*. More rare than any other family homicide, it occurs in 1.5 percent of the total criminal deaths in the United States. It is estimated that in sibling murders, females were the perpetrators in 15 percent of the cases.

Investigative Strategies

Since 1976, more than 52,000 men and women have been murdered by those with whom they shared an intimate relationship (Greenfeld et al., 1998). The implication of a domestic relationship is far more significant for female murder victims than male murder victims, however. Males are most often the perpetrators and the victims in homicides, and they are nine times more likely than females to commit a murder; both male and female offenders are more likely to target male than female victims (Fox & Zawitz, 1999). Without obvious signs of a theft-, gang-, or drug-related murder, the investigator looks from the intimate relations outward toward the strangers Figure 11–6.)

The investigation of death begins with an examination of the area immediately surrounding the body. Clues within the circle of death aid in the primary first step of

Figure 11–6 The circle of death surrounds the body of the homicide victim.

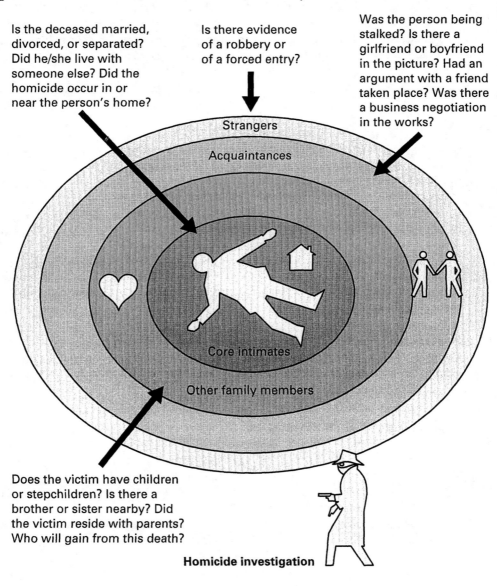

Is the deceased married, divorced, or separated? Did he/she live with someone else? Did the homicide occur in or near the person's home?

Is there evidence of a robbery or of a forced entry?

Was the person being stalked? Is there a girlfriend or boyfriend in the picture? Had an argument with a friend taken place? Was there a business negotiation in the works?

Strangers

Acquaintances

Core intimates

Other family members

Does the victim have children or stepchildren? Is there a brother or sister nearby? Did the victim reside with parents? Who will gain from this death?

Homicide investigation

determining if the death is due to homicide, suicide, or attributable to natural causes. If the victim has been shot or otherwise physically wounded, it may appear self-evident but cannot be considered conclusive until a forensic medical autopsy has been performed. Police officers work closely with a *medical examiner*, sometimes called a *coroner*, to determine the cause of death. If the person died under the care of a physician for a known fatal illness, an autopsy may not be necessary. For violent or sudden deaths that were not witnessed by another person, it is often standard procedure. Confirmation of a sexual assault may be necessary and is considered regardless of the age or gender of the deceased. The coroner is a medical doctor who has received additional training in conducting the forensic autopsy. Officially pronouncing the victim dead and naming the cause of death are the responsibilities of the coroner.

The collection of evidence also begins within the circle and moves outward. The victim tells a story: the place where the body is found, its gender, injury, and even the positioning of the body speak to the circumstances surrounding the death. Some police departments employ specialists who are called immediately to work on evidence collection; some departments train their own police officers to do this step. Whether or not forensic specialists are called by the police depends on the severity of the crime, the apparent signs of the cause of death, and the policy in the jurisdiction of the crime. Experts in ballistics, hair and fiber analysis, DNA analysis, fingerprint analysis, and photography are among the more common forensic specialists involved in the initial murder investigation, in addition to law enforcement. As more is learned about the death, others may be called to assist the primary investigators.

Approximately half of homicide victims know their assailants, either as intimates, family members, or acquaintances. The expectation of privacy that may exist due to a domestic relationship underscores the need for a search warrant in homicide investigations. Evidence seized without a warrant may otherwise fall prey to the exclusionary rule. The rule excludes the use of evidence to prove a person's guilt when it has been seized in violation of the offender's constitutional rights.

Guidelines have been established to assist police officers and to assure that the rights inherent under the *Mincey v. Arizona* decision are protected. An example of a form that is consistent with the requirements is provided in Figure 11–7. The information contained in an affidavit must be particular to the crime committed, give the exact location of the evidence, and detail exactly what the officer seeks to seize.

The search to identify the perpetrator of the murder also begins in the circle immediately surrounding the victim. The vast majority of intimate murders occur in the victim's home. Likely suspects are considered from the *core intimates* outward. The core intimate refers to the husband, wife, boyfriend, or girlfriend of the victim. If the person slain is female, the probability that the suspect is someone other than a stranger is increased substantially.

The victim–offender relationship varies with the age of the victim. Of all known murders, a family member most often commits the killing of a young child. In other words, when a child is murdered in the United States, the most likely killer is a family member (Greenfeld, 1996). People over the age of 50 make up 12 percent of the murder

Figure 11-7   Sample Mincey warrant application.

* This is a Mere Evidence Search Warrant Affidavit and Application pursuant to
Mincey v. Arizona (1978) 437 U.S. 385.

A.)   Blood, semen, saliva, physiological fluids and secretions, hair fibers, fingerprints, palm prints, footprints, shoeprints, weapons and firearms including pistols, rifles, revolvers, shotguns, hatchets, axes, cutting instruments and cutting tools, blunt force instruments, projectiles, ammunition, bullet casings and fragments; dirt, dust and soil, paint samples, glass and plastic fragments, marks of tools used to gain access to locked premises or containers, and items containing traces of any of the above mentioned articles.

B.)   Constitutes evidence of an offense, or that a particular person participated in the commission of an offense, to wit: **Murder**

C.)   **Description of the location of the place to be searched goes here.**

D.)   **(The following paragraphs should be added to the wording of the Search Warrant application at the end of the Affidavit).**

1.   That the affient, _____ , is a regular member of the _____ Police Department and has been a member for the past _____ years. That I am presently assigned to the Detective Division's Major Crime Squad Scene processing Unit and have been so assigned for the past _____ years. That I have investigated and processed numerous serious and violent crimes, including murder, and have received specialized training and experience in the collection of physical evidence, crime scene processing and the investigation of such cases. That I have personal knowledge of the facts and circumstances hereinafter related as a result of my own investigative efforts and those of brother officers who have reported their findings to me.

(One of the two affiants should be a member of the crime scene processing unit. The second affient should be an investigator and should include his customary paragraph of introduction.)

2.   That the affiants do believe that the offense herein before stated was committed at the location to be searched in that: (Specify circumstances indicating commission of the offenses at the place to be searched: include information as to when the crime was first reported, what first officer on the scene observed, a description of the scene, etc. This information may require several paragraphs.)

3.   That the affiants have personal knowledge, based on their experience and training, that crimes of violence involve a struggle, a break, the use of weapons and other instrumentality, and/or the element of unpredictability. That the person or persons participating in the commission of a violent offense is in contact with physical surroundings in a forceful or otherwise detectable manner. That there is often an attempt to alter, destroy, remove, clean up or cover up evidence of a crime. That traces may be left in the form of blood, semen, saliva, physiological fluids and secretions, hair, fibers, fingerprints, palm prints, footprints, shoeprints, weapons and firearms including pistols, rifles, revolvers, shotguns, hatchets, axes, cutting instruments and cutting tools, blunt force instruments, projectiles, ammunition, bullet casings and fragments; dirt, dust and soil, paint samples, glass and plastic fragments, marks of tools used to gain access to locked premises or containers, and items containing traces of any of the above mentioned articles. That many of the above items are minute and microscopic, thus requiring additional specialized examination by forensic laboratory techniques.

4.   That the affiants have personal knowledge based upon their experience and training, that crime scene, such as described above, will contain physical evidence, herein before itemized, which will aid in establishing the identity of the perpetrator (s), the circumstances under which the crime was committed, and/or which in general will assist in the discovery of the pertinent facts; and that such evidence requires a systematic search to located, seize, record and process.

5.   That based on the foregoing facts and information, the affiants have probable cause to believe and do believe that evidence of the MURDER will be found within and upon (specify the place to be searched).

More about It: The Mincey Warrant Requirement

A common misconception is that an investigation into the death of a person does not require a search warrant to seize evidence. Although many exceptions to the Fourth Amendment warrant requirement do exist, the death of a human being is not among them. Precedence for homicide investigations conducted within private homes was established in *Mincey v. Arizona* (1978) when the U.S. Supreme Court struck down the "murder scene exception" of that state. The case involved an undercover police officer who was killed during a drug buy at Mincey's apartment. Following the murder, police officers secured the scene, then conducted a four-day search of the apartment. They subsequently seized hundreds of items. The Court held that the exhaustive search of the apartment of Mincey was unreasonable and a violation of his privacy, even though the police were lawfully in the apartment.

Without a warrant, a police officer may be on the premises legally to conduct an "emergency" response, such as a search for other victims and for the killer. Hot pursuit and imminent danger to people are examples of recognized emergencies. The possibility of evidence destruction is considered an exigent circumstance. The officers may search only for evidence establishing the circumstances of death or circumstances relevant to motive, intent, or knowledge.

A person can waive his or her personal rights to Fourth Amendment protection and consent to a search of his or her property. This consent must be given prior to the commencement of the search and must be made freely and intelligently by the person or a proper third party. Consent searching is the most frequently challenged exception and should be used judicially in a homicide investigation. A search warrant is necessary, according to the *Mincey* decision, for a homicide crime scene investigation, in the absence of other recognized exceptions.

---

victims in the United States. For victims over age 60, their children represent the most frequent killer, committing approximately 42 percent of these murders. When the murder of an elder is committed by a family member, the spouse is the perpetrator in approximately 24 percent of cases (Dawson & Langan, 1994).

CONCLUSIONS

This chapter began with an introduction to the crime of stalking. It is a newly defined crime that had been linked to celebrities. The crime is called gender neutral because it affects both female and male victims, although the majority are women. A major difference between stalking and other crimes is that it consists of a series of actions rather than a single act. It may involve activities that are otherwise legal if not committed within the context of other criminal behavior. Extreme fear is often felt by those victimized in this manner.

Following or harassing constitutes a major element of the crime. The actions are purposeful, and a specific person is targeted for the unwanted attention. A stalker can be anyone: a former intimate or acquaintance, or a perfect stranger. Every report should be taken seriously, as the behavior is known to turn violent in approximately one-fourth of cases. An important note relative to the role of law enforcement is the changing role of the police officer to involve prevention in addition to crime response. This means that a threat assessment should be conducted to learn if the victim is in imminent danger.

Also included in this chapter was a discussion on domestic homicide. A substantial number of Americans have been touched by a tragic death of a close friend or family member. Although some forms of purposeful death are justified or excused in our society, this does not mean that the practice of taking a life is taken lightly or without controversy. Recent statistics suggest that the homicide rate of intimates has declined, most pronouncedly in the number of men killed by an intimate. This may be due to the increased information, services, and options that are available to victims of abuse. Another explanation is the decline in the frequency of marriage.

The circle of death for both adults and children is used to illustrate the investigative strategy when a victim of homicide is discovered. The family and friends of the victim are eliminated as suspects through this method. Evidence is also located within the area surrounding the body. For these reasons, the crime scene must be protected and a search conducted that protects the legal rights of domestic killers. A search warrant should be sought whenever possible, due to the possibility of a relationship between the victim and the killer.

KEY TERMS

Battered women's syndrome
Clemency
Erotomania
Excusable homicide
False victimization syndrome
Familicide
Felonious homicide
Filicide
Fratricide

Harassing
Infanticide
Justifiable homicide
Love obsessional stalker
Matricide
Parricide
Patricide
Simple obsessional stalker
Stalking

QUESTIONS for REVIEW

1. Describe the crime of stalking.

2. What are the most common behaviors of stalking?

3. What makes these behaviors illegal?

4. Why does the "threat requirement" of some statutes become a difficult obstacle to overcome?

5. Describe the three types of stalkers that were presented in this chapter. Are there any characteristics common to other forms of domestic violence offenders?

6. Although false allegations in reports of violent crime are rare, why are they significant?

7. Explain some common safety precautions for stalking victims. Why would they be necessary?

8. What is the most frequently noted factor contributing to all forms of homicide?

9. Choose one of the family relationships and describe the prevalence of murder within it.

10. What is a Mincey warrant? Why is it important?

*R*EFERENCES

Amick-McMullen, A., D. G. Kilpatrick, and H. S. Resnick. 1991. "Homicide as a Risk Factor for PTSD among Surviving Family Members." *Behavioral Modification* 15(4):545–59.

Balos, Beverly and Mary L. Fellows. 1994. *Law and Violence against Women: Cases and Materials on Systems of Oppression*. Durham, NC: Carolina Academic Press.

Black, Henry C. 1990. *Black's Law Dictionary*. St. Paul, MN: West Publishing Company.

Block, Carolyn R. and Antigone Christakos. 1996. "Chicago Intimate Partner Homicide: Patterns and Trends across Three Decades." In *Lethal Violence: Proceedings of the 1995 Meeting of the Homicide Research Working Group*. Washington, DC: U.S. Department of Justice.

Burnley, Jane et al. (eds.). 1996. *National Victim Assistance Academy Textbook*. Washington, DC: Office for Victims of Crime.

_____. 1998. "Chapter 16 Supplement." In *Homicide: Its Impact and Consequences: Statistical Overview*. 1997–1998 Academy Text Supplement edition. Washington, DC: U.S. Department of Justice.

Dawson, J. and P. Langan. 1994. *Murder in Families*. NCJ 143498. Washington, DC: U.S. Department of Justice.

Fein, Robert A. and Bryan Vossekuil. 1998. *Protective Intelligence Threat Assessment Investigations: A Guide for State and Local Law Enforcement Officials*. NCJ 170612. Washington, DC: U.S. Department of Justice.

Fein, Robert A., Bryan Vossekuil, and Gwen Holden. 1995. *Threat Assessment: An Approach to Prevent Targeted Violence*. NCJ 155000. Washington, DC: U.S. Department of Justice.

Fox, James A. and Marianne W. Zawitz. 1999. *Homicide Trends in the United States*. NCJ 173956. Washington, DC: U.S. Department of Justice.

Gelles, Richard J. 1996. *The Book of David: How Preserving Families Can Cost Children's Lives*. New York: Basic Books.

Greenfeld, Lawrence. 1996. *Child Victimizers: Violent Offenders and Their Victims*. Bureau of Justice Statistics, Executive Summary. NIJ 158625. Washington, DC: U.S. Department of Justice.

Greenfeld, Lawrence, Michael Rand, Diane Craven, Patsy Klaus, Craig Perkins, Cheryl Ringel, Greg Warchol, Cathy Maston, and James Fox. 1998. *Violence by Intimates: Analysis of Crimes by Current or Former Spouses, Boyfriends, and Girlfriends*. NCJ 167237. Washington, DC: U.S. Department of Justice.

Heide, Kathleen M. 1992. *Why Kids Kill Parents: Child Abuse and Adolescent Homicide*. Columbus, OH: Ohio State University Press.

Langan, Patrick A. and John M. Dawson. 1995. *Spouse Murder Defendants in Large Urban Counties*. NCJ 153256. Washington, DC: U.S. Department of Justice.

Lardner, George, Jr. 1997. *The Stalking of Kristin: A Father Investigates the Murder of His Daughter*. New York: Onyx.

Moenssens, Andre et al. 1995. *Scientific Evidence in Civil and Criminal Cases*, 4th ed. Westbury, NY: Foundation Press.

Mohandie, Kris, Chris Hatcher, and Douglas Raymond. 1998. "False Victimization Syndromes in Stalking." Pp. 225–56 in *The Psychology of Stalking: Clinical and Forensic Perspectives*, Reid Meloy (ed.). San Diego, CA: Academic Press.

Moret, Jim. 1997. "Technology Brings Stalkers One Step Closer to Celebrities." July. *http://cgi.cnn.com*. January 1999.

National Conference on State Legislatures. "Feds Address 'Stalking,' While Courts Review State Laws." February 1997. *www.ncsl.org/programs/cj/CJL4297.HTM*. January 1999.

National Institute of Justice. 1998. *Stalking and Domestic Violence: The Third Annual Report to Congress under the Violence Against Women Act*. NCJ 172204. Washington, DC: U.S. Department of Justice.

Orion, Doreen R. 1998. *I Know You Really Love Me: A Psychiatrist's Account of Stalking and Obsessive Love*. New York: Dell Publishing Company.

Parnell, Teresa F. and Deborah O. Day (eds.). 1997. *Munchausen by Proxy Syndrome: Misunderstood Child Abuse*. Thousand Oaks, CA: Sage Publications.

Rosenfeld, Richard. 1997. *Changing Relationships between Men and Women and the Decline in Intimate Partner Homicide*. NCJ 166149. Washington, DC: U.S. Department of Justice.

Sarlat, Rick. 1999. "Wife of Detective Is Murdered." January 30. *Philadelphia Tribune* On-Line Edition.

Schaum, Melita and Karen Parrish. 1995. *Stalked: Breaking the Silence on the Crime of Stalking in America*. New York: Simon & Schuster.

Tjaden, Patricia. 1997. *The Crime of Stalking: How Big Is the Problem?* FS 000186. Washington, DC: National Institute of Justice.

Tjaden, Patricia and Nancy Thoennes. 1998. *Prevalence, Incidence, and Consequences of Violence against Women: Findings from the National Violence Against Women Survey*. NCJ 172837. Washington, DC: U.S. Department of Justice.

U.S. Department of Health and Human Services. 1996. "Reduction in SIDS Deaths Helps Bring Low Infant Mortality." *Health and Human Services News*.

Wang, Ching-Tung and Deborah Daro. 1998. *Current Trends in Child Abuse Reporting and Fatalities: The Results of the 1997 Annual Fifty State Survey*. Working Paper 808. Chicago: National Committee to Prevent Child Abuse.

Weisman, Adam and Kaushal Sharma. 1997. "Parricide and Attempted Parricide." In *The Nature of Homicide: Trends and Changes—Proceedings of the 1996 Meeting of the Homicide Research Working Group*. NCJ 16149. Washington, DC: U.S. Department of Justice.

Wiese, D. and Deborah Daro. 1995. *Current Trends in Child Abuse Reporting and Fatalities: The Results of the 1994 Annual Fifty State Survey*. Chicago: National Committee to Prevent Child Abuse.

Wilson, Margo and Martin Daly. 1996. "Familicide: Uxoricide Plus Filicide?" In *Lethal Violence: Proceedings of the 1995 Meeting of the Homicide Research Working Group*. Washington, DC: U.S. Department of Justice.

Case

Mincey v. Arizona, 437 U.S. 385 (1978).

Statutes

Massachusetts General Laws ch. 265, §43; ch. 233, §23F.
New York Public Law Code, §240.30.

Part Five

The Future

Chapter 12, "Research on the Internet," is the solitary section in Part Five. This distinction is earned because the Internet truly is the future in domestic violence research. Do you know how to access the valuable information that is now available there? Where do you start in searching the World Wide Web? How will you find what you want to know? Are some sites more reliable than others? What are the criteria for evaluating the information when you find it? These questions are answered in Chapter 12. In addition, many site addresses are made available for you to begin exploring. Don't get overwhelmed, but the journey to learn more about domestic violence has just begun with this final chapter.

Research on the Internet

INTRODUCTION

Domestic violence is an emerging field of study that is frequently changing and being updated with new and exciting information. The Internet is an important resource on domestic violence, since all studies conducted with federal government funding are now available there. State and federal laws are often posted on the Internet along with a legal analysis. U.S. Supreme Court decisions are available more quickly on the Internet than from traditional sources. Nonprofit organizations and self-help groups are accessible and share resources over the Internet. Even job postings are listed. Keeping up with this technology is more important than ever before. Currency in the field now demands knowledge on accessing the wealth of data available. For students who would like to know more on a specific topic and for those conducting research, get on the World Wide Web!

What is the Internet? The Internet is like the electric wiring of a house. It does not provide service, it provides the access to services. It supports *applications* that can run within the system, containing the language that allows computers to talk together regardless of the system you are using—such as Unix, Windows, and Mac OS. E-mail (electronic messages), Gopher, telnet, and FTP (file transfer protocol) are examples of services available over the Internet that are text-based.

The Internet provides a link that ties together computers around the world. This electronic network makes it possible to access and share information between computers through a protocol called TCP/IP. The *protocol* is a special language that first divides information into little data packets and addresses each one for transportation.

The *router*, a machine that sits at network intersections, determines the best path for the data to travel on. At its destination, a *gateway* receives the information and reassembles the packets that might have traveled along different routes.

Developed for use by the Department of Defense, the Internet became international in 1973. It has been growing at a phenomenal rate since then. With the advent of satellites as a means of communication, the Internet was abandoned by the military. A communication system on the ground was no longer needed.

The InterNIC, developed by the National Science Foundation in 1993, maintains domain name registration through the *domain name system* (DNS). Domain names identify a location on the Internet as an address known as the *uniform resource locator* (URL). The first part of any domain name identifies the person, place, or organization that is located at the address. The second part of the domain name identifies the group to which the address belongs. It is like having a name or street address followed by the city or state. In some instances, the second part of the domain name identifies a country other than the United States. This gives you the exact location of an address within a group. For example, the five original domain groups that were organized specified these basic categories:

Commercial sites	.com
Educational sites	.edu or .ac
Government sites	.gov
Military sites	.mil
Organizations	.org

The most popular network service on the Internet is called the World Wide Web. Born in 1991, the Web, or WWW, supports graphics, audio, and video in addition to text. Many people think of the Internet and the World Wide Web as being the same thing. This is not the case; WWW is merely one of the many services that can be accessed over the Internet. Due to its wide public use, however, it is not uncommon for people to refer to the Internet when they really mean the World Wide Web.

With the development of the World Wide Web, the superhighway of information was opened for public use through Web *browsers* that are used to navigate it. Browsers run on your personal computer and allow you to view the World Wide Web pages. The two most popular browsers are the Netscape Navigator and Microsoft Internet Explorer. There are others; Mosaic is one that is also well known.

This chapter is a peek into the World Wide Web—that service on the Internet where you can locate information, although not necessarily reliable information, on just about anything that is of interest to you. Some of the sites are animated, some contain video and audio clips. In particular, some URLs for sites that are related to domestic violence will be offered for you to explore on your own.

Before beginning, it is important to note that anyone can post information on the World Wide Web. All one needs is an *internet service provider* (ISP), a computer that will offer access to the Internet and store that information for others to retrieve. That means that there is a lot of junk out there. Discriminating surfers understand that information obtained through the World Wide Web must be scrutinized for its credibility. Don't believe everything you see out there!

How do you find what you are looking for? How do you know that the information is reliable? More important, how do you start? All you need are the basics and a sense of adventure. The best way to learn is to "log on" and "surf." Remember: The Internet can be fun! The more you explore, the more comfortable it becomes.

GETTING ONTO THE WORLD WIDE WEB

To get on to the World Wide Web, you need a personal computer, a browser, and an Internet connection. Most computers will support a browser; any machine that is a 486 or better will do; the Pentiums will allow better performance and are preferred, however. IBM-compatible computers that come with software installed will typically have Windows 95, Windows 98, or Windows NT already. Microsoft Internet Explorer is the browser that comes prepackaged with the Windows software and requires that you set it up with your Internet connection through your Internet service provider. Instructions on how to set up your browser are contained within the program. Updated copies of both Microsoft Internet Explorer and Netscape Navigator can be downloaded if you are not running the most current version. They are also available for purchase from most computer software stores.

The next step is to actually connect to the Internet. Many college and university campuses have their own computer service; the local area network (LAN) is called a *direct connection*. You must establish an account with the school in order to access their computer network. If you are not sure, just ask someone if there is a direct Internet connection available. Once you have the browser installed on your computer and you are plugged in to a direct connection, you can just log on. If you do not have your own computer, go to the university library or computer center and find out which computers are Internet connected. Some local libraries also have one or more computers that are Internet connected and available for public use.

Another way to access the Internet is through a *dial-up connection*. This requires that you have a modem connected to your computer. America Online is a popular example, although others are also available. You pay a monthly fee and in return receive Internet access, e-mail, and a variety of other on-line services. The alternative to a dial-up connection is an *Internet service provider*. Some service providers offer unlimited use of the Internet for a monthly fee; others prorate the cost with your estimated use. If you are not sure that you will use the Internet for long periods of time, the estimated usage fee may work for you. Be careful, though; going over your allotted time may cost heavily!

The most common use of the Internet is to communicate. It is not necessary to be on the World Wide Web for this purpose, although many people use the World Wide Web to communicate with others. Communications can occur in two ways, on a personal level or the group level. Personal communication is accomplished through e-mail. Sending an electronic message requires that both people have an e-mail address. These are assigned by your Internet service provider regardless of the form of connection that you have. Typically, it is your name (or some variation of your name), followed by a designation of your service provider (Figure 12–1). E-mail can be sent from within your Internet browser.

Notice that the end of the address contains the group designation. EDU refers to the education group and would be part of an address obtained through a university. The second method of communication is on the group level. This refers to user and chat groups. Explore those on your own if you would like to "speak" with others who share your interests.

Once connected to the Internet, you are ready to browse the World Wide Web. What next? The World Wide Web is your library, literally an entrance to the world of knowledge. Open your browser and you will see an area in which to type in the URL of the site that you want to visit. The *uniform resource locator* (URL) is a specific address on the Internet. Later in this chapter, you will be provided with the URLs of many sites that I have visited that pertain to domestic violence. Sometimes Web sites change the URL and others close down completely. If you experience difficulty in finding one of the Web sites that is listed, conduct a "search" using the name of the organization that had posted the original URL. Type one of these in the area marked

Figure 12–1   This is a *POP* (Post Office Protocol) mail address.

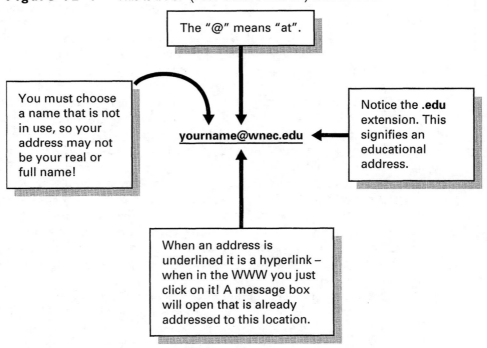

"address" on the home page of your browser to visit these sites and press "enter." Your browser will load the page that corresponds with the URL you type in. It is important to type the URL exactly or your browser will not load the proper page. Now look at the sources that have been provided for you. Later in the chapter, you will learn how to conduct your own search.

THE BASICS OF INTERNET RESEARCH

The most basic elements of Internet research are finding information and then evaluating it for your use. Search engines help with the first element, rely on common sense and some guidelines to satisfy the second. Finally, cite the information that you use. For an excellent detailed description on how to cite Internet sources, go to "How to cite electronic media" (National Center for Health Statistics, 1995):

http://www.cdc.gov/nchswww/howto/sitelec/citelec.htm

Search Engines

If you do not know the URL for the site you want to visit, you can find information by conducting a search. To do a search, you need to use a *search engine*. These reside on the World Wide Web ready and waiting for you to choose the one that works best for you. There are literally hundreds of search engines on the Internet. Within your Internet browser, you can type in the URL to go to a specific search engine, or you can use one that is on the home page of your browser. Whichever search engine you use, it is advisable to conduct more than one search to optimize your choices. Here is a directory of search engines that provides links to many of them: Beaucoup!

http://www.beaucoup.com/engines.html

The three major categories of search engines are the directory, the robot, and the multisearch. The difference between them is that robots produce indiscriminate quantity, whereas directories produce small amounts of quality information resources. Robots deal in millions of Web sites. Directories deal in perhaps thousands of Web sites.

1. *Directory search engines* are like catalogs of Web sites that have been divided into categories. Examples of this type are Yahoo (*www.yahoo.com*) and Excite (*http://www.excite.com*). Directory search engines get the information from people who enter it into the search engine's database. A directory search is more likely to produce high-quality information, since it is more focused.

2. *Robots* are sometimes called worms, spiders, harvesters, or wanderers. They use a program to search, catalog, and organize information on the Internet. In the middle of the night, they go out and visit Web sites and other Internet resources and take key information from them which they act upon when you employ them in a search. Examples of robots are HotBot

(*http://www.hotbot.com/*) and AltaVista (*http://www.alta-vista.net/*). The robot will give you a greater quantity of information, but the sources may be only remotely connected to the subject that you are researching.

3. One way to overcome the dilemma of choosing the proper search engine is to use a *multisearch engine*. These search robot search engines and directory search engines and can produce different results. Some integrate the results from various search engines by eliminating the duplicate results returned. Integration takes longer to show results on your screen because the engine must process more information before producing the results. One of my favorites is DogPile (*http://www.dogpile.com*). DogPile produces the closest links to your search; it retrieves and ranks the best responses from a variety of search engines. It also "times out" your search inquiry. This means that if no results to your query are found in a specified time period, it will skip over to the next engine and conduct that search. This is helpful if you are not sure whether or not you have conducted your inquiry using the best search words possible.

Typically, you should try to use search words or words that best describe what you are looking for when conducting a search. Beginners sometimes have difficulty with choosing accurate search phrases. One way to get around that problem is to use the multisearch engine that lets you ask in question form: Ask Jeeves! (*http://aj.com/*).

Evaluating Your Source

You will need to scrutinize your resources on the Internet, if for no other reason than the volume. How do you choose the best to use? First determine your purpose: Why do you need this information? If it is to expand your knowledge and gain insight from different perspectives, the Internet is your garden! Harvest it all and don't worry. A word of caution: Don't rely on the graphics and setup of the page to make your decision on reliability; a Web page expert may not know anything about domestic violence.

On the other hand, if you are writing a paper yourself and looking for legitimate sources, you must evaluate what you find. Although some suggest that the reputation of the author is most important, this criterion is not helpful if you are new to the field of study and unfamiliar with the experts. It is more important to consider the credibility of the producer. Where does the information come from? Can you determine if the source is from a perspective that you can identify? Is this posted through a police department, or other government agency? Alternatively, is the information posted by NAMBLA? Do you know the difference?

Another criterion used for evaluating the value of an Internet resource is the bibliography and/or references. Can you document or research the information on which the article is based? Are these legitimate sources? Consider also the date of the article and its relevance to your project. The University of Wisconsin–Eau Claire McIntyre Library posted its method of evaluating Internet resources, suggesting you look at the "Ten C's" (Richmond, 1996).

More about It: N A M B L A

The use of an acronym or other name that appears professional can be deceiving. Make sure that you know what the organization stands for before you cite it as a source! For example, NAMBLA stands for North American Man–Boy Love Association. It is a pederast organization that advocates legal reform allowing for the decriminalization of sex between adult males and boys. A sexual relationship between adults and children is child abuse. It is behavior that is prohibited by law in every state in the United States. This perspective would not be a creditable one to cite on child issues. Be careful; they, too, are located on the Internet!

THE EXTENT OF PERSONAL CRIME

Three major sources contribute to the body of knowledge that exists today on the extent of personal crime: the Uniform Crime Reports, the National Crime Victimization Surveys, and Self-Report Surveys. Measuring the characteristics of crime is the most important function of each of the major methods. They seek to determine when and where criminal acts are perpetrated; the type or severity of the crime; and how often the offenses are committed. The characteristics of the criminal, of the victim, and of the victim–criminal relationship are quantified to enhance theoretical explanations and to develop social policy. Without these contemporary methods of gathering information, our knowledge on victimization would not exist.

The Uniform Crime Reporting System

In the 1920s, the International Association of Chiefs of Police (IACP) identified the desirability of gathering information on crime and tracking national crime statistics. The Federal Bureau of Investigation (FBI) was authorized to serve as the national clearinghouse for this voluntary collection on police data in 1929. It is called the Uniform Crime Reporting System (UCR). Besides being the oldest source of crime data, it is the most frequently cited source of information.

The Uniform Crime Reports can be found by going to the home page of the FBI at

http://www.fbi.gov/

Monthly arrest reports from law enforcement agencies across the nation are sent to the FBI, which publishes them in an annual report, *Crime in the United States*. In addition to crime counts and trends, the report includes data on crimes cleared, persons arrested (age, gender, and race), law enforcement officers killed or assaulted, and the characteristics of homicides (including victim–offender relationships).

THE TEN C'S FOR EVALUATING INTERNET RESOURCES

1. *Content.* What is the intent of the content? Are the title and author identified? Is the content "juried"? Is the content "popular" or "scholarly," satiric or serious? What is the date of the document or article? Is the "edition" current? Do you have the latest version? (Is this important?) How do you know?

2. *Credibility.* Is the author identifiable and reliable? Is the content credible? Authoritative? Should it be? What is the purpose of the information, that is, is it serious, satiric, humorous? Is the URL extension .edu, .com, .gov, or .org? What does this tell you about the "publisher"?

3. *Critical thinking.* How can you apply critical thinking skills, including previous knowledge and experience, to evaluate Internet resources? Can you identify the author, publisher, edition, and so on, as you would a "traditionally" published resource? What criteria do you use to evaluate Internet resources?

4. *Copyright.* Even if the copyright notice does not appear prominently, someone wrote, or is responsible for, the creation of a document, graphic, sound, or image, and the material falls under the copyright conventions. "Fair use" applies to short, cited excerpts, usually as an example for commentary or research. Materials are in the "public domain" if this is stated explicitly. Just as users of print media, Internet users must respect copyrights.

5. *Citation.* Internet resources should be cited to identify sources used, both to give credit to the author and to provide the reader with avenues for further research. Standard style manuals (print and on line) provide some examples of how to cite Internet documents, although standards have not yet been formally established.

6. *Continuity.* Will the Internet site be maintained and updated? Is it now, and will it continue to be, free? Can you rely on this source over time to provide up-to-date information? Some good .edu sites have moved to .com, with possible cost implications. Other sites offer partial use for free, and charge fees for continued or in-depth use.

7. *Censorship.* Is you discussion list "moderated"? What does this mean? Does your search engine or index look for all words, or are some words excluded? Is this censorship? Does your institution, based on its mission, parent organization, or space limitations, apply restrictions to Internet use? Consider censorship and privacy issues when using the Internet.

8. *Connectivity.* If more than one user will need to access a site, consider each users' access and "functionality." How do users connect to the Internet, and what kind of connection does the assigned resource require? Does access to the resource require

(c o n t ' d)

a graphical user interface? If it is a popular (busy) resource, will it be accessible in the time frame needed? Is it accessible by more than one Internet tool? Do users have access to the same Internet tools and applications? Are users familiar with the tools and applications? Is the site "viewable" by all Web browsers?

9. *Comparability*. Does the Internet resource have an identified comparable print or CD-ROM data set or source? Does the Internet site contain comparable and complete information? (For example, some newspapers have partial but not full text information on the Internet.) Do you need to compare data or statistics over time? Can you identify sources for comparable earlier or later data? Comparability of data may or may not be important, depending on your project.

10. *Context*. What is the context for your research? Can you find "anything" on your topic, that is, commentary, opinion, narrative, statistics, and your quest will be satisfied? Are you looking for current or historical information? Definitions? Research studies or articles? How does Internet information fit in the overall information context of your subject? Before you start searching, define the research context and research needs and decide what sources might be best to use to fill information needs successfully without data overload.

Source: Elizabeth B. Richmond, Assistant Professor and Reference Librarian, University of Wisconsin–Eau Claire, Wisconsin. For further information or to reprint, contact Ms. Richmond at *richmoeb@uwec.edu.*

Drawbacks of the Uniform Crime Reporting System.   Critics cite numerous limitations in the Uniform Crime Reporting System. First, it represents only those crimes that are reported to the police. It does not reflect the actual number of crimes committed. The second limitation is the manner in which the crimes are reported to the FBI. When several crimes are committed in one event, for example, only the most serious is included in the UCR; the rest are not reported. In the past, crimes that were not indexed in the UCR could not be included. For example, "rape" was an offense that could only be committed against women by strangers. Therefore, the report of a woman who had been raped by a spouse would not be recorded. The report of a male raped by a domestic partner would also not be included. Another complaint about this source is the limited amount of information that has been gathered on the victim-to-offender relationship. To address these complaints, the UCR program is currently being converted to a more comprehensive and detailed one, the National Incident-Based Reporting System.

National Incident-Based Reporting System.   To improve the quality, quantity, and timeliness of crime statistical data collected by the law enforcement community and to improve the methodology of analyzing, auditing, and publishing the collected data, a new reporting system has been designed. Eventually, the National Incident-Based Reporting System (NIBRS) will replace the UCR. As of November 1996, ten states have been NIBRS certified, twenty more are in the process of testing the program, and another ten states are developing plans to test in the near future.

The most significant difference between UCR and NIBRS is that it will report on *incidents* of crime in addition to *arrests* in a category called group A offenses. The designation as "attempted" or "completed" has also been added. Expanded victim-to-offender relationships will be reported for all crimes where a crime against a person has been committed, such as rape or assault, in addition to homicide. An increased emphasis on the circumstances of the crime, such as aggravated assaults, is another notable change. NIBRS holds great promise to increase the information on crime characteristics, in particular for domestic violence crimes.

The FBI is also authorized to collect data under NIBRS. More information about NIBRS can be found at

http://www.fbi.gov/crimestats.htm

Drawbacks to National Incident-Based Reporting System.   Even with the improvements in crime statistics that are being implemented through NIBRS, one major limitation remains. The statistics will only reflect the crimes that people are willing to report to the police; therefore, they will not accurately depict crime in some categories. For example, the findings from the National Violence Against Women Survey found that there is a difference in the prevalence of reported rape and physical assault among women of different racial and ethnic backgrounds (Tjaden & Thoennes, 1998):

Native American/Alaska Native women	Most likely to report victimization
Asian/Pacific Islander women	Least likely to report victimization
Hispanic women	Less likely to report being raped
Non-Hispanic women	More likely to report being raped

National Crime Victimization Survey

The National Crime Victimization Survey (NCVS) attempts to address the problem of reporting. NCVS is the primary source of information on criminal victimization in the United States. A component of the Department of Justice, the Bureau of Justice Statistics began the NCVS program in 1973. It provides details on crime incidents, victims, and trends. A redesign of the survey was completed in 1993 to improve the questions, update the survey methods, and broaden the scope of crimes measured.

Commercial crimes and homicide are not included in this survey, which is conducted by personnel from the U.S. Census Bureau. A representative sample of approximately 45,000 households with over 94,000 persons interviewed is included to determine the extent of crime, regardless of whether or not it was reported to law enforcement. The survey includes detailed information about victims, offenders, and the nature of the criminal conduct.

Results of the National Crime Victimization Survey are compiled by the Bureau of Justice Statistics and can be accessed at their Web site:

http://www.ojp.usdoj.gov/bjs/welcome.html

Drawbacks to the National Crime Victimization Survey.   As stated earlier, the NCVS does not include all the crimes covered by the UCR. It is also criticized because it relies on people's memories of their victimization. Some people may exaggerate their victimization; others will fail to view themselves as victims at all. Incidents may have been forgotten or fabricated. There is no way to confirm the victimization reports.

Self-Report Studies

The third way to determine the extent of crime is a category of information rather than a specific source. Self-report studies are questionnaires or interviews given by researchers who query people on how much crime they have committed. Frequently, studies of this sort are conducted with college and high school students or in prisons. They are important because they have refuted the idea that only a small population commits crime. They suggest a large discrepancy between official statistics and the reality of criminal behavior.

On the World Wide Web, the most comprehensive source of criminal justice information to include self-report studies is the Justice Information Center (JIC) (Figure 12–2). The site is a clearinghouse for research and statistics, as well as a database of criminal justice abstracts. Publications and research from the U.S. Department of Justice (DOJ), Office of Justice Programs (OJP), the Bureau of Prevention (OJJDP), the Bureau of Justice Statistics (BJS), the Bureau of Justice Assistance (BJA), and the Office for Victims of Crime (OVC) can all be accessed from the JIC at

http://www.ncjrs.org/

It would probably take months to access all the documents available at the JIC site. The image map is searchable, which means that you can click on any of the categories listed and the page will bring you to a listing of available documents within the section. You can also do a search by key word, typing in words that relate to your area of interest. Another advantage of JIC is the abstract database, which is also searchable. This provides an abstract of documents that you can obtain in full from other sources.

If this information is not what you are looking for, conduct a search in another way. Click on *Research and Evaluation*, and look at the document list to see what might answer your question. Here you would find full text versions of the report. This is an example of the information that you would find.

Figure 12–2   The Justice Information Center home page is a wealth of information at your fingertips.

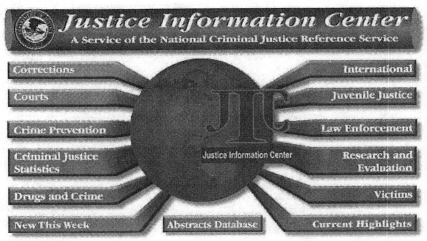

Jeffrey Fagan, Ph.D.
Series: NIJ Research Preview
Published: January 1998
8 pages
12,000 bytes
Adolescent Violence: A View from the Street

Figures, charts, forms, and tables are not included in this ASCII plain-text file. To view this document in its entirety, download the Adobe Acrobat graphic file available from this Web site or order a print copy from NCJRS at 800-851-3420.

U.S. Department of Justice
Office of Justice Programs
National Institute of Justice

Note that it contains information on how to obtain the document:

1. In *ASCII*. This would be a text-only, but full version of the document.

2. In *Adobe Acrobat*. This would contain all charts and graphics of the original file. Adobe Acrobat is a free download that you can obtain by clicking on the "download Adobe Acrobat now" sign and follow the directions on how to install it on your computer. It is easy and allows you to read full graphic documents. They can be printed on your personal printer exactly as they appear on the screen.

3. In *Print Copy*. By calling the toll-free number, you can order files that will be mailed to you. This is particularly helpful if the report is long. Some of the documents available are over 200 pages!

More about It: An Abstract Database Search in JIC

Want to know more about self-report studies? Go to the JIC home page and click on *Abstract Database*; on the next page, type in "self-report study." A WWW page opens that lists document abstracts that contain the phrase. Click on the hyperlink, and this is an example of what you would see:

NCJ Doc. No.: 103420
Personal Author: Eskridge, C W

Date of Publication: 86
Number of Pages: 24
Country of Origin: United States
Note: Presented at annual meetings of the American Society of Criminology, Atlanta, Ga., November 1986.

Title: Deviants among College Students? A Self-Report Study
Results from a self-report deviance survey completed by 789 students at the University of Nebraska-Lincoln during 1985-86 showed that, on the average, students said they committed approximately 8 different types of deviant activities.

Drawbacks to the Self-Report Studies.   Critics cite the unreliability of offender reports as a major flaw in this kind of research. There is no way to determine if the person is exaggerating his or her participation in criminal activity to impress the researcher. Another limitation of self-report studies is that they typically investigate involvement in minor crimes, not major criminal activities. As you have noted, there are limitations to each of the different major sources of information that researchers use to determine the prevalence of crime. Together they balance each other out, offering different perspectives on similar problems. On the WWW, there is the opportunity to search for a general picture on crime or to delve deeply into specific areas. Therefore, in addition to conducting general research on crime and victimization, you may want to limit your search and focus on a particular form of domestic violence. In the next section we offer some excellent starting points for research into child abuse.

CHILD ABUSE

Wherever you see the term *clearinghouse*, you have hit a gold mine. Keep looking on that Web page until you find everything you want to know. Be sure and bookmark the home page so that you can return to it later, and select another area to delve into.

Otherwise, it is easy to follow a number of hotlinks off a major source and then forget how to get back to where you started.

A "must have" site for people interested in child abuse is the *National Clearinghouse on Child Abuse and Neglect Information* (Figure 12–3). Affiliated with the U.S. Department of Health and Human Services, this is a national resource for professionals seeking information on the prevention, identification, and treatment of child abuse and neglect and related child welfare issues.

http://www.calib.com/nccanch/index.htm

Another major site for child abuse information is found at the home page of the *National Committee to Prevent Child Abuse.* This research center conducts an annual national survey of child abuse protective agencies. The 50-state survey provides the most current data available on the number and characteristics of child abuse reports and fatalities.

http://www.childabuse.org/

The most recent survey is entitled *Current Trends in Child Abuse Reporting and Fatalities: The Results of the 1997 Annual Fifty State Survey* (Wang & Daro, 1998). The report can also be obtained via postal mail by calling (312) 663-3520.

In Chapters 6 and 9, the problem of parental kidnapping was addressed. High divorce rates contribute to the concern about children who are illegally seized by an estranged parent. The *National Center for Missing and Exploited Children* maintains a national registry on children who are reported missing. Photographs of missing children are posted on their Web page with names and descriptions. In addition to accepting tips over the Internet, the center also maintains a 24-hour hotline for reports: 1-800-THE-LOST.

http://www.missingkids.com/

The *Child Abuse Prevention Network*, maintained by Cornell University, provides Internet resources for the prevention of child abuse. Access to additional information for professionals who work in the field can be obtained by becoming a member of this organization.

http://child.cornell.edu/

More about It: Bookmark

Bookmarks are a way to keep track of the URLs that you have visited and may want to return to at a future time. In Netscape Navigator, just click on the word *Bookmarks*, which is located at the top left side of the monitor screen. Next, click on *Add Bookmark*. That's it! In Microsoft Internet Explorer, click on the icon *Favorites*.

Figure 12–3   National Clearinghouse on child abuse and neglect information contains weekly updates.

National Clearinghouse on Child Abuse and Neglect Information

The Clearinghouse is a national resource for professionals seeking information on the prevention, identification, and treatment of child abuse and neglect and related child welfare issues. Go to "Services" for more information in these areas. Also, see our Highlights area for weekly updates!

What's New!   New!   Catalog

Publications   Databases

Calendar   Funding Sources

Services   Links

Site Map   Prevention Resources

Highlights

- New annotated bibliographies available online!

A Service of the Children's Bureau,
Administration for Children and Families,
Department of Health and Human Services

For more information, contact:

National Clearinghouse on Child Abuse and Neglect Information
330 C Street, SW
Washington, DC 20447
Phone: (800) 394-3366 or (703) 385-7565
Fax: (703) 385-3206

Nancy Faulkner's *Pandora's Box* provides links to over 200 pages on the subject of child abuse. It has links to Internet crimes, child abuse resources, child laws, and more.

http://www.prevent-abuse-now.com/

An interesting page with links on male child sexual abuse is provided by Jim Hopper. Data on prevention, prevalence, and more are available through this source.

http://www.jimhopper.com/abstats

Remember the term *guardian ad litem* from Chapter 6? The guardian ad litem is a person appointed by the court to represent the best interests of a child and to speak on his or her behalf. The *National Association of Guardian Ad Litem* (NAGAL) can be found on the WWW by pointing your browser to

http://www.nagal.org/

CHILD DEATH INVESTIGATION

According to a recent report on child homicide in California between 1992 and 1995 (State Child Death Review Board, 1997): "...484 children under 6 years of age were murdered between 1992–1995 in California. Of these deaths, 396 (82 percent) were recorded as resulting from child abuse. In 304 of these homicides (63 percent), the suspected perpetrator was the victim's parent or stepparent. Many child abuse homicides are thought to have been perpetrated by other caregivers, including unmarried partners of the parents (e.g., a boyfriend of the victim's mother), but the data do not provide enough detail to determine an exact number."

The full report on child homicide in California is available at the *Interagency Council on Child Abuse and Neglect* site (ICAN). In addition, ICAN administers the *National Center on Child Fatality Review* (NCFR). Their searchable online database allows a person to type in a particular state to receive the name of a contact person who heads up the local child death review team. Child death review teams (CDRTs) have been formed in California and many other states because of concerns of professionals on the increasing number of children who were being killed by abuse and neglect. The teams, made up of professionals from many fields, look into cases of child death.

http://child.cornell.edu/ncfr/home.html

For more information on CDRTs and the effort by the *New York City Multidisciplinary Child Fatality Review* (NMCFR) to aid professionals and interested parties in conducting investigations into the deaths and abuse of children, visit the New York site:

http://www.roadluge.com/~browning/index.htm

Concerned about child deaths? Learn more about the shaken baby syndrome, which was discussed in Chapter 9. This site is maintained by the *Shaken Baby Alliance*, a nonprofit organization dedicated to assisting shaken baby syndrome victims and their families. It is a source of education for the general public on the syndrome.

http://www.shakenbaby.com/

CRIMINAL JUSTICE SITES

The *Crime Prevention Evaluation Library* is an annotated compilation of all scientific evaluations of crime prevention programs. Look here to find what the experts have to say about the criminal justice efforts to prevent crime. What works?

http://www.preventingcrime.org/

The *Institute for Law and Justice* is a private nonprofit company that provides research, consulting, and services in criminal justice.

http://www.ilj.org/

Personal web pages frequently provide links to valuable resources. The *Law Offices of Kim Kruglick* have many criminal law links of interest.

http://www.kruglaw.com/lawlink.html

ELDER ABUSE

The *Administration on Aging* page, maintained by the U.S. Department of Health and Human Services, offers up-to-date information on the concerns of elders. Follow the link on their home page to the first *National Elder Abuse Incidence Study*, Final Report (September 1998): "This study estimates that at least one-half million older persons in domestic settings were abused and/or neglected, or experienced self neglect during 1996, and that for every reported incident of elder abuse, neglect or self neglect, approximately five go unreported."

http://www.aoa.dhhs.gov/

Another great source of information on elders is the *National Center on Elder Abuse*, supported by the U.S. Department of Health and Human Services. Elder law, statistics, and publications are all available from links off this Web page. The *Clearinghouse on Abuse and Neglect of the Elderly* (CANE), the largest computerized collection of elder abuse resources with over 3,500 holdings, is available as a searchable database.

http://www.gwjapan.com/NCEA/

GAY AND LESBIAN DOMESTIC VIOLENCE SITES

Domestic violence in the gay and lesbian community may be as frequent as family violence in other relationships. For a bibliography on issues that affect these relationships, visit the *Gay and Lesbian Domestic Violence Bibliography* page.

http://www.xq.com/cuav/dvbibl.htm

The *Advocates for Abused and Battered Lesbians* (AABL) is a local service in the Seattle, Washington area. The site contains a global directory with information on how to obtain services for abused and battered lesbians nationwide.

http://www.aabl.org/

The *New South Wales Police Department* in Australia employs special liaison officers who are police officers, administrative staff, and volunteers, who work with Aboriginal, ethnic, youth, aged, domestic violence and other victims, gay and lesbian communities, and the tourism industry to help victims. Officers who are specially trained to respond to battering in same-sex relationships are on call.

http://www.police.nsw.gov.au/

The *Community United Against Violence* (CUAV) addresses common misconceptions about gay battering relationships. The site suggests that 15 to 25 percent of gay couples experience severe violence in their relationships.

http://www.xq.com/cuav/domviol.htm

The Domestic Violence page has general information about the dynamics of abuse and provides numerous links and resources for lesbian survivors of battering.

http://www.en.com/users/allison/dvpage.html

Stop Abuse For Everyone (SAFE) is a nonprofit organization that provides advocacy, information, and support for men and women who are the victims of domestic violence. They set up and advocate for services for men and women, straight, gay, or lesbian. SAFE concentrates on domestic violence against straight men, gay men, and lesbian women, because few services exist for these groups.

http://www.dgp.toronto.edu/~jade/safe/

GENERAL INFORMATION

An excellent source for information on violence against women, the *safety zone* was featured on CNET TV's program *The Web*, aired on the Sci-Fi channel during the week of September 27, 1997. It was also featured in *Internet Week*, September 14, 1998.

http://www.serve.com/zone/

The *Family Violence Prevention Fund* (FUND) is a national nonprofit organization that focuses on domestic violence education, prevention, and public policy reform. It specifically addresses domestic violence committed by athletes.

http://www.igc.org/fund/

An electronic clearinghouse on domestic violence data appears at the *Minnesota Center Against Violence and Abuse* (MINCAVA).

http://www.mincava.umn.edu/

The Domestic Violence Section of the *Metro Nashville Police Department* offers some warning signs of domestic abuse. They address *separation abuse*, abuse occurring *after* the victim has separated from the abuser, which results in a high injury rate for women.

http://www.telalink.net/~police/abuse/index.html

ANTISTALKING SITES

The *antistalking Web site* is a site for anyone interested in the crime of stalking. It is meant to be a resource not only for stalking victims, but also for law enforcement, mental health professionals, researchers, educators, legislators, and security personnel.

http://www.antistalking.com/Default.htm

Cyberstalking is explained by the *Cyberangels* in a site that was recently named the recipient of the 1998 President's Service Award.

http://www.cyberangels.org/safetyandprivacy/stalking.html

GOVERNMENT SITES

The *Social Security Administration* announced on November 4, 1998, that it was taking additional steps to make it easier for abused, battered women to establish a new identity and obtain a new Social Security number, reducing the risk of further violence. Read about this at their Web site:

http://www.ssa.gov/press/domestic_violence.html

Created in 1984 by the Justice Assistance Act, the *Office of Justice Programs* (OJP) works within its established partnership arrangements with federal, state, and local agencies and national and community-based organizations to develop, fund, and evaluate a wide range of criminal and juvenile justice programs. OJP's mission is to provide federal leadership in developing the nation's capacity to prevent and control crime, administer justice, and assist crime victims. Here you can search for information from specific OJP Program Offices, such as the Violence Against Women Office (VAWO); OJP bureaus, such as the Office for Victims of Crime; or OJP support bureaus, such as the Office for Civil Rights.

http://www.ojp.usdoj.gov/

The Research and Development Branch of OJP is the *National Institute of Justice*. Its searchable database has a wealth of information.

http://www.ojp.usdoj.gov/nij/

As you learned in Chapter 6, people convicted of a domestic violence crime (misdemeanor or felony) may no longer be licensed to buy weapons or ammunition. You can find out more information at the *Bureau of Alcohol, Tobacco and Firearms'* Web site:

http://www.atf.treas.gov

Drugs are increasingly being associated with the crime of rape, as noted in Chapter 5. You will find more information on date rape at the SAIP page cited below under "Marital and Date Rape." Information on the date rape drug Rohypnol ("roofies") appears at the *Drug Enforcement Administration* (DEA) site, along with information on law enforcement seizure of this drug, which is often brought in from Mexico.

http://www.usdoj.gov/dea/pubs/rohypnol/rohypnol.htm

INTERNATIONAL SITES

Women's Rights Center (Poland):

http://free.ngo.pl/temida/index.htm

Women's Aid (Ireland):

http://www.ilinxmedia.com/waiddub/waidmyths.html

The *Family Violence Prevention Fund* provides updates on national and international domestic violence news:

http://www.igc.org/fund

LAW ENFORCEMENT SITES

Dr. Frank Schmalleger's Criminal Justice Cybrary of 3,109 criminal justice links provides links to information on just about any topic of interest to the profession. It can be found at *http://talkjustice.com/files/cybrary.htm*

Dr. Cecil Greek's criminal justice pages at Florida State University provide the most comprehensive view of resources available on the Internet that relates to the field of criminal justice. A must see!

http://www.criminology.fsu.edu/cj.html

Police Sites

International Association of Chiefs of Police:

http://www.kcilink.com/~patrick/

The Danvers, Massachusetts, Police Department maintains a great source of information and links on their *Domestic Violence Resource and Information Page*. This site provides invaluable information about domestic law, duties of police officers, and victim rights specific to Massachusetts. It has links to some very interesting sources.

http://www.star.net/people/~danvrspd/domviol.htm

LEGAL SITES

The *State and Local Government Web Page* is a Library of Congress Internet resource page. It provides links to Web, Gopher, telnet, and FTP sites that contain the full text of state statutes, state constitutions, and other legislative resources. Unsure of the laws in your state that relate to domestic violence? Try this site!

http://www.loc.gov/global/state/stategov.html

The *American Bar Association*, Commission on Domestic Violence, takes a strong stand against family violence. The site offers information and resources for victims of abuse. The site contains a link to the Model Code on Domestic and Family Violence, the new ABA Guide for Judges Handling Interstate Cases Involving Children and Families, and more. Internship opportunities are available.

http://www.abanet.org/domviol/home.html

Maintained by Indiana University School of Law, the *World Wide Web Virtual Library: Law* is searchable. It includes pages of links to matters of interest to criminal justice, everything from the electric chair to the Texas Department of Public Safety Criminal Records Database.

http://www.law.indiana.edu/law/v-lib/criminal.html#search

The *Legal Information Institute* (LII and Hermes) offers U.S. Supreme Court opinions under the auspices of Project Hermes, the court's electronic-dissemination project. This archive will soon contain all opinions of the court issued since May 1990.

http://supct.law.cornell.edu/supct/

A law browser that provides links and information on legal matters that contains a searchable database is *Find Law: Internet Legal Resources.*

http://www.findlaw.com/

JUDICIAL SITES

The stated purpose of the *American Judges Association* is to improve the effective and impartial administration of justice, to enhance the independence and status of the judiciary, to provide for continuing education of its members, and to promote the interchange of ideas of a judicial nature among judges, court organizations and the public.

http://www.theaja.org/

MARITAL AND DATE RAPE

The *National Clearinghouse on Marital and Date Rape* is well known for having waged a 20-year campaign to change customs, policies, behaviors, and laws relative to acquaintance and marital rape. They claim success for having assured through their efforts that marital/cohabitant/date rape be considered a crime in all 50 states, at least where force is used (1993). They offer an informative Web site and offer student volunteer internship positions.

http://members.aol.com/ncmdr/index.html

The *Date Rape* page entitled "'Friends' Raping Friends—Could It Happen to You?" was written by Jean O'Gorman Hughes, Research Associate, and Bernice R. Sandler, Executive Director, Project on the Status and Education of Women, Association of American Colleges (April 1987).

http://www.cs.utk.edu/~bartley/acquaint/acquaintRape.html

The *Sexual Assault Information Page* (SAIP) is a not-for-profit information and referral service created and maintained by Chris Bartley. SAIP provides information concerning acquaintance rape, child sexual abuse/assault, incest, rape, ritual abuse, sexual assault, and sexual harassment.

http://www.cs.utk.edu/~bartley/saInfoPage.html

VICTIMS' ASSISTANCE

Under a grant from the U.S. Department of Justice, the *National Victim Assistance Academy* coordinates the activities of the following program offices and bureaus: Bureau of Justice Assistance, Bureau of Justice Statistics, National Institute of Justice, Office of Juvenile Justice and Delinquency Prevention, and the Office for Victims of Crime.

http://www.ojp.usdoj.gov/ovc/assist/nvaa/

Partnerships Against Violence Network (PAVNET) is a "virtual library" of information about violence and youth at risk, representing data from seven federal agencies. It is a "one-stop," searchable information resource to help reduce redundancy in information management and to provide clear and comprehensive access to information for states and local communities.

http://www.pavnet.org/

WOMAN BATTERING

"Women, and particularly poor women, were much more likely to be victims of violent crime committed by an intimate (a current or former partner) or relative. In 1992–93 the victimization rate of women by intimates was nearly 7 times as high for women as for men, and for women in the lowest income group more than 4 times that for women in the highest income group" (U.S. Department of Health and Human Services, 1995).

For publications and statistics on the associated health concerns due to family violence, visit the *National Center for Health Statistics*. NCHS is the primary federal organization responsible for the collection, analysis, and dissemination of health statistics.

http://www.cdc.gov/nchswww/default.htm

The *National Center for Victims of Crime* is the largest nonprofit organization advocating for all victims. This Web site contains information on stalking and domestic violence generally, in addition to other concerns of victims. It contains a virtual library, discussion forum, online publications, and more.

http://www.nvc.org/

A comprehensive guide to family violence is provided in the *DV Survival Kit*:

http://www.dvguide.com/content.html

The *National Victim Assistance Academy Textbook* (Burnley et al., 1996) is an entire book online—read it chapter by chapter! Its topics include all forms of victimization, including child abuse, domestic violence, and elderly victims.

http://www.ojp.usdoj.gov/ovc/assist/nvaa/

The *National Coalition against Domestic Violence* located in Denver, Colorado is a grassroots nonprofit membership organization that has been working since 1978 to end violence in the lives of women and children. They provide a national network for state coalitions and local programs serving battered women and their children, public policy at the national level, technical assistance, community awareness campaigns, general

information and referrals, and publications on the issue of domestic violence; they
sponsor a national conference every two years for battered women and their advocates.

http://webmerchants.com/ncadv/

JUST FOR FUN

All work and no play makes the World Wide Web a dull place to surf! When you are
finished with your research, don't forget to enjoy yourself. Not only will you find neat
places to visit, you will also increase your skill at navigating the World Wide Web. A
good place to find a game to relax with is through use of the search engine *CNET
Gamecenter*, with links to game reviews, hardware, and downloads.

http://www.gamecenter.com/

Do you still prefer television? Go to *TV Guide Online!*

http://www.tvguide.com/

What about a night on the town? Not sure which movie you should see?
Perhaps the *Internet Movie Database* can help you decide.

http://us.imdb.com/

For the computer shopper who is looking for a good deal, check out the auctions
at *Egghead.Com*. Upgrade your personal computer, buy accessories or software, and do
it all on line.

http://www.egghead.com

CONCLUSIONS

Valuable resources for domestic violence research reside on the Internet. Knowing
how to connect, what might be obtained, and how to access the information are the
focus of this chapter. The electronic network that we call the Internet is described in
order to note the difference between it and the World Wide Web. WWW is a service
that resides on the Internet—the most popular one.

Connecting to the Internet requires a computer, an Internet connection, and a
browser. Unless you are accessing a direct connection through a college or university
network, you will need a modem to access a dial-up or Internet service provider. Once
you have the hardware, you need software—a browser. The browser resides on your
computer and reads the language of the Internet. Locating the Web site that you want
to access is done by using the URL.

You find information on the World Wide Web by using a search engine. There
are so many search engines that you can choose the best one for your purposes. The

directory type will be focused, resulting in a higher-quality search. The robot search will fetch more resources, allowing for you to pick and choose from a variety of sources. A multisearch will collect the closest sites, from a number of engines, and allow you to choose what best suits your needs.

An important step in the process of Internet research is evaluation of your source. Determine your purpose, and consider the creditability of the producer of the data. Look also for a bibliography and for references, an indication that the data originate from legitimate sources. Finally, determine if the information is current and relevant to your project.

The major sources of criminal justice knowledge may sound familiar to you: the Uniform Crime Reporting System, the National Victimization Survey, and Self-Report Surveys. These sources are accessible over the Internet, in addition to hard copies that can be found in many libraries across the country. Obtaining information from these major sources directly over the Internet may expedite your research. For those who have never examined these sources, you will be amazed at the ease with which they may be accessed! In the future, the UCR will be replaced by the National Incident-Based Reporting System, and even more data will develop from this source.

The remainder of the chapter contains URLs from numerous sites that are relevant to the study of domestic violence. This can be only a partial list, as the availability of family violence data grows daily. These are good places to start your search for information.

$\mathcal{K}$EY $\mathcal{T}$ERMS

Browser
Dial-up connection
Direct server
Directory search engines
Domain name system
E-mail address
Gateway
Internet service provider
Multisearch engine
National crime victimization survey

National incident-based reporting system
Protocol
Robot
Router
Self-report studies
Separation abuse
Uniform crime reporting system
Uniform resource locator
World Wide Web

$\mathcal{Q}$UESTIONS $\mathcal{f}$OR $\mathcal{R}$EVIEW

1. Describe the Internet.

2. What is a domain name?

3. What is the most popular service on the Internet?

4. Describe the three major types of search engine.

5. How do you evaluate an Internet source?

6. What are the ten C's for evaluating Internet sources?

7. What are the three major sources for information regarding the extent of personal crime?

8. Explain the NIBRS. Who is responsible for collecting data under this system? Why has the system been developed?

9. What is the most comprehensive source of criminal justice information on the World Wide Web?

10. Visit at least two sites in a category of domestic violence. What have you learned from those Web pages?

$\mathcal{R}$ EFERENCES

Burnley, Jane et al. (eds.). 1996. *National Victim Assistance Academy Textbook*. Washington, DC: Office for Victims of Crime.

National Center for Health Statistics. 1995. "How to Cite Electronic Media." *http://www.cdc.gov/nchswww/howto/sitelec/citelec.htm*. 1998.

Richmond, Betsy (ed.). 1996. "Ten C's for Evaluating Internet Resources." *www.uwec.edu/Admin/Library/10cs.html*. 1999.

State Child Death Review Board. 1997. "Child Deaths in California." March. *http://child.cornell.edu/ncfr/calif.html*. 1999.

Tjaden, Patricia and Nancy Thoennes. 1998. *Prevalence, Incidence, and Consequences of the Violence Against Women: Findings from the National Violence Against Women Survey*. NCJ 172837. Washington, DC: U.S. Department of Justice.

U.S. Department of Health and Human Services. 1995. "Health, United States Report, with Special Profile of Women's Health." *http://www.cdc.gov/nchswww/releases/96news/hus95rel.htm*. 1999.

Wang, Ching-Tung and Deborah Daro. 1998. *Current Trends in Child Abuse Reporting and Fatalities: The Results of the 1997 Annual Fifty State Survey*. Working Paper 808. Chicago: National Committee to Prevent Child Abuse.

Index

A

Abuse:
    institutional, 14
    legality of, 12
    physical,
        defined, 11
        of elderly, 22
    psychological, damage from, 12
    sexual,
        defined, 11
        signs of, 12
    See also specific abuse.
Abuse prevention:
    acts on, as remedy, 10
    police procedures and, 162
    police strategies for, 203–205
Abusers, guises of, 202–203
Abusive relationships, defined, 5
Administration on Aging, as Internet
    resource, 365
Adoption, under Code of Hammurabi, 32
Advocates, role of, 205

Africans:
    legal helplessness of, 37–38
    marriage rights of, 37–38
Aid: *See* Intervention.
Alcohol, implicated, 84, 104
American Breeders' Association, origin of, 68
Amir, Menachem, rape study by, 125
Anger:
    and rape, 114
    therapy programs on, 98
    and violence, 104
Animal abuse, as intimidation, 4
Apprenticeship, for chilren, 44
Arrest:
    allowable, questions for, 234
    domestic violence, types of, 162–163
    for elderly abuse, 309
        mandated, 309, 310
    mailed warrants as, 237
    mandatory, 226, 227
        effects of, 196–200
    of mutal accusants, 239
    preferred, 226

C

Canada, protective movement in, 48–49
Caregiver, defined, 14
Castration:
    chemical, 69, 117, 226
    for child abusers, 226
    controversy over, 69
    forced, origin of, 68
Child abuse:
    by age, 260–261
    agencies monitoring, 168, 169
    awareness of, 19
    claims of,
        false, 195–196
        inflated, 195
    criminalization of, 255–256
    deaths from, 336
    defined, 13–14
    direct *vs.* indirect, 128
    "discovered," 45
    documenting, difficulty of, 20–21
    early American, 44
    emotional, 263–264
        criminal, 264
    evidence of, 246, 257
    extent of, determining, 270
    false charges of, 266
    and family income, 19, 109
    and family makeup, 109
    by family relationship, 20, 108–109
    and family size, 19, 109
    form reporting, 231–232
    by gender, 261–262
    indirect, 256
    to infants, 264–265
    information sources on, 169
    Internet sources on, 361–364, 362,
        364
    laws against, 20
    by maltreatment, 256–257
    multidisciplinary-team investigation
        of, 265

    physical, 264
        accidental *vs.* inflicted, 264
        locations of, 264–265
    police role in, 194–196
    prevalence of, 18–20
    prevention of, Internet source on,
        362
    by race, 262–263
    reporting of, mandated, 168,
        281–282
    Roman, 42
    secondary, 258
    by sex, 19, 20–21
    sexual,
        by age, 20
        in child sex rings, 277, 278
        exhibitionism, 276
        forced prostitution, 276
        incest, 276
        legal elements of, 274–275
        molestation, 275
        pornography, 276
        prevalence of, 20
        rape, 275
        symptoms of, 276–277
        voyeurism, 275
    statistics on, 258–259
    See also Burns; Injuries; Interviews;
        Maltreatment; Munchausen by
        proxy; Neglect; Pedophiles.
Child Abuse Prevention and Treatment
    Act:
    discussed, 168
    on failure to seek medical care, 280
Child Abuse Prevention Network, as
    Internet resource, 362
Child Abuse Protection and Treatment Act,
    provisions of, 180
Child abusers:
    imprisonment of, mandatory, 226
    indictability of, determining, 256
    male, 116–117
        juvenile, 117–118